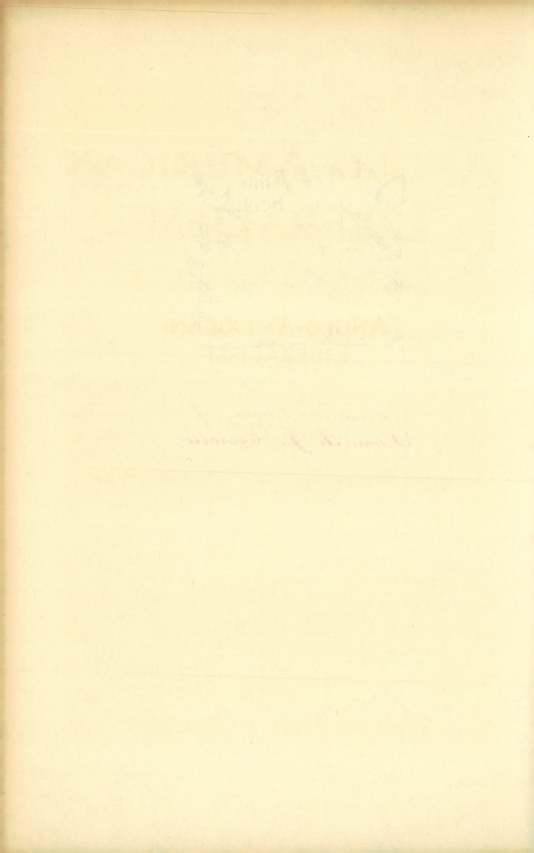

ANGLO-AMERICAN LIBERALISM

ANGLO-AMERICAN LIBERALISM:

Readings in Normative Political Economy

Edited by

Conrad Waligorski and Thomas Hone

Nelson-Hall nh Chicago

LIBRARY OF CONGRESS CATALOGING IN PUBLICATION DATA
Main entry under title:

Anglo-American liberalism.

  Bibliography: p.
  1. Liberalism—Addresses, essays, lectures.
2. Laissez-faire—Addresses, essays, lectures.
I. Waligorski, Conrad. II. Hone, Thomas.
JC571.A546   320.5'12   81-4008
ISBN 0-88229-617-5 (cloth)   AACR2
ISBN 0-88229-785-6 (paper)

Manufactured in the United States of America

10 9 8 7 6 5 4 3 2 1

The paper in this book is pH neutral (acid-free).

To Robert Booth Fowler

Contents

Acknowledgments   ix

Preface   xi

Introduction: Anglo-American Political-Economic Liberalism,
  by Conrad Waligorski   1

Section One: Liberalism, Human Rights and the
Purpose of the State   23
  1. The Putney Debates   25
  2. The Agreement of the People   35
  3. James Harrington: 43
    Oceana
  4. John Locke: 53
    Second Treatise of Government
  5. James Mill: 66
    Essay on Government
  6. John Stuart Mill: 73
    Representative Government

Section Two: Revolution and Political Change   87
  7. Thomas Jefferson: 89
    Notes on Virginia, letters, and *Inauguration Address: March 4,*
    1801
  8. Thomas Paine: *Rights of Man*   101
  9. Jeremy Bentham: 112
    An Introduction to the Principles of Morals and Legislation

Section Three: Individualism and Tolerance   123
  10. John Locke: 124
    A Letter Concerning Toleration
  11. Voltaire: 138
    A Treatise on Toleration, A Philosophical Dictionary, and *The*
    Ignorant Philosopher
  12. John Stuart Mill: 147
    On Liberty

13. David Spitz: 156
   A Liberal Perspective on Liberalism and Conservatism
14. John Rawls: 164
   A Theory of Justice

Section Four: Liberalism and Laissez-Faire Economics   175
15. John Locke: 177
   Of Property
16. Adam Smith: 180
   The Wealth of Nations
17. Thomas Malthus: 192
   An Essay on the Principle of Population
18. Herbert Spencer: 204
   Social Statics

Section Five: The Response to Laissez-Faire within Liberalism   217
19. John Stuart Mill: 219
   Principles of Political Economy
20. Thomas Hill Green: 229
   Liberal Legislation and Freedom of Contract
21. John Maynard Keynes: 237
   The End of Laissez-Faire, Art and the State, The Means to Prosperity, and *The General Theory of Employment. . . .*

Section Six: Liberalism Confronts the Authoritarianism and Value Confusion of the Twentieth Century   255
22. C. B. Macpherson: 256
   The Maximization of Democracy
23. John Dewey: 265
   Liberalism and Social Action
24. Theodore Lowi: 274
   The Politics of the Second Republic of the United States
25. Richard Wollheim: 288
   Without Doubt or Dogma: The Logic of Liberalism
26. Jervis Anderson, Jeanne Kirkpatrick, Dennis H. Wrong: 293
   A Symposium: What Is a Liberal—Who Is a Conservative?
27. Donald Hanson: 300
   What Is Living and What Is Dead in Liberalism?

Suggested Readings   315
Notes   317

Acknowledgments

We could not have compiled this collection of papers and essays without the assistance of the libraries of the University of Arkansas, Southern Illinois University at Carbondale, and Indiana University. Part of the manuscript was typed at the Office of Research and Sponsored Programs at the University of Arkansas, and we thank the University for its assistance.

Proper credit, too, is due our typists: Vickie Hilliard at Arkansas, and Nancy Kiefer, Janis Shepherd, and Linda Smith at Indiana. Janis Shepherd merits our particular appreciation for piecing the manuscript together. Also, we wish to thank our wives, Ann Waligorski and Teresa Hone, for their support and assistance.

Finally, our editors at Nelson-Hall, especially Jeanne Berger, deserve mention. Their assistance was quite important to our finishing this collection.

Preface

Modern liberalism developed initially as a revolutionary doctrine. In the name of individual freedom, liberals from the seventeenth through the early nineteenth centuries questioned the legitimacy and authority of every existing political and economic system. On occasion they raised embarrassing questions about class relations and the distribution of social power. Though it is no longer fashionable to talk about liberalism as either revolutionary or as a model for other parts of the world, a core of values, principles, institutions, and ideas remains, a set of arguments and assumptions that form the basic framework for the entire spectrum of Western political discourse. These values still serve as the basic justification and model for many of our political institutions and organize much of our political discourse. Liberalism is an important and diverse political philosophy, though it is often misunderstood. North Americans, Western Europeans, and people most heavily influenced by these cultures still live with the institutions and values which modern liberals created. Though liberalism is on the defensive, even its strongest critics have adopted some of the language and forms of liberalism— freedom, liberty, representative institutions—while denying or distorting their meaning into authoritarian forms.

In this book we are concerned with the basic principles of Anglo-American liberalism. This focus is based on the assumption that what people think and believe affects politics. Values, ideals, moral assumptions, and principles shape our perceptions of society and enable us to assess our place in it. Organized into ideologies or held as inarticulate expectations about politics, values provide a set of shared pictures, a justification for specific actions, and a framework for analyzing and evaluating the world. At their worst these values form the basis for the kind of galloping abstractions which simplify reality into the saved and the damned, giving their adherents immunity from worry about the pain they inflict upon those too benighted to see the truth. At their best, values may provide common ground for agreement on how our political, economic, and social systems should operate and what they should attempt to achieve, even though simple agreement on fundamental political values was not and never will be sufficient to ensure unified conclusions about specific programs, policies, and institutions. In literally inventing much of the language and institutional structure of modern liberalism, Anglo-American liberalism has had a deep impact on Western politics. If we are to understand the nature and meaning of our beliefs and values (as well as those of people who disagree) we must understand the origin of and continuing debate over those values.

With the exception of Voltaire, who admired the English liberal tradition, all of our selections are either English, American, or Canadian, because it is in these countries that liberalism has had its deepest impact. France, Italy, and Germany had extensive liberal movements, but their roots tended to be more shallow. These movements had less of an impact on public policy and mass attitudes than in the United States and in England, where liberal arguments received wide support, and after ceasing to be merely party creeds, reflected the attitudes and approaches of most significant power contenders.

Introduction:

Anglo-American Political-Economic Liberalism

by Conrad Waligorski

The Anglo-American tradition of political and political-economic liberalism began in the seventeenth and eighteenth centuries with the migration of people and ideas from England to the North American colonies. Particularly in New England, these people and ideas were from the radical and populist end of the English political spectrum. Throughout the seventeenth, eighteenth, and nineteenth centuries, and well into the twentieth in terms of people such as John Maynard Keynes, liberal ideas crossed the Atlantic, encouraging similar concerns and independent political traditions. Linked by a semicommon language, British and American liberals addressed common problems and issues with a shared core of assumptions and values. This is clearest in the early period with the Puritans, Thomas Paine, and Thomas Jefferson, and in the later period among political economists. This common tradition has always been concerned with problems such as mass democracy, making representative government work, protecting individual rights and, starting in the nineteenth century, the concerns of industrialization, capitalism, economic freedom, and the often explosive interaction of politics and economics. The liberal tradition values individualism, freedom, rights, limited governmental power, reason, constitutionalism, and tolerance. Though there are different justifications within this tradition—religion, contract theory, utility, and idealism—and different and changing emphases among these shared concerns and values, the Anglo-American liberal tradition has rarely concentrated on any single value to the exclusion of the others.

Speaking in broad terms, this simple enumeration reveals the difference between the Anglo-American and continental European liberal traditions. Despite a partial merging by such people as John Stuart Mill, T.H. Green, and C.B. Macpherson, the Anglo-American liberal tradition has remained largely separate. Our authors are mainly part of the individualist strain in liberalism, as opposed to the continental strain with its emphasis on the state or nation as superior to the individual. Individualist liberalism does not assume there is such a thing as an individual's true or real will which is perfected or embodied by the state. Rather it has assumed that no matter how important state or society may be, that it is the individual who is the real center for policy.

There are other common concerns in the Anglo-American tradition, all of which are illustrated in the readings. The United Kingdom and the North American colonies are the historic homes of modern liberalism, models for other liberals well into the twentieth century. This tradition has always emphasized real consent, the individual's agreement to obey reasonable government. Individualist in orientation, it has generally seen rights as adhering in or belonging to individuals, not as gifts from either state or society. In doing so, it placed limits on the state and eventually social relations; individuals could never be forced to be free, only permitted and encouraged to be free. Anglo-American liberals have rarely emphasized the anticlericalism of their continental counterparts. Rather, Anglo-American liberalism has deep roots in dissenting religions. These liberals emphasized first the necessity of religious and then political-social tolerance. Anglo-American liberals often argued that social relations are distinct from the state. They developed from these arguments the idea that government officials and those who command large concentrations of economic power are subject to the law, not superior to it. Yet unlike some continental liberals, they argued that nature, interest, and accommodation, not will, are the source of rights and freedom. Whether emphasizing individual or collective action, however, Anglo-American liberals have generally attempted to balance the rival claims of individual and society or state, of equality and freedom, of liberalism and democracy. In doing so, Anglo-American liberalism has constantly returned, after occasional excesses in one or another direction, to its traditional concern with rights, tolerance, and balance, even when it has encouraged resistance or revolution by those who were deprived of their rights.

We feel that this focus, which unites North American and English writers for the first time, will make up in coherence and depth what it may lack in breadth. In making our choices we have attempted to avoid the coal shovel approach which often jumbles together different intellectual traditions and makes it very difficult to discover what is unique to each or what they have in common. This does not mean that other liberals are unimportant, only that the individualist theme of Anglo-American liberalism is a separate tradition which needs to be analyzed in its own right.

In making these selections we have tried to avoid a rigid and dogmatic definition of liberalism. Not only would this further confuse the nature of modern liberalism, but it would itself be illiberal. We have refused to focus on any single characteristic as defining liberalism, but rather have chosen a number of characteristics, such as individualism, rights, freedom, equality, and tolerance, all of which combine to form the content of liberalism. In this process we have focused on values, not policies. Rather than strictly defining liberalism, we will allow liberals to speak for themselves.

Finally, we have attempted to avoid an artificial distinction between politics and economics. A glance at the daily newspaper illustrates that these are not watertight, separate worlds. Political and economic theory and policy are interdependent. Today we are debating the politics and economics of welfare, tax policy, health care, energy shortages, inflation, the balance of payments, foreign aid, regional integration, and multinational corporations, all of which link political and economic concerns and issues. The important liberals recognized and appreciated this link. Whether or not they attempted to make a sharp distinction between the legitimate areas of politics and economics, they realized that politics and economics are part of the same social reality. As such they deeply affect each other. Even though many liberals wanted public policy to be excluded from involvement in the economy they admitted that what occurs in one part of society affects the other parts. This mutual interaction is a major theme from Adam Smith to John Maynard Keynes (selections 16, 17, 18, and 21 by Smith, Malthus, Spencer, and Keynes). It has continually entered into the Anglo-American discussion of individualism, freedom, and rights.

These edited selections present the basic arguments which still form the background of most contemporary arguments over what government (especially government in America) should or should not do. We have attempted to present the essentials of arguments, stripped of unnecessary or obsolete language and examples. In confronting these value arguments we confront our own and thereby discover which of these values we hold only formally and which are really part of the core of our being. Many of these authors engaged in a dialogue with each other and we hope you will engage in a dialogue with them. Though their concerns and language, as well as ours, have changed over time, basic values and assumptions have remained remarkably stable. The common liberal concern with human liberation allows us to speak to each other even though separated by decades and centuries.

Varieties of Liberalism

Liberalism has deep and extremely complex roots in the history of Western culture and politics. A number of its basic themes originated in the ancient and medieval worlds. Greek and Roman communities left a legacy of written law and rule of law—important aspects of liberalism—which has dominated Western thinking to this day. From the medieval world liberals inherited ideas of constitutionalism, communal liberty, distinctions between church and state, limited government, higher law, a renewed respect for law as a limit on governors, and inchoate representative bodies which in some countries developed into powerful parliamentary institutions embodying a wide variety of liberal values.

Modern liberalism, however, does not date from antiquity nor the middle ages, nor is it synonymous with the Western political tradition.[1] Liberalism, as we know it today, began to develop in England during the civil war of the 1640s, as both a doctrine and a party. The civil war began over questions such as parliamentary rights, monarchical prerogative, and taxation, but rapidly developed a popular character which raised new and fundamental questions about politics, religion, and the individual's relation to the community. As will be seen from the Putney Debates and the "Agreement of the People" (selections 1 and 2), English liberals developed many of the political arguments and assumptions of liberalism nearly 150 years before liberals acquired real political power anywhere in Europe or North America.[2] Starting as an essentially middle-class ideology, the English revolutionaries' universalistic claims and language helped ensure that liberalism's benefits would not be confined only to one class.

Rather than attempting a history of liberalism in this short space, we can illustrate its development by briefly examining some of its major varieties. As a political and then an economic doctrine, liberalism has developed in many directions since its modern beginnings in seventeenth century England.

Classical liberalism (selections 3 and 4 by Harrington and Locke) began to develop in England in the 1640s and was the dominant form of liberalism until the early nineteenth century. Even today, elements of classical liberalism form a major component of contemporary liberalism. Classical liberals focused on securing and defending individual human rights through political reform. They advocated the rule of law, limited government, extension of the franchise, and constitutional guarantees of religious freedom, or tolerance. In England these reforms were partially secured, at least for some groups, by the Revolution of 1688. The "Glorious Revolution" was a virtually bloodless coup which replaced the increasingly autocratic government of James II with a more reduced role for monarchy under William and Mary and subsequent English monarchs. In 1689, the Parliament adopted a "Bill of Rights," which among other things limited the power of the king, guaranteed freedom of speech and debate within Parliament, opposed "excessive bail," forbade "cruel and unusual punishment," and further guaranteed traditional rights and privileges. The "Glorious Revolution" helped ensure the dominance of the "Whig tradition" in English and American politics, with its emphasis on limited government, rights, civil liberties, toleration for most religious groups, and at least some popular political participation. Extension of the values of religious tolerance to politics helped develop the idea that organized opposition to government policies and efforts to develop alternatives is legitimate and not treason. The modern party system and all interest group activities are based on this belief. As a careful reading of Federalist Paper Number 10 will reveal, even the men who wrote the American Constitution were uncertain whether organized opposition was completely legitimate. Much of the popular political activity of the late eighteenth and early nineteenth centuries, as well as writing by such people as Thomas Paine, Richard Price, Joseph Priestley, and Thomas Jefferson was directed at expanding classical liberalism to include larger and larger parts of the population.

Toward the end of the eighteenth and beginning of the nineteenth century, some liberals began a movement to overhaul government to make it less an impediment to individual freedom. Associated in England with Jeremy Bentham and with the utilitarian movement (see selections 9 and 5 by Bentham and James Mill), these liberals often emphasized administrative and judicial reform, and improvement in legal codes as keys to improving human welfare. Utilitarians also developed a defense of rights and a more democratic form of government based on their principle that the greatest good for the greatest number should be the object of governmental policy. In the United States, the drafting of the American Constitution represented a move toward increased governmental efficiency and though many of the drafters were not liberals, the document reflected some classic liberal policies such as limited government, human rights, and at least limited individual participation in government.

Most of these principles form the core of liberalism to this day. They were based in the first instance on negative freedom—the idea that there is a sphere of human activity within which government should not interfere. Often associated with the doctrines of social contract, natural law, and natural rights, the notion of negative freedom assumed that if government left people alone they would be able to accomplish their own purposes and goals. Early liberals emphasized negative liberty because they feared that state power would always be expansive, always threatening liberty and rights, always endangering social relations, and always capable of arbitrary action. Therefore, it required limitations and surveillance. Though some of them also feared private power (Jefferson was prominent among them), most early liberals saw government as the enemy (selection 4 by Locke on revolution) and for good reason. If government was the enemy, then it logically followed that the way to prevent destruction of freedom was to limit government and ensure participation of the governed.

This classic political doctrine had strong implications for economics (see laissez-faire readings). Laissez-faire liberalism, which emphasized that the government should not become involved in the economy, grew out of classic political liberalism. The basic assumptions of laissez-faire liberalism have hardly changed in the two centuries since their first systematic statement by Adam Smith, though there have been significant changes in their application. Essentially they are based on a belief in the value of voluntarism in the social sphere, a belief that people are capable of deciding how best to fulfill their own wants and needs and that it is through individual effort and competition that all great social advances occur.

Laissez-faire liberals have assumed that a self-regulating market is the essential and *only* legitimate social device for allocating goods, services, and resources among individuals. Each product, service, and person's labor is offered for sale on this market, with the price received depending solely on unregulated supply and demand. In the ideal self-regulating market, individuals are assumed to be able to bargain equally with each other, with no one having either an inherent advantage over anyone else or such a large share of the market that he could arbitrarily affect price. Both monopoly and government restrictions are banished as interferences with the right and ability of individuals to freely bargain with each other. In this free bargaining each individual seeks his own advantage. This naturally leads to competition and an effort to gain more by increasing one's share of the market. Under free competition and the discipline of an open, unregulated market, one can gain more of the market only by improving one's product, lowering its price, or both. This requires greater efficiency and such efficiency, achieved solely for personal gain, benefits everyone.

Thus competition and a free market are not only natural but lead to a natural harmony of interests because if each person seeks his own advantage he will naturally cater to the wants and needs of other people. Individualism, self-concern, and total freedom of action lead to social good by increasing efficiently the total amount of goods and services available for consumption. In the process a "natural" market reduces the need for conscious political interference in the kinds of allocative activities that could be performed well only by free self-seeking individuals. Politics, as a clash over public policy and struggle for decision-making power on public issues is thus eliminated from a large part of social life.

While classic political liberals allowed some role for governmental action, laissez-faire liberals sought to banish government to nothing more than a protector of markets and enforcer of contracts. In essence they replaced political struggle and political participation with the free market, where all were assumed equally free and able to compete with all. In this sense laissez-faire was profoundly apolitical as well as antipolitical. Laissez-faire liberals argued that economics must be completely separate from politics. Politics could not aid the natural working of the market. All it could do was interfere, destroying the natural laws of competition and reward for effort, produce inefficiency, and in the process destroy liberty.

In terms of concern for economic freedom, property rights, and a respect for private enterprise, laissez-faire liberalism has deeply colored contemporary liberalism. However, the actual effects of nonintervention were horrendous and many modern liberals have sought to remove these. Early industrialization led to savage working and living conditions. In the name of liberty, many liberals denied that the state could remedy unhealthy working conditions, regulate hours of employment and child labor, or require children to attend school. In the name of freedom of contract they focused on the form of a contract and forgot that people may be unable to enter into contracts as equals, or that an individual worker needs a job much more than any large employer needs one worker (see selection 20 by Green). Seeing freedom largely in economic terms—freedom to compete—they refused to see that competition could destroy freedom for those who lacked the power of a large industrialist. Failing to admit that competition itself had changed with the growth of enterprise, they clung to the form of freedom while undermining its reality. Even natural law, which had originally referred to political relations, was reduced to natural economic laws emphasizing competition.

Many laissez-faire liberals thus had a narrow interpretation of freedom and politics. They demoted, almost annihilated, politics. Power relations became private economic affairs. If social relations in general, and market relations in particular, were the only source of good, then politics became radically irrelevant to the central concerns of life. By banishing government from the market, laissez-faire liberalism promised to end tyranny and produce more abundance. These attitudes typified English liberalism until the mid-nineteenth century and American liberalism until the early twentieth.

Ultimately this kind of thinking led to a dead end, as it defined freedom too heavily in competitive-economic terms and tended to see political and social liberty largely in formal, nondynamic terms. Such liberalism merges into the modern laissez-faire conservatism of thinkers such as Milton Friedman and Ayn Rand.[3] Because such liberalism demoted politics and political speculation, and was associated in many peoples' minds with economic exploitation, some liberals attempted to recast their doctrine. This redefinition included "the nature of liberty, and the relationship between liberty and legal coercion" as well as "the relationship between individual human nature and its social *milieu*."[4] Three major types of liberalism emerged[5]: social darwinism, idealism, and the multifaceted reform liberalism.[6] The last two attempted to rescue the principles of freedom from laissez-faire doctrines and to reconstruct a new rationale for political action.

Writers such as Herbert Spencer (selection 18) accepted laissez-faire and attempted to apply biological concepts to society and the economy. They claimed that human society was analogous to animal societies, and that the Darwinian "laws" which governed animal evolution applied also to human communities. Moreover, they argued that the main evolutionary struggle now occurred in the economy. Interference with this struggle on the part of the state in the form of minimum wages, maximum hours, or free schools violated freedom and would ensure the survival of the weakest at the expense of the strong. Those who excelled in the economic (not political) competition were society's natural leaders and benefactors, dragging the rest of us along behind them in the painful evolutionary struggle for a better society. They reaffirmed the older laissez-faire emphasis on noninterference, lending it the apparent prestige of modern biological science as the justification for allowing great economic inequalities to exist. In heavy moralistic tones (the Horatio Alger series of books popularly illustrated this), such writers argued that success went to those who worked hard and sacrificed. Poverty, ignorance, even disease were viewed as personal or parental faults or failings, not the result of economic or social inequalities. Anyone could succeed, if only he or she tried hard enough.

But everyone did not succeed. In England and America a wide variety of socialists, reformers, conservatives, and liberals protested the assumptions and results of this kind of thinking. Thomas Hill Green's version of idealism (selection 20) emphasized man's social nature and the interdependence of the individual personality and its social environment. Green rejected the pure individualism of earlier, especially laissez-faire, liberalism. He attempted to recapture the ancient Greek sense of public life with its appreciation of man's interrelation with his environment. In the process, Green developed the notion of positive freedom. As understood in the Anglo-American individualist tradition, positive freedom accepts and expands the idea that freedom means that no one will interfere with one's legitimate activities. It refers to the actual opportunity to carry out those activities which no one may interfere with.[7] Thus, negative freedom would be sustained if no person interfered with one's right to speak or to vote. But if I do not exercise these rights because I do not know they exist, or I do not have the necessary skills, money, or education to do so, that failure to exercise them is not a violation of freedom. Thus according to laissez-faire liberalism, workers' poverty did not interfere with their freedom. Proponents of positive freedom, however, argued that such obstacles must be removed, and the state has the duty to help remove them, before people can be called free. People must have the capacity to exercise freedom to be free. Government action becomes necessary in the name of freedom. Here we have one basis of the modern welfare state, and the liberals' occasional support for it. John Dewey and John Maynard Keynes were heavily influenced by this school of thought (selections 23 and 21).

Many contemporary liberals accept a combination of these elements. Reform liberalism, while not the only form of contemporary liberalism, represents an attempt to maintain and expand the political emphases of classical liberalism, while enlarging basic notions of freedom, participation, and equality into social and economic relations. Reform liberalism is not a single theory, nor is it an ideology. Rather it is an attempt to apply and to extend the basic principles of liberalism to the profoundly new and dangerous conditions of contemporary political economy. Rather than defending only the forms and policy preferences of past liberalisms, it attempts to modify these where they no longer serve their functions of promoting and ensuring human freedom. Thus most reform liberals have abandoned a pure laissez-faire approach and have accepted the notion that government and society have an obligation to promote positive human freedom. At the same time they still maintain a distrust of any concentration of political or economic power. Selections by John Dewey and John Maynard Keynes illustrate the degree to which reform liberals have concerned themselves with the distribution of economic resources. Obviously, in any such enterprise among people who value freedom and individualism, disagreements are inevitable concerning proper policy, the real spirit of liberalism, and the exact role of government. Most reform liberals would also say that disagreement is necessary.

John Stuart Mill stands at the head of a century of British reform liberalism. Mill is an extremely important transitional figure in liberalism. Groomed by his father, James Mill, and by Jeremy Bentham to become the intellectual leader of utilitarianism, Mill eventually saw and rejected the narrow confines of both utilitarianism and laissez-faire liberalism. Though he never developed as deep an appreciation for positive freedom as did T. H. Green, Mill became one of the most widely read and influential liberals of the nineteenth and twentieth centuries. In *On Liberty,* Mill accepted and argued for the full range of classic liberal rights, for freedom of thought, freedom of action, freedom from social interference with private action, and freedom to form associations. In *On Representative Government* and *The Subjection of Women* he argued for the extension of voting rights to workers and women respectively. Mill favored extension of state power only to redress the imbalance of power and opportunity between individuals. His state, however, was to be a representative state, which would also help create conditions for active competition. Though Mill in his *Principles of Political Economy* favorably examined socialism and the stationary state, he never abandoned a favorable attitude toward private property (selection 19).

In his proposals and doubts, Mill foreshadowed much of the program of twentieth-century reform liberalism. Many individuals and groups accepted and incorporated bits and pieces of the program Mill presented, but it was not until well into the twentieth century that large numbers of people began to consciously adopt and modify the liberal political inheritance to current economic conditions. Keynes represents one such effort in England. In the United States the New Deal represents yet another. The battle over the proper meaning of liberalism, how to justify and extend liberal values to all social groups, and whether liberalism could meet the political challenges posed by twentieth-century ideologies and totalitarian movements are discussed in selections by John Rawls, Richard Wollheim, John Dewey, and Donald Hanson. Some of these people might be surprised to find themselves categorized as liberals, or in the company of some of the others. All of them, however, argue that some aspect of what we call reform liberalism is at least a partial answer to our increasingly chaotic world.

Potentially, there are other ways to categorize the many varieties of liberalism. We could distinguish liberalism across time and between countries, or distinguish political from social and economic liberalism. This last distinction would violate the interrelation and interdependence of liberty and freedom as well as politics and economics in all aspects of life, because liberalism does not rest on a single dimension. It is highly possible to be "liberal" on extension of political rights, and "nonliberal" on economic relations. Such a distinction might violate our concern with liberal principles, separating thinkers and issues which belong together. Our collection, however, focuses on major themes which Anglo-Ameri-

can liberals themselves have focused on over time. We feel this essentially the-
matic approach, foreshadowed by our distinction between types of liberalism,
will provide the easiest and most systematic approach to Anglo-American liberal
thought.

Liberal Principles and Policies

By now many readers are probably wondering how we dare call all of the thinkers we have mentioned ''liberal.'' Many of our students have asked us how something can be called ''liberal'' in one period and ''conservative'' in another. For
example, they often ask how limited government may be considered ''liberal'' in
1776 (by Adam Smith and the American Revolutionaries) and ''conservative''
today. Their confusion reflects a much wider confusion over the use of terms such
as ''liberal'' or ''conservative'' that one commonly sees in the press or hears from
news commentators. The answer lies in looking beyond single ideas and misapplied labels to the principles, purposes, and assumptions which lie behind specific
proposals.

At its heart, liberalism refers to liberation, largely *individual* liberation. If all
liberals assume that human beings are capable of liberation and freedom, the issue
then becomes where, how, and how much. Here we must distinguish basic principles and values from secondary principles or policies designed to implement principles. Though the distinction between principle and policy can never be completely clear, fundamental goals which liberals have advocated include personal
freedom, political liberty, and ''individualism.'' Many policies or ''methods''
have been urged to protect these goals, such as tolerance, rule of law, free
inquiry, and limited government. Each of these has often been elevated to virtually a first principle in itself. Certainly it is difficult to imagine how we could have
any kind of individual freedom without tolerance, the rule of law, or free inquiry.
All of these seem absolutely necessary to protect freedom and individual welfare.
But in saying this, we have made them instrumental. Yes, they are vital and
perhaps indispensible, but they are still instrumental to the ends of freedom, liberty, and individual welfare.

But, you may ask, what has happened to limited government? Surely if that is a
vital and perhaps absolutely necessary instrument for freedom, then anyone concerned for liberty must advocate limited government. Our answer is ''not
proven.'' It is logical to deny that anyone who advocated freedom and liberty
could give their unconditional loyalty to any state (leaving aside Hegel's notion of
freedom), and still be consistent. But that does not mean that we must rush into
the either/or fallacy and reject governmental involvement as illegitimate. If total
government means no freedom, no government does not logically nor necessarily
mean total freedom (for if it did, social contract theorists such as John Locke and
John Rawls could not explain why people have created government).

We must say that the answer is indeterminate—it depends. Upon what? Circumstances. But "circumstances" seems to confuse the issue. Surely that reduces us to relativism and then it might be best to stick with what we have— representative, fragmented government—and at least be certain of something. After all, the liberal faith in limited, representative government does reflect the traditional liberal fear that anyone with power will tend to abuse that power unless checked. All liberals do worry about the abuse of governmental power, but many know well that private individuals in "private" institutions may also abuse power. It is an act of faith, and nothing more, to argue that only governments abuse power or have power that is relative to freedom. Economic power (control over jobs, interest rates, and vital resources), and social power (control over access to desirable status, education, and hierarchical structures in social relations) affect freedom.

In one period limited government may be a means to freedom, if it is the government that is the major obstacle to freedom. If not, then emphasis on limited government may undermine freedom and encourage the abuse of private power. In such situations people may turn to government in an effort to increase freedom, both freedom *from* the abuse of economic and social power and freedom *to* participate in these areas. Thus one can consistently maintain that for Adam Smith to argue for limited government was "liberal" because, within the circumstances of his environment, government regulation of the economy was an obstacle to the liberation of an important source of human energy and freedom. At the same time it can be "liberal" to argue that the private powers liberated by reduced government power eventually need regulation to prevent the abuse of this power, and that government (today) is the only instrument sufficiently powerful to do so. Those who argue only for limited government (today) are often called "conservatives" because they are opposed to the changes contained in this shift of focus.

If this seems complex, it is. But then reality is complex, and any effort to reduce political reality to a simple formula is bound to hinder real understanding. As Hanson notes in the section reprinted in the readings, "the cause of liberty must simultaneously rely upon and mistrust the coercive powers of government."[8] We must constantly be alert to the principles people advocate and ask if their means implement or retard those principles. We must separate "time-bound" and "timeless" elements in their arguments. Time-bound elements refer to the specific proposals which liberals advocate to implement and apply their values. Though policies cannot be infinitely flexible, they can and must change in response to fairly specific conditions. Timeless elements refer to basic values and principles, such as reason, individualism, and rights, which are the basis for and purpose behind specific policies. These remain fairly constant even if there is a major reemphasis or reinterpretation (such as development of the idea of positive freedom), which affects policy proposals and opportunities in concrete situations. A means which in one age helps ensure liberty, may, in another, become an obstacle to liberty. Thus we must constantly be aware of the circumstances within which arguments and proposals take place. For many reform liberals laissez-faire principles are the result of specific historical conditions, and these thinkers criticize the defenders of laissez-faire for making principles of what were only means. Indeed, laissez-faire liberals often call themselves "conservatives," acknowledging the difference of principle. As a consequence, we must avoid defining "liberal" and "conservative" by policy alone and look to principles, while still asking if a specific policy will implement basic principles. Even if "liberals" and "conservatives" seemingly favor or oppose the same policy, their reasons and expectations may be different, or the context and content of the policy may be very different. Attitudes on quotas, busing, and increased governmental influence in the economy are current examples.

Granted all of this, we must still ask if there is a common thread which enables us to call Adam Smith and John Maynard Keynes, John Locke and John Stuart Mill liberals. After all, the meaning and content of liberalism have changed. We believe there are common characteristics, despite changes in specific policy recommendations. Each of these takes on meaning and significance within the controversies of a specific period of time. Thus even though liberals might agree to all of these across time, their exact definition has changed, and will continue to change, based on specific issues and personalities.

Common Characteristics

"Liberal" and "liberalism" appear to many people to defy definition. Yet many other basic terms, such as "democracy," "socialism," "rights," and even "political party" also lack a precise definition, perhaps because they are so important. Still, we use them and convey meaning with them. This is so because they retain a shared meaning even when they are used as fighting words, slogans, pejoratives, or expletives. There are a number of crucial ideas and principles which are constant to liberalism. These principles, assumptions, and basic policies need to be taken as a group, or at least in combination, because they supplement and limit each other. Liberals have believed that these principles must be weighed and balanced together. No single principle if taken to its logical conclusion is capable of producing a good society. Thus individualism, if carried too far, means the end of society; if ignored, the end of liberty. These are not either/or questions, but rather efforts to achieve the maximization of each principle in combination with the others.

One of liberalism's most important assumptions is that *human beings are essentially rational and competent,* that they are able to perceive their own interests. Of course, liberals and others have violently disagreed over what is in a person's interest, but the concept of interest forms the historical core of liberalism. Despite its innocent look, this concept has not been used very often by political thinkers and was virtually nonexistent before the development of seventeenth-century English liberalism. This assumption forms the basis for liberal arguments in support of mass political participation and free public education. This does not mean that liberals assume that all people are good or completely rational (though some have said as much). Rather it points to a hopeful series of alternatives—people can understand their situation; they are more than victims of emotion, fate, or chance; they can be taught; trust *can* be placed in ordinary people; common people are capable of being a little better; and people who are encouraged to think and reason make better citizens than those who are kept in ignorance. Thomas Jefferson put this as well as anyone else: "We believed . . . that man was a rational animal, endowed by nature with rights . . . and that he could be restrained from wrong and protected in the right by moderate powers confided to persons of his own choice, and held to their duties by dependence on his own will. . . . [Men] habituated to think for themselves and to follow their reason as their guide would be more easily and safely governed than with minds nourished in error and vitiated and debased, as in Europe, by ignorance, indigence, and oppression" (selection 7).

Even if it can be proven empirically that everyone is not rational and competent, this does not undermine the moral argument that all people should be treated as if they were. Nor, in the absence of universally agreed upon distinctions, does it mean that we can easily separate the competent from those who are not, particularly if you believe that unchecked power will be abused. Strip liberalism of this assumption about competence and you undermine its faith in freedom, individualism, and rights. That is why liberals such as John Locke, Thomas Jefferson, and John Dewey have emphasized the importance of education to develop human talents as a basic support for free government and human happiness.

This assumption has also divided liberals from conservatives of all varieties. If people are more rational and competent than not, then it becomes possible to view them as masters of their situation or at least able to improve their situation. Starting with the Putney Radicals through the Enlightenment and even today, this assumption has led liberals to downgrade tradition and history as limits on human possibilities. Though this downgrading has often led them to ignore historical conditioning and limits, it has also promised that people need not forever remain the same as their ancestors, and that they can plan, modify, and change their lives and their societies. Classic, laissez-faire, and reform liberals often disagree about where and how to apply this principle, but they hold it in common.

Individualism is a second basic liberal principle. Liberals have held it as a value in itself, as a means to other ends, and as a corollary of their belief in rights and human abilities. Individualism means that we assume that individual persons are the basic building blocks of society even if man is social by nature. Society and government exist to serve individual welfare, not the other way around. In this sense, liberalism is in fundamental disagreement with all organic models of society, whether they be traditional, conservative, fascist, or some variety of Marxism. Thus liberals have held that individuals are both the key to and reason for social-political-economic improvement. Moreover, they have assumed that individuals seeking their own interests need little direction in doing so. This assumption further implies that individual interests are compatible, or at least capable of being reconciled with each other and the common interest. Many liberals still believe that the common interest can be attained by, or is expressed in, the pursuit of private interests. This assumption has been under constant attack, and, in light of energy and resource problems, is undergoing re-examination. Such re-examination, however, is unlikely to affect the central place of individual welfare in liberal thinking, even if it leads to a change in assumptions about how to achieve that welfare.

Liberals have never completely agreed on the meaning of individualism nor how individualism is best expressed. Seventeenth-century liberals emphasized religious tolerance and pluralism. Laissez-faire liberals emphasized economic liberty and a free marketplace as the means of pursuing and reconciling individual interests. They emphasized minimum government and maximum individual action. This idea was convenient for the expanding middle classes of the eighteenth and nineteenth century, but often left other groups at an extreme disadvantage. Moreover, it ignored political liberty and the consequences of pushing any single liberal principle to extreme conclusions while ignoring others. Reform liberals have therefore argued that organization and governmental intervention to create the conditions of freedom are necessary if everyone is to be ensured the benefits of individualism. Liberals have agreed on the desirability of making the individual the center of social activity and policy, but have disagreed about the means to do this.

Individualism, placing individuals at the focus of policy and value, is not the same as a philosophy of individuality which often ignores the social context of human activity. Liberalism does not necessarily mean a loss of community or an ignoring of the common interest or common good, any more than does concern for the common interest mean we must sacrifice the individual to the state. T. H. Green, Thomas Jefferson, John Maynard Keynes, and to a lesser extent Jeremy Bentham are examples of liberals who were deeply concerned with creating a community supportive of individuals. But, though important, the community and communal framework are not exclusive concerns. T. H. Green argued that a discussion of freedom makes sense only when discussing individuals. Liberals often argue that it is only by treating people as ends in themselves that we can ensure that they will not be treated as means to some other, or someone else's end.

Rights and Freedom and Liberty as liberal principles are both implied by competence and individualism and accepted as ends in themselves, even though one person's rights may clash with another person's exercise of individual freedom. Anglo-American liberals have agreed that rights and freedom belong to or adhere in individuals, and are related, though not synonymous. The idea of having a right refers to having a privilege or claim to do something. This privilege may be based upon custom or tradition, on natural law/rights or on positive law. The concept of freedom asserts that a person may be free of some particular interference in his or her life, or that he or she may do something unhindered, such as vote or enjoy free speech. If such a claim is enforceable under the law we call it a positive right, one which is easier to protect in the event of conflict. If it is not enforceable under the law, or is claimed against the letter of the positive law, we refer to it as a moral right. Then its protection will be more precarious, but a long and still growing tradition asserts that such rights are real.

Individual freedom/liberty (from here on in we will not attempt to distinguish them) is part of the core of liberalism, even though there is a centuries old debate over what they mean and where and to whom they apply. Perhaps freedom/liberty is too important a concept to consign to one definition. Like rights which are often, but not exclusively, an expression of individual freedom, the concept refers to being able to hold and carry out those actions which a person may wish to hold or to carry out. The list of potential claims at first appears endless. For example, the United States Constitution lists at least forty-five political rights and other documents and nations discuss economic and social rights not found in the Constitution. Each claim, however, carries with it the demand that some area of human life must be free from either private or governmental interference. That is, there is some area of activity where an individual or group may think or do as they choose. For early liberals this often meant a distinction between state and society. Classic liberals were first concerned with the idea of religious freedom—that people should have the right to hold and practice their own religious beliefs. This was expanded to include a wide area of political activity including equality before the law, the suffrage, speech, press, and assembly (see "Agreement of the People," selection 2). Historically this idea developed into an attack on privileged status and unequal treatment by the law, a common theme which runs from the first to the last selection in this book. Targets have varied over time—monarchy, churches, economic monopolies, discrimination—but freedom/liberty has been a thread uniting all liberals.

But to what areas of human life does a claim to freedom/liberty apply? Does it apply to all areas or only a few, such as voting and investing? Laissez-faire liberals emphasized economic freedom, largely defined as allowing people to compete freely with each other. They viewed government as the major institutional threat to freedom. Many nonliberals and reform liberals have argued, on the other hand, that government is not the only threat, and that many noninstitutional factors such as discrimination against the aging are impediments to freedom/liberty. Today liberals disagree among themselves over whether to include questions of schools, race, and sex on the agenda of liberty, and whether, and in what areas, freedom/liberty refers only to removal of restraints or to the active supply of the means and opportunities to exercise formal freedom, that is, positive freedom.

Moreover, individual freedom requires individual choice. The person who has no choice, or only an extremely limited choice, is not free, though liberals constantly argue over which areas of life choice should extend to. Currently arguments rage over abortion, the status of women, preference for minorities in hiring or admission to professional schools, homosexuality, drug use, and control over the mass media. In each of these areas liberals are asking where their basic values fit, and how best to extend those values. What areas we will emphasize in freeing the individual vary depending on what we see as a threat to individuals in carrying out the activities which we and they accept as legitimate. The permanent problem of freedom ''is the need to recognize the relativity of freedom to conditions of time and place. Liberty in any age will mean freedom from those forces felt as oppressive in that age.''[9] In all ages, however, vested privilege and claims of superiority are the common targets, regardless of the source of such claims.

Many people have asserted that there is an inherent conflict between freedom/liberty and our next characteristic, *equality*. There is some tension here, but tensions are inevitable where there are no rigid rules which take the place of thinking and individual responsibility. These become irreconcilable concepts only if each is pushed to its ultimate limit. Then total freedom can destroy equality, as some will claw their way ahead of others and then claim that their competition is the only legitimate expression of freedom. Total equality will destroy freedom, for then it is conceivable that all would receive the same reward poured into the same mold. Either of these extremes would destroy the creative tension between these concepts, a tension that has allowed liberalism to adapt to changing circumstances. Moreover each extreme would violate the liberal concern for individualism, for individualism can exist only where people have the chance to express themselves without fear or stifling inequalities. When most liberals discuss equality they do not mean equality of results or reward but an equal opportunity to exercise freedom and self-choice.

This notion of equality means much more than an absence of legal obstacles to achievement but includes elements of political, social, and economic equality. It means the elimination of gross inequalities in wealth and status, even if they result from the exercise of a limited notion of freedom. This is necessary because sometimes the exercise of one person's freedom may make it impossible for other people to exercise their potential choices—i.e., their freedom. Thus free schools and the income tax do not violate freedom more than they contribute to the equality that is often necessary for people to be free. Today the issue is whether the proposed Equal Rights Amendment, busing, and national health insurance might make freedom a greater reality for more people, by allowing more people to choose their life regardless of sex, race, or economic condition. The search for balance between freedom and equality must go on, as does the search for freedom/liberty itself, because a tension between these values is built into liberalism and liberal societies.

Tolerance (represented in this volume by Locke, Voltaire, Jefferson, and John Stuart Mill) is accepted by all forms of liberals as necessary to individual freedom and good in itself. Liberals defend tolerance by pointing to the great dangers of intolerance, which has led to wars of religion, vast amounts of persecution, and is the backbone of all forms of modern dictatorship. However, liberals go beyond a negative defense to argue that not only is diversity legitimate, but it may be a positive good. Diversity can enhance choice by providing more alternatives, thereby increasing the range of freedom. Moreover, many liberals believe that it is only by tolerating differences that we can search for and hope to find the truth or a reasonable approximation thereof. Yet even if tolerance does not lead to discovery of *the truth,* liberals argue it is necessary because it may help us to decide what is error and lead us to better understand and defend what we believe. Moreover, tolerance testifies to a belief in the moral autonomy of individuals, an autonomy that is destroyed by censorship and intolerance. Thus a defense of free inquiry is closely associated with tolerance, and this defense often includes an attack on dogmatism and inflexibility in thinking and in politics.

Liberals also share a number of basic *political assumptions* which are conclusions from the preceding principles and are often argued for as principles themselves. One of these is a deep concern for *methods* in politics—how we proceed in our political activities and whether we follow a known set of rules of procedure. Liberals often tend to argue that it is more important to agree on a *process* for decision making to ensure fairness and nonarbitrary action than to agree on any one single decision, so long as fundamental principles are not systematically violated in the process. Thus it is often argued that if we short circuit the normal processes of decision making, no matter how noble the end, we open up the possibility of arbitrary action which will deprive everyone of their freedom. Critics claim this makes a fetish of procedure at the cost of ignoring and even oppressing those who cannot participate. They cite especially those who have been excluded from participation by law or custom or who lack significant power and hence the ability to participate in the decision-making process. This is a serious problem because any decision-making system will be unfair from someone's perspective. Liberals who take their values seriously acknowledge that no procedure is perfect and work to correct the problems, even acknowledging the legitimacy of actions such as civil disobedience. While outside the accepted procedures, this tactic is often directed toward opening and expanding both the procedures and the principles those procedures are supposed to protect.

The basic principles of liberalism must also defend a right of *dissent.* Tolerance, respect for individualism, and the belief in rights demands this. At the minimum, as part of the methods of government, liberals accept the *right of people to oppose government.* The right and legitimacy of opposition to government is one of the great liberal inventions and is obviously related to tolerance and freedom. It makes political parties and interest groups possible. Legitimation of opposition also helps to solve the problem of finding alternatives to government policies and, perhaps more importantly, helps solve the problem of transition between one and another government or group of office holders. That the right to oppose government policy and to actively oppose it by organizing has not always been an obvious and accepted right is illustrated by the fact that many of the founders of the United States deeply feared factionalism and the organization of political parties. Centuries of political and religious censorship testify to the common fear that opposition is the same as treason, as well as to the belief that there is but one truth which must be imposed, by force if necessary.

While many people agree that opposition parties, newspapers, and interest groups are legitimate, what about opposition that goes beyond these channels? Is civil disobedience legitimate, and if so, when and under what restrictions? No political ideology has ever completely justified disobedience, resistance, or revolution against those that hold that ideology, but the liberal tradition, as opposed to particular liberal politicians, has consistently argued that people may have a right to oppose governments, even popularly elected ones, if those governments flagrantly abuse rights. This question takes us beyond our immediate concerns, but several of our authors will address it.

Generally liberals have accepted participation and representative institutions. As Jefferson points out (selection 7) these processes not only help protect the interests of the people at large, but also help to improve people by educating them to political understanding and public affairs. This belief reveals a common concern with and fear of power. Liberals have generally stood for limited government. Even today, when many liberals have turned to strong government to protect individualism and freedom, they have often done so with reluctance. Though we can distinguish principle (here freedom) from policy (attitudes toward government), no person concerned with freedom and individualism can fully give any institution, whether it be government or the market place, total power. Thus many reform liberals seek both to use government for their ends and to limit the ability of governors to act without restraint. Constitutionalism, separation of powers, bureaucracies responding to different constituencies, court actions, and the liberal's bad conscience all act to balance expanded government.

The energy and resource crises will bring into deeper focus the problem of employing government to protect rights, freedom, and individualism. These crises have the potential to reduce choice and thus freedom, increase planning and governmental involvement in social and economic relations, and acutely raise the problem of equitable distribution among groups and classes. Though all contemporary ideologies fail to deal with this issue, only liberalism is deeply concerned with the individual freedom and mobility which may be curtailed. A strong reaffirmation of fundamental liberal values, coupled with the kind of rethinking of policy to protect basic values that John Maynard Keynes engaged in during the 1930s, is necessary to begin to cope with this challenge. How we answer the question of expanded governmental involvement to protect liberal values depends on your perception of who or what is the greatest threat to freedom at a particular time.

These principles and assumptions represent the common intellectual core of liberalism. While specific policies and proposals change, these principles have largely remained the same, though there have been major changes in emphasis among them. At heart these differences involve skepticism about any claim to absolute truth, especially if such a claim will arbitrarily limit what people may think, say, and do. There is a persistent refusal in the history of liberalism to elevate any single principle to the highest value, where it is pursued to the exclusion of all others that might also be of benefit to people. Rather, there is a consistent argument that we must adjust claims and principles and not allow even liberty or individualism to be carried to their possible extremes. Thus liberalism implies mistrust of fanaticism, and requires balancing, listening to other sides, weighing claims, and some skepticism. It proudly acknowledges what some critics charge: that it attempts to achieve both liberty/freedom and equality, individualism and democracy, freedom and workable government. This in turn involves a certain amount of ambiguity. Though the basic principles are accepted as unchallengeable, their specific application may change. To many this appears as indecisiveness. To liberals it is necessary to human survival and justice.

Liberalism and Democracy

Liberalism and democracy are linked but conceptually distinct. Under the proper conditions each may support the other. Though many of the classic liberal writers were not thoroughgoing democrats (selection 5 by James Mill), the universalistic logic of their arguments, especially about consent and rights, implied mass participation. The development of representative government encouraged a merging of liberal and democratic thinking and institutions. This blending is readily apparent in The Putney Debates, Thomas Jefferson, Thomas Paine, and C. B. Macpherson (selections 1, 7, 8, and 22). Yet there is a tension between liberalism and democracy. Most of our students are surprised, even shocked, when we mention that there can be a great deal of conflict between democratic and liberal values. Though Americans often attempt to link them, they are not always compatible. This is especially true of pure majoritarian democracy, which often emphasizes majority rule to the exclusion of other considerations.[10] If majorities have an absolute right to rule, if there will be no limit upon the rights of a majority, then we cannot consider minority rights. Minorities will have only those rights allowed to them by the majority. They can have no rights against the majority without the consent of the majority.[11] Even where people enjoy legal tolerance and rights they may still find their behavior excessively limited due to what John Stuart Mill called the tyranny of the majority—extreme social pressure to conform to a very narrow range of accepted values, beliefs, and practices. People may then find that it is very costly to exercise formal rights of which the majority or powerful minorities disapprove.

The Anglo-American liberal tradition has rarely defined democracy in purely majoritarian terms but continental tradition has occasionally done so. The bad reputation that democracy suffered from in early modern times was due to the contention, based on some ancient Greek writers, that democracy was simply rule by the ignorant masses, without any regard for talent or distinction. Jean-Jacques Rousseau's *Social Contract* is an example of conflict between majoritarianism and liberalism. Rousseau argued that the individual gives himself up to the community, having no rights against it. Individuals have only the rights of citizens, the most important of which is to participate in the deliberations which determine the General Will. Presumably this is determined by some sort of consensus. Once the General Will has been determined, it becomes the real will of each individual within the community. Individuals cannot disagree with the General Will, because then they would be disagreeing with themselves. Individuals who persist in disagreeing with the General Will, or in disobeying it, can be forced to be free, to obey their real will, by being forced into conformity with the General Will. Individuals thus have no rights against the General Will. If you contend that only a small group or a gifted individual can interpret the General Will, you move from radical democracy to tyranny in one step, which is why Rousseau was opposed by many of his liberal contemporaries.

The American Civil Rights movement in the 1950s and 1960s is a classic illustration of the potential conflict between majoritarian and liberal claims. Protesters attacked segregation on classic liberal grounds: violation of natural and civil rights; unequal treatment of persons by the law; unequal education, job, and residential opportunities; violation of government trusts; denial of liberty and freedom. Men such as Martin Luther King appealed over the heads of segregationists and local law to the Bill of Rights, American tradition, notions of religion, natural rights, and natural justice to justify their claims for inclusion into American society. Segregationists, on the other hand, often emphasized local majority rule. Again and again they appealed to the right of a majority of the people in a local community or a state to decide for themselves what social, political, economic, and educational relations would be allowed in that area. Ultimately their majoritarian claim became illiberal; that is, they argued that majorities have the right to determine what rights will be allowed to minorities.

Liberals are, and should be, troubled by this kind of conflict. Though liberals have repeatedly emphasized processes of decision making, rather than any one single substantive result, they have traditionally argued for participation and majority rule as fundamental rights. When liberal values and majority wishes come into severe conflict, neither liberalism nor democracy wins. Such conflict is an inevitable part of complex politics, and liberals argue that we must weigh and balance rival claims, admitting there will always be some element of ambiguity, but attempting to resolve these claims in the direction of the maximum amount of individual freedom and development. Ultimately liberal values support democracy, and democratic forms can protect liberal values only if, with Jefferson, we work for both massive participation and minority rights. Jefferson pointed the way toward the development of liberal democracy, a combination of rights and participation within a framework of majority government.

Liberty, individualism, rights, and participation are related. Liberals and liberalism have contributed more to removing restraints upon people and creating an humanitarian climate than the adherents of any other ideology. In their skepticism, tolerance, lack of belief in absolutes, emphasis on making improvements when possible, providing a critical alternative to ideological bombast, mistrust of arbitrary power, and emphasis on free discussion, liberalism and liberals keep the path to alternative futures open.[12] In an age when many are armed with ideologies to justify repression of any ideas or institutions with which they disagree, when torture and mass murder are made common by the pursuit of ends which only a privileged few are presumed to see or understand, this is no small accomplishment. Today only liberalism and those ideologies closely related to liberalism encourage pluralism, legitimate the search for alternatives, allow the questioning of their own values, and admit it is legitimate (even if not always encouraged) to question and criticize them when they turn into orthodoxy. In comparing liberalism with other ideologies, programs, and value systems we must keep in mind what John Stuart Mill in his *Principles of Political Economy* insisted upon (selection 19): we must compare ideals with ideals, policy with policy, result with result, for if we do not then one system will inevitably appear superior to another, but we will not in fact be comparing them as they are. Rather, we will compare how one might ideally be with how one actually is, and this will ensure we will not understand either one.

Liberalism, Human Rights,
and the Purpose
of the State

The doctrine of human rights has very deep roots in Western culture and thinking, but it was not until the sixteenth century that large numbers of people began to consciously claim individual rights. Previously, rights were considered to be communal in nature. They belonged to the community. A person's rights depended on his or her membership in a group or guild or position in society, but rights did not belong to a person simply as a human being. Serfs had the rights that pertained to serfs, and noblemen those to noblemen. Anglo-American liberalism began with a claim to individual religious and political rights and a concern with how they can be protected. This theme is illustrated by the first three sections.

The desire to protect and expand rights was a basic cause of the English, American, and French revolutions. The liberals in this section, and many of the others in the book, argue that the purpose of the state and government is to protect people and their rights. The search for an institutional basis—a constitutional order or settlement—to protect rights ties together the authors in this and the next section. This concern for institutions and how they embody and protect basic values is characteristic of Anglo-American liberalism.

In discussing rights we must make a number of fundamental distinctions to help us decide what we are talking about. The first question we must consider is what do we mean by rights. This has been a point of violent disagreement for more than three hundred years. People with rights assert a claim, though some say that the word "claim" is too weak. What do people claim? Essentially two things. First, to be allowed to do something. This may be to speak freely, worship by choice, participate in politics, or lead a self-determined life. The important point is that no one should interfere with the exercise of this claim. Second, people claim the right of having certain things done to them or provided for them. A claim to economic and social rights such as health care or social security falls into this category. Until this century most liberals defined rights solely in the first sense, but many reform liberals have extended the notion to the provision of services. Even if we agree on one or both of these notions of rights there may still be disagreement over specific rights.

An analysis of rights also requires that we do not confuse a right as a claim with the justification or proof it is based on. There is much confusion and conflict over why people have rights. We may distinguish moral claims from positive claims though sometimes these may refer to the same rights. People have claimed moral rights based on social contracts, utility, custom, natural law, psychology, and religion. Whether or not we believe these can provide the foundation for rights will help determine what we mean by rights. Some people have argued, however, that the only rights which it makes sense to discuss are positive rights enforceable under the written law, that is, rights guaranteed by the law of a specific nation. If this is true then there can be no appeal beyond the written law, whatever it may be, a position many but not all liberals disagree with.

We must also consider what areas rights apply to. Are rights limited to classic political claims such as freedom and participation? Many classic liberals and contemporary conservatives claim these are the only rights. Yet since the late eighteenth century more and more liberals (Thomas Paine was one of the first) have argued that rights include social and economic rights. Today these may include protection from unemployment and a guarantee of a minimum level of welfare.

In mentioning guarantees we raise the question of *who* guarantees *what* to *whom*. Are rights applicable only against government or are they also applicable against private persons or groups? With the exception of protection of person and property, many classic liberals and contemporary conservatives have emphasized government. Yet starting with at least John Stuart Mill and his concern with the "tyranny of the majority," liberals have become more and more concerned with the conditions and relations under which people work, live, and study. If people do not have any appeal from arbitrary power in these areas they cannot be truly free.

Next, who possesses rights, groups or individuals? In the Middle Ages rights were linked with role and status, as they are informally to this day. Most of the Anglo-American liberal tradition, along with contemporary Anglo-American conservatives, have argued that individuals as individuals possess rights, even if there is disagreement over their content and source. Rights are not given by any status, class, race, nation, government, or state but belong to people as people. In this sense they are universal. But many continental liberals and traditional conservatives have argued that people have only those rights which are given to them by their position, nation, or state. Consequently there are no universal rights or the rights of man, only the rights of an American, an Englishman, a German, etc.

Finally we face the problem of translating principles into policies. What policies actually protect what kinds of rights, under what circumstances, and for whom? What kinds of trade-offs will we accept (such as a decrease in petroleum sales) because of our demand that other nations protect rights? Different liberals have answered these and the other five questions in terms of their perceptions of the dangers and opportunities inherent in each. These distinctions are relevant to understanding the continuing debate over rights at home and in other countries such as in the Soviet Union or the developing nations. Which set of choices we accept in defining rights will largely determine our reactions to contemporary rights claims and conflicts.

1   THE PUTNEY DEBATES

The English Civil War (1641-1649) shattered the old forms of government, making new arrangements necessary. The Putney Debates illustrate one major facet of the search for new ideas, values, and institutions. They took place within the revolutionary army at a General Council of Officers on October 28, 29 and November 1, 1647. The General Council included leading army officers, such as Oliver Cromwell and Henry Ireton, as well as elected representatives of the rank and file of the Parliamentary army—"agitators." The debates centered on what should be the nature of a constitutional settlement because the king had been defeated in battle. More "radical" elements, such as Rainborough, defended the first "Agreement of the People" while the "conservatives" argued for the "Heads of the Proposals."[1] This document would have allowed a larger role for the king and a smaller role for the victorious middle classes. Both sides agreed that there must be a change in the form of government, but disagreed over what obligates people to obey, who would be allowed to participate, and what should be the role of the king and the House of Lords in any new government. In the process of debating whether the rank and file were obliged to obey an agreement which the officers might make with Parliament, the debate raised some of the most fundamental questions of political theory[2]: obligation, consent, representation, participation, rights, justice, freedom, rule of law, contracts, and the idea of a written constitution. These debates represent the issues being discussed in England in the 1640s and point out the shape of liberal discourse for the next three centuries. In the selection below we can easily see how different pictures of human nature and rights lead to different policy conclusions. In discussing the extent of the franchise, Ireton argued that widespread participation would destroy property, as people without property would take the property of the rich. Rainborough and others distinguished property from political rights, appealed to justice and reason, and argued that everyone's property needs protection by having a voice in government.

These selections are from the second day of debates, October 29, 1647. On this day most of the speakers focused on the nature and extent of participation, starting a debate (see James Mill below) which ended in universal adult suffrage only in this century. In the United States all women were guaranteed the right to vote through passage of the Nineteenth Amendment to the Constitution in 1920. In Great Britain all men twenty-one and over who had not been given the vote in the reforms of 1832, 1867, and 1884, and most women thirty and older were granted the right to vote in 1918. All women were given the right to vote in 1928. Recent legislation, such as the Civil Rights acts of 1964, 1965, 1967, and 1969, as well as Supreme Court decisions such as in *Baker* v. *Carr* (369 U.S. 186, 1962), *Gray* v. *Sanders* (372 U.S. 368, 1963), *Wesberry* v. *Sanders* (376 U.S. 1, 1964) and *Reynolds* v. *Simms* (377 U.S. 533, 1964) have extended, refined, and guaranteed the right to participate through an equal vote.

THE SECOND DAY
OF THE PUTNEY DEBATES*

[Debate Begins Over "The Agreement of the People"]

Mr. Pettus.

Wee judge that all inhabitants that have not lost their birthright should have an equall voice in Elections.

Col. Rainborow. [i.e. Rainborough]

I desir'd that those that had engaged in itt [should speak] for really I thinke that the poorest hee that is in England hath a life to live as the greatest hee; and therfore truly, Sir, I thinke itt's cleare, that every man that is to live under a Governement ought first by his owne consent to putt himself under that Governement; and I doe thinke that the poorest man in England is nott att all bound in a stricte sence to that Governement that hee hath not had a voice to putt himself under; and I am confident that when I have heard the reasons against itt, somethinge will bee said to answer those reasons, insoemuch that I should doubt whether he was an Englishman or noe that should doubt of these thinges.

---

*C. H. Firth, ed., *The Clarke Papers,* Vol. 1 (London: Camden Society, 1891). Reprinted by permission of the Royal Historical Society.

Commissary Ireton.

That's [the meaning of] this ["according to the number of the inhabitants."] Give mee leave to tell you, that if you make this the rule I thinke you must flie for refuge to an absolute naturall Right, and you must deny all Civill Right; and I am sure itt will come to that in the consequence. This I perceive is prest . . . as that wee must for this right lay aside all other considerations; this is soe just, this is soe due, this is soe right to them. And that those that they doe thus chuse must have such a power of binding all, and loosing all, according to those limitations; this is prest, as soe due, and soe just as [it] is argued, that itt is an Engagement paramount [to] all others: and you must for itt lay aside all others: if you have engaged any others you must breake itt. . . . For my parte I thinke itt is noe right att all. I thinke that noe person hath a right to an interest or share in the disposing or determining of the affaires of the Kingdome, and in chusing those that shall determine what lawes wee shall bee rul'd by heere, noe person hath a right to this, that hath nott a permanent fixed interest in this Kingedome; and those persons together are properly the Represented of this Kingedome, and consequentlie are to make uppe the Representors of this Kingedome, who taken together doe comprehend whatsoever is of reall or permanent interest in the Kingedome. . . . Wee talke of birthright. Truly [by] birthright there is thus much claime. Men may justly have by birthright, by their very being borne in England, that wee should nott seclude them out of England, that wee should nott refuse to give them aire, and place, and ground, and the freedome of the high wayes and other thinges, to live amongst us. . . . That I thinke is due to a man by birth. Butt that by a man's being borne heere hee shall have a share in that power that shall dispose of the lands heere, and of all thinges heere, I doe nott thinke itt a sufficient ground. I am sure if wee looke uppon that which is the utmost within man's view of what was originally the constitution of this Kingedome, [if wee] looke uppon that which is most radicall and fundamentall, and which if you take away there is noe man hath any land, any goods, [or] any civill interest, that is this: that those that chuse the Representors for the making of Lawes by which this State and Kingedome are to bee govern'd, are the persons who taken together doe comprehend the locall interest of this Kingedome; that is, the persons in whome all land lies, and those in Corporations in whome all trading lies. This is the most fundamentall Constitution of this Kingedome, which if you doe nott allow you allow none att all. This Constitution hath limitted and determined itt that onely those shall have voices in Elections. Itt is true as was said by a Gentleman neere mee, the meanest man in England ought to have [a voice in the election of the government he lives under]. . . . I say this, that those that have the meanest locall interest, that man that hath butt fourty shillinges a yeare, hee hath as great voice in the Election of a Knight for the shire as hee that hath ten thousand a yeare or more, if hee had never soe much; and therfore there is that regard had to itt. . . . If wee shall goe to take away this fundamentall parte of the civill constitution wee shall plainly goe to take away all property and interest that any man hath, either in land by inheritance, or in estate by possession, or any thinge else. There is all the reason and justice that can bee if I will come to live in a Kingedome being a forraigner to itt, or live in a Kingedome having noe permanent interest in itt—if I will desire as a stranger, or claime as one freeborne heere, the ayre, the free passage of highwayes, the protection of lawes and all such things, if I will either desire them, or claime them, I [if I have no permanent interest in that Kingdom], must submitt to those lawes and those rules which those shall choose who taken together doe comprehend the whole interest of the Kingedome.

Col. Rainborow

Truly, Sir, I am of the same opinion I was; and am resolved to keepe itt till I know reason why I should nott. . . . I doe hear nothing att all that can convince mee, why any man that is borne in England ought nott to have his voice in Election of Burgesses. Itt is said, that if a man have nott a permanent interest, hee can have noe claime, and wee must bee noe freer then the lawes will lett us to bee, and that there is noe Chronicle will lett us bee freer then that wee enjoy. Something was said to this yesterday. I doe thinke that the maine cause why Almighty God gave men reason, itt was, that they should make use of that reason, and that they should improve itt for that end and purpose that God gave itt them. And truly, I thinke that halfe a loafe is better then none if a man bee an hungry, yett I thinke there is nothing that God hath given a man that any else can take from him. Therfore I say, that either itt must bee the law of God or the law of man that must prohibite the meanest man in the Kingdome to have this benefitt[3] as well as the greatest. I doe nott finde any thinge in the law of God, that a Lord shall chuse 20 Burgesses and a Gentleman butt two, or a poore man shall chuse none. I finde noe such thinge in the law of nature, nor in the law of nations. Butt I doe finde, that all Englishmen must bee subject to English lawes, and I doe verily believe, that there is noe man butt will say, that the foundation of all law lies in the people, and if [it lie] in the people, I am to seeke for this exemption. And truly I have thought somethinge [else], in what a miserable distressed condition would many a man that hath fought for the Parliament in this quarrell bee? I will bee bound to say, that many a man whose zeale and affection to God and this Kingedome hath carried him forth in this cause hath soe spent his estate that in the way the State, the Army are going hee shall nott hold uppe his head; and when his estate is lost, and nott worth 40s a yeare, a man shall nott have any interest; and there are many other wayes by which estates men have doe fall to decay, if that bee the rule which God in his providence does use. A man when hee hath an estate hath an interest in making lawes, when hee hath none, hee hath noe power in itt. Soe that a man cannott loose that which hee hath for the maintenance of his family, butt hee must loose that which God and nature hath given him. Therfore I doe [think] and am still of the same opinion; that every man born in England cannot, ought nott, neither by the law of God nor the law of nature, to bee exempted from the choice of those who are to make lawes, for him to live under, and for him, for ought I know, to loose his life under. Therfore I thinke there can bee noe great sticke in this.

Truly I thinke that there is nott this day raigning in England a greater fruite or effect of Tyranny then this very thinge would produce. Truly I know nothing free butt onely the Knight of the shire, nor doe I know any thinge in a Parliamentary way that is cleare from the heighth and fulnesse of Tyranny, but onlie [that]. . . .
Ireton.

. . . I think I agreed to this matter, that all should bee equallie distributed. Butt the question is, whether itt should bee distributed to all persons, or whether the same persons that are the electors [now] should bee the Electors still, and itt [be] equallie distributed amongst them. . . .

All the maine thinge that I speake for is because I would have an eye to propertie. I hope wee doe nott come to contend for victorie, butt lett every man consider with himself that hee doe nott goe that way to take away all propertie. For heere is the case of the most fundamentall parte of the Constitution of the Kingedome, which if you take away, you take away all by that. Heere are men of this and this qualitie are determined to bee the Electors of men to the Parliament, and they are all those who have any permanent interest in the Kingedome, and who taken together doe comprehend the whole interest of the Kingedome. I meane by permanent, locall, that is nott any where else. . . . Now I wish wee may all consider of what right you will challenge, that all the people should have right to Elections. Is itt by the right of nature? If you will hold forth that as your ground, then I thinke you must deny all property too, and this is my reason. For thus: by that same right of nature, whatever itt bee that you pretend, by which you can say, "one man hath an equall right with another to the chusing of him that shall governe him"— by the same right of nature, hee hath an equal right in any goods hee see: meate, drinke, cloathes, to take and use them for his sustenance. Hee hath a freedom to the land, [to take] the ground, to exercise itt, till itt; he hath the same freedome to any thinge that any one doth account himself to have any propriety in. Why now I say then, if you, against this most fundamentall parte of [the] civill Constitution [which I have now declar'd], will pleade the law of nature, that a man should, paramount [to] this, and contrary to this, have a power of chusing those men that shall determine what shall bee law in this state, though he himself have noe permanent interest in the State, [but] whatever interest hee hath hee may carry about with him. If this be allowed, [because by the right of nature], wee are free, wee are equall, one man must have as much voice as another, then shew mee what steppe or difference [there is], why by the same right of necessity to sustaine nature [I may not claim property as well]? Itt is for my better being [I may say], and possibly nott for itt neither, possibly I may nott have soe reall a regard to the peace of the Kingedom as that man who hath a permanent interest in itt. Hee that is heere to day and gone to morrow, I doe nott see that hee hath such a permanent interest . . . if upon these grounds you doe paramount [to] all Constitutions hold uppe this law of nature, I would faine have any man shew mee their bounds, where you will end, and [why you should not] take away all propertie?

Col. Rainborow.

I shall now bee a little more free and open with you than I was before. . . . For my parte, as I thinke, you forgott somethinge that was in my speech, and you doe nott only your selves beleive that [we] are inclining to anarchy, butt you would make all men beleive that. And Sir, to say because a man pleades, that every man hath a voice [by the right of nature], that therefore itt destroyes [by] the same [argument all property]—that there's a propertie the law of God sayes itt; else why [hath] God made that law, ''Thou shalt nott steale?'' If I have noe interest in the Kingedome I must suffer by all their lawes bee they right or wronge. I am a poore man, therfore I must bee prest. Nay thus; a Gentleman lives in a country and hath three or fower Lordshippes as some men have—God knowes how they gott them—and when a Parliament is call'd hee must bee a Parliament man; and itt may bee hee sees some poore men, they live neere this man, hee can crush them—I have knowne an evasion to make sure hee hath turned the poore man out of doores; and I would faine know whether the potencie of men doe nott this, and soe keepe them under the greatest tyranny that was thought off in the world. Therefore I thinke that to that itt is fully answered. God hath sett downe that thinge as to propriety with this law of his, ''Thou shalt not steale.'' For my parte I am against any such thought, and as for yourselves I wish you would nott make the world beleive that wee are for anarchy.

Lieut. Generall.

. . . Noe man sayes that you have a minde to anarchy, butt the consequence of this rule tends to anarchy, must end in anarchy; for where is there any bound or limitt sett if you take away this [limit], that men that have noe interest butt the interest of breathing [shall have no voices in elections]? Therfore I am confident on't wee should nott bee soe hott one with another.

Ireton.

Now then, as I say, I would misrepresent nothing; the answer which had any thing of matter in itt, the great and maine answer upon which that which hath bin said against this rests, that seem'd to be: that itt will nott make the breach of propertie: that there is a law, ''Thou shalt nott steale.'' The same law sayes, ''Honour thy Father and Mother''; and that law doth likewise extend to all that are our governours in that place where wee are in. Soe that, by that there is a forbidding of breaking a Civill Law when wee may live quietly under itt, and a Divine Law. Againe itt is said indeed before, that there is noe Law, noe Divine Law, that tells us, that such a Corporation must have the Election of Burgesses, or such a shire, or the like. . . . That Divine Law doth nott determine particulars butt generalls, in relation to man and man, and to propertie, and all thinges else. . . .

Col. Rainborow.

To the thinge itt self propertie. I would faine know how itt comes to bee the propertie [of some men, and not of others]. As for estates, and those kinde of thinges, and other thinges that belonge to men, itt will bee granted that they are propertie; butt I deny that that is a propertie, to a Lord, to a Gentleman, to any man more then another in the Kingdome of England. Iff itt bee a propertie, itt is a propertie by a law; neither doe I thinke, that there is very little propertie in this thinge by the law of the land, because I thinke that the law of the land in that thinge is the most tyrannicall law under heaven, and I would faine know what wee have fought for, and this is the old law of England and that which inslaves the people of England that they should bee bound by lawes in which they have noe voice att all.[4] [So with respect to the law which says 'Honour thy father and thy mother.'] The great dispute is who is a right Father and a right Mother. I am bound to know who is my Father and Mother, and I take it in the same sence you doe, I would have a distinction, a character whereby God commands mee to honour [them], and for my parte I looke uppon the people of England soe, that wherin they have nott voices in the chusing of their Fathers and Mothers, they are nott bound to that commandement.

Mr. Pettus.

I desire to adde one worde, concerning the worde Propertie. Itt is for somethinge that anarchy is soe much talk't of. For my owne parte I cannott beleive in the least that itt can bee clearlie derived from the paper. Tis true, that somewhat may bee derived in the paper against the power of the Kinge, and somewhat against the power of the Lords. . . . Butt I hope that they may live to see the power of the Kinge and the Lords throwne downe, that yett may live to see propertie preserved. And for this of changing the Representative of the Nation, of changing those that chuse the Representative, making of them more full, taking more into the number then formerly, I had verily thought wee had all agreed that more should have chosen, and that all had desir'd a more equall Representative then wee now have. For now those onely chuse who have 40s. freehold. A man have a lease for 100£ a yeare, a man may have a lease for three lives [but he has no voice]. Butt [as] for this [argument] that itt destroyes all right [to property] that every Englishman that is an inhabitant of England should chuse and have a choice in the Representatives, I suppose itt is [on the contrary] the onely meanes to preserve all propertie. For I judge every man is naturally free; and I judge the reason why men when they were in soe great numbers [choose representatives was] that every man could nott give his voice; and therefore men agreed to come into some forme of Governement that they who were chosen might preserve propertie. I would faine know, if we were to begin a Governement, [whether you would say]

'you have nott 40s. a yeare, therfor you shall not have a voice.' Wheras before
there was a Governement every man had such a choice, and afterwards for this
very cause they did chuse Representatives, and putt themselves into formes of
Governement that they may preserve propertie, and therfore itt is nott to destroy
itt [to give every man a choice].

Ireton.

. . . I doe nott speake of not inlarging this att all, butt of keeping this to the most
fundamentall Constitution in this Kingedome, that is, that noe person that hath
nott a locall and permanent interest in the Kingedome should have an equall
dependance in Elections [with those that have]. Butt if you goe beyond this law, if
you admitt any man that hath a breath and being, I did shew you how this will
destroy propertie. Itt may come to destroy propertie thus: you may have such men
chosen or att least the major parte of them [as have no local and permanent inter-
est]. Why may nott those men vote against all propertie?. . . Shew mee what you
will stoppe att, wherin you sill fence any man in a property by this rule.

Col. Rainborow.

I should nott have spoken againe . . . butt there is much danger and itt may
seeme to some, that there is some kinde of remedy, I thinke that wee are better as
wee are. That the poore shall chuse many, still the people are in the same case, are
over voted still. And therfore truly, Sir, I should desire to goe close to the busi-
nesse; and the thinge that I am unsatisfied in is how itt comes about that there is
such a propriety in some freeborne Englishmen, and nott [in] others.

Cowling.

Why Election was only 40 [shillings] a yeare,[5] which was more than 40
[pounds] a yeare now, the reason was [this], that the Commons of England were
overpowr'd by the Lords, who had abundance of vassalls, butt that they might
still make their lawes good against incroaching prerogatives, therefore they
did exclude all slaves. Now the case is nott soe; all slaves have bought their
freedomes. They are more free that in the common wealth are more
beneficiall. . . .

Mr. Wildman.

Unless I bee very much mistaken wee are very much deviated from the first
Question. Instead of following the first proposition to inquire what is just, I conceive wee looke to prophesies, and looke to what may bee the event, and judge of
the justnesse of a thinge by the consequence. I desire wee may recall [ourselves to
the question] whether itt bee right or noe. I conceive all that hath bin said against
itt will be reduc't to this and another reason; that itt is against a fundamentall law,
[and] that every person ought to have a permanent interest, because itt is nott fitt
that those should chuse Parliaments that have noe lands to bee disposed of by
Parliament. . . . The case is different from the native Inhabitant and forraigner
[i.e. foreigner]. If a forraigner shall bee admitted to bee an Inhabitant in the
Nation, soe hee will submitt to that forme of Governement as the natives doe, hee

hath the same right as the natives, but in this particular. Our case is to bee consider'd thus, that wee have bin under slavery. That's acknowledged by all. Our very lawes were made by our Conquerours; and wheras itt's spoken much of Chronicles, I conceive there is noe creditt to bee given to any of them; and the reason is because those that were our Lords, and made us their vassalls, would suffer nothing else to bee chronicled. Wee are now engaged for our freedome; that's the end of Parliaments, nott to constitute what is already according to the just rules of Governement.[6] Every person in England hath as cleere a right to Elect his Representative as the greatest person in England. I conceive that's the undeniable maxime of Governement: that all governement is in the free consent of the people. If [so], then uppon that account, there is noe person that is under a just Governement, or hath justly his owne, unlesse hee by his owne free consent bee putt under that Governement. This hee cannott bee unlesse hee bee consenting to itt, and therfore according to this maxime there is never a person in England [but ought to have a voice in elections]; if as that Gentleman[7] says bee true, there are noe lawes that in this strictnesse and rigour of justice [any man is bound to] that are nott made by those who heè doth consent to. And therfore I should humbly move, that if the Question bee stated—which would soonest bringe thinges to an issue—itt might rather bee this: whether any person can justly bee bound by law, who doth nott give his consent that such persons shall make lawes for him?

Ireton.

. . . A man ought to bee subject to a law that did nott give his consent, butt with this reservation, that if this man doe thinke himself unsatisfied to bee subject to this law hee may goe into another Kingedome. And soe the same reason doth extend in my understanding to that man that hath noe permanent interest in the Kingedome. If he hath mony, his monie is as good in another place as heere; hee hath nothing that doth locally fixe him to this Kingedome. If this man will live in this Kingedome to trade amongst us, that man ought to subject himself to the law made by the people who have the interest of this Kingedome in us; and yett I doe acknowledge that which you take to bee soe generall a maxime, that in every Kingedome, within every land, the originall of power, of making lawes, of determining what shall bee law in the land, does lie in the people that are possess't of the permanent interest in the land. . . .

Major Rainborow.

I thinke if itt can bee made to appeare, that itt is a just and reasonable thinge, and that is for the preservation of all the freeborne men, itt ought to bee made good unto them. The reason is, that the cheif end of this Governement is to preserve persons as well as estates, and if any law shall take hold of my person itt is more deare than my estate.

Col. Rainborow.

. . . Then I say the one parte shall make hewers of wood and drawers of water of the other five, and soe the greatest parte of the Nation be enslav'd. Truly I thinke wee are still where wee were; and I doe not heare any argument given butt only that itt is the present law of the Kingedome. I say still, what shall become of those many [men] that have laid out themselves for the Parliament of England in this present warre, that have ruined themselves by fighting, by hazarding all they had? They are Englishmen. They have now nothing to say for themselves.

For my parte I thinke wee cannott engage one way or other in the Army if wee doe nott thinke of the people's liberties. If wee can agree where the liberty and freedome of the people lies, that will doe all.

Mr. Wildman.[8]

Truly, Sir, I being desired by the Agents yesterday to appeare att Councill or Committees either, att that time, I suppose I may bee bold to make knowne what I know of their sence, and a little to vindicate them in their way of proceeding, and to shew the necessity of this way of proceeding that they have entred upon. Truly, Sir, as to breaking of Engagements: the Agents doe declare their principle, that whensoever any Engagement cannott bee kept justly they must breake that Engagement. Now though itt's urg'd they ought to condescend to what the Generall Councill doe [resolve], I conceive itt's true [only] soe longe as itt is for their safetie. I conceive [itt's] just and righteous for them to stand uppe for some more speedy vigorous actinges. I conceive itt's noe more than what the Army did when the Parliament did nott only delay deliverance butt oppos'd itt; and I conceive this way of their appearing hath nott appear'd to bee in the least way anythinge tending to devision, since they proceede to cleare the rights of the people; and soe longe as they proceede uppon those righteous principles [for which we first engaged],[9] itt cannot bee laid to their charge that they are deviders. And though itt bee declared [that they ought to stand only as soldiers and not as Englishmen], that the malice of the enemies would have bereaved you of your liberties as Englishmen; therefore as Englishmen they are deeply concerned to regard the due observation of their rights, [and have the same right to declare their apprehensions] as I, or any Commoner, have right to propound to the Kingedome my conceptions what is fitt for the good of the Kingedome. . . . I finde itt to bee their minds . . . a very vast difference in the whole matter of proposalls. The foundation of slavery was rivetted more strongly then before. As where the militia is instated in the Kinge and Lords, and nott in the Commons, there is a foundation of a future quarrell constantlie laid. However the maine thing was that they found by the proposalls propounded the right of the Militia was acknowledged to bee in the Kinge, before any redresse of any one of the people's greivances or any one of their burthens; and [the King was] soe to bee brought in as with a negative voice. . . . And finding [this] they perceived they were as they thought in a sad case, for they thought, hee coming in thus with a negative, the Parliament are butt as soe many cyphers, soe many round O. . . . The godly people are turn'd over and trampled uppon already in the most places of the Kingedome. I speake butt the words of the agents, and I finde this to bee their thoughts. Butt wheras itt is said, "how will this paper [Agreement of the People] provide for anythinge for that purpose?" I say, that this paper doth lay downe the foundations of freedome for all manner of people. Itt doth lay the foundations of souldiers [freedom], wheras they found a great uncertainty in the proposalls: that they should goe to the Kinge for an act of indempnity, and thus the Kinge might command his Judges to hange them uppe for what they did in the warres; because the present Constitution being left as itt was, nothing was law butt what the Kinge sign'd, and nott any ordnance of Parliament. And considering this, they thought itt should bee by an Agreement with the people, wherby a rule betweene the Parliament and the people might bee sett, that soe they might bee destroyed neither by the Kinge's Prerogative, nor Parliament's priviledges. . . . They thought there must bee a necessity of a rule betweene the Parliament and the people, soe that the Parliament should know what they were intrusted to, and what they were nott; and that there might bee noe doubt of the Parliament's power to lay foundations for future quarrells. . . . That there might bee noe dispute betweene Lords and Commons, butt these thinges being setled, there should bee noe more disputes, butt that the Parliament should redresse the peoples grievances.

---

2   THE AGREEMENT

OF THE PEOPLE

Radical groups in England, such as the Levellers, proposed the Agreement of the People as the constitutional settlement for England. The Agreement itself went through several stages of development. The Second Agreement, reprinted here, was presented to Parliament by the Army, January 20, 1649, ten days before the execution of Charles I. It differs from the First Agreement, which was debated at Putney, in being longer and more detailed while omitting some demands. One of the omitted passages required, "that the laws ought to be equal, so they must be good, and not evidently destructive to the safety and well-being of the People." More significantly, the Second Agreement no longer referred to members of Parliament as "deputies" as had the first.

The Agreement of the People argues that government is legitimate only when it is based on consent. It assumes that people are capable of reason and of exercising reason in politics. Even though the Agreements were never implemented they are the ancestors of all modern liberal-democratic constitutions. The authors of the

Agreements intended them to be a contract submitted to the people of England for their approval in creating a new form of government. The Agreements would have protected freedom of conscience and religion, and would have created equality before the law, separation of powers, frequent elections, an expanded franchise, and more equal voting districts. The first version would have excluded persons who did not agree to be bound by the Agreement. Other rights were not included in the Second Agreement on the assumption that the new Parliament would pass protective legislation for them.[1] These provided protection from testifying against oneself, placed limits on capital punishment, required reform of the system of punishment, and guaranteed the right to call witnesses. They also included economic affairs such as limits on restraint of trade and on interest charges.

AN AGREEMENT OF THE PEOPLE OF ENGLAND, AND THE PLACES THEREWITH INCORPORATED, FOR A SECURE AND PRESENT PEACE, UPON GROUNDS OF COMMON RIGHT, FREEDOM, AND SAFETY.*

Having, by our late labours and hazards, made it appear to the world at how high a rate we value our just freedom; and God having so far owned our cause as to deliver the enemies thereof into our hands, we do now hold ourselves bound, in mutual duty to each other, to take the best care we can, for the future, to avoid both the danger of returning into a slavish condition, and the chargeable remedy of another war: for as it cannot be imagined that so many of our countrymen would have opposed us in this quarrel, if they had understood their own good, so may we hopefully promise to ourselves, that when our common Rights and Liberties shall be cleared, their endeavours will be disappointed that seek to make themselves our masters; since therefore our former oppressions and not-yet-ended troubles, have been occasioned either by want of frequent national meetings in council, or by the undue or unequal constitution thereof, or by rendering those meetings ineffectual, we are fully agreed and resolved, God willing, to provide, That hereafter our Representatives be neither left to an uncertainty for times nor be unequally constituted, nor made useless to the ends for which they are intended. In order whereunto we declare and agree.

---

[1]A.S.P. Woodhouse, *Puritanism and Liberty* (Chicago: University of Chicago Press, 1951), pp. 364–67.
*Cobbett's Parliamentary History of England, vol. 3 (London, 1808).

First, That, to prevent the many inconveniences apparently arising from the long continuance of the same persons in Supreme Authority, this present parliament end and dissolve upon, or before, the last day of April, 1649.

Secondly, That the People of England (being at this day very unequally distributed by counties, cities, and boroughs, for the election of their representatives) be indifferently proportioned; and, to this end, that the representative of the whole nation shall consist of 400 persons, or not above. . . . [The Agreement then listed the number of representatives allowed to each county, city, or town.]

Provided, That, the first or second Representative may, if they see cause, assign the remainder of the 400 representers, not hereby assigned, or so many of them as they shall see cause for, unto such counties as shall appear in this present distribution to have less than their due proportion. Provided also, That where any city or borough, to which one representer or more is assigned, shall be found in a due proportion, not competent alone to elect a representer, or the number of representers assigned thereto, it is left to future representatives to assign such a number of parishes or villages near adjoining to such city or borough, to be joined therewith in the elections, as may make the same proportionable.

Thirdly, That the people do, of course, choose themselves a representative once in 2 years, and shall meet for that purpose upon the first Thursday in every second May, by 11 in the morning; and the representatives so chosen to meet upon the second Thursday in the June following, at the usual place in Westminster, or such other place as, by the foregoing Representative, or the Council of State in the interval, shall be, from time to time, appointed and published to the people, at the least 20 days before the time of election: and to continue their sessions there, or elsewhere, until the second Thursday in December following, unless they shall adjourn, or dissolve themselves sooner; but not to continue longer. The election of the first representative to be on the first Thursday in May, 1649; and that, and all future elections, to be according to the Rules prescribed for the same purpose in this Agreement, viz. 1. That the electors in every division shall be natives or denizens of England; not persons receiving alms, but such as are assessed ordinarily towards the relief of the poor; not servants to, and receiving wages from, any particular person. And in all elections, except for the Universities, they shall be men of 21 years of age, or upwards, and housekeepers, dwelling within the division for which the election is: Provided, That (until the end of 7 years next ensuing the time herein limited for the end of this present parliament) no person shall be admitted to, or have any hand or voice in, such elections, who hath adhered unto or assisted the king against the parliament in any of the late wars or insurrections; or who shall make, or join in, or abet, any forcible opposition against this Agreement. 2. That such persons, and such only, may be elected to be of the Representative, who, by the rule aforesaid, are to have voice in elections in one place or other.— Provided, That of those none shall be eligible for the first or second Representative, who have not voluntarily assisted the parliament against the king, either in person before the 14th of June, 1645, or else in money, plate, horse, or arms, lent upon the Propositions, before the end of May, 1643; or who have joined in, or abetted, the treasonable Engagement in London, in 1647; or who declared or engaged themselves for a Cessation of Arms with the Scots that invaded this nation the last summer; or for compliance with the actors in any insurrections of the same summer; or with the Prince of Wales, or his accomplices, in the revolted Fleet. Provided also, That such persons as, by the Rules in the preceding Article, are not capable of electing until the end of 7 years, shall not be capable to be elected until the end of 14 years next ensuing. And we desire and recommend it to all men, that, in all times, the persons to be chosen for this great trust may be men of courage, fearing God and hating covetousness; and that our representatives would make the best provisions for that end. 3. That whoever, by the Rules in the two preceding Articles, are incapable of electing, or to be elected, shall presume to vote in, or be present at, such election for the first or second Representative; or, being elected, shall presume to sit or vote in either of the said representatives, shall incur the pain of confiscation of the moiety [half] of his estate, to the use of the public, in case he have any visible estate to the value of 50£. and if he has not such an estate, then shall incur the pain of imprisonment for 3 months. And if any person shall forcibly oppose, molest, or hinder the people, capable of electing as aforesaid, in their quiet and free election of repre- senters, for the first Representative, then each person so offending shall incur the penalty of Confiscation of his whole estate, both real and personal; and, if he has not an estate to the value of 50£. shall suffer imprisonment during one whole year without bail or mainprize. Provided, That the offender in each such case be con- victed within 3 months next after the committing of his offence, and the first Representative is to make further provision for the avoiding of these evils in future elections. 4. That to the end all officers of state may be certainly accounta- ble, and no factions made to maintain corrupt interests, no member of a council of state, nor any officer of any salary-forces in army or garrison, nor any treasurer or receiver of public money, shall, while such, be elected to be of a representative: and in case any such election shall be, the same to be void. And in case any lawyer shall be chosen into any Representative, or council of State, then he shall be incapable of practice as a lawyer during the trust. 5. For the more convenient election of representatives, each county, wherein more than three representers are to be chosen, with the towns corporate and cities, if there be any, lying within the compass thereof, to which no Representers are herein assigned, shall be divided by a due proportion into so many, and such parts, as each part may elect two, and no part above three representers. For the setting forth of which divisions, and the ascertaining of other circumstances hereafter expressed, so as to make the elec- tions less subject to confusion or mistake, in order to the next Representative, Thomas Lord Grey of Grooby, sir John Danvers, sir Henry Holcroft, knights;

Moses Wall, gentleman; Samuel Moyer, John Langley, Wm. Hawkins, Abraham Babington, Daniel Taylor, Mark Hilsey, Rd. Price, and col. John White, citizens of London, or any 5 or more of them, are intrusted to nominate and appoint, under their hands and seals, three or more fit persons in each county, and in each city and borough, to which one representer or more is assigned, to be as commissioners, for the ends aforesaid, in the respective counties, cities, and boroughs; and, by like writing under their hands and seals, shall certify into the Parliament Records, before the 14th of Feb. next, the Names of the Commissioners so appointed for the respective counties, cities, and boroughs; which commissioners, or any three or more of them, for the respective counties, cities, and boroughs, shall, before the end of Feb. next, by writing under their hands and seals, appoint two fit and faithful persons, or more, in each hundred, lath, or wapontake, within the respective counties, and in each ward within the city of London, to take care for the orderly taking of all voluntary Subscriptions to this Agreement, by fit persons to be employed for that purpose in every parish; who are to return the subscription, so taken, to the persons that employed them, keeping a transcript thereof to themselves; and those persons, keeping like transcripts, to return the original Subscriptions to the respective commissioners by whom they were appointed, at, or before, the 14th of April next, to be registered and kept in the County Records for the said counties respectively; and the Subscriptions in the city of London to be kept in the chief Court of Record for the said city. And the commissioners for the other cities and boroughs respectively, are to appoint two or more fit persons in every parish within their precincts, to take such Subscriptions. . . . And the same commissioners, or any three or more of them, for the several counties, cities, and boroughs, respectively, shall, where more than 3 Representers are to be chosen, divide such counties, as also the city of London, into so many, and such parts as are aforementioned; and shall set forth the bounds of such divisions; and shall, in every county, city, and borough, where any Representers are to be chosen, and in every such division as aforesaid within the city of London, and within the several counties so divided, respectively, appoint one place certain wherein the people shall meet for the choice of the Representers; and some one fit person, or more, inhabiting within each borough, city, county, or division, respectively, to be present at the time and place of election, in the nature of Sheriffs, to regulate the elections; and by pole, or otherwise, clearly to distinguish and judge thereof, and to make return of the person or persons elected, as is hereafter expressed; and shall likewise, in writing under their hands and seals, make certificates of the several divisions, with the bounds thereof, by them set forth, and of the certain places of meeting, and persons, in the nature of Sheriff, appointed in them respectively as aforesaid; and cause such certificates to be returned into the parliament Records before the end of April next; and before that time shall also cause the same to be published in every parish within the counties, cities, and boroughs respectively; and shall in every such

parish likewise nominate and appoint, by warrant under their hands and seals, one
trusty person, or more, inhabiting therein, to make a true List of all the persons
within their respective parishes, who, according to the rules aforegoing, are to
have voice in the elections; and, expressing who amongst them are, by the same
rules, capable of being elected; and such list, with the said warrant, to bring in
and return, at the time and place of election, unto the person appointed in the
nature of Sheriff, as aforesaid, for that borough, city, county, or division respectively; which person so appointed as sheriff, being present at the time and place of
election; or, in case of his absence, by the space of one hour after the time limited
for the people's meeting, then any person present that is eligible, as aforesaid,
whom the people then and there assembled shall chuse for that end, shall receive
and keep the said Lists, and admit the persons therein contained, or so many of
them as are present, unto a free vote in the said election; and, having first caused
this Agreement to be publickly read in the audience of the people, shall proceed
unto, and regulate and keep peace and order in the elections; and, by pole, or
otherwise, openly distinguish and judge of the same; and thereof, by certificate or
writing under the hands and seals of himself, and 6 or more of the electors, nomi-
nating the person or persons duly elected, shall make a true return into the parliament Records, within 21 days after the election, under pain for default thereof,
or, for making any false return, to forfeit 100£. to the public use: and also cause
Indentures to be made, and inchangeably sealed and delivered, betwixt himself,
and six or more of the said electors, on the one part, and the persons, or each
person, elected severally, on the other part, expressing their election of him as a
Representer of them according to this Agreement, and his acceptance of that trust,
and his promise accordingly to perform the same with faithfulness, to the best of
his understanding and ability, for the glory of God, and good of the people. This
course is to hold for the first Representative, which is to provide for the ascertaining of these circumstances in order to future representatives.

Fourthly, That 150 members at least be always present in each sitting of the
Representative, at the passing of any law or doing of any act whereby the people
are to be bound; saving, That the number of 60 may make a house for debates or
Resolutions that are preparatory thereunto.

Fifthly, That each Representative shall, within 20 days after their first meeting,
appoint a Council of State for the managing of public affairs, until the 10th day
after the meeting of the next representative, unless that next representative thinks
fit to put an end to that trust sooner. And the same council to act and proceed
therein, according to such instructions and limitations as the Representative shall
give and not otherwise.

Sixthly, That, in each interval betwixt biennial representatives, the Council of
State, in case of imminent danger or extreme necessity, may summon a Representative to be forthwith chosen, and to meet; so as the session thereof continue not
above 80 days; and so as it dissolve, at least, 50 days before the appointed time

for the next biennial representative; and upon the 50th day so preceding it shall dissolve of course, if not otherwise dissolved sooner.

Seventhly, That no member of any Representative be made either receiver, treasurer, or other officer, during that employment, saving to be a member of the council of the state.

Eighthly, That the representatives have, and shall be understood to have, the supreme trust in order to the preservation and government of the whole; and that their power extend, without the consent or concurrence of any other person or persons, to the erecting and abolishing of Courts of Justice and public Offices, and to the enacting, altering, repealing, and declaring of laws, and the highest and final judgment, concerning all natural or civil things, but not concerning things spiritual or evangelical. Provided that, even in things natural and civil, these six Particulars next following are, and shall be, understood to be excepted and reserved from our Representatives, viz. 1. We do not impower them to impress or constrain any person to serve in foreign war, either by sea or land, nor for any military service within the kingdom; save that they may take order for the forming, training, and exercising of the people, in a military way, to be in readiness for resisting of foreign invasions, suppressing of sudden insurrections, or for assisting in execution of the laws; and may take order for the employing and conducting of them for those ends; provided, That, even in such cases, none be compellable to go out of the county he lives in, if he procure another to serve in his room. 2. That, after the time herein limited for the commencement of the First Representative, none of the people may be at any time questioned for anything said or done in relation to the late wars or public differences, otherwise than in execution or pursuance of the determinations of the present house of commons, against such as have adhered to the king, or his interest, against the people; and saving, that accomptants for public monies received, shall remain accountable for the same. 3. That no securities given, or to be given, by the public faith of the nation, nor any Engagements of the public faith for satisfaction of debts and damages, shall be made void or invalid by the next, or any future representatives; except to such creditors as have, or shall have, justly forfeited the same: and saving, That the next Representative may confirm or make null, in part or in whole, all gifts of lands, monies, offices, or otherwise, made by the present parliament to any member or attendant of either house. 4. That, in any laws hereafter to be made, no person, by virtue of any tenure, grant, charter, patent, degree, or birth, shall be privileged from subjection thereto, or from being bound thereby, as well as others. 5. That the Representative may not give judgment upon any man's person or estate, where no law hath before provided; save only in calling to account and punishing public officers for abusing or failing in their trust. 6. That no Representative may in any wise render up, or give, or take away, any of the foundations of common right, liberty, and safety contained in this Agreement, nor level men's estates, destroy property, or make all things common and that, in all matters of such fundamental concernment, there shall be a liberty to particular members of the said Representatives to enter their Dissents from the major Vote.

Ninthly, Concerning Religion, we agree as followeth. 1. It is intended that the Christian Religion be held forth and recommended as the public profession in this nation, which we desire may, by the grace of God, be enformed to the greatest purity in doctrine, worship, and discipline, according to the Word of God; the instructing of the people there unto in a public way, so it be not compulsive; as also the maintaining of able Teachers for that end, and for the confutation or discovery of heresy, error, and whatsoever is contrary to sound doctrine, is allowed to be provided for by our Representatives; the maintenance of which Teachers may be out of a public treasury, and we desire, not by tithes. Provided, That Popery or Prelacy be not held forth as the public way or profession in this nation. 2. That, to the public profession so held forth, none be compelled by penalties or otherwise; but only may be endeavoured to be won by sound doctrine, and the example of a good conversation. 3. That such as profess faith in God by Jesus Christ, however differing in judgment from the doctrine, worship, or discipline publicly hold forth, as aforesaid, shall not be restrained from but shall be protected in, the profession of their faith and exercise of religion, according to their consciences, in any place except such as shall be set apart for the public worship; where we provide not for them, unless they have leave, so as they abuse not this liberty to the civil injury of others, or to actual disturbance of the public peace on their parts. Nevertheless, it is not intended to be hereby provided, That this liberty shall necessarily extend to Popery or Prelacy. 4. That all laws, ordinances, statutes, and clauses in any law, statute, or ordinance to the contrary of the liberty herein provided for, in the two particulars next preceding concerning Religion, be, and are hereby, repealed and made void.

Tenthly, It is agreed, That whosoever shall, by force of arms, resist the orders of the next or any future Representative (except in case where such Representative shall evidently render up or give, or take away the foundations of common right, liberty, and safety contained in this Agreement) he shall forthwith, after his or their such resistance, lose the benefit and protection of the laws, and shall be punishable with death, as an enemy and traitor to the nation. Of the things expressed in this Agreement: The certain ending of this parliament, as in the first Article; the equal or proportionable distribution of the number of the Representers to be elected, as in the second; the certainty of the people's meeting to elect for Representatives biennal, and their Freedom in Elections; with the certainty of meeting, sitting, and ending of representatives so elected, which are provided for in the third Article; as also the Qualifications of persons to elect or be elected, as in the first and second Particulars under the third Article; also the certainty of a number for passing a law or preparatory debates, provided for in the fourth Article; the matter of the fifth Article, concerning the Council of State, and of the sixth, concerning the calling, sitting, and ending of Representatives extraordinary; also the power of representatives to be, as in the eighth Article, and limited, as in the six Reserves next following the same: likewise the second and third Particulars under the ninth Article concerning Religion, and the whole matter of the tenth Article: All these we do account and declare to be fundamental to our Common Right, Liberty, and Safety; and therefore do both agree thereunto, and resolve to maintain the same, as God shall enable us. The rest of the matters in this Agreement, we account to be useful and good for the public; and the particular circumstances of numbers, times, and places expressed in the several Articles, we account not fundamental; but we find them necessary to be here determined, for the making the Agreement certain and practicable; and do hold these most convenient that are here set down; and therefore do positively agree thereunto. . . .

3   JAMES HARRINGTON

James Harrington (1611–1677) was both a friend of King Charles I (1600–1649) and a republican. He published *Oceana* in 1656 as a model for the creation of a republic in England. Harrington argued that the form of government depends on the nature of land ownership. In his famous law of the balance, he stated that the person or group who controlled most of the land would also control the government. Thus, if one person owned most of the land the government would necessarily be a monarchy. If a large number of people owned most of the land, as was happening in England, the government would necessarily be a republic. Harrington preferred republics because they protected rights and popular interests and encouraged widespread participation. He believed that it was possible to create an "immortal" commonwealth or republic which would never collapse due to internal stress. An agrarian law must encourage widespread land ownership by forbidding anyone from acquiring more land than would produce £2,000 income a year. This would ensure that the land would be divided among at least five thousand owners, and in practice among more. Political institutions must reflect this widespread economic power. Harrington proposed a system of separation of powers: a senate, elected by and from the richer classes, which would propose laws; a system whereby the people would vote to accept or reject these laws; and, an executive to carry out the laws. Frequent rotation in office and an elaborate secret ballot would prevent anyone from gaining enough power to oppress the majority. With an agrarian law settling the pattern of land ownership and proper political institutions, it would not matter what kind of people you had in a country. Self-interest and limits on economic concentrations would keep the system in balance. They would encourage fidelity to the laws which gave people a share in power and prevent anyone from gaining enough power to overthrow the system from the inside. Harrington, who actively worked to implement his system, was imprisoned after restoration of the monarchy in 1660.

Harrington wrote *Oceana* in the form of an imaginary history of an island nation which had overthrown its monarchy and instituted a republic. In the selection reprinted below, Harrington discusses the nature of the agrarian law. The part from Hermes de Caducco's speech to the end records part of Oceana's leaders' debate over basic laws for Oceana. Though Harrington's scheme was not successful many people read *Oceana*. In America, John Adams continually drew on it in the 1770s and 1780s, as a model for the new republic.

OCEANA*

Janotti, the most excellent describer of the commonwealth of Venice, divides the whole series of government into two times or periods: the one ending with the liberty of Rome, which was the course or empire, as I may call it, of ancient prudence, first discovered to mankind by God Himself in the fabric of the commonwealth of Israel, and afterwards picked out of His footsteps in Nature, and unanimously followed by the Greeks and Romans; the other beginning with the arms of Caesar, which, extinguishing liberty, were the transition of ancient into modern prudence, introduced by those inundations of Huns, Goths, Vandals, Lombards, Saxons, which, breaking the Roman empire, deformed the whole face of the world with those ill features of government, which at this time are become far worse in these Western parts, except Venice, which, escaping the hands of the Barbarians by virtue of its impregnable situation, has had its eye fixed upon ancient prudence, and is attained to a perfection even beyond the copy.

Relation being had to these two times, government (to define it *de jure,* or according to ancient prudence) is an art whereby a civil society of men is instituted and preserved upon the foundation of common right or interest; or, to follow Aristotle and Livy, it is the empire of laws, and not of men.

And government (to define it *de facto,* or according to modern prudence) is an art whereby some man, or some few men, subject a city or a nation, and rule it according to his or their private interest; which, because the laws in such cases are made according to the interest of a man, or of some few families, may be said to be the empire of men, and not of laws.

The Commonwealth of Oceana (London, 1887), parts 1, 3. First published in 1656.

To go my own way, and yet to follow the ancients, the principles of government are twofold: internal, or the goods of the mind; and external, or the goods of fortune. The goods of the mind are natural or acquired virtues, as wisdom, prudence, and courage, &c. The goods of fortune are riches. . . .

To begin with riches, in regard that men are hung upon these, not of choice as upon the other, but of necessity and by the teeth; forasmuch as he who wants bread is his servant that will feed him, if a man thus feeds a whole people, they are under his empire.

Empire is of two kinds, domestic and national, or foreign and provincial.

Domestic empire is founded upon dominion.

Dominion is property, real or personal; that is to say, in lands, or in money and goods.

Lands, or the parts and parcels of a territory, are held by the proprietor or proprietors, lord or lords of it, in some proportion; and such (except it be in a city that has little or no land, and whose revenue is in trade) as is the proportion or balance of dominion or property in land, such is the nature of the empire.

If one man be sole landlord of a territory, or overbalance the people, for example, three parts in four, he is Grand Seignior; for so the Turk is called from his property, and his empire is absolute monarchy.

If the few or a nobility, or a nobility with the clergy, be landlords, or overbalance the people to the like proportion, it makes the Gothic balance . . . and the empire is mixed monarchy, as that of Spain, Poland, and late of Oceana.

And if the whole people be landlords, or hold the lands so divided among them that no one man, or number of men, within the compass of the few or aristocracy, overbalance them, the empire (without the interposition of force) is a commonwealth.

If force be interposed in any of these three cases, it must either frame the government to the foundation, or the foundation to the government; or holding the government not according to the balance, it is not natural, but violent; and therefore if it be at the devotion of a prince, it is tyranny; if at the devotion of the few, oligarchy; or if in the power of the people, anarchy. Each of which confusions, the balance standing otherwise, is but of short continuance, because against the nature of the balance, which, not destroyed, destroys that which opposes it.

But there be certain other confusions, which, being rooted in the balance, are of longer continuance, and of worse consequence; as, first, where a nobility holds half the property, or about that proportion, and the people the other half; in which case, without altering the balance there is no remedy but the one must eat out the other, as the people did the nobility in Athens, and the nobility the people in Rome. Secondly, when a prince holds about half the dominion, and the people the other half . . . the government becomes a very shambles, both of the princes and the people. Somewhat of this nature are certain governments at this day, which are said to subsist by confusion. In this case, to fix the balance, is to entail misery;

but in the three former, not to fix it, is to lose the government. Wherefore it being unlawful in Turkey that any should possess land but the Grand Seignior, the balance is fixed by the law, and that empire firm. Nor, though the kings often sell, was the throne of Oceana known to shake, until the statute of alienations broke the pillars, by giving way to the nobility to sell their estates. While Lacedemon held to the division of land made by Lycurgus, it was immovable; but, breaking that, could stand no longer. This kind of law fixing the balance in lands is called Agrarian, and was first introduced by God himself, who divided the land of Canaan to His people by lots, and is of such virtue, that wherever it has held that government has not altered, except by consent; as in that unparalleled example of the people of Israel, when being in liberty they would needs choose a king. But without an Agrarian law, government, whether monarchical, aristocratical, or popular, has no long lease.

An equal commonwealth is such a one as is equal both in the balance or foundation, and in the superstructure; that is to say, in her Agrarian law, and in her rotation.

An equal Agrarian is a perpetual law, establishing and preserving the balance of dominion by such a distribution, that no one man or number of men, within the compass of the few or aristocracy, can come to overpower the whole people by their possessions in lands.

As the Agrarian answers to the foundation, so does rotation to the superstructures.

Equal rotation is equal vicissitude in government, or succession to magistracy conferred for such convenient terms, enjoying equal vacations, as take in the whole body by parts, succeeding others, through the free election or suffrage of the people.

The contrary, whereunto is prolongation of magistracy, which, trashing the wheel of rotation, destroys the life or natural motion of a commonwealth.

The election or suffrage of the people is most free, where it is made or given in such a manner that it can neither oblige nor disoblige another, nor through fear of an enemy, or bashfulness towards a friend, impair a man's liberty.

An equal commonwealth (by that which has been said) is a government established upon an equal Agrarian, arising into the superstructures or three orders, the senate debating and proposing, the people resolving, and the magistracy executing, by an equal rotation through the suffrage of the people given by the ballot. For though rotation may be without the ballot, and the ballot without rotation, yet the ballot not only as to the ensuing model includes both, but is by far the most equal way; for which cause under the name of the ballot I shall hereafter understand both that and rotation too.

Hermes de Caducco, lord orator of the tribe of Nubia, [spoke to the people].

"This freeborn nation lives not upon the dole or bounty of one man, but distributing her annual magistracies and honours with her own hand, is herself King People. . . .

"For, neither by reason nor by experience is it impossible that a common-wealth should be immortal; seeing the people being the materials, never die; and the form, which is motion, must, without opposition, be endless. . . .

"And forasmuch as sovereign power is a necessary but a formidable creature, not unlike the powder which (as you are soldiers)[1] is at once your safety and your danger, being subject to take fire against you as well as for you, how well and securely is she by your galaxies so collected as to be in full force and vigour, and yet so distributed that it is impossible you should be blown up by your own maga-zine? Let them who will have it, that power if it be confined cannot be sovereign, tell us, whether our rivers do not enjoy a more secure and fruitful reign within their proper banks, than if it were lawful for them, in ravaging our harvests, to spill themselves? whether souls, not confined to their peculiar bodies, do govern them any more than those of witches in their trances? whether power, not con-fined to the bounds of reason and virtue, has any other bounds than those of vice and passion? or if vice and passion be boundless, and reason and virtue have certain limits, on which of these thrones holy men should anoint their sovereign? But to blow away this dust, the sovereign power of a commonwealth is no more bounded, that is to say straitened, than that of a monarch; but is balanced. The eagle mounts not to her proper pitch, if she be bounded, nor is free, if she be not balanced. And lest a monarch should think he can reach further with his sceptre, the Roman eagle upon such a balance spread her wings from the ocean to Euphra-tes. Receive the sovereign power; you have received it, hold it fast, embrace it for ever in your shining arms. The virtue of the loadstone is not impaired or limited, but receives strength and nourishment, by being bound in iron."

The centre, or basis of every government, is no other than the fundamental laws of the same.

Fundamental laws are such as state what it is that a man may call his own, that is to say, property; and what the means be whereby a man may enjoy his own, that is to say, protection. The first is also called dominion, and the second empire or sovereign power, whereof this (as has been shown) is the natural product of the former; for such as is the balance of dominion in a nation, such is the nature of its empire.

Wherefore the fundamental laws of Oceana, or the centre of this common-wealth, are the Agrarian and the ballot: the Agrarian by the balance of dominion preserving equality in the root; and the ballot by an equal rotation conveying it into the branch, or exercise of sovereign power, as, to begin with the former, appears by:

The thirteenth order, "Constituting the Agrarian laws of Oceana, Marpesia, and Panopea,[2] whereby it is ordained, first, for all such lands as are lying and being within the proper territories of Oceana, that every man who is at present possessed, or shall hereafter be possessed, of an estate in land exceeding the revenue of £2,000 a year, and having more than one son, shall leave his lands either equally divided among them, in case the lands amount to above £2,000 a year to each, or so near equally in case they come under, that the greater part or portion of the same remaining to the eldest exceed not the value of £2,000 revenue. And no man, not in present possession of lands above the value of £2,000 by the year, shall receive, enjoy (except by lawful inheritance), acquire, or purchase to himself lands within the said territories, amounting, with those already in his possession, above the said revenue. And if a man has a daughter, or daughters, except she be an heiress, or they be heiresses, he shall not leave or give to any one of them in marriage, or otherwise, for her portion, above the value of £1500 in lands, goods, and moneys. Nor shall any friend, kinsman, or kinswoman, add to her or their portion or portions that are so provided for, to make any one of them greater. Nor shall any man demand or have more in marriage with any woman. Nevertheless an heiress shall enjoy her lawful inheritance, and a widow, whatsoever the bounty or affection of her husband shall bequeath to her, to be divided in the first generation, wherein it is divisible according as has been shown.

"Secondly, For lands lying and being within the territories of Marpesia, the Agrarian shall hold in all parts as it is established in Oceana, except only in the standard or proportion of estates in land, which shall be set for Marpesia, at five hundred pounds.

"Thirdly, For Panopea, the Agrarian shall hold in all parts, as in Oceana. And whosoever possessing above the proportion allowed by these laws, shall be lawfully convicted of the same, shall forfeit the overplus to the use of the State."

Agrarian laws of all others have ever been the greatest bugbears, and so in the institution were these, at which time it was ridiculous to see how strange a fear appeared in everybody of that which, being good for all, could hurt nobody. But instead of the proof of this order, I shall out of those many debates that happened ere it could be passed, insert two speeches that were made at the council of legislators, the first by the right honourable Philautus de Garbo, a young man, being heir-apparent to a very noble family, and one of the councillors, who expressed himself as follows:

"May it please your Highness, my Lord Archon of Oceana.

"If I did not, to my capacity, know from how profound a councillor I dissent, it would certainly be no hard task to make it as light as the day: first, That an Agrarian is altogether unnecessary. Secondly, That it is dangerous to a commonwealth. Thirdly, That it is insufficient to keep out monarchy. Fourthly, That it ruins families. Fifthly, That it destroys industry. And last of all, That though it were indeed of any good use, it will be a matter of such difficulty to introduce in this nation, and so to settle that it may be lasting, as is altogether invincible."

[The Lord Archon Answered]

"My Lords, the Legislators of Oceana.

"First, Whereas my lord, upon observation of the modern commonwealths, is of opinion that an Agrarian is not necessary: it must be confessed that at the first sight of them there is some appearance favouring his assertion, but upon accidents of no precedent to us. For the commonwealths of Switzerland and Holland, I mean of those leagues, being situated in countries not alluring the inhabitants to wantonness, but obliging them to universal industry, have an implicit Agrarian in the nature of them: and being not obnoxious to a growing nobility . . . are of no example to us, whose experience in this point has been to the contrary. But what if even in these governments there be indeed an explicit Agrarian? For when the law commands an equal or near equal distribution of a man's estate in land among his children, as it is done in those countries, a nobility cannot grow; and so there needs no Agrarian, or rather there is one . . . if a commonwealth has been introduced at once, as those of Israel and Lacedemon, you are certain to find her underlaid with this as the main foundation. . . . But, not to restrain a fundamental of such latitude to any one kind of government, do we not yet see that if there be a solo landlord of a vast territory, he is the Turk? that if a few landlords overbalance a populous country, they have store of servants? that if a people be in an equal balance, they can have no lords? that no government can otherwise be erected, than upon some one of these foundations? that no one of these foundations (each being else apt to change into some other) can give any security to the government, unless it be fixed? that through the want of this fixation, potent monarchy and commonwealths have fallen upon the heads of the people, and accompanied their own sad ruins with vast effusions of innocent blood? Let the fame, as was the merit of the ancient nobility of this nation, be equal to or above what has been already said, or can be spoken, yet have we seen not only their glory, but that of a throne, the most indulgent to and least invasive for so many ages upon the liberty of a people that the world has known, through the mere want of fixing her foot by a proportionable Agrarian upon her proper foundation, to have fallen with such horror as has been a spectacle of astonishment to the whole earth. . . . Aristotle . . . says that democracies, when a less part of their citizens overtop the rest in wealth, degenerate into oligarchies and principalities; and, which comes nearer to the present purpose, that the greater part of the nobility of Tarentum coming accidentally to be ruined, the government of the few came by consequence to be changed into that of the many.

  "These things considered, I cannot see how an Agrarian, as to the fixation or security of a government, can be less than necessary. And if a cure be necessary, it excuses not the patient, his disease being otherwise desperate, that it is dangerous; which was the case of Rome. . . . As if when a senator was not rich (as Crassus held) except he could pay an army, that commonwealth could expect nothing but ruin whether in strife about the Agrarian, or without it. "Of late," says Livy, "riches have introduced avarice, and voluptuous pleasures abounding, have through lust and luxury begot a desire of blasting and destroying all good orders." If the greatest security of a commonwealth consists in being provided with the proper antidote against this poison, her greatest danger must be from the absence of an Agrarian, which is the whole truth of the Roman example. For the

Laconic, I shall reserve the farther explication of it . . . and first see whether an Agrarian proportioned to a popular government be sufficient to keep out monarchy. My lord is for the negative, and fortified by the people of Israel electing a king. To which I say, that the action of the people therein expressed is a full answer to the objection of that example; for the monarchy neither grew upon them, nor could, by reason of the Agrarian, possibly have invaded them, if they had not pulled it upon themselves by the election of a king. Which being an accident, the like whereof is not to be found in any other people so planted, nor in this till, as it is manifest, they were given up by God to infatuation (for says He to Samuel, 'They have not rejected thee, but they have rejected Me, that I should not reign over them'), has something in it which is apparent, by what went before, to have been besides the course of Nature, and by what followed. For the king having no other foundation than the calamities of the people, so often beaten by their enemies, that despairing of themselves they were contented with any change, if he had peace as in the days of Solomon, left but a slippery throne to his successor, as appeared by Rehoboam. And the Agrarian, notwithstanding the monarchy thus introduced, so faithfully preserved the root of that commonwealth, that it shot forth oftener, and by intervals continued longer than any other government, as may be computed from the institution of the same by Joshua, 1465 years before Christ, to the total dissolution of it, which happened in the reign of the Emperor Adrian, 135 years after the Incarnation. A people planted upon an equal Agrarian, and holding to it, if they part with their liberty, must do it upon goodwill, and make but a bad title of their bounty. As to instance yet further in that which is proposed by the present order to this nation, the standard whereof is at £2,000 a year; the whole territory of Oceana being divided by this proportion, amounts to five thousand lots. So the lands of Oceana bring thus distributed, and bound to this distribution, can never fall to fewer than five thousand proprietors. But five thousand proprietors so seised will not agree to break the Agrarian, for that were to agree to rob one another; nor to bring in a king, because they must maintain him, and can have no benefit by him; nor to exclude the people, because they can have as little by that, and must spoil their militia. So the commonwealth continuing upon the balance proposed, though it should come into five thousand hands, can never alter, and that it should ever come into five thousand hands, is as improbable as anything in the world that is not altogether impossible.

"My lord's other considerations are more private; as that this order destroys families; which is as if one should lay the ruin of some ancient castle to the herbs which usually grow out of them, the destruction of those families being that indeed which naturally produced this order. For we do not now argue for that which we would have, but for that which we are already possessed of, as would appear if a note were but taken of all such as have at this day above £2,000 a year in Oceana. If my lord should grant (and I will put it with the most) that they who are proprietors in land, exceeding this proportion, exceed not three hundred, with what brow can the interest of so few be balanced with that of the whole nation? or rather, what interest have they to put in such a balance? they would live as they had been accustomed to do; who hinders them? they would enjoy their estates; who touches them? they would dispose of what they have according to the interest of their families; it is that which we desire. A man has one son, let him be called; would he enjoy his father's estate? it is his, his son's, and his son's son's after him. A man has five sons, let them be called; would they enjoy their father's estate? It is divided among them. . . . If a man shall dispute otherwise, he must draw his arguments from custom and from greatness, which was the interest of the monarchy, not of the family; and we are now a commonwealth. If the monarchy could not bear with such divisions because they tended to a commonwealth, neither can a commonwealth connive at such accumulations because they tend to a monarchy. If the monarchy might make bold with so many for the good of one, we may make bold with one for the good of so many, nay, for the good of all. . . . Really, my lords, it is a flinty custom [primogeniture]. . . . And this is that interest of a family, for which we are to think ill of a government that will not endure it. But quiet ourselves; the land through which the river Nilus wanders in one stream, is barren; but where it parts into seven, it multiplies its fertile shores by distributing, yet keeping and improving, such a propriety and nutrition, as is a prudent Agrarian to a well-ordered commonwealth.

"Nor (to come to the fifth assertion) is a political body rendered any fitter for industry by having one gouty and another withered leg, than a natural. It tends not to the improvement of merchandise that there be some who have no need of their trading, and others that are not able to follow it. If confinement discourages industry, an estate in money is not confined, and lest industry should want whereupon to work, land is not engrossed or entailed upon any man, but remains at its devotion. I wonder whence the computation can arise, that this should discourage industry. Two thousand pounds a year a man may enjoy in Oceana, as much in Panopea, £500 in Marpesia; there be other plantations, and the commonwealth will have more. Who knows how far the arms of our Agrarian may extend themselves? and whether he that might have left a pillar, may not leave a temple of many pillars to his more pious memory? Where there is some measure in riches, a man may be rich, but if you will have them to be infinite, there will be no end of starving himself, and wanting what he has: and what pains does such a one take to be poor! Furthermore, if a man shall think that there may be an industry less greasy or more noble, and so cast his thoughts upon the commonwealth, he will have leisure for her, and she riches and honours for him . . . in giving encouragement to industry, we also remember that covetousness is the root of all evil. And our Agrarian can never be the cause of those seditions threatened by my lord, but is the proper cure of them, as Lucan notes well in the state of Rome before the civil wars, which happened through the want of such an antidote.

[The Archon here ends the discussion of the laws and constitution of Oceana]

"A government of this make is a commonwealth for increase. . . .

"Rome was said to be broken by her own weight, but poetically; for that weight by which she was pretended to be ruined, was supported in her emperors by a far slighter foundation. And in the common experience of good architecture, there is nothing more known than that buildings stand the firmer and the longer for their own weight, nor ever swerve through any other internal cause than that their materials are corruptible; but the people never die, nor, as a political body, are subject to any other corruption than that which derives from their government. Unless a man will deny the chain of causes, in which he denies God, he must also acknowledge the chain of effects; wherefore there can be no effect in Nature that is not from the first cause, and those successive links of the chain without which it could not have been. Now except a man can show the contrary in a commonwealth, if there be no cause of corruption in the first make of it, there can never be any such effect. Let no man's superstition impose profaneness upon this assertion; for as man is sinful, but yet the universe is perfect, so may the citizen be sinful, and yet the commonwealth be perfect. And as man, seeing the world is perfect, can never commit any such sin as shall render it imperfect, or bring it to a natural dissolution, so the citizen, where the commonwealth is perfect, can never commit any such crime as will render it imperfect, or bring it to a natural dissolution. To come to experience: Venice, notwithstanding we have found some flaws in it, is the only commonwealth in the make whereof no man can find a cause of dissolution; for which reason we behold her (though she consists of men that are not without sin) at this day with one thousand years upon her back, yet for any internal cause, as young, as fresh, and free from decay, or any appearance of it, as she was born; but whatever in Nature is not sensible of decay by the course of a thousand years, is capable of the whole age of Nature; by which calculation, for any check that I am able to give myself, a commonwealth, rightly ordered, may for any internal causes be as immortal or long-lived as the world. But if this be true, those commonwealths that are naturally fallen, must have derived their ruin from the rise of them. Israel and Athens died not natural but violent deaths, in which manner the world itself is to die. We are speaking of those causes of dissolution which are natural to government; and they are but two, either contradiction or inequality. If a commonwealth be a contradiction, she must needs destroy herself; and if she be unequal, it tends to strife, and strife to ruin. By the former of these fell Lacedemon, by the latter Rome. Lacedemon being made altogether for war, and yet not for increase, her natural progress became her natural dissolution, and the building of her own victorious hand too heavy for her foundation, so that she fell indeed by her own weight. But Rome perished through her native inequality, which how it inveterated the bosoms of the senate and the people each against other, and even to death, has been shown at large.

"Look well to it, my Lords, for if there be a contradiction or inequality in your commonwealth, it must fall; but if it has neither of these, it has no principle of mortality. . . . But a commonwealth, as we have demonstrated, swerves not from her principles, but by and through her institution; if she brought no bias into the world with her, her course for any internal cause must be straightforward, as we see is that of Venice. She cannot turn to the right hand, nor to the left, but by some rub, which is not an internal but external cause: against such she can be no way fortified, but through her situation, as is Venice, or through her militia, as was Rome, by which examples a commonwealth may be secure of those also. Think me not vain, for I cannot conceal my opinion here; a commonwealth that is rightly instituted can never swerve, nor one that is not rightly instituted be secured from swerving. . . . But your commonwealth is founded upon an equal Agrarian; and if the earth be given to the sons of men, this balance is the balance of justice, such a one as in having due regard to the different industry of different men, yet faithfully judges the poor. 'And the king that faithfully judges the poor, his throne shall be established for ever'; much more the commonwealth, seeing that equality, which is the necessary dissolution of monarchy, is the generation, the very life and soul of a commonwealth. . . .''

---

4 JOHN LOCKE

John Locke (1632-1704) is one of those theorists whom we often take for granted. His ideas have influenced and shaped our thinking to such an extent that they seem commonplace when we first read them. They are not. Locke stands at the beginning of three centuries of liberal thought and expansion of human liberty. Throughout his work he argued and assumed that people are rational and competent enough to understand their interests and achieve their goals if they are allowed to freely pursue them. This assumption represents a startling and potentially liberating change from hitherto accepted notions. It challenges the legitimacy of all authoritarian and even paternalistic governments. In *Two Treatises of Government*, Locke argues that people have rights and are capable of exercising those rights, therefore only government based on consent is legitimate. Government is created for no other purpose than to protect the natural rights and property—land, personal goods, one's person and rights—of free individuals who contract together to create it or consent to an existing government. As such, government is limited in scope and power. It is a trust which the people may revoke when the government exceeds its limited power and purposes. When that occurs the governors rebel against the people and any resulting violence is the fault of

governors who have violated their trust. During such a rebellion, society continues to exist and the people may reconstitute government on any grounds which
they choose, as long as the new government does not violate natural rights.

Locke published his *Two Treatises of Government* in 1690. Our selection is
from the *Second Treatise*. Though many people have assumed that Locke wrote
his *Two Treatises* as an apology and vindication of the Glorious Revolution of
1688, Locke probably began them ten years earlier during the Exclusion Crisis.
This involved an attempt to pass a law excluding a Catholic from becoming king
of England. Though Locke had a minor role in this affair he eventually went into
exile in Holland and did not return to England until after the Glorious Revolution.

SECOND TREATISE OF GOVERNMENT*

Of the State of Nature

4. To understand political Power, right, and derive it from its Original, we
must consider, what State all Men are naturally in, and that is, a *State of perfect
Freedom* to order their Actions, and dispose of their Possessions, and Persons as
they think fit, within the bounds of the Law of Nature, without asking leave, or
depending upon the Will of any other Man.

A *State* also *of Equality,* wherein all the Power and Jurisdiction is Reciprocal,
no one having more than another; there being nothing more evident, than that
Creatures of the same species and rank, promiscuously born to all the same
advantages of Nature, and the use of the same Faculties, should also be equal one
amongst another without Subordination or Subjection. . . .

6. But though this be *a State of Liberty,* yet *it is not a State of Licence;* though
Man in that State have an uncontrolable Liberty, to dispose of his Person or Pos-
sessions, yet he has not Liberty to destroy himself, or so much as any Creature in
his Possession, but where some nobler Use, than its bare Preservation calls for it.
The *State of Nature* has a Law of Nature to govern it, which obliges every one:
And Reason, which is that Law, teaches all Mankind, who will but consult it, that
being all *equal and independent,* no one ought to harm another in his Life,
Health, Liberty, or Possessions. . . .

19. And here we have the plain *Difference between the State of Nature, and the
State of War,* which however some Men have confounded, are as far distant, as a
State of Peace, good Will, mutual Assistance and Preservation; and a State of
Enmity, Malice, Violence and mutual Destruction are one from another. Men
living together according to Reason, without a common superior on Earth, with

---

The Works of John Locke (London, 1714), chapters 2, 3, 7, 8, 9, 19.

Authority to judge between them, is *properly the State of Nature.* But force, or a declared design of Force upon the Person of another, where there is no common Superior on Earth to appeal to for Relief, *is the State of War:* And 'tis the want of such an Appeal gives a Man the right of War even against an *Aggressor,* though he be in Society and a fellow Subject. Thus a *Thief,* whom I cannot harm, but by Appeal to the Law, for having stolen all that I am worth, I may kill, when he sets on me to rob me but of my Horse or Coat; because the Law, which was made for my Preservation where it cannot interpose to secure my Life from present Force, which if lost, is capable of no Reparation, permits me my own Defence, and the right of War, a Liberty to kill the Aggressor, because the Aggressor allows not time to appeal to our common Judge, nor the decision of the Law, for Remedy in a Case, where the Mischief may be irreparable. *Want of a common Judge with Authority, puts all Men in a state of Nature: Force without Right, upon a Man's Person, makes a state of War,* both where there is, and is not, a common Judge.

20. But when the actual Force is over, the *State of War ceases* between those that are in Society, and are equally on both Sides subjected to the fair Determination of the Law; because then there lies open the remedy of Appeal for the past Injury, and to prevent future Harm. . . .

21. To avoid this *State of War* (wherein there is no Appeal but to Heaven, and wherein ever the least Difference is apt to end . . .), is one great *reason of Mens putting themselves into Society,* and quitting the State of Nature. . . .

[Absolute Government]

90. Hence it is evident, that *absolute Monarchy,* which by some Men is counted the only Government in the World, is indeed *inconsistent with civil Society,* and so can be no form of Civil-Government at all. For the *end of civil Society,* being to avoid, and remedy those inconveniencies of the State of Nature, which necessarily follow from every Man's being Judge in his own Case, by setting up a known Authority, to which every one of that Society may appeal upon any Injury received, or Controversie that may arise, and which every one of the Society ought to obey; wherever any Persons are, who have not such an Authority to appeal to, for the decision of any Difference between them, there those Persons are still *in the State of Nature.* And so is every *absolute Prince* in respect of those who are under his *Dominion.*

91. For he being suppos'd to have all, both legislative and executive Power in himself alone, there is no Judge to be found, no appeal lies open to any one, who may fairly, and indifferently, and with Authority decide, and from whose Decision Relief and Redress may be expected of any Injury or Inconveniency, that may be suffered from the Prince, or by his Order: So that such a Man, however entitled, *Czar,* or *Grand Seignior,* or how you please, is as much *in the state of Nature,* with all under his Dominion, as he is with the rest of Mankind. For wherever any two Men are, who have no standing Rule, and common Judge to appeal

to on Earth, for the determination of Controversies of Right betwixt them, there they are still *in the State of Nature,* and under all the inconveniencies of it, with only this woeful Difference to the Subject, or rather Slave of an absolute Prince: That whereas, in the ordinary State of Nature, he has a Liberty to judge of his Right, and according to the best of his Power, to maintain it; now whenever his Property is invaded by the will and order of his Monarch, he has not only no Appeal, as those in Society ought to have, but as if he were degraded from the common State of rational Creatures, is denied a Liberty to judge of, or to defend his Right; and so is exposed to all the Misery and Inconveniencies, that a Man can fear from one, who being in the unrestrained State of Nature, is yet corrupted with Flattery, and armed with Power.

93. *In absolute Monarchies* indeed, as well as other Governments of the World, the Subjects have an Appeal to the Law, and Judges to decide any Controversies, and restrain any Violence that may happen betwixt the Subjects themselves, one amongst another. . . . But whether this be from a true Love of Mankind and Society, and such a Charity as we owe all one to another, there is Reason to doubt. For this is no more, than what every Man, who loves his own Power, Profit, or Greatness, may and naturally must do, keep those Animals from hurting, or destroying one another, who labour and drudge only for his Pleasure and Advantage; and so are taken care of, not out of any Love the Master has for them, but Love of himself, and the Profit they bring him. For if it be asked, what Security, *what Fence* is there, in such a State, *against the Violence and Oppression of this absolute Ruler*? The very Question can scarce be born. They are ready to tell you, that it deserves Death only to ask after Safety. Betwixt Subject and Subject, they will grant, there must be Measures, Laws and Judges, for their mutual Peace and Security: But as for the Ruler, he ought to be *absolute,* and is above all such Circumstances. . . .

Of the Beginning of Political Societies

95. Men being, as has been said, by Nature, all free, equal, and independent, no one can be put out of this Estate, and subjected to the political Power of another, without his own Consent. The only Way whereby any one devests himself of his natural Liberty, and puts on the *Bonds of civil Society* is by agreeing with other Men to joyn and unite into a Community, for their comfortable, safe, and peaceable Living one amongst another, in a secure Enjoyment of their Properties, and a greater Security against any, that are not of it. This any number of Men may do, because it injures not the Freedom of the rest; they are left as they were in the Liberty of the State of Nature. When any number of Men have so *consented to make one Community or Government,* they are thereby presently incorporated, and make *one Body politick,* wherein the *Majority* have a Right to act and conclude the rest.

96. For when any number of Men have, by the consent of every individual, made a *Community,* they have thereby made that *Community* one body, with a Power to act as one Body, which is only by the Will and Determination of the *Majority*. For that which acts any Community, being only the consent of the individuals of it, and it being necessary to that which is one Body to move one way; it is necessary the Body should move that way whither the greater force carries it, which is the *consent of the Majority:* Or else it is impossible it should act or continue one Body, *one Community,* which the consent of every individual that united into it, agreed that it should; and so every one is bound by that consent to be concluded by the *Majority.* And therefore we see, that in Assemblies, impowered to act by positive Laws, where no number is set by that positive Law which impowers them, the *Act of the Majority* passes for the Act of the whole, and of course determines, as having by the Law of Nature and Reason, the Power of the whole.

97. And thus every Man, by consenting with others to make one Body Politick under one Government, puts himself under an Obligation, to every one of that Society, to submit to the determination of the *Majority,* and to be concluded by it; or else this *original Compact,* whereby he with others incorporates into *one Society,* would signifie nothing, and be no Compact. . . .

119. *Every Man* being, as has been shewed, *naturally free,* and nothing being able to put him into Subjection to any earthly Power, but only his own *Consent,* it is to be consider'd, what shall be understood to be a *sufficient Declaration* of a Man's *Consent, to make him subject* to the Laws of any Government. There is a common distinction of an express and a tacit Consent, which will concern our present Case. No Body doubts but an express *Consent,* of any Man, entering into any Society, makes him a perfect member of that Society, a Subject of that Government. The Difficulty is, what ought to be look'd upon as a *tacit Consent,* and how far it binds, i.e. how far any one shall be looked on to have consented, and thereby submitted to any Government, where he has made no Expressions of it at all. And to this I say, that every Man, that hath any Possessions, or Enjoyment, of any part of the Dominions of any Government, doth thereby give his *tacit Consent,* and is as far forth obliged to Obedience to the Laws of that Government, during such Enjoyment, as any one under it; whether this his Possession be of Land, to him and his Heirs for ever, or a Lodging only for a Week; or whether it be barely travelling freely on the Highway; and in Effect, it reaches as far as the very being of any one within the Territories of that Government.

120. To understand this the better, it is fit to consider, that every Man, when he, at first, incorporates himself into any Commonwealth, he, by his uniting himself thereunto, annexed also, and submits to the Community those Possessions, which he has, or shall acquire, that do not already belong to any other Government. For it would be a direct Contradiction, for any one, to enter into Society

with others for the securing and regulating of Property: And yet to suppose his Land, whose Property is to be regulated by the Laws of the Society, should be exempt from the Jurisdiction of that Government, to which he himself, the Proprietor of the Land, is a Subject. By the same Act therefore, whereby any one unites his Person, which was before free, to any Commonwealth; by the same he unites his Possessions, which were before free, to it also; and they become, both of them, Person and Possession, subject to the Government and Dominion of that Commonwealth, as long as it hath a Being. Whoever therefore, from thenceforth, by Inheritance, Purchase, Permission, or otherways, *enjoys any part of the Land*, so annext to, and under the Government *of that Commonwealth, must take it with the Condition* it is under; that is, *of submitting to the Government of the Commonwealth*, under whose Jurisdiction it is, as far forth as any Subject of it.

121. But since the Government has a direct Jurisdiction only over the Land, and reaches the Possessor of it, (before he has actually incorporated himself in the Society) only as he dwells upon, and enjoys that: The Obligation any one is under, by Virtue or such Enjoyment, to *submit to the Government, begins and ends with the Enjoyment;* so that whenever the Owner, who has given nothing but such a *tacit Consent* to the Government, will, by Donation, Sale, or otherwise, quit the said Possession, he is at Liberty to go and incorporate himself into any other Commonwealth; or to agree with others to begin a new one, *in vacuis locis*, in any part of the World, they can find free and unpossessed: Whereas he, that has once, by actual Agreement, and any *express* Declaration, given his *Consent* to be of any Commonweal, is perpetually and indispensably obliged to be, and remain unalterably a Subject to it, and can never be again in the Liberty of the state of Nature; unless, by any Calamity, the Government, he was under, comes to be dissolved; or else by some publick Act cuts him off from being any longer a Member of it.

122. But submitting to the Laws of any Country, living quietly, and enjoying Privileges and Protection under them, *makes not a Man a Member of that Society:* This is only a local Protection and Homage due to, and from all those, who, not being in a state of War, come within the Territories belonging to any Government, to all Parts whereof the force of its Law extends. . . . And thus we see, that *Foreigners,* by living all their Lives under another Government, and enjoying the Privileges and Protection of it, though they are bound, even in Conscience, to submit to its Administration, as far forth as any Denison; yet do not thereby come to be *Subjects or Members of that Commonwealth.* Nothing can make any Man so, but his actually entering into it by positive Engagement, and express Promise and Compact. . . .

Of the Ends of Political Society and Government

123. If Man in the state of Nature be so free, as has been said; if he be absolute Lord of his own Person and Possessions, equal to the greatest and subject to no

Body, why will he part with his Freedom? Why will he give up this Empire, and subject himself to the Dominion and Control of any other Power? To which 'tis obvious to answer, that though in the state of Nature he hath such a Right, yet the Enjoyment of it is very uncertain, and constantly exposed to the Invasion of others. For all being Kings as much as he, every Man his Equal and the greater Part no strict Observers of Equity and Justice, the enjoyment of the Property he has in this State, is very unsafe, very unsecure. This makes him willing to quit this Condition, which however free, is full of Fears and continual Dangers: And 'tis not without Reason, that he seeks out, and is willing to joyn in Society with others, who are already united, or have a Mind to unite, for the mutual *Preservation* of their Lives, Liberties and Estates, which I call by the general Name, *Property*.

124. The great and *chief End* therefore, of Mens uniting into Commonwealths, and putting themselves under Government, *is the Preservation of their Property*. To which in the state of Nature there are many things wanting.

First, There wants an *establish'd*, settled, known *Law*, received and allowed by common Consent to be the Standard of right and wrong, and the common Measure to decide all Controversies between them. For though the Law of Nature be plain and intelligible to all rational Creatures; yet Men being biassed by their Interest, as well as ignorant for want of Study of it, are not apt to allow of it as a Law binding to them in the application of it to their particular Cases.

125. *Secondly,* In the state of Nature there wants *a known and indifferent Judge,* with Authority to determine all Differences according to the established Law. For every one in that State being both Judge and Executioner of the Law of Nature, Men being partial to themselves, Passion and Revenge is very apt to carry them too far, and with too much Heat, in their own Cases; as well as Negligence, and unconcernedness, to make them too remiss in others. . . .

126. *Thirdly,* In the state of Nature there often wants *Power* to back and support the Sentence when right, and to *give* it due *Execution*. They who by any Injustice offended, will seldom fail, where they are able, by Force to make good their Injustice; such Resistance many times makes the Punishment dangerous, and frequently destructive, to those who attempt it.

127. Thus Mankind, notwithstanding all the Privileges of the state of Nature, being but in an ill Condition, while they remain in it, are quickly driven into Society. Hence it comes to pass, that we seldom find any number of Men live any time together in this State. The Inconveniencies that they are therein exposed to, by the irregular, and uncertain exercise of the Power every Man has of punishing the transgressions of others, make them take Sanctuary under the establish'd Laws of Government, and therein seek *the preservation of their Property*. 'Tis this makes them so willingly give up every one his single Power of punishing, to be exercised by such alone, as shall be appointed to it, amongst them; and by such Rules as the Community, or those authorized by them to that purpose, shall agree

on. And in this we have the original *right and rise of both the Legislative and Executive Power,* as well as of the Governments, and Societies themselves.

128. For in the State of Nature, to omit the liberty he has of innocent Delights, a Man has two Powers.

The first is to do whatsoever he thinks fit for the preservation of himself, and others within the permission of the *Law of Nature;* by which Law common to them all, he and all the rest of *Mankind are one Community,* make up one Society, distinct from all other Creatures. And were it not for the Corruption and Viciousness of degenerate Men, there would be no need of any other; no Necessity that Men should separate from this great and natural Community, and by positive agreements combine into smaller and divided Associations.

The other Power a Man has in the state of Nature, is the *power to punish the Crimes* committed against that Law. Both these he gives up, when he joyns in a private, if I may so call it, or particular Political Society, and incorporates into any Commonwealth, separate from the rest of Mankind.

129. The first *Power, viz. of doing whatsoever he thought fit for the preservation of himself,* and the rest of Mankind, *he gives up* to be regulated by Laws made by the Society, so far forth as the preservation of himself, and the rest of that Society shall require; which Laws of the Society in many things confine the liberty he had by the Law of Nature.

130. *Secondly,* The *Power of punishing he wholly gives up,* and engages his natural Force, (which he might before imploy in the Execution of the Law of Nature, by his own single Authority, as he thought fit) to assist the Executive Power of the Society, as the Law thereof shall require. For being now in a new State, wherein he is to enjoy many Conveniencies, from the Labour, Assistance, and Society of others in the same Community, as well as Protection from its whole Strength; he is to part also with as much of his natural Liberty, in providing for himself, as the Good, Prosperity, and Safety of the Society shall require; which is not only necessary, but just; since the other Members of the Society do the like.

131. But though Men when they enter into Society, give up the Equality, Liberty, and Executive Power they had in the state of Nature, into the hands of the Society, to be so far disposed of by the Legislative, as the good of the Society shall require; yet it being only with an intention in every one the better to preserve himself his Liberty and Property; (For no rational Creature can be supposed to change his condition with an intention to be worse) the Power of the Society, or *Legislative* constituted by them, can *never be suppos'd to extend farther than the common good;* but is obliged to secure every ones Property, by providing against those three defects above-mentioned, that made the State of Nature so unsafe and uneasie. And so whoever has the Legislative or supream Power of any Commonwealth, is bound to govern by establish'd *standing Laws,* promulgated and known to the People, and not by Extemporary Decrees[1]; by *indifferent* and upright

Judges, who are to decide Controversies by those Laws; And to imploy the force of the Community at home, *only in the Execution of such Laws,* or abroad to prevent or redress Foreign Injuries, and secure the Community from Inroads and Invasion. And all this to be directed to no other *End,* but the *Peace, Safety,* and *publick good* of the People.

Of the Dissolution of Government

211. He that will with any clearness speak of the *Dissolution of Government,* ought in the first place to distinguish between the *Dissolution of the Society,* and the *Dissolution of the Government.* That which makes the Community, and brings Men out of the loose state of Nature, into *one Politick Society,* is the Agreement which every one has with the rest to incorporate, and act as one Body, and so be one distinct Commonwealth. The usual, and almost only way whereby *this Union is dissolved,* is the Inroad of Foreign Force making a Conquest upon them. For in that Case, (not being able to maintain and support themselves, as *one intire* and *independent Body*) the Union belonging to that Body which consisted therein, must necessarily cease, and so every one return to the state he was in before, with a liberty to shift for himself, and provide for his own Safety as he thinks fit in some other Society. Whenever the *Society is dissolved,* 'tis certain the Government of that Society cannot remain. . . .

212. Besides this over-turning from without, *Governments are dissolved from within,*

First, When the *Legislative* is *altered.* Civil Society being a state of Peace, amongst those who are of it, from whom the state of War is excluded by the Umpirage, which they have provided in their Legislative, for the ending all Differences, that may arise amongst any of them, 'tis in their *Legislative,* that the Members of a Commonwealth are united, and combined together into one coherent living Body. This *is the Soul that gives Form, Life, and Unity* to the Commonwealth: From hence the several Members have their mutual Influence, Sympathy, and Connexion: And therefore when the *Legislative* is broken, or *dissolved,* Dissolution and Death follows. For the *Essence and Union of the Society* consisting in having one Will, the Legislative, when once established by the Majority, has the declaring, and as it were keeping of that Will. The *Constitution of the Legislative* is the first and fundamental Act of Society, whereby provision is made for the *Continuation of their Union,* under the Direction of Persons, and Bonds of Laws, made by Persons authorized thereunto, by the Consent and Appointment of the People, without which no one Man, or number of Men, amongst them, can have Authority of making Laws, that shall be binding to the rest. When any one or more, shall take upon them to make Laws, whom the People have not appointed so to do, they make Laws without Authority, which the People are not therefore bound to Obey; by which means they come again to be out of Subjection, and may constitute to themselves a *new Legislative,* as they think best, being in full liberty to resist the force of those, who without Authority would impose any thing upon them. . . .

214. . . . Whoever introduces new Laws, not being thereunto authorized by the fundamental appointment of the Society, or subverts the old, disowns and over-turns the Power by which they were made, and so sets up a *new Legislative*.

215. *Secondly,* When the Prince hinders the Legislative from assembling in its due time, or from acting freely, pursuant to those ends, for which it was consti-tuted, the *Legislative is altered*. For 'tis not a certain number of Men, no, nor their meeting, unless they have also Freedom of debating, and Leisure of perfect-ing, what is for the good of the Society, wherein the Legislative consists; when these are taken away or altered, so as to deprive the Society of the due exercise of their Power, the *Legislative* is truly altered. For it is not Names, that constitute Governments, but the Use and Exercise of those Powers, that were intended to accompany them, so that he, who takes away the Freedom, or hinders the acting of the Legislative in its due Seasons, in effect takes *away the Legislative,* and *puts an end to the Government*.

216. *Thirdly,* When by the arbitrary Power of the Prince, the Electors, or ways of Election are altered, without the Consent, and contrary to the common Interest of the People, there also the *Legislative is altered*. For if others, than those whom the Society hath authorized thereunto, do chuse, or in another Way, than what the Society hath prescribed, those chosen are not the Legislative appointed by the People.

217. *Fourthly,* the Delivery also of the People into the Subjection of a foreign Power, either by the Prince, or by the Legislative, is certainly a *Change of the Legislative,* and so a *Dissolution of the Government*. . . .

220. In these and the like Cases, *when the Government is dissolved,* the People are at Liberty to provide for themselves, by erecting a new Legislative, differing from the other, by the change of Persons, or Form, or both, as they shall find it most for their Safety and Good. For the *Society* can never, by the Fault of another, lose the Native and Original Right it has to preserve it self, which can only be done by a settled Legislative, and a fair and impartial execution of the Laws made by it. But the state of Mankind is not so miserable that they are not capable of using this Remedy, till it be too late to look for any. To tell *People* they *may provide for themselves,* by erecting a new Legislative, when by Oppression, Arti-fice, or being delivered over to a foreign Power, their old one is gone, is only to tell them, they may expect Relief, when it is too late, and the evil is past Cure. This is in effect no more, than to bid them first be Slaves, and then to take care of their Liberty; and when their Chains are on, tell them, they may act like Freemen. This, if barely so, is rather Mockery, than Relief; and Men can never be secure from Tyranny, if there be no means to escape it, till they are perfectly under it: And therefore it is, that they have not only a Right to get out of it, but to prevent it.

221. There is . . . another Way whereby *Governments are dissolved,* and that is, when the Legislative, or the Prince either of them act contrary to their Trust.

First, The *Legislative acts against the Trust* reposed in them, when they endeavour to invade the Property of the Subject, and to make themselves, or any part of the Community, Masters, or arbitrary Disposers of the Lives, Liberties, or Fortunes of the People.

222. The Reason why Men enter into Society, is the preservation of their Property; and the End why they chuse and authorize a Legislative, is, that there may be Laws made, and Rules set, as Guards and Fences to the Properties of all the Members of the Society, to limit the Power, and moderate the Dominion of every part and member of the Society. For since it can never be supposed to be the will of the Society, that the Legislative should have a Power to destroy that, which every one designs to secure, by entering into Society, and for which the People submitted themselves to Legislators of their own making, whenever the *Legislators endeavour to take away, and destroy the property of the People,* or to reduce them to Slavery under arbitrary Power, they put themselves into a state of War with the People, who are thereupon absolved from any farther Obedience, and are left to the common Refuge, which God hath provided for all Men, against Force and Violence. Whensoever therefore the *Legislative* shall transgress this fundamental Rule of Society . . . By this breach of Trust they *forfeit the Power,* the People had put into their Hands, for quite contrary ends, and it devolves to the People, who have a Right to resume their original Liberty, and by the establishment of a new Legislative, (such as they shall think fit) provide for their own Safety and Security. . . . What I have said here, concerning the Legislative in general, holds true also concerning the supreme Executor. . . .

223. To this perhaps it will be said, that the People being ignorant, and always discontented, to lay the foundation of Government in the unsteady Opinion and uncertain Humour of the People, is to expose it to certain Ruin; And *no Government will be able long to subsist,* if the People may set up a new Legislative, whenever they take offence at the old one. To this I answer, quite the contrary. People are not so easily got out of their old Forms, as some are apt to suggest. They are hardly to be prevailed with to amend the acknowledg'd Faults, in the Frame they have been accustom'd to. And if there be any original Defects, or adventitious ones introduced by time, or Corruption; 'tis not an easie thing to get them changed, even when all the World sees there is an Opportunity for it. . . .

224. But 'twill be said, this *Hypothesis* lays a *ferment for* frequent *Rebellion.* To which I Answer,

First, No more than any other *Hypothesis.* . . . *The People generally ill treated,* and contrary to right, will be ready upon any Occasion to ease themselves of a Burden, that sits heavy upon them. They will wish, and seek for the Opportunity, which in the change, weakness and accidents of human Affairs, seldom delays long to offer it self. . . .

225. *Secondly* . . . such *Revolutions happen* not upon every little Mismanagement in publick Affairs. *Great Mistakes* in the ruling Part, many wrong and inconvenient Laws, and all the *Slips* of human Frailty will be *born by the People* without Mutiny or Murmur. But if a long train of Abuses, Prevarications and Artifices, all tending the same Way, make the Design visible to the People, and they cannot but feel, what they lie under, and see, whither they are going; 'tis not to be wonder'd, that they should then rouze themselves, and endeavour to put the rule into such Hands, which may secure to them the ends for which Government was at first erected; and without which, ancient Names, and specious Forms, are so far from being better, that they are much worse, than the state of Nature, or pure Anarchy. . . .

226. *Thirdly* . . . *this Doctrine* of a Power in the People of providing for their Safety a-new, by a new Legislative, when their Legislators have acted contrary to their Trust, by invading their Property, is *the best Fence against Rebellion,* and the probablest Means to hinder it. For *Rebellion* being an Opposition, not to Persons, but Authority, which is founded only in the Constitutions and Laws of the Government; those whoever they be, who by Force break through, and by Force justifie their Violation of them, are truly and properly *Rebels.* For when Men by entering into Society and Civil-Government, have excluded Force, and introduced Laws for the preservation of Property, Peace, and Unity amongst themselves, those who set up Force again in Opposition to the Laws, do *rebellare,* that is, bring back again the state of War, and are properly Rebels: Which they who are in Power, (by the Pretence they have to Authority, the temptation of Force they have in their Hands, and the Flattery of those about them) being likeliest to do; the properest Way to prevent the Evil, is to shew them the Danger and Injustice of it, who are under the greatest Temptation to run into it.

227. In both the forementioned Cases, when either the Legislative is changed, or the Legislators act contrary to the End for which they were constituted; those who are guilty are *guilty of Rebellion.* . . .

228. But if they, who say *it lays a Foundation for Rebellion,* mean that it may occasion civil Wars, or intestine Broils, to tell the People they are absolved from Obedience, when illegal Attempts are made upon their Liberties or Properties, and may oppose the unlawful Violence of those, who were their Magistrates, when they invade their Properties contrary to the Trust put in them; and that therefore this Doctrine is not to be allow'd, being so destructive to the Peace of the World. They may as well say upon the same Ground, that honest Men may not oppose Robbers or Pirats, because this may occasion disorder or bloodshed. If any *Mischief* come in such Cases, it is not to be charged upon him who defends his own Right, but *on him, that invades* his Neighbours. If the innocent honest Man must quietly quit all he has for Peace sake, to him, who will lay violent Hands upon it, I desire it may be consider'd, what a kind of Peace there will be in the World, which consists only in Violence and Rapine; and which is to be maintain'd only for the benefit of Robbers and Oppressors. . . .

232. Whosoever uses *force without Right,* as every one does in Society, who does it without Law, puts himself into a *state of War* with those, against whom he so uses it, and in that state all former Ties are cancelled, all other Rights cease, and every one has a right to defend himself, and *to resist the Aggressor. . . .*

240. Here, 'tis like, the common Question will be made, *Who shall be Judge,* whether the Prince or Legislative act contrary to their Trust? This, perhaps, ill affected and factious Men may spread amongst the People, when the Prince only makes use of his due Prerogative. To this I reply; *The People shall be Judge;* for who shall be *Judge* whether his Trustee or Deputy acts well, and according to the Trust reposed in him, but he who deputes him, and must, by having deputed him, have still a Power to discard him, when he fails in his Trust? If this be reasonable in particular Cases of private Men, why should it be otherwise in that of the greatest moment, where the Welfare of Millions is concerned, and also where the Evil, if not prevented, is greater, and the Redress very difficult, dear, and dangerous?

242. If a Controversie arise betwixt a Prince and some of the People, in a matter, where the Law is silent, or doubtful, and the thing be of great Consequence, I should think the proper *Umpire,* in such a Case, should be the Body of the *People.* For in Cases where the Prince hath a Trust reposed in him, and is dispensed from the common ordinary Rules of the Law; there, if any Men find themselves aggrieved, and think the Prince acts contrary to, or beyond that Trust, who so proper to *judge* as the Body of the *People,* (who, at first, lodg'd that Trust in him) how far they meant it should extend? But if the Prince, or whoever they be in the Administration, decline that way of Determination, the Appeal then lies no where but to Heaven. Force between either Persons, who have no known Superior on Earth, or which permits no Appeal to a Judge on Earth, being properly a state of War, wherein the Appeal lies only to Heaven, and in that State the *injured Party must judge* for himself, when he will think fit to make use of that Appeal, and put himself upon it.

243. To conclude, The *Power that every Individual gave the Society,* when he entered into it, can never revert to the Individuals again, as long as the Society lasts, but will always remain in the Community; because without this, there can be no Community, no Commonwealth, which is contrary to the original Agreement: So also when the Society hath placed the Legislative in any Assembly of Men, to continue in them and their Successors, with Direction and Authority for providing such Successors, *the Legislative can never revert to the People* whilst that Government lasts: Because having provided a Legislative with Power to continue for ever, they have given up their Political Power to the Legislative, and cannot resume it. But if they have set Limits to the Duration of their Legislative, and made this supreme Power in any Person, or Assembly, only temporary: Or else, when by the Miscarriages of those in Authority, it is forfeited; upon the Forfeiture, or at the Determination of the Time set, *it reverts to the Society,* and the People have a Right to act as Supreme, and continue the Legislative in them-

selves; or erect a new Form, or under the old Form place it in new Hands, as they think good.

---

5 JAMES MILL

James Mill (1773-1836), the father of John Stuart Mill, made his assumptions very clear. As a utilitarian closely associated with Jeremy Bentham, Mill believed that human happiness is determined by the balance between pains and pleasure. He assumed that man is essentially a laborer and consumer and that individuals and society would be happiest if each person is assured of retaining ''the greatest possible quantity of the produce of his labour.'' Government is necessary to protect people in the enjoyment of the results of their labor. It has no other function, yet to carry out this duty it requires power. Mill assumes, however, that everyone—governors to common citizens—will abuse power if they have the opportunity to do so. Therefore government should be both limited and represent the interests of the whole community, because only the whole community will not have an interest in abusing power. Mill argues that only representative government could be sufficiently limited yet powerful enough to protect people. Though his principles justified universal suffrage, Mill limited his policy demands to middle-class adult male suffrage on the assumption that the poor do not understand their interest and women's interests are so closely tied to those of their husbands or fathers as to not require the right to vote.

Mill's ''Essay on Government'' was written for the *Supplement* of the *Encyclopaedia Britannica*, 1819. It was published in separate form in 1825.

ESSAY ON GOVERNMENT*

That dissection of human nature which would be necessary for exhibiting, on proper evidence, the primary elements into which human happiness may be resolved, it is not compatible with the present design to undertake. We must content ourselves with assuming certain results.

Essays on Government, Jurisprudence, Liberty of the Press and Law of Nations (London, 1825).

We may allow, for example, in general terms, that the lot of every human being is determined by his pains and pleasures; and that his happiness corresponds with the degree in which his pleasures are great, and his pains are small.

Human pains and pleasures are derived from two sources:—They are produced, either by our fellow-men, or by causes independent of other men.

We may assume it as another principle, that the concern of Government is with the former of these two sources; that its business is to increase to the utmost the pleasures, and diminish to the utmost the pains, which men derive from one another.

Of the laws of nature, on which the condition of man depends, that which is attended with the greatest number of consequences, is the necessity of labour for obtaining the means of subsistence, as well as the means of the greatest part of our pleasures. This is, no doubt, the primary cause of Government: for, if nature had produced spontaneously all the objects which we desire, and in sufficient abundance for the desires of all, there would have been no source of dispute or of injury among men; nor would any man have possessed the means of ever acquiring authority over another.

The results are exceedingly different, when nature produces the objects of desire not in sufficient abundance for all. The source of dispute is then exhaustless: and every man has the means of acquiring authority over others, in proportion to the quantity of those objects which he is able to possess.

In this case, the end to be obtained, through Government as the means, is, to make that distribution of the scanty materials of happiness, which would insure the greatest sum of it in the members of the community, taken altogether, preventing every individual, or combination of individuals, from interfering with that distribution, or making any man to have less than his share.

When it is considered that most of the objects of desire, and even the means of subsistence, are the product of labour, it is evident that the means of insuring labour must be provided for as the foundation of all.

The means for the insuring of labour are of two sorts: the one made out of the matter of evil, the other made out of the matter of good.

The first sort is commonly denominated force; and, under its application, the labourers are slaves. This mode of procuring labour we need not consider; for, if the end of Government be to produce the greatest happiness of the greatest number, that end cannot be attained by making the greatest number slaves.

The other mode of obtaining labour is by allurement, or the advantage which it brings. To obtain all the objects of desire in the greatest possible quantity, we must obtain labour in the greatest possible quantity; and, to obtain labour in the greatest possible quantity, we must raise to the greatest possible height the advantage attached to labour. It is impossible to attach to labour a greater degree of advantage that the whole of the product of labour. Why so? Because, if you give more to one man than the produce of his labour, you can do so only by taking it away from the produce of some other man's labour. The greatest possible happiness of society is, therefore, attained by insuring to every man the greatest possible quantity of the produce of his labour.

How is this to be accomplished? for it is obvious that every man, who has not all the objects of his desire, has inducement to take them from any other man who is weaker than himself: and how is he to be prevented?

One mode is sufficiently obvious; and it does not appear that there is any other: The union of a certain number of men, to protect one another. The object, it is plain, can best be attained when a great number of men combine, and delegate to a small number the power necessary for protecting them all. This is Government.

With respect to the end of Government, or that for the sake of which it exists, it is not conceived to be necessary, on the present occasion, that the analysis should be carried any further. What follows is an attempt to analyze the means.

The Means of attaining the End of Government; viz. Power, and Securities against the Abuse of that Power

Two things are here to be considered; the power with which the small number are entrusted; and the use which they are to make of it.

With respect to the first, there is no difficulty. The elements, out of which the power of coercing others is fabricated, are obvious to all. . . .

All the difficult questions of Government relate to the means of restraining those, in whose hands are lodged the powers necessary for the protection of all, from making a bad use of it.

Whatever would be the temptations under which individuals would lie, if there was no Government, to take the objects of desire from others weaker than themselves, under the same temptations the members of Government lie, to take the objects of desire from the members of the community, if they are not prevented from doing so. Whatever, then, are the reasons for establishing Government, the very same exactly are the reasons for establishing securities, that those entrusted with the powers necessary for protecting others make use of them for that purpose solely, and not for the purpose of taking from the members of the community the objects of desire.

An Objection stated—and answered

That one human being will desire to render the person and property of another subservient to his pleasures, notwithstanding the pain or loss of pleasure which it may occasion to that other individual, is the foundation of Government. The desire of the object implies the desire of the power necessary to accomplish the object. The desire, therefore, of that power which is necessary to render the persons and properties of human beings subservient to our pleasures, is a grand governing law of human nature.

What is implied in that desire of power; and what is the extent to which it carries the actions of men; are the questions which it is necessary to resolve, in order to discover the limit which nature has set to the desire on the part of a King, or an Aristocracy, to inflict evil upon the community for their own advantage.

Power is a means to an end. The end is every thing, without exception, which the human being calls pleasure, and the removal of pain. The grand instrument for attaining what a man likes is the actions of other men. Power, in its most appropriate signification, therefore, means security for the conformity between the will of one man and the acts of other men. This, we presume, is not a proposition which will be disputed. The master has power over his servant, because when he wills him to do so and so,—in other words, expresses a desire that he would do so and so, he possesses a kind of security that the actions of the man will correspond to his desire. The General commands his soldiers to perform certain operations, the King commands his subjects to act in a certain manner, and their power is complete or not complete, in proportion as the conformity is complete or not complete between the actions willed and the actions performed. The actions of other men, considered as means for the attainment of the objects of our desire, are perfect or imperfect, in proportion as they are or are not certainly and invariably correspondent to our will. There is no limit, therefore, to the demand of security for the perfection of that correspondence. A man is never satisfied with a smaller degree if he can obtain a greater. And as there is no man whatsoever, whose acts, in some degree or other, in some way or other, more immediately or more remotely, may not have some influence as means to our ends, there is no man, the conformity of whose acts to our will we would not give something to secure. The demand, therefore, of power over the acts of other men is really boundless. It is boundless in two ways; boundless in the number of persons to whom we would extend it, and boundless in its degree over the actions of each.

. . . With respect to the rulers of a community, this at least is certain, that they have a desire for the uniformity between their will and the actions of every man in the community. And for our present purpose, this is as wide a field as we need to embrace.

With respect to the community, then, we deem it an established truth, that the rulers, one or a few, desire an exact conformity between their will and the acts of every member of the community. . . .

In the Representative System alone the Securities for good Government are to be found

What then is to be done? For, according to this reasoning, we may be told that good Government appears to be impossible. The people, as a body, cannot perform the business of Government for themselves. If the powers of Government are entrusted to one man, or a few men, and a Monarchy, or governing Aristocracy, is formed, the results are fatal: And it appears that a combination of the simple forms is impossible.

Notwithstanding the truth of these propositions, it is not yet proved that good Government is impossible. For though the people, who cannot exercise the powers of Government themselves, must entrust them to some one individual or set of individuals, and such individuals will infallibly have the strongest motives to make a bad use of them, it is possible that checks may be found sufficient to prevent them. The next subject of inquiry, then, is the doctrine of checks. It is sufficiently conformable to the established and fashionable opinions to say, that, upon the right constitution of checks, all goodness of Government depends. To this proposition we fully subscribe. Nothing, therefore, can exceed the importance of correct conclusions upon this subject. . . .

In the grand discovery of modern times, the system of representation, the solution of all the difficulties, both speculative and practical, will perhaps be found. If it cannot, we seem to be forced upon the extraordinary conclusion, that good Government is impossible. For as there is no individual, or combination of individuals, except the community itself, who would not have an interest in bad Government, if entrusted with its powers; and as the community itself is incapable of exercising those powers, and must entrust them to some individual or combination of individuals, the conclusion is obvious: The Community itself must check those individuals, else they will follow their interest, and produce bad Government.

But how is it the Community can check? The community can act only when assembled: And then it is incapable of acting.

The community, however, can chuse Representatives: And the question is, whether the Representatives of the Community can operate as a check?

What is required in a Representative Body to make it a Security for good Government?

We may begin by laying down two propositions, which appear to involve a great portion of the inquiry; and about which it is unlikely that there will be any dispute.

I. The checking body must have a degree of power sufficient for the business of checking.

II. It must have an identity of interest with the community; otherwise it will make a mischievous use of its power.

I. To measure the degree of power which is requisite upon any occasion, we must consider the degree of power which is necessary to be overcome. Just as much as suffices for that purpose is requisite, and no more. We have then to inquire what power it is which the Representatives of the community, acting as a check, need power to overcome. The answer here is easily given. It is all that power, wheresoever lodged, which they, in whose hands it is lodged, have an interest in misusing. We have already seen, that to whomsoever the community entrusts the powers of Government, whether one, or a few, they have an interest in misusing them. All the power, therefore, which the one or the few, or which the one and the few combined, can apply to insure the accomplishment of their sinister ends, the checking body must have power to overcome, otherwise its check will be unavailing. In other words, there will be no check.

This is so exceedingly evident, that we hardly think it necessary to say another word in illustration of it. If a King is prompted by the inherent principles of human nature to seek the gratification of his will; and if he finds an obstacle in that pursuit, he removes it, of course, if he can. If any man, or any set of men, oppose him, he overcomes them, if he is able; and to prevent him, they must, at the least, have equal power with himself.

The same is the case with an Aristocracy. To oppose them with success in pursuing their interest at the expense of the community, the checking body must have power successfully to resist whatever power they possess. If there is both a King and an Aristocracy, and if they would combine to put down the checking force, and to pursue their mutual interest at the expense of the community, the checking body must have sufficient power successfully to resist the united power of both King and Aristocracy.

These conclusions are not only indisputable, but the very theory of the British Constitution is erected upon them. The House of Commons, according to that theory, is the checking body. It is also an admitted doctrine, that if the King had the power of bearing down any opposition to his will that could be made by the House of Commons; or if the King and the House of Lords combined had the power of bearing down its opposition to their joint will, it would cease to have the power of checking them; it must, therefore, have a power sufficient to overcome the united power of both.

II. All the questions which relate to the degree of power necessary to be given to that checking body, on the perfection of whose operations all the goodness of Government depends, are thus pretty easily solved. The grand difficulty consists in finding the means of constituting a checking body, whose powers shall not be turned against the community for whose protection it is created.

There can be no doubt, that if power is granted to a body of men, called Representatives, they, like any other men, will use their power, not for the advantage of the community, but for their own advantage, if they can. The only question is, therefore, how they can be prevented? in other words, how are the interests of the Representatives to be identified with those of the community?

Each Representative may be considered in two capacities; in his capacity of Representative, in which he has the exercise of power over others, and in his capacity of Member of the Community, in which others have the exercise of power over him.

If things were so arranged, that, in his capacity of Representative, it would be impossible for him to do himself so much good by misgovernment, as he would do himself harm in his capacity of member of the community, the object would be accomplished. We have already seen, that the amount of power assigned to the checking body cannot be diminished beyond a certain amount. It must be sufficient to overcome all resistance on the part of all those in whose hands the powers of Government are lodged. But if the power assigned to the Representative cannot be diminished in amount, there is only one other way in which it can be diminished, and that is, in duration.

This, then, is the instrument; lessening of duration is the instrument, by which, if by any thing, the object is to be attained. The smaller the period of time during which any man retains his capacity of Representative, as compared with the time in which he is simply a member of the community, the more difficult it will be to compensate the sacrifice of the interests of the longer period, by the profits of misgovernment during the shorter.

This is an old and approved method of identifying as nearly as possible the interests of those who rule with the interests of those who are ruled. It is in pursuance of this advantage, that the Members of the British House of Commons have always been chosen for a limited period. If the Members were hereditary, or even if they were chosen for life, every inquirer would immediately pronounce that they would employ, for their own advantage, the powers entrusted to them; and that they would go just as far in abusing the persons and properties of the people, as their estimate of the powers and spirit of the people to resist them would allow them to contemplate as safe.

As it thus appears, by the consent of all men, from the time when the Romans made their Consuls annual, down to the present day, that the end is to be attained by limiting the duration, either of the acting, or (which is better) of the checking power, the next question is, to what degree should the limitation proceed?

The general answer is plain. It should proceed, till met by overbalancing inconveniences on the other side. What then are the inconveniences which are likely to flow from a too limited duration?

They are of two sorts; those which affect the performance of the service, for which the individuals are chosen, and those which arise from the trouble of election. It is sufficiently obvious, that the business of Government requires time to perform it. The matter must be proposed, deliberated upon, a resolution must be taken, and executed. If the powers of Government were to be shifted from one set of hands to another every day, the business of Government could not proceed. Two conclusions, then, we may adopt with perfect certainty; that whatsoever time is necessary to perform the periodical round of the stated operations of Government, this should be allotted to those who are invested with the checking powers; and secondly, that no time, which is not necessary for that purpose, should by any means be allotted to them. With respect to the inconvenience arising from frequency of election, though, it is evident, that the trouble of election, which is always something, should not be repeated oftener than is necessary, no great allowance will need to be made for it, because it may easily be reduced to an inconsiderable amount.

As it thus appears, that limiting the duration of their power is a security against the sinister interest of the people's Representatives, so it appears that it is the only security of which the nature of the case admits. The only other means which could be employed to that end, would be punishment on account of abuse. It is easy, however, to see, that punishment could not be effectually applied. In order for punishment, definition is required of the punishable acts; and proof must be established of the commission. But abuses of power may be carried to a great extent, without allowing the means of proving a determinate offence. No part of political experience is more perfect than this.

If the limiting of duration be the only security, it is unnecessary to speak of the importance which ought to be attached to it.

In the principle of limiting the duration of the power delegated to the Representatives of the people, is not included the idea of changing them. The same individual may be chosen any number of times. The check of the short period, for which he is chosen, and during which he can promote his sinister interest, is the same upon the man who has been chosen and re-chosen twenty times, as upon the man who has been chosen for the first time. And there is good reason for always re-electing the man who has done his duty, because the longer he serves, the better acquainted he becomes with the business of the service. Upon this principle of rechoosing, or of the permanency of the individual, united with the power of change, has been recommended the plan of permanent service with perpetual power of removal. This, it has been said, reduces the period within which the Representative can promote his sinister interest to the narrowest possible limits; because the moment when his Constituents begin to suspect him, that moment they may turn him out. On the other hand, if he continues faithful, the trouble of election is performed once for all, and the man serves as long as he lives.

---

6 JOHN STUART MILL

Representative Government is the culmination of liberal utilitarian thinking about the nature and purpose of the state. It contains an argument for popular representation and a defense of limited, constitutional government. And it is, moreover, an argument which attempts to balance and to reconcile two different liberal values: widespread participation in the affairs of the community and the desire to have the community led by its finest citizens.

English liberals such as Locke and Mill (1806-1873) did not believe all men had the same skills, equal talents, or similar degrees of moral concern. They never flinched (as their political successors do now) from arguing that human quality, and not social or economic equality, was their goal. Mill, especially, argued, against the conservatives, that "ordinary" human beings had great potential. At the same time, however, Mill was no democrat. He had little faith in "common" men. His efforts were bent toward creating a society where, *eventually,* even "common" citizens would be uncommonly competent and humane. The argument of *Representative Government,* therefore, is that only representative political institutions allow for the efficient and just regulation of society and for the development of citizens capable of conducting the community's affairs responsibly.

Representative Government has not been popular among twentieth-century liberals. They have found its moralistic tone naive or condescending. There are also whole sections where Mill argues that flaws in the national character of some peoples must inhibit or prohibit their adoption of representative institutions. That sort of "anthropology" (which still lingers on in the form of speculation about the political consequences of cultural norms) is disparaged by contemporary liberal philosophers. Yet much of what Mill has to say about the proper development of representative institutions is relevant to current problems and developments in the United States and elsewhere. The purpose of, and the proper form of representation must remain fundamental concerns for liberals, and there is probably no better place to begin a study of representation than *Representative Government.*

REPRESENTATIVE GOVERNMENT*

Chapter I

. . . Let us remember, then, in the first place, that political institutions (however the proposition may be at times ignored) are the work of men; owe their origin and their whole existence to human will. Men did not wake on a summer morning and find them sprung up. Neither do they resemble trees, which, once planted, 'are aye growing' while men 'are sleeping.' In every stage of their existence they are made what they are by human voluntary agency. Like all things, therefore, which are made by men, they may be either well or ill made; judgment

---

Considerations on Representative Government (London: Parker, Son, and Bourn, 1861).

and skill may have been exercised in their production, or the reverse of these. And again, if a people have omitted, or from outward pressure have not had it in their power, to give themselves a constitution by the tentative process of applying a corrective to each evil as it arose, or as the sufferers gained strength to resist it, this retardation of political progress is no doubt a great disadvantage to them, but it does not prove that what has been found good for others would not have been good also for them, and will not be so still when they think fit to adopt it.

On the other hand, it is also to be borne in mind that political machinery does not act of itself. As it is first made, so it has to be worked, by men, and even by ordinary men. It needs, not their simple acquiescence, but their active participation; and must be adjusted to the capacities and qualities of such men as are available. This implies three conditions. The people for whom the form of government is intended must be willing to accept it; or at least not so unwilling, as to oppose an insurmountable obstacle to its establishment. They must be willing and able to do what is necessary to keep it standing. And they must be willing and able to do what it requires of them to enable it to fulfil its purposes. The word "do" must be understood as including forbearances as well as acts. They must be capable of fulfilling the conditions of action, and the conditions of self-restraint, which are necessary either for keeping the established polity in existence, or for enabling it to achieve the ends, its conduciveness to which forms its recommendation. . . .

We have now examined the three fundamental conditions of the adaptation of forms of government to the people who are to be governed by them. If the supporters of what may be termed the naturalistic theory of politics, mean but to insist on the necessity of these three conditions; if they only mean that no government can permanently exist, which does not fulfil the first and second conditions, and, in some considerable measure, the third; their doctrine, thus limited, is incontestable. Whatever they mean more than this, appears to me altogether untenable. All that we are told about the necessity of an historical basis for institutions, of their being in harmony with the national usages and character, and the like, means either this, or nothing to the purpose. There is a great quantity of mere sentimentality connected with these and similar phrases, over and above the amount of rational meaning contained in them. But, considered practically, these alleged requisites of political institutions are merely so many facilities for realizing the three conditions. When an institution, or set of institutions, has the way prepared for it by the opinions, tastes, and habits of the people, they are not only more easily induced to accept it, but will more easily learn, and will be, from the beginning, better disposed to do what is required of them both for the preservation of the institutions, and for bringing them into such action as enables them to produce their best results. It would be a great mistake in any legislator not to shape his measures so as to take advantage of such pre-existing habits and feelings, when available. On the other hand, it is an exaggeration to elevate these mere aids and facilities into necessary conditions. People are more easily induced to do, and do more easily, what they are already used to; but people also learn to do things new to them. Familiarity is a great help; but much dwelling on an idea will make it familiar, even when strange at first. There are abundant instances in which a whole people have been eager for untried things. The amount of capacity which a people possess for doing new things, and adapting themselves to new circumstances, is itself one of the elements of the question. It is a quality in which different nations, and different stages of civilization, differ much from one another. The capability of any given people for fulfilling the conditions of a given form of government, cannot be pronounced on by any sweeping rule. Knowledge of the particular people, and general practical judgment and sagacity, must be the guides. There is also another consideration not to be lost sight of. A people may be unprepared for good institutions; but to kindle a desire for them is a necessary part of the preparation. To recommend and advocate a particular institution or form of government, and set its advantages in the strongest light, is one of the modes, often the only mode within reach, of educating the mind of the nation, not only for accepting or claiming, but also for working, the institution. What means had Italian patriots, during the last and present generation, of preparing the Italian people for freedom in unity, but by inciting them to demand it? Those, however, who undertake such a task, need to be duly impressed, not solely with the benefits of the institution or polity which they recommend, but also with the capacities, moral, intellectual, and active, required for working it; that they may avoid, if possible, stirring up a desire too much in advance of the capacity.

The result of what has been said is, that, within the limits set by the three conditions so often adverted to, institutions and forms of government *are* a matter of choice. To inquire into the best form of government in the abstract (as it is called) is not a chimerical, but a highly practical employment of scientific intellect; and to introduce into any country the best institutions which, in the existing state of that country, are capable of, in any tolerable degree, fulfilling the conditions, is one of the most rational objects to which practical effort can address itself. Everything which can be said by way of disparaging the efficacy of human will and purpose in matters of government, might be said of it in every other of its applications. In all things there are very strict limits to human power. It can only act by wielding some one or more of the forces of nature. Forces, therefore, that can be applied to the desired use, must exist; and will only act according to their own laws. We cannot make the river run backwards; but we do not therefore say that watermills 'are not made, but grow.' In politics as in mechanics, the power which is to keep the engine going must be sought for *outside* the machinery; and if it is not forthcoming, or is insufficient to surmount the obstacles which may reasonably be expected, the contrivance will fail. This is no peculiarity of the political art; and amounts only to saying that it is subject to the same limitations and conditions as all other arts.

At this point we are met by another objection, or the same objection in a different form. The forces, it is contended, on which the greater political phenomena depend, are not amenable to the direction of politicians or philosophers. The government of a country, it is affirmed, is, in all substantial respects, fixed and determined beforehand by the state of the country in regard to the distribution of the elements of social power. Whatever is the strongest power in society will obtain the governing authority; and a change in the political constitution cannot be durable unless preceded or accompanied by an altered distribution of power in society itself. A nation, therefore, cannot choose its form of government. The mere details, and practical organization, it may choose; but the essence of the whole, the seat of the supreme power, is determined for it by social circumstances.

That there is a portion of truth in this doctrine, I at once admit; but to make it of any use, it must be reduced to a distinct expression and proper limits. When it is said that the strongest power in society will make itself strongest in the government, what is meant by power? Not thews and sinews; otherwise pure democracy would be the only form of polity that could exist. To mere muscular strength, add two other elements, property and intelligence, and we are nearer the truth, but far from having yet reached it. Not only is a greater number often kept down by a less, but the greater number may have a preponderance in property, and individually in intelligence, and may yet be held in subjection, forcible or otherwise, by a minority in both respects inferior to it. To make these various elements of power politically influential, they must be organized; and the advantage in organization is necessarily with those who are in possession of the government. A much weaker party in all other elements of power, may greatly preponderate when the powers of government are thrown into the scale; and may long retain its predominance through this alone: though, no doubt, a government so situated is . . . unstable. . . .

But there are still stronger objections to this theory of government in the terms in which it is usually stated. The power in society which has any tendency to convert itself into political power, is not power quiescent, power merely passive, but active power; in other words power actually exerted; that is to say, a very small portion of all the power in existence. Politically speaking, a great part of all power consists in will. How is it possible, then, to compute the elements of political power, while we omit from the computation anything which acts on the will? To think that, because those who wield the power in society wield in the end that of government, therefore it is of no use to attempt to influence the constitution of the government by acting on opinion, is to forget that opinion is itself one of the greatest active social forces. One person with a belief, is a social power equal to ninety-nine who have only interests. They who can succeed in creating a general persuasion that a certain form of government, or social fact of any kind, deserves to be preferred, have made nearly the most important step which can possibly be taken towards ranging the powers of society on its side. . . .

It was not by any change in the distribution of material interests, but by the spread of moral convictions, that negro slavery has been put an end to in the British Empire and elsewhere. The serfs in Russia will owe their emancipation, if not to a sentiment of duty, at least to the growth of a more enlightened opinion respecting the true interest of the State. It is what men think, that determines how they act; and though the persuasions and convictions of average men are in much greater degree determined by their personal position than by reason, no little power is exercised over them by the persuasions and convictions of those whose personal position is different, and by the united authority of the instructed. When, therefore, the instructed in general can be brought to recognise one social arrangement, or political or other institution, as good, and another as bad, one as desirable, another as condemnable, very much has been done towards giving to the one, or withdrawing from the other, that preponderance of social force which enables it to subsist. And the maxim, that the government of a country is what the social forces in existence compel it to be, is true only in the sense in which it favours, instead of discouraging, the attempt to exercise, among all forms of government practicable in the existing condition of society, a rational choice.

Chapter II

The form of government for any given country being (within certain definite conditions) amenable to choice, it is now to be considered by what test the choice should be directed; what are the distinctive characteristics of the form of government best fitted to promote the interests of any given society.

Before entering into this inquiry, it may seem necessary to decide what are the proper functions of government: for, government altogether being only a means, the eligibility of the means must depend on their adaptation to the end. But this mode of stating the problem gives less aid to its investigation than might be supposed, and does not even bring the whole of the question into view. For, in the first place, the proper functions of a government are not a fixed thing, but different in different states of society; much more extensive in a backward than in an advanced state. And, secondly, the character of a government or set of political institutions cannot be sufficiently estimated while we confine our attention to the legitimate sphere of governmental functions. For though the goodness of a government is necessarily circumscribed within that sphere, its badness unhappily is not. Every kind and degree of evil of which mankind are susceptible, may be inflicted on them by their government; and none of the good which social existence is capable of, can be any further realized than as the constitution of the government is compatible with, and allows scope for, its attainment. Not to speak of indirect effects, the direct meddling of the public authorities has no necessary limits but those of human life; and the influence of government on the well-being of society can be considered or estimated in reference to nothing less than the whole of the interests of humanity. . . .

If we ask ourselves on what causes and conditions good government in all its senses, from the humblest to the most exalted, depends, we find that the principal of them, the one which transcends all others, is the qualities of the human beings composing the society over which the government is exercised. . . .

The first element of good government, therefore, being the virtue and intelligence of the human beings composing the community, the most important point of excellence which any form of government can possess is to promote the virtue and intelligence of the people themselves. The first question in respect to any political institutions is, how far they tend to foster in the members of the community the various desirable qualities, moral or intellectual; or rather (following Bentham's more complete classification) moral, intellectual, and active. The government which does this the best, has every likelihood of being the best in all other respects, since it is on these qualities, so far as they exist in the people, that all possibility of goodness in the practical operations of the government depends.

We may consider, then, as one criterion of the goodness of a government, the degree in which it tends to increase the sum of good qualities in the governed, collectively and individually; since, besides that their well-being is the sole object of government, their good qualities supply the moving force which works the machinery. This leaves, as the other constituent element of the merit of a government, the quality of the machinery itself; that is, the degree in which it is adapted to take advantage of the amount of good qualities which may at any time exist, and make them instrumental to the right purposes. . . .

All government which aims at being good, is an organization of some part of the good qualities existing in the individual members of the community, for the conduct of its collective affairs. A representative constitution is a means of bringing the general standard of intelligence and honesty existing in the community, and the individual intellect and virtue of its wisest members, more directly to bear upon the government, and investing them with greater influence in it, than they would have under any other mode of organization; though, under any, such influence as they do have is the source of all good that there is in the government, and the hindrance of every evil that there is not. The greater the amount of these good qualities which the institutions of a country succeed in organizing, and the better the mode of organization, the better will be the government.

We have now, therefore, obtained a foundation for a twofold division of the merit which any set of political institutions can possess. It consists partly of the degree in which they promote the general mental advancement of the community, including under that phrase advancement in intellect, in virtue, and in practical activity and efficiency; and partly of the degree of perfection with which they organize the moral, intellectual, and active worth already existing, so as to operate with the greatest effect on public affairs. A government is to be judged by its action upon men, and by its action upon things; by what it makes of the citizens, and what it does with them; its tendency to improve or deteriorate the people themselves, and the goodness or badness of the work it performs for them, and by means of them. Government is at once a great influence acting on the human mind, and a set of organized arrangements for public business: in the first capacity its beneficial action is chiefly indirect, but not therefore less vital, while its mischievous action may be direct. . . .

Chapter III

. . . There is no difficulty in showing that the ideally best form of government is that in which the sovereignty, or supreme controlling power in the last resort, is vested in the entire aggregate of the community; every citizen not only having a voice in the exercise of that ultimate sovereignty, but being, at least occasionally, called on to take an actual part in the government, by the personal discharge of some public function, local or general.

To test this proposition, it has to be examined in reference to the two branches into which, as pointed out in the last chapter, the inquiry into the goodness of a government conveniently divides itself, namely, how far it promotes the good management of the affairs of society by means of the existing faculties, moral, intellectual, and active of its various members, and what is its effect in improving or deteriorating those faculties.

The ideally best form of government, it is scarcely necessary to say, does not mean one which is practicable or eligible in all states of civilization, but the one which, in the circumstances in which it is practicable and eligible, is attended with the greatest amount of beneficial consequences, immediate and prospective. A completely popular government is the only polity which can make out any claim to this character. It is pre-eminent in both the departments between which the excellence of a political Constitution is divided. It is both more favourable to present good government, and promotes a better and higher form of national character, than any other polity whatsoever.

Its superiority in reference to present well-being rests upon two principles, of as universal truth and applicability as any general propositions which can be laid down respecting human affairs. The first is, that the rights and interests of every or any person are only secure from being disregarded, when the person interested is himself able, and habitually disposed, to stand up for them. The second is, that the general prosperity attains a greater height, and is more widely diffused, in proportion to the amount and variety of the personal energies enlisted in promoting it.

Putting these two propositions into a shape more special to their present application; human beings are only secure from evil at the hands of others, in proportion as they have the power of being, and are, self-*protecting;* and they only achieve a high degree of success in their struggle with Nature in proportion as they are self-*dependent,* relying on what they themselves can do, either separately or in concert, rather than on what others do for them. . . .

Now there can be no kind of doubt that the passive type of character is favoured by the government of one or a few, and the active self-helping type by that of the Many. Irresponsible rulers need the quiescence of the ruled more than they need any activity but that which they can compel. Submissiveness to the prescriptions of men as necessities of nature, is the lesson inculcated by all governments upon those who are wholly without participation in them. The will of superiors, and the law as the will of superiors, must be passively yielded to. But no men are mere instruments or materials in the hands of their rulers, who have will or spirit or a spring of internal activity in the rest of their proceedings: and any manifestation of these qualities, instead of receiving encouragement from despots, has to get itself forgiven by them. Even when irresponsible rulers are not sufficiently conscious of danger from the mental activity of their subjects to be desirous of repressing it, the position itself is a repression. Endeavour is even more effectually restrained by the certainty of its impotence, than by any positive discouragement. Between subjection to the will of others, and the virtues of self-help and self-government, there is a natural incompatibility. This is more or less complete, according as the bondage is strained or relaxed. Rulers differ very much in the length to which they carry the control of the free agency of their subjects, or the supersession of it by managing their business for them. But the difference is in degree, not in principle; and the best despots often go the greatest lengths in chaining up the free agency of their subjects. A bad despot, when his own personal indulgences have been provided for, may sometimes be willing to let the people alone; but a good despot insists on doing them good, by making them do their own business in a better way than they themselves know of. . . .

Very different is the state of the human faculties where a human being feels himself under no other external restraint than the necessities of nature, or mandates of society which he has his share in imposing, and which it is open to him, if he thinks them wrong, publicly to dissent from, and exert himself actively to get altered. No doubt, under a government partially popular, this freedom may be exercised even by those who are not partakers in the full privileges of citizenship. But it is a great additional stimulus to any one's self-help and self-reliance when he starts from an even ground, and has not to feel that his success depends on the impression he can make upon the sentiments and dispositions of a body of whom he is not one. It is a great discouragement to an individual, and a still greater one to a class, to be left out of the constitution; to be reduced to plead from outside the door to the arbiters of their destiny, not taken into the consultation within. The maximum of the invigorating effect of freedom upon the character is only obtained, when the person acted on either is, or is looking forward to become, a citizen as fully privileged as any other. What is still more important than even this matter of feeling, is the practical discipline which the character obtains, from the occasional demand made upon the citizens to exercise, for a time and in their turn, some social function. It is not sufficiently considered how little there is in most men's ordinary life to give any largeness either to their conceptions or to their sentiments. Their work is a routine; not a labour of love, but of self-interest in the most elementary form, the satisfaction of daily wants; neither the thing done, nor the process of doing it, introduces the mind to thoughts or feelings extending beyond individuals; if instructive books are within their reach, there is no stimulus to read them; and in most cases the individual has no access to any person of cultivation much superior to his own. Giving him something to do for the public, supplies, in a measure, all these deficiencies. If circumstances allow the amount of public duty assigned him to be considerable, it makes him an educated man. Notwithstanding the defects of the social system and moral ideas of antiquity, the practice of the dicastery and the ecclesia raised the intellectual standard of an average Athenian citizen far beyond anything of which there is yet an example in any other mass of men, ancient or modern. . . . A benefit of the same kind, though far less in degree, is produced on Englishmen of the lower middle class by their liability to be placed on juries and to serve parish offices; which, though it does not occur to so many, nor is so continuous, nor introduces them to so great a variety of elevated considerations, as to admit of comparison with the public education which every citizen of Athens obtained from her democratic institutions, makes them nevertheless very different beings, in range of ideas and development of faculties, from those who have done nothing in their lives, but drive a quill, or sell goods over a counter. Still more salutary is the moral part of the instruction afforded by the participation of the private citizen, if even rarely, in public functions. He is called upon, while so engaged, to weigh interests not his own; to be guided, in case of conflicting claims, by another rule than his private partialities; to apply, at every turn, principles and maxims which have for their reason of existence the general good: and he usually finds associated with him in the same work minds more familiarized than his own with these ideas and operations, whose study it will be to supply reasons to his understanding, and stimulation to his feeling for the general good. He is made to feel himself one of the public, and whatever is their interest to be his interest. Where this school of public spirit does not exist, scarcely any sense is entertained that private persons, in no eminent social situation, owe any duties to society, except to obey the laws and submit to the government. There is no unselfish sentiment of identification with the public. Every thought and feeling, either of interest or of duty, is absorbed in the individual and in the family. The man never thinks of any collective interest, of any objects to be pursued jointly with others, but only in competition with them, and in some measure at their expense. A neighbour, not being an ally or an associate, since he is never engaged in any common undertaking for the joint benefit, is therefore only a rival. Thus even private morality suffers, while public is actually extinct. Were this the universal and only possible state of things, the utmost aspirations of the lawgiver or the moralist could only stretch to making the bulk of the community a flock of sheep innocently nibbling the grass side by side.

From these accumulated considerations it is evident that the only government which can fully satisfy all the exigencies of the social state, is one in which the whole people participate; that any participation, even in the smallest public function, is useful; that the participation should everywhere be as great as the general degree of improvement of the community will allow; and that nothing less can be ultimately desirable, than the admission of all to a share of the sovereign power of the state. But since all cannot, in a community exceeding a single small town, participate personally in any but some very minor portions of the public business, it follows that the ideal type of a perfect government must be representative.

Chapter V

. . . The meaning of representative government is, that the whole people, or some numerous portion of them, exercise through deputies periodically elected by themselves, the ultimate controlling power, which, in every constitution, must reside somewhere. This ultimate power they must possess in all its completeness. They must be masters, whenever they please, of all the operations of government. . . .

But while it is essential to representative government that the practical supremacy in the state should reside in the representatives of the people, it is an open question what actual functions, what precise part in the machinery of government, shall be directly and personally discharged by the representative body. Great varieties in this respect are compatible with the essence of representative government, provided the functions are such as secure to the representative body the control of everything in the last resort.

There is a radical distinction between controlling the business of government, and actually doing it. The same person or body may be able to control everything, but cannot possibly do everything; and in many cases its control over everything will be more perfect, the less it personally attempts to do. The commander of an army could not direct its movements so effectually if he himself fought in the ranks, or led an assault. It is the same with bodies of men. Some things cannot be done except by bodies; other things cannot be well done by them. It is one question, therefore, what a popular assembly should control, another what it should itself do. It should, as we have already seen, control all the operations of government. . . .

But it is equally true, though only of late and slowly beginning to be acknowledged, that a numerous assembly is as little fitted for the direct business of legislation as for that of administration. There is hardly any kind of intellectual work which so much needs to be done not only by experienced and exercised minds, but by minds trained to the task through long and laborious study, as the business of making laws. This is a sufficient reason, were there no other, why they can never be well made but by a committee of very few persons. A reason no less conclusive is, that every provision of a law requires to be framed with the most accurate and long-sighted perception of its effect on all the other provisions; and the law when made should be capable of fitting into a consistent whole with the previously existing laws. It is impossible that these conditions should be in any degree fulfilled when laws are voted clause by clause in a miscellaneous assembly. The incongruity of such a mode of legislating would strike all minds, were it not that our laws are already, as to form and construction, such a chaos, that the confusion and contradiction seem incapable of being made greater by any addition to the mass. . . .

Instead of the function of governing, for which it is radically unfit, the proper office of a representative assembly is to watch and control the government: to throw the light of publicity on its acts; to compel a full exposition and justification of all of them which any one considers questionable; to censure them if found condemnable, and, if the men who compose the government abuse their trust, or fulfil it in a manner which conflicts with the deliberate sense of the nation, to expel them from office, and either expressly or virtually appoint their successors. This is surely ample power, and security enough for the liberty of the nation. In addition to this, the Parliament has an office, not inferior even to this in importance; to be at once the nation's Committee of Grievances, and its Congress of Opinions: an arena in which not only the general opinion of the nation, but that of every section of it, and as far as possible of every eminent individual whom it contains, can produce itself in full light and challenge discussion; where every person in the country may count upon finding somebody who speaks his mind, as well or better than he could speak it himself—not to friends and partisans exclusively, but in the face of opponents, to be tested by adverse controversy; where those whose opinion is overruled, feel satisfied that it is heard, and set aside not by a mere act of will, but for what are thought superior reasons, and commend themselves as such to the representatives of the majority of the nation; where every party or opinion in the country can muster its strength, and be cured of any illusion concerning the number or power of its adherents; where the opinion which prevails in the nation makes itself manifest as prevailing, and marshals its hosts in the presence of the government, which is thus enabled and compelled to give way to it on the mere manifestation, without the actual employment, of its strength; where statesmen can assure themselves, far more certainly than by any other signs, what elements of opinion and power are growing, and what declining, and are enabled to shape their measures with some regard not solely to present exigencies, but to tendencies in progress. Representative assemblies are often taunted by their enemies with being places of mere talk and *bavardage*. There has seldom been more misplaced derision. I know not how a representative assembly can more usefully employ itself than in talk, when the subject of talk is the great public interests of the country, and every sentence of it represents the opinion either of some important body of persons in the nation, or of an individual in whom some such body have reposed their confidence. A place where every interest and shade of opinion in the country can have its cause even passionately pleaded, in the face of the government and of all other interests and opinions, can compel them to listen and either comply, or state clearly why they do not, is in itself, if it answered no other purpose, one of the most important political institutions that can exist anywhere, and one of the foremost benefits of free government. Such 'talking' would never be looked upon with disparagement if it were not allowed to stop 'doing;' which it never would, if assemblies knew and acknowledged that talking and discussion are their proper business, while *doing*, as the result of discussion, is the task not of a miscellaneous body, but of individuals specially trained to it; that the fit office of an assembly is to see that those individuals are honestly and intelligently chosen, and to interfere no further with them, except by unlimited latitude of suggestion and criticism, and by applying or withholding the final seal of national assent. It is for want of this judicious reserve, that popular assemblies attempt to do what they cannot do well—to govern and legislate—and provide no machinery but their own for much of it, when of course every hour spent in talk is an hour withdrawn from actual business. But the very fact which most unfits such bodies for a Council of Legislation, qualifies them the more for their other office—namely, that they are not a selection of the greatest political minds in the country, from whose opinions little could with certainty be inferred concerning those of the nation, but are, when properly constituted, a fair sample of every grade of intellect among the people which is at all entitled to a voice in public affairs. Their part is to indicate wants, to be an organ for popular demands, and a place of adverse discussion for all opinions relating to public matters, both great and small; and, along with this, to check by criticism, and eventually by withdrawing their support, those high public officers who really conduct the public business, or who appoint those by whom it is conducted. Nothing but the restriction of the function of representative bodies within these rational limits, will enable the benefits of popular control to be enjoyed in conjunction with the no less important requisites (growing ever more important as human affairs increase in scale and in complexity) of skilled legislation and administration. There are no means of combining these benefits, except by separating the functions which guarantee the one from those which essentially require the other; by disjoining the office of control and criticism from the actual conduct of affairs, and devolving the former on the representatives of the Many, while securing for the latter, under strict responsibility to the nation, the acquired knowledge and practised intelligence of a specially trained and experienced Few.

Revolution
and Political Change

Liberals, even when they have been revolutionaries, have rarely been comfortable with the idea and the practice of revolution. Liberal thinkers with a few exceptions have seen revolution as a last alternative, as something good men are driven to by unresponsive or tyrannical institutions. American liberals have not been so cautious in their approach to change, but that may be due to the peculiar circumstances of American history and not to the "radical" leanings of American liberalism. American liberals have not had to deal philosophically or politically with a serious conservative challenge, but American liberalism, like liberalism in England, has had since its beginnings a strong Whig component.

Even American liberal revolutionaries, though, have not called for a fundamental transformation of man or of society. Thomas Paine, who certainly was a revolutionary, did not perceive liberal institutions and concepts as radical; instead, like so many of his liberal contemporaries, he saw them as "natural," as the products of "common sense." Paine did not argue that private property or the family should be abolished. His goal was political equality, not social or economic equality, although it appears Paine believed that, once the former were achieved, inequalities of wealth and position would decline.

It is no accident, then, that this section is entitled "Revolution and Political Change." Liberals saw (and still see) revolution as a form of political change, not as the consequence of patterned historical development or as the opportunity to create a "new man." Consequently, the liberal approach to change—even to revolution—has been optimistic but realistic, hopeful but honest. The willingness of liberals to accept change in lieu of revolution (because revolution is only one form of change) has allowed liberals to preserve private property and inequalities of wealth in societies where poor voters greatly outnumber the rich.

Critics of liberalism (see Section 6) have been saying for over a century that such societies cannot persevere, that there must, inevitably, erupt in those societies a conflict between those with real economic power and those with potential political power. If such confrontations do not occur, it will be the "fault" of liberals like Bentham, who proposed grounds for major social change which did not work clearly to the benefit of only one social class. Bentham's utilitarianism is revolutionary because it is the first "public" (instead of class) ideology.

Revolution must nevertheless remain a problem for liberals. Liberals still believe that consent is the proper basis of political authority. The claim of "no taxation without representation" is a summary statement of this belief. But what if a liberal government acts without the consent of its citizens or ignores the petitions presented to it by groups of citizens who fear that most of their fellows are unwilling or unable to protect their rights? As the responsibilities of modern government have grown, this problem has become more serious. In consequence, liberal thinkers have argued about the value of civil disobedience, and they have also devoted more and more time to the question of political obligation. Should the moral citizen ignore or disobey the immoral state? Can people in nations like the United States *ever* be said to have consented to the laws of their country? These are not just matters for debate, as the conflict in America during the war in Viet Nam showed. These issues are, however, rooted in the basic goal of the liberal revolutions—giving individuals responsibility for the affairs of the community.

Finally, we should point out that the Anglo-American liberal tradition provides real grounds for resisting community authority. In this it is the only major intellectual tradition to admit the possibility that people may sometimes legitimately resist governments which adhere to that tradition. Yet liberals have not been successful in institutionalizing resistance. That is, they have not developed a protected area within the law where people may sometimes disobey or resist the law. They *have* done this with dissent, but not with resistance.

This is an important problem because liberal and liberal-democratic principles may sometimes justify disobedience or resistance but not provide the means to protect those who then decide to disobey or resist. This is a dilemma which Jefferson acknowledges in the selection reprinted here. It is a continuing problem for liberals, because if rights, liberty, consent, contracts, and individualism are to be meaningful one must accept the possibility that people will occasionally come into conflict with government or the law over matters of principle or because of disagreements over the proper means to implement accepted principles.

Indeed, some people have claimed that the violation of specific rules is sometimes necessary to protect fundamental liberal principles. The occasional violence that surrounded the American civil rights movement or the opposition to the war in Viet Nam raised again the question of what is to be done with citizens who in good conscience and in the name of freedom, rights, and individualism resist government policies. Liberals have not answered that question successfully.

Though many liberals reject the notion that obedience to the law must be the primary liberal value, they are still in doubt as to what to do with those who do resist. Nowhere else is the gap between principle and policy as wide as it is here. Liberals are troubled by this gap. When constitutional principles, juries, or the discretion of judges or prosecutors will not fill it, which is most of the time, liberals, and only liberals, are faced with a severe dilemma.

7 THOMAS JEFFERSON

Thomas Jefferson (1743-1826) wrote voluminously on a wide variety of topics. As a politician, diplomat, scientist, elder statesman, farmer, musician, architect, and educator he knew many of the important persons of his era. Jefferson emphasized rights and participation throughout his long career. From his first major work, *A Summary View of the Rights of British America*, 1774, until his last letter, written to Roger O. Weightman, June 24, 1826, he argued that government is a limited trust, designed to protect each person's inalienable rights. In his *Summary View*, in terms reminiscent of Locke, Jefferson reminded George III that government is created to protect rights. When governors abuse power they rebel against the people, forfeiting their trust, giving the people the right to resist these encroachments on their rights. In his last letter, two weeks before his death, Jefferson argued "the mass of mankind has not been born with saddles on their backs, nor a favored few booted and spurred, ready to ride them legitimately, by the grace of God." People were beginning to recognize their rights and Jefferson saw in this great hope for the future.

Jefferson assumed that there is a hopeful alternative for people, that people and society can gradually improve. Improvement requires tolerance, respect for rights, and widespread participation. The people, who are the source of all authority, have the right to change government to suit their wants and needs, but even majorities must respect rights of minorities. Policies to protect these rights included equal representation, education, tolerance, separation of church and state, limited terms in office, frequent amendment of the constitution, and the creation of a system of democratically controlled wards. Ultimately, people possessed the right to rebel if governors or majorities violated their trusts. All of these themes are illustrated in the following selections. They emphasize Jefferson's later letters in which he summed up his lifelong reflections on politics and liberty.

NOTES ON VIRGINIA, 1782, QUERY XVII.*

The error seems not sufficiently eradicated, that the operations of the mind, as well as the acts of the body, are subject to the coercion of the laws. But our rulers can have authority over such natural rights, only as we have submitted to them. The rights of conscience we never submitted, we could not submit. We are answerable for them to our God. The legitimate powers of government extend to such acts only as are injurious to others. But it does me no injury for my neighbor to say there are twenty gods, or no god. It neither picks my pocket nor breaks my leg. If it be said his testimony in a court of justice cannot be relied on, reject it then, and be the stigma on him. Constraint may make him worse by making him a hypocrite, but it will never make him a truer man. It may fix him obstinately in his errors, but will not cure them. Reason and free inquiry are the only effectual agents against error. Give a loose to them, they will support the true religion by bringing every false one to their tribunal, to the test of their investigation. They are the natural enemies of error, and of error only. Had not the Roman government permitted free inquiry, Christianity could never have been introduced. Had not free inquiry been indulged, at the era of the reformation, the corruptions of Christianity could not have been purged away. If it be restrained now, the present corruptions will be protected, and new ones encouraged. Was the government to prescribe to us our medicine and diet, our bodies would be in such keeping as our souls are now. Thus in France the emetic was once forbidden as a medicine, and the potatoe as an article of food. Government is just as infallible, too, when it fixes systems in physics. Galileo was sent to the inquisition for affirming that the earth was a sphere; the government had declared it to be as flat as a trencher, and Galileo was obliged to abjure his error. This error however at length prevailed, the earth became a globe, and Descartes declared it was whirled round its axis by a vortex. The government in which he lived was wise enough to see that this was no question of civil jurisdiction, or we should all have been involved by authority in vortices. In fact the vortices have been exploded, and the Newtonian principles of gravitation is now more firmly established, on the basis of reason, than it would be were the government to step in and to make it an article of necessary faith. Reason and experiment have been indulged, and error has fled before them. It is error alone which needs the support of government. Truth can stand by itself.

---

*P. L. Ford, ed., *The Works of Thomas Jefferson* (New York: G.P. Putnam's Sons, 1904).

Subject opinion to coercion: whom will you make your inquisitors? Fallible men; men governed by bad passions, by private as well as public reasons. And why subject it to coercion? To produce uniformity. But is uniformity of opinion desireable? No more than of face and stature. Introduce the bed of Procrustes then, and as there is danger that the large men may beat the small, make us all of a size, by lopping the former and stretching the latter. Difference of opinion is advantageous in religion. The several sects perform the office of a Censor morum over each other. Is uniformity attainable? Millions of innocent men, women and children, since the introduction of Christianity, have been burnt, tortured, fined, imprisoned: yet we have not advanced one inch towards uniformity. What has been the effect of coercion? To make one half the world fools, and the other half hypocrites. To support roguery and error all over the earth. Let us reflect that it is inhabited by a thousand millions of people. That these profess probably a thousand different systems of religion. That ours is but one of that thousand. That if there be but one right, and ours that one, we should wish to see the 999 wandering sects gathered into the fold of truth. But against such a majority we cannot effect this by force. Reason and persuasion are the only practicable instruments. To make way for these, free inquiry must be indulged; and how can we wish others to indulge it while we refuse it ourselves. But every state, says an inquisitor, has established some religion. "No two, say I, have established the same." Is this a proof of the infallibility of establishments? Our sister states of Pennsylvania and New York, however, have long subsisted without any establishment at all. The experiment was new and doubtful when they made it. It has answered beyond conception. They flourish infinitely. Religion is well supported; of various kinds indeed, but all good enough; all sufficient to preserve peace and order: or if a sect arises whose tenets would subvert morals, good sense has fair play, and reasons and laughs it out of doors, without suffering the state to be troubled with it. They do not hang more malefactors than we do. They are not more disturbed with religious dissentions. On the contrary, their harmony is unparalleled, and can be ascribed to nothing but their unbounded tolerance, because there is no other circumstance in which they differ from every nation on earth. They have made the happy discovery, that the way to silence religious disputes, is to take no notice of them. Let us too give this experiment fair play, and get rid, while we may, of those tyrannical laws. It is true we are as yet secured against them by the spirit of the times. I doubt whether the people of this country would suffer an execution for heresy, or a three years imprisonment for not comprehending the mysteries of the trinity. But is the spirit of the people an infallible, a permanent reliance? Is it government? Is this the kind of protection we receive in return for the rights we give up? Besides, the spirit of the times may alter, will alter. Our rulers will become corrupt, our people careless. A single zealot may commence persecuter, and better men be his victims. It can never be too often repeated, that the time for fixing every essential right on a legal basis is while our rulers are honest, and ourselves united. . . .

TO JAMES MADISON: JAN. 30, 1787*[1]

I am impatient to learn your sentiments on the late troubles in the Eastern states. So far as I have yet seen, they do not appear to threaten serious consequences. Those states have suffered by the stoppage of the channels of their commerce, which have not yet found other issues. This must render money scarce, and make the people uneasy. This uneasiness has produced acts absolutely unjustifiable; but I hope they will provoke no severities from their governments. A consciousness of those in power that their administration of the public affairs has been honest, may perhaps produce too great a degree of indignation: and those characters wherein fear predominates over hope may apprehend too much from these instances of irregularity. They may conclude too hastily that nature has formed man insusceptible of any other government but that of force, a conclusion not founded in truth, nor experience. Societies exist under three forms sufficiently distinguishable. 1. Without government, as among our Indians. 2. Under governments wherein the will of every one has a just influence, as is the case in England in a slight degree, and in our states, in a great one. 3. Under governments of force: as is the case in all other monarchies and in most of the other republics. To have an idea of the curse of existence under these last, they must be seen. It is a government of wolves over sheep. It is a problem, not clear in my mind, that the first condition is not the best. But I believe it to be inconsistent with any great degree of population. The second state has a great deal of good in it. The mass of mankind under that enjoys a precious degree of liberty & happiness. It has its evils too: the principal of which is the turbulence to which it is subject. But weigh this against the oppressions of monarchy, and it becomes nothing. . . . Even this evil is productive of good. It prevents the degeneracy of government, and nourishes a general attention to the public affairs. I hold it that a little rebellion now and then is a good thing, & as necessary in the political world as storms in the physical. Unsuccessful rebellions indeed generally establish the encroachments on the rights of the people which have produced them. An observation of this truth should render honest republican governors so mild in their punishment of rebellions, as not to discourage them too much. It is a medicine necessary for the sound health of government. . . .

---

*P. L. Ford, ed., *The Works of Thomas Jefferson* (New York: G.P. Putnam's Sons, 1904).

To William Stephens Smith: Nov. 13, 1787†

. . . [C]an history produce an instance of rebellion so honourably conducted? I say nothing of its motives. They were founded in ignorance, not wickedness. God forbid we should ever be 20 years without such a rebellion. The people cannot be all, & always, well informed. The part which is wrong will be discontented in proportion to the importance of the facts they misconceive. If they remain quiet under such misconceptions it is a lethargy, the forerunner of death to the public liberty. . . . What country can preserve its liberties if their rulers are not warned from time to time that their people preserve the spirit of resistance? Let them take arms. The remedy is to set them right as to facts, pardon & pacify them. . . .

To James Madison: Dec. 20, 1787*

. . . The late rebellion in Massachusetts has given more alarm than I think it should have done. Calculate that one rebellion in 13 states in the course of 11 years, is but one for each state in a century & a half. No country should be so long without one. Nor will any degree of power in the hands of government prevent insurrections. France, with all its despotism, and two or three hundred thousand men always in arms has had three insurrections in the three years I have been here in every one of which greater numbers were engaged than in Massachusetts & a great deal more blood was spilt. In Turkey, which Montesquieu supposes more despotic, insurrections are the events of every day. In England, where the hand of power is lighter than here, but heavier than with us they happen every half dozen years. Compare again the ferocious depredations of their insurgents with the order, the moderation & the almost self-extinguishment of ours.

To P. S. DuPont De Nemours: April 24, 1816*†

. . . We of the United States, you know, are constitutionally and conscientiously democrats. We consider society as one of the natural wants with which man has

---

†P. L. Ford, ed., *The Works of Thomas Jefferson* (New York: G.P. Putnam's Sons, 1904).
*P. L. Ford, ed., *The Works of Thomas Jefferson* (New York: G.P. Putnam's Sons, 1904).
*†P.L. Ford, ed., *The Works of Thomas Jefferson* (New York: G.P. Putnam's Sons, 1904).

been created; that he has been endowed with faculties and qualities to effect its satisfaction by concurrence of others having the same want; that when, by the exercise of these faculties, he has procured a state of society, it is one of his acquisitions which he has a right to regulate and control, jointly indeed with all those who have concurred in the procurement, whom he cannot exclude from its use or direction more than they him. We think experience has proved it safer, for the mass of individuals composing the society, to reserve to themselves personally the exercise of all rightful powers to which they are competent, and to delegate those to which they are not competent to deputies named, and removable for unfaithful conduct, by themselves immediately. Hence, with us, the people (by which is meant the mass of individuals composing the society) being competent to judge of the facts occurring in ordinary life, they have retained the functions of judges of facts, under the name of jurors; but being unqualified for the management of affairs requiring intelligence above the common level, yet competent judges of human character, they chose, for their management, representatives, some by themselves immediately, others by electors chosen by themselves. Thus our President is chosen by ourselves, directly in *practice*, for we vote for A as elector only on the condition he will vote for B, our representatives by ourselves immediately, our Senate and judges of law through electors chosen by ourselves. And we believe that this proximate choice and power of removal is the best security which experience has sanctioned for ensuring an honest conduct in the functionaries of society. . . .

But when we come to the moral principles on which the government is to be administered, we come to what is proper for all conditions of society. . . . I believe with you that morality, compassion, generosity, are innate elements of the human constitution; that there exists a right independent of force; that a right to property is founded in our natural wants, in the means with which we are endowed to satisfy these wants, and the right to what we acquire by those means without violating the similar rights of other sensible beings; that no one has a right to obstruct another, exercising his faculties innocently for the relief of sensibilities made a part of his nature; that justice is the fundamental law of society; that the majority, oppressing an individual, is guilty of a crime, abuses its strength, and by acting on the law of the strongest breaks up the foundations of society; that action by the citizens in person, in affairs within their reach and competence, and in all others by representatives, chosen immediately, and removable by themselves, constitutes the essence of a republic; that all governments are more or less republican in proportion as this principle enters more or less into their composition; and that a government by representation is capable of extension over a greater surface of country than one of any other form. These, my friend, are the essentials in which you and I agree; however, in our zeal for their maintenance, we may be perplexed and divaricate, as to the structure of society most likely to secure them.

. . . Enlighten the people generally, and tyranny and oppressions of body and mind will vanish like evil spirits at the dawn of day. Although I do not, with some enthusiasts, believe that the human condition will ever advance to such a state of perfection as that there shall no longer be pain or vice in the world, yet I believe it susceptible of much improvement, and most of all, in matters of government and religion: and that the diffusion of knowledge among the people is to be the instrument by which it is to be effected. . . .

INAUGURATION ADDRESS: MARCH 4, 1801*

During the contest of opinion through which we have passed, the animation of discussion and of exertions has sometimes worn an aspect which might impose on strangers unused to think freely and to speak and to write what they think; but this being now decided by the voice of the nation, announced according to the rules of the constitution, all will, of course, arrange themselves under the will of the law, and unite in common efforts for the common good. All, too, will bear in mind this sacred principle, that though the will of the majority is in all cases to prevail, that will, to be rightful, must be reasonable; that the minority possess their equal rights, which equal laws must protect, and to violate which would be oppression. Let us, then, fellow citizens unite with one heart and one mind. Let us restore to social intercourse that harmony and affection without which liberty and even life itself are but dreary things. And let us reflect that having banished from our land that religious intolerance under which mankind so long bled and suffered, we have yet gained little if we countenance a political intolerance as despotic, as wicked, and capable of as bitter and bloody persecutions. During the throes and convulsions of the ancient world, during the agonizing spasms of infuriated man, seeking through blood and slaughter his long-lost liberty, it was not wonderful that the agitation of the billows should reach even this distant and peaceful shore; that this should be more felt and feared by some and less by others; that this should divide opinions as to measures of safety. But every difference of opinion is not a difference of principle. We have called by different names brethren of the same principle. We are all republicans—we are all federalists. If there be any among us who would wish to dissolve this Union or to change its republican form, let them stand undisturbed as monuments of the safety with which error of opinion may be tolerated where reason is left free to combat it. I know, indeed, that some honest men fear that a republican government cannot be strong; that this government is not strong enough. But would the honest patriot, in the full tide of

---

*H. A. Washington, ed., *The Writings of Thomas Jefferson* (New York: Riker, Thorne and Co., 1854).

successful experiment, abandon a government which has so far kept us free and firm, on the theoretic and visionary fear that this government, the world's best hope, may by possibility want energy to preserve itself? I trust not. I believe this, on the contrary, the strongest government on earth. I believe it is the only one where every man, at the call of the laws, would fly to the standard of the law, and would meet invasions of the public order as his own personal concern. Sometimes it is said that man cannot be trusted with the government of himself. Can he, then, be trusted with the government of others? Or have we found angels in the forms of kings to govern him? Let history answer this question.

Let us, then, with courage and confidence pursue our own federal and republican principles, our attachment to our union and representative government. Kindly separated by nature and a wide ocean from the exterminating havoc of one quarter of the globe; too high-minded to endure the degradations of the others; possessing a chosen country, with room enough for our descendants to the hundredth and thousandth generation; entertaining a due sense of our equal right to the use of our own faculties, to the acquisitions of our industry, to honor and confidence from our fellow citizens, resulting not from birth but from our actions and their sense of them; enlightened by a benign religion, professed, indeed, and practiced in various forms, yet all of them including honesty, truth, temperance, gratitude, and the love of man; acknowledging and adoring an overruling Providence, which by all its dispensations proves that it delights in the happiness of man here and his greater happiness hereafter; with all these blessings, what more is necessary to make us a happy and prosperous people? Still one thing more, fellow citizens—a wise and frugal government, which shall restrain men from injuring one another, which shall leave them otherwise free to regulate their own pursuits of industry and improvement, and shall not take from the mouth of labor the bread it has earned. This is the sum of good government, and this is necessary to close the circle of our felicities.

About to enter, fellow citizens, on the exercise of duties which comprehend everything dear and valuable to you, it is proper that you should understand what I deem the essential principles of our government, and consequently those which ought to shape its administration. I will compress them within the narrowest compass they will bear, stating the general principle, but not all its limitations. Equal and exact justice to all men, of whatever state or persuasion, religious or political; peace, commerce, and honest friendship, with all nations—entangling alliances with none; the support of the state governments in all their rights, as the most competent administrations for our domestic concerns and the surest bulwarks against anti-republican tendencies; the preservation of the general government in its whole constitutional vigor, as the sheet anchor of our peace at home and safety abroad; a jealous care of the right of election by the people—a mild and safe corrective of abuses which are lopped by the sword of the revolution where peaceable remedies are unprovided; absolute acquiescence in the decisions of the majority—the vital principle of republics, from which there is no appeal but to force, the vital principle and immediate parent of despotism; a well-disciplined militia—our best reliance in peace and for the first moments of war, till regulars may relieve them; the supremacy of the civil over the military authority; economy in the public expense, that labor may be lightly burdened; the honest payment of our debts and sacred preservation of the public faith; encouragement of agriculture, and of commerce as its handmaid; the diffusion of information and the arraignment of all abuses at the bar of public reason; freedom of religion; freedom of the press; freedom of person under the protection of the *habeas corpus*; and trial by juries impartially selected—these principles form the bright constellation which has gone before us, and guided our steps through an age of revolution and reformation. The wisdom of our sages and the blood of our heroes have been devoted to their attainment. They should be the creed of our political faith—the text of civil instruction—the touchstone by which to try the services of those we trust; and should we wander from them in moments of error or alarm, let us hasten to retrace our steps and to regain the road which alone leads to peace, liberty, and safety.

To Samuel Kercheval: July 12, 1816*[2]

. . . At the birth of our republic, I committed that opinion to the world, in the draught of a constitution annexed to the *Notes on Virginia*, in which a provision was inserted for a representation permanently equal. The infancy of the subject at that moment, and our inexperience of self-government, occasioned gross departures in that draught from genuine republican canons. In truth, the abuses of monarchy had so much filled all the space of political contemplation, that we imagined everything republican which was not monarchy. We had not yet penetrated to the mother principle, that "governments are republican only in proportion as they embody the will of their people, and execute it." Hence, our first constitutions had really no leading principles in them. But experience and reflection have but more and more confirmed me in the particular importance of the equal representation then proposed. . . .

But it will be said, it is easier to find faults than to amend them. I do not think their amendment so difficult as is pretended. Only lay down true principles, and adhere to them inflexibly. Do not be frightened into their surrender by the alarms of the timid, or the croakings of wealth against the ascendency of the people. If

---

*P. L. Ford, ed., *The Works of Thomas Jefferson* (New York: G. P. Putnam's Sons, 1904).

experience be called for, appeal to that of our fifteen or twenty governments for forty years, and show me where the people have done half the mischief in these forty years, that a single despot would have done in a single year; or show half the riots and rebellions, the crimes and the punishments, which [as] have taken place in any single nation, under kingly government, during the same period. The true foundation of republican government is the equal right of every citizen, in his person and property, and in their management. Try by this, as a tally, every provision of our constitution, and see if it hangs directly on the will of the people. Reduce your legislature to a convenient number for full, but orderly discussion. Let every man who fights or pays, exercise his just and equal right in their election. Submit them to approbation or rejection at short intervals. Let the executive be chosen in the same way, and for the same term, by those whose agent he is to be; and leave no screen of a council behind which to skulk from responsibility. It has been thought that the people are not competent electors of judges *learned in the law*. But I do not know that this is true, and, if doubtful, we should follow principle. In this, as in many other elections, they would be guided by reputation, which would not err oftener, perhaps, than the present mode of appointment. . . .

The organization of our county administrations may be thought more difficult. But follow principle, and the knot unties itself. Divide the counties into wards of such size as that every citizen can attend, when called on, and act in person. Ascribe to them the government of their wards in all things relating to themselves exclusively. A justice, chosen by themselves, in each, a constable, a military company, a patrol, a school, the care of their own poor, their own portion of the public roads, the choice of one or more jurors to serve in some court, and the delivery, within their own wards, of their own votes for all elective officers of higher sphere, will relieve the county administration of nearly all its business, will have it better done, and by making every citizen an acting member of the government, and in the offices nearest and most interesting to him, will attach him by his strongest feelings to the independence of his country, and its republican constitution. The justices thus chosen by every ward, would constitute the county court, would do its judiciary business, direct roads and bridges, levy county and poor rates, and administer all the matters of common interest to the whole country. These wards called townships in New England, are the vital principle of their governments, and have proved themselves the wisest invention ever devised by the wit of man for the perfect exercise of self-government, and for its preservation. We should thus marshal our government into, 1, the general federal republic, for all concerns foreign and federal; 2, that of the State, for what relates to our own citizens exclusively; 3, the county republics, for the duties and concerns of the county; and 4, the ward republics, for the small, and yet numerous and interesting concerns of the neighborhood; and in government, as well as in every other business of life, it is by division and subdivision of duties alone, that all matters, great and small, can be managed to perfection. And the whole is cemented by giving to every citizen, personally, a part in the administration of the public affairs.

The sum of these amendments is, 1. General Suffrage. 2. Equal representation in the legislature. 3. An executive chosen by the people. 4. Judges elective or amovable. 5. Justices, jurors, and sheriffs elective. 6. Ward divisions. And 7. Periodical amendments of the constitution.

I have thrown out these as loose heads of amendment, for consideration and correction; and their object is to secure self-government by the republicanism of our constitution, as well as by the spirit of the people; and to nourish and perpetuate that spirit. I am not among those who fear the people. They, and not the rich, are our dependence for continued freedom. And to preserve their independence, we must not let our rulers load us with perpetual debt. We must make our election between *economy and liberty*, or *profusion and servitude*. If we run into such debts, as that we must be taxed in our meat and in our drink, in our necessaries and our comforts, in our labors and our amusements, for our callings and our creeds, as the people of England are, our people, like them, must come to labor sixteen hours in the twenty-four, give the earnings of fifteen of these to the government for their debts and daily expenses; and the sixteenth being insufficient to afford us bread, we must live, as they now do, on oatmeal and potatoes; have no time to think, no means of calling the mismanagers to account; but be glad to obtain subsistence by hiring ourselves to rivet their chains on the necks of our fellow-sufferers. Our landholders, too, like theirs, retaining indeed the title and stewardship of estates called theirs, but held really in trust for the treasury, must wander, like theirs, in foreign countries, and be contented with penury, obscurity, exile, and the glory of the nation. This example reads to us the salutary lesson, that private fortunes are destroyed by public as well as by private extravagance. And this is the tendency of all human governments. A departure from principle in one instance becomes a precedent for a second; that second for a third; and so on, till the bulk of the society is reduced to be mere automatons of misery, and to have no sensibilities left but for sinning and suffering. Then begins, indeed, the *bellum omnium in omnia*, which some philosophers observing to be so general in this world, have mistaken it for the natural, instead of the abusive state of man. And the fore horse of this frightful team is public debt. Taxation follows that, and in its train wretchedness and oppression.

Some men look at constitutions with sanctimonious reverence, and deem them like the ark of the covenant, too sacred to be touched. They ascribe to the men of the preceding age a wisdom more than human, and suppose what they did to be beyond amendment. I knew that age well; I belonged to it, and labored with it. It deserved well of its country. It was very like the present, but without the experience of the present; and forty years of experience in government is worth a century of book-reading; and this they would say themselves, were they to rise from the dead. I am certainly not an advocate for frequent and untried changes in laws and constitutions. I think moderate imperfections had better be borne with; because, when once known, we accommodate ourselves to them, and find practical means of correcting their ill effects. But I know also, that laws and institutions must go hand in hand with the progress of the human mind. As that becomes more developed, more enlightened, as new discoveries are made, new truths disclosed, and manners and opinions change with the change of circumstances, institutions must advance also, and keep pace with the times. We might as well require a man to wear still the coat which fitted him when a boy, as civilized society to remain ever under the regimen of their barbarous ancestors. It is this preposterous idea which has lately deluged Europe in blood. Their monarchs, instead of wisely yielding to the gradual change of circumstances, of favoring progressive accommodation to progressive improvement, have clung to old abuses, entrenched themselves behind steady habits, and obliged their subjects to seek through blood and violence rash and ruinous innovations, which, had they been referred to the peaceful deliberations and collected wisdom of the nation, would have been put into acceptable and salutary forms. Let us follow no such examples, nor weakly believe that one generation is not as capable as another of taking care of itself, and of ordering its own affairs. Let us, as our sister States have done, avail ourselves of our reason and experience, to correct the crude essays of our first and unexperienced, although wise, virtuous, and well-meaning councils. And lastly, let us provide in our constitution for its revision at stated periods. . . . Here, then, would be one of the advantages of the ward divisions I have proposed. The mayor of every ward, on a question like the present, would call his ward together, take the simple yea or nay of its members, convey these to the county court, who would hand on those of all its wards to the proper general authority; and the voice of the whole people would be thus fairly, fully, and peaceably expressed, discussed, and decided by the common reason of the society. If this avenue be shut to the call of sufferance, it will make itself heard through that of force, and we shall go on, as other nations are doing, in the endless circle of oppression, rebellion, reformation; and oppression, rebellion, reformation, again; and so on forever.

To William Johnson: June 12, 1823*

. . . The doctrines of Europe were, that men in numerous associations cannot be restrained within the limits of order and justice, but by forces physical and moral,

---

*P. L. Ford, ed., *The Works of Thomas Jefferson* (New York: G.P. Putnam's Sons, 1904).

wielded over them by authorities independent of their will. Hence their organization of kings, hereditary nobles, and priests. Still further to constrain the brute force of the people, they deem it necessary to keep them dcwn by hard labor, poverty and ignorance, and to take from them, as from bees, so much of their earnings, as that unremitting labor shall be necessary to obtain a sufficient surplus barely to sustain a scanty and miserable life. And these earnings they apply to maintain their privileged orders in splendor and idleness, to fascinate the eyes of the people, and excite in them an humble adoration and submission, as to an order of superior beings. . . . We believed . . . that man was a rational animal, endowed by nature with rights, and with an innate sense of justice; and that he could be restrained from wrong and protected in right, by moderate powers, confided to persons of his own choice, and held to their duties by dependence on his own will. We believed that the complicated organization of kings, nobles, and priests, was not the wisest nor best to effect the happiness of associated man; that wisdom and virtue were not hereditary; that the trappings of such a machinery, consumed by their expense, those earnings of industry, they were meant to protect, and, by the inequalities they produced, exposed liberty to sufferance. We believed that men, enjoying in ease and security the full fruits of their own industry, enlisted by all their interests on the side of law and order, habituated to think for themselves, and to follow their reason as their guide, would be more easily and safely governed, than with minds nourished in error, and vitiated and debased, as in Europe, by ignorance, indigence and oppression. . . .

8 THOMAS PAINE

Thomas Paine (1737-1809) was an agitator, propagandist, and revolutionary. Not content with an important role in one revolution (America), he participated actively in a second (France) and attempted to foment a third (in his native England). Paine was a genuine revolutionary, unafraid of drastic social change and quite confident in his radicalism. He was not schooled in political philosophy, but his pamphlets and papers were often quite persuasive and always direct and clear. Paine's targets were hereditary monarchs, aristocrats, and established churches, and he gave them no rest. But this intelligent, energetic, and creative man turned his argumentative and rhetorical skills against even former friends (such as George Washington) whom he believed no longer cared for the great goal of the liberal revolutions: the creation of free republics composed of enlightened, energetic citizens.

We tend to forget that such republics were radical institutions in Paine's day and that revolutionaries such as Paine were set on overturning centuries of tradition and some of the most hallowed of all society's conventions. Paine's goal was to replace convention with reason. To do so, however, he had first to subvert established conventions and institutions and then to offer alternatives which could be defended. His defense of republican government linked natural rights and "common sense." This confident appeal to a common (rather than elite) sense of what was right is what most distinguishes Paine's writings. Later liberals, though they often failed to share Paine's optimism, nevertheless still assumed that political problems could be resolved by decent citizens employing separately and together the "common sense" which, as human beings, they all possessed.

RIGHTS OF MAN*

Reason and ignorance, the opposites of each other, influence the great bulk of mankind. If either of these can be rendered sufficiently extensive in a country, the machinery of government goes easily on. Reason shows itself, and ignorance submits to whatever is dictated to it.

The two modes of government which prevail in the world, are, first, government by election and representation; second, government by hereditary succession. The former is generally known by the name of republic; the latter by that of monarchy and aristocracy.

Those two distinct and opposite forms, erect themselves on the two distinct and opposite bases of reason and ignorance. As the exercise of government requires talents and abilities, and as talents and abilities cannot have hereditary descent, it is evident that hereditary succession requires a belief from man, to which his reason cannot subscribe, and which can only be established upon his ignorance; and the more ignorant any country is, the better it is fitted for this species of government.

On the contrary, government in a well constituted republic, requires no belief from man beyond what his reason authorizes. He sees the *rationale* of the whole system, its origin, and its operation; and as it is best supported when best understood, the human faculties act with boldness, and acquire, under this form of government, a gigantic manliness.

As, therefore, each of those forms acts on a different basis, the one moving freely by the aid of reason, the other by ignorance; we have next to consider, what it is that gives motion to that species of government which is called mixed govern-

---

The Political Writings of Thomas Paine, Vol. 2 (Boston: J. P. Mendum, 1859), pp.137-43, 333-44.

ment, or, as it is sometimes ludicrously styled, a government of *this, that, and t'other*.

The moving power in this species of government is, of necessity, corruption. However imperfect election and representation may be in mixed governments, they still give exertion to a greater portion of reason than is convenient to the hereditary part; and therefore it becomes necessary to buy the reason up. A mixed government is an imperfect every-thing, cementing and soldering the discordant parts together, by corruption, to act as a whole. . . .

In mixed governments, there is no responsibility; the parts cover each other till responsibility is lost; and the corruption which moves the machine, contrives at the same time its own escape. When it is laid down as a maxim, that *a king can do no wrong*, it places him in a state of similar security with that of idiots and persons insane, and responsibility is out of the question, with respect to himself. It then descends upon the minister, who shelters himself under a majority in parliament, which, by places, pensions, and corruption, he can always command; and that majority justifies itself by the same authority with which it protects the minister. In this rotary motion, responsibility is thrown off from the parts, and from the whole.

When there is a part in a government which can do no wrong, it implies that it does nothing; and is only the machine of another power, by whose advice and direction it acts. What is supposed to be the king, in mixed governments, is the cabinet; and as the cabinet is always a part of the parliament, and the members justifying in one character what they act in another, a mixed government becomes a continual enigma; entailing upon a country, by the quantity of corruption necessary to solder the parts, the expense of supporting all the forms of government at once, and finally resolving itself into a government by committee; in which the advisers, the actors, the approvers, the justifiers, the persons responsible, and the persons not responsible, are the same person.

By this pantomimical contrivance, and change of scene and character, the parts help each other out in matters, which, neither of them singly, would presume to act. When money is to be obtained, the mass of variety apparently dissolves, and a profusion of parliamentary praises passes between the parts. Each admires, with astonishment, the wisdom, the liberality and disinterestedness of the other; and all of them breathe a pitying sigh at the burdens of the nation.

But in a well-conditioned republic, nothing of this soldering, praising and pitying, can take place; the representation being equal throughout the country, and complete in itself, however it may be arranged into legislative and executive, they have all one and the same natural source. The parts are not foreigners to each other, like democracy, aristocracy, and monarchy. As there are no discordant distinctions, there is nothing to corrupt by compromise, nor confound by contrivance. Public measures appeal of themselves to the understanding of the nation, and resting on their own merits, disown any flattering application to vanity. The continual whine of lamenting the burden of taxes, however successfully it may be practised in mixed governments, is inconsistent with the sense and spirit of a republic. If taxes are necessary, they are of course advantageous; but if they require an apology, the apology itself implies an impeachment. Why then is man thus imposed upon, or why does he impose upon himself?

When men are spoken of as kings and subjects, or when government is mentioned under distinct or combined heads of monarchy, aristocracy, and democracy, what is it that *reasoning* man is to understand by the terms? If there really existed in the world two more distinct and separate *elements* of human power, we should then see the several origins to which those terms would descriptively apply; but as there is but one species of man, there can be but one element of human power, and that element is man himself. Monarchy, aristocracy, and democracy are but creatures of imagination; and a thousand such may be contrived as well as three. . . .

When we survey the wretched condition of man, under the monarchical and hereditary systems of government, dragged from his home by one power, or driven by another, and impoverished by taxes more than by enemies, it becomes evident that those systems are bad, and that a general revolution in the principle and construction of governments is necessary.

What is government more than the management of the affairs of a nation? It is not, and from its nature cannot be, the property of any particular man or family, but of the whole community at whose expense it is supported; and though by force or contrivance it has been usurped into an inheritance, the usurpation cannot alter the right of things. Sovereignty, as a matter of right, appertains to the nation only, and not to any individual; and a nation has at all times an inherent, indefeasible right to abolish any form of government it finds inconvenient, and establish such as accords with its interest, disposition, and happiness. The romantic and barbarous distinctions of men into kings and subjects, though it may suit the condition of courtiers cannot that of citizens; and is exploded by the principle upon which governments are now founded. Every citizen is a member of the sovereignty, and as such can acknowledge no personal subjection; and his obedience can be only to the laws.

When men think of what government is, they must necessarily suppose it to possess a knowledge of all the objects and matters upon which its authority is to be exercised. In this view of government, the republican system, as established by America and France, operates to embrace the whole of a nation: and the knowledge necessary to the interest of all the parts, is to be found in the centre, which the parts by representation form: but the old governments are on a construction that excludes knowledge as well as happiness; government by monks, who know nothing of the world beyond the walls of a convent, is as consistent as government by kings.

What were formerly called revolutions, were little more than a change of persons, or an alteration of local circumstances. They rose and fell like things of course, and had nothing in their existence or their fate that could influence beyond the spot that produced them. But what we now see in the world, from the revolutions of America and France, are a renovation of the natural order of things, a system of principles as universal as truth and the existence of man, and combining moral with political happiness and national prosperity.

"I. Men are born, and always continue, free and equal, in respect to their rights. Civil distinctions, therefore, can be founded only on public utility.

"II. The end of all political associations is the preservation of the natural and imprescriptible rights of man, and these rights are liberty, property, security, and resistance of oppression.

"III. The nation is essentially the source of all sovereignty, nor can any individual, or any body of men, be entitled to any authority which is not expressly derived from it."

In these principles there is nothing to throw a nation into confusion, by inflaming ambition. They are calculated to call forth wisdom and abilities, and to exercise them for the public good, and not for the emolument or aggrandizement of particular descriptions of men or families. Monarchical sovereignty, the enemy of mankind and the source of misery, is abolished; and sovereignty itself is restored to its natural and original place, the nation. —Were this the case throughout Europe, the cause of wars would be taken away. . . .

As war is the system of government on the old construction, the animosity which nations reciprocally entertain is nothing more than what the policy of their governments excites to keep up the spirit of the system. Each government accuses the other of perfidy, intrigue, and ambition as a means of heating the imagination of their respective nations and increasing them to hostilities. Man is not the enemy of man but through the medium of a false system of government. Instead, therefore, of exclaiming against the ambition of kings, the exclamation should be directed against the principle of such governments; and instead of seeking to reform the individual, the wisdom of a nation should apply itself to reform the system.

Whether the forms and maxims of governments which are still in practice were adapted to the condition of the world at the period they were established is not in this case the question. The older they are, the less correspondence can they have with the present state of things. Time and change of circumstances and opinions have the same progressive effect in rendering modes of government obsolete as they have upon customs and manners. Agriculture, commerce, manufactures, and the tranquil arts, by which the prosperity of nations is best promoted, require a different system of government and a different species of knowledge to direct its operations than what might have been required in the former condition of the world.

As it is not difficult to perceive, from the enlightened state of mankind, that hereditary governments are verging to their decline and that revolutions on the broad basis of national sovereignty and government by representation are making their way in Europe, it would be an act of wisdom to anticipate their approach and produce revolutions by reason and accommodation, rather than commit them to the issue of convulsions.

From what we now see, nothing of reform in the political world ought to be held improbable. It is an age of revolutions, in which everything may be looked for. The intrigue of courts, by which the system of war is kept up, may provoke a confederation of nations to abolish it; and a European congress to patronize the progress of free government and promote the civilization of nations with each other is an event nearer in probability than once were the revolutions and alliance of France and America. . . .

That every nation, *for the time being*, has a right to govern itself as it pleases, must always be admitted, but government by hereditary succession is government for another race of people, and not for itself; and as those on whom it is to operate are not yet in existence, or are minors, so neither is the right in existence to set it up for them, and to assume such a right is treason against the rights of posterity. . . .

Reasoning by exclusion, if *hereditary government* has not a right to exist, and that it has not is proveable, *representative government* is admitted of course.

In contemplating government by election and representation, we amuse not ourselves in inquiring when or how, or by what right it began. Its origin is ever in view. Man is himself the origin and evidence of the right. It appertains to him in right of his existence, and his person is the title-deed.

The true and only true basis of representative government is equality of rights. Every man has a right to one vote, and no more, in the choice of representatives. The rich have no more right to exclude the poor from the right of voting, or of electing and being elected, than the poor have to exclude the rich; and wherever it is attempted, or proposed, on either side, it is a question of force, and not of right. Who is he that would exclude another? That other has a right to exclude him.

That which is now called aristocracy implies an inequality of rights; but who are the persons that have a right to establish this inequality? Will the rich exclude themselves? No! Will the poor exclude themselves? No! By what right then can any be excluded? It would be a question, if any man, or class of men, have a right to exclude themselves; but be this as it may, they cannot have the right to exclude another. The poor will not delegate such a right to the rich, nor the rich to the poor, and to assume it is not only to assume arbitrary power, but to assume a right to commit robbery. Personal rights, of which the right of voting for representatives is one, are a species of property of the most sacred kind; and he that would employ his pecuniary property, or presume upon the influence it gives him, to dispossess or to rob another of his property of rights, uses that pecuniary property as he would use fire-arms, and merits to have it taken from him.

Inequality of rights is created by a combination in one part of the community to exclude another part from its rights. Whenever it may be made an article of a constitution, or a law, that the right of voting, or of electing and being elected, shall appertain exclusively to persons possessing a certain quantity of property, be it little or much, it is a combination of the persons possessing that quantity, to exclude those who do not possess the same quantity. It is investing themselves with powers as a self-created part of society, to the exclusion of the rest.

It is always to be taken for granted, that those who oppose an equality of rights, never mean the exclusion should take place on themselves; and in this view of the case, pardoning the vanity of the thing, aristocracy is a subject of laughter. This self-soothing vanity is encouraged by another idea not less selfish, which is that the opposers conceive they are playing a safe game, in which there is a chance to gain and none to lose; that at any rate the doctrine of equality includes *them*, and that if they cannot get more rights than those whom they oppose and would exclude, they shall not have less. This opinion has already been fatal to thousands, who, not contented with *equal rights*, have sought more till they lost all, and experienced in themselves the degrading *inequality* they endeavored to fix upon others.

In any view of the case it is dangerous and impolitic, sometimes ridiculous, and always unjust, to make property the criterion of the right of voting. If the sum, or value of the property upon which the right is to take place be considerable, it will exclude a majority of the people, and unite them in a common interest against the government, and against those who support it, and as the power is always with the majority, they can overturn such a government and its supporters whenever they please.

If, in order to avoid this danger, a small quantity of property be fixed, as the criterion of the right, it exhibits liberty in disgrace, by putting it in competition with accident and insignificance. When a brood-mare shall fortunately produce a foal or a mule, that by being worth the sum in question, shall convey to its owner the right of voting, or by its death take it from him, in whom does the origin of such a right exist? Is it in the man, or in the mule? When we consider how many ways property may be acquired without merit, and lost without a crime, we ought to spurn the idea of making it a criterion of rights.

But the offensive part of the case is, that this exclusion from the right of voting implies a stigma on the moral character of the persons excluded; and this is what no part of the community has a right to pronounce upon another part. No external circumstance can justify it; wealth is no proof of moral character; nor poverty of the want of it. On the contrary, wealth is often the presumptive evidence of dishonesty; and poverty the negative evidence of innocence. If, therefore, property, whether little or much, be made a criterion, the means by which that property has been acquired, ought to be made a criterion also.

The only ground upon which exclusion from the right of voting is consistent with justice, would be to inflict it as a punishment for a certain time, upon those who should propose to take away that right from others. The right of voting for representatives is the primary right by which other rights are protected. To take away this right is to reduce a man to slavery, for slavery consists in being subject to the will of another, and he that has not a vote in the election of representatives, is in this case. The proposal, therefore, to disfranchise any class of men is as criminal as the proposal to take away property. When we speak of right, we ought always to unite with it the idea of duties: rights become duties by reciprocity. The right which I enjoy it becomes my duty to guarantee to another, and he to me; and those who violate the duty justly incur a forfeiture of the right.

In a political view of the case, the strength and permanent security of government is in proportion to the number of people interested in supporting it. The true policy, therefore, is to interest the whole by an equality of rights, for the danger arises from exclusions. It is possible to exclude men from the right of voting, but it is impossible to exclude them from the right of rebelling against that exclusion; and when all other rights are taken away, the right of rebellion is made perfect.

While men could be persuaded they had no rights, or that rights appertained only to a certain class of men, or that government was a thing existing in right of itself, it was not difficult to govern them authoritatively. The ignorance in which they were held, and the superstition in which they were instructed, furnished the means of doing it; but when the ignorance is gone, and the superstition with it; when they perceive the imposition that has been acted upon them; when they reflect that the cultivator and the manufacturer are the primary means of all the wealth that exists in the world, beyond what nature spontaneously produces; when they begin to feel their consequence by their usefulness and their right as members of society, it is then no longer possible to govern them as before. The fraud once detected cannot be retracted. To attempt it is to provoke derision or invite destruction.

That property will ever be unequal is certain. Industry, superiority of talents, or dexterity of management, extreme frugality, fortunate opportunities, or the opposite, or the mean of those things, will ever produce that effect, without having recourse to the harsh, ill-sounding names of avarice and oppression; and besides this, there are some men who, though they do not despise wealth, will not stoop to the drudgery of the means of acquiring it, nor will be troubled with it beyond their wants or their independence; whilst in others there is an avidity to obtain it by every means not punishable; it makes the sole business of their lives, and they follow it as a religion. All that is required, with respect to property, is to obtain it *honestly*, and not employ it *criminally*; but it is always criminally employed, when it is made the criterion for exclusive rights.

In institutions that are purely pecuniary, such as that of a bank, or a commercial company, the rights of the members composing that company are wholly created by the property they invest therein; and no other rights are represented in the government of that company, than what arise out of that property; neither has that government cognizance of *any thing but property*.

But the case is totally different with respect to the institution of civil government, organized on the system of representation. Such a government has cognizance of *every thing*, and of *every man* as a member of the national society, whether he has property or not; and, therefore, the principle requires that every man, and *every kind of right*, be represented, of which the right to acquire and to hold property is but one, and that not of the most essential kind. The protection of a man's person is more sacred than the protection of property; and, besides this, the faculty of performing any kind of work or services by which he acquires a livelihood, or maintaining his family, is of the nature of property. It is property to him; he has acquired it; and it is as much the object of his protection, as exterior property, possessed without that faculty, can be the object of protection to another person.

I have always believed that the best security for property, be it much or little, is to remove from every part of the community, as far as can possibly be done, every cause of complaint, and every motive to violence; and this can only be done by an equality of rights. When rights are secure, property is secure in consequence. But when property is made a pretense for unequal or exclusive rights, it weakens the right to hold the property, and provokes indignation and tumult; for it is unnatural to believe that property can be secure under the guarantee of a society injured in its rights by the influence of that property. . . .

It is at all times necessary, and more particularly so during the progress of a revolution, and until right ideas confirm themselves by habit, that we frequently refresh our patriotism by reference to first principles. It is by tracing things to their origin that we learn to understand them: and it is by keeping that line and that origin always in view that we never forget them.

An inquiry into the origin of rights will demonstrate to us that *rights* are not *gifts* from one man to another, nor from one class of men to another; for who is he who could be the first giver, or by what principle, or on what authority, could he possess the right of giving? A declaration of rights is not a creation of them, nor a donation of them. It is a manifest of the principle by which they exist, followed by a detail of what the rights are; for every civil right has a natural right for its foundation, and it includes the principle of a reciprocal guarantee of those rights from man to man. As, therefore, it is impossible to discover any origin of rights otherwise than in the origin of man, it consequently follows, that rights appertain to man in right of his existence only, and must therefore be equal to every man. The principle of an *equality of rights* is clear and simple. Every man can understand it, and it is by understanding his rights that he learns his duties; for where the rights of men are equal, every man must finally see the necessity of protecting the rights of others as the most effectual security for his own. But if in the formation of a constitution we depart from the principle of equal rights, or attempt any modification of it, we plunge into a labyrinth of difficulties from which there is no way out but by retreating. Where are we to stop? Or by what principle are we to find out the point to stop at, that shall discriminate between men of the same country, part of whom shall be free, and the rest not? If property is to be made the criterion, it is a total departure from every moral principle of liberty, because it is attaching rights to mere matter, and making man the agent of that matter. It is, moreover, holding up property as an apple of discord, and not only exciting but justifying war against it; for I maintain the principle, that when property is used as an instrument to take away the rights of those who may happen not to possess property, it is used to an unlawful purpose, as fire-arms would be in a similar case.

In a state of nature all men are equal in rights, but they are not equal in power; the weak cannot protect themselves against the strong. This being the case, the institution of civil society is for the purpose of making an equalization of powers that shall be parallel to, and a guarantee of, the equality of rights. The laws of a country, when properly constructed, apply to this purpose. Every man takes the arm of the law for his protection as more effectual than his own; and therefore every man has an equal right in the formation of the government, and of the laws by which he is to be governed and judged. In extensive countries and societies, such as America and France, this right in the individual can only be exercised by delegation, that is, by election and representation; and hence it is that the institution of representative government arises.

Hitherto, I have confined myself to matters of principle only. First, that hereditary government has not a right to exist; that it cannot be established on any principle of right; and that it is a violation of all principle. Secondly, that government by election and representation has its origin in the natural and eternal rights of man; for whether a man be his own lawgiver, as he would be in a state of nature; or whether he exercises his portion of legislative sovereignty in his own person, as might be the case in small democracies where all could assemble for the formation of the laws by which they were to be governed; or whether he exercises it in the choice of persons to represent him in a national assembly of representatives, the origin of the right is the same in all cases. The first, as is before observed, is defective in power; the second, is practicable only in democracies of small extent; the third, is the greatest scale upon which human government can be instituted.

Next to matters of *principle*, are matters of *opinion*, and it is necessary to distinguish between the two. Whether the rights of men shall be equal is not a matter of opinion but of right, and consequently of principle; for men do not hold their rights as grants from each other, but each one in right of himself. Society is the guardian but not the giver. And, as in extensive societies, such as America and France, the right of the individual in matters of government, cannot be exercised but by election and representation, it consequently follows, that the only system of government, consistent with principle, where simple democracy is impracticable, is the representative system. But as to the organical part, or the manner in which the several parts of government shall be arranged and composed, it is altogether *matter of opinion*. It is necessary that all the parts be conformable with the *principle of equal rights*; and so long as this principle be religiously adhered to, no very material error can take place, neither can any error continue long in that part that falls within the province of opinion.

In all matters of opinion, the social compact, or the principle by which society is held together, requires that the majority of opinions becomes the rule for the whole, and that the minority yields practical obedience thereto. This is perfectly conformable to the principle of equal rights; for, in the first place, every man has a *right to give an opinion*, but no man has a right that his own should govern the rest. In the second place, it is not supposed to be known beforehand on which side of any question, whether for or against, any man's opinion will fall. He may happen to be in a majority upon some questions, and in a minority upon others; and by the same rule that he expects obedience in the one case, he must yield it in the other. All the disorders that have arisen in France, during the progress of the revolution, have had their origin, not in the *principle of equal rights*, but in the violation of that principle. The principle of equal rights has been repeatedly violated, and that not by the majority, but by the minority, and *that minority has been composed of men possessing property, as well as of men without property; property, therefore, even upon the experience already had, is no more a criterion of character than it is of rights*. It will sometimes happen that the minority are right, and the majority are wrong, but as soon as experience proves this to be the case, the minority will increase to a majority, and the error will reform itself by the tranquil operation of freedom of opinion and equality of rights. Nothing, therefore, can justify an insurrection, neither can it ever be necessary, where rights are equal and opinions free. . . .

I shall conclude this discourse with offering some observations on the means of *preserving liberty*; for it is not only necessary that we establish it, but that we preserve it.

It is, in the first place, necessary that we distinguish between the means made use of to overthrow despotism, in order to prepare the way for the establishment of liberty, and the means to be used after despotism is overthrown.

The means made use of in the first case are justified by necessity. Those means are, in general, insurrections; for whilst the established government of despotism continues in any country, it is scarcely possible that any other means can be used. It is also certain that in the commencement of a revolution, the revolutionary party permit to themselves a *discretionary exercise of power* regulated more by circumstances than by principle, which, were the practice to continue, liberty would never be established, or if established, would soon be overthrown. It is never to be expected in a revolution, that every man is to change his opinion at the same moment. There never yet was any truth or any principle so irresistibly obvious, that all men believed it at once. Time and reason must co-operate with each other to the final establishment of any principle; and, therefore, those who may happen to be first convinced, have not a right to persecute others, on whom conviction operates more slowly. The moral principle of revolutions is to instruct, not to destroy.

Had a constitution been established two years ago (as ought to have been done), the violences that have since desolated France and injured the character of the revolution, would, in my opinion, have been prevented. The nation would then have had a bond of union, and every individual would have known the line of conduct he was to follow. But, instead of this, a revolutionary government, a thing without either principle or authority, was substituted in its place; virtue and crime depended upon accident; and that which was patriotism one day, became treason the next. All these things have followed from the want of a constitution; for it is the nature and intention of a constitution to *prevent governing by party*, by establishing a common principle that shall limit and control the power and impulse of party, and that says to all parties, *thus far shalt thou go and no further*. But in the absence of a constitution, men look entirely to party; and instead of principle governing party, party governs principle.

An avidity to punish is always dangerous to liberty. It leads men to stretch, to misinterpret, and to misapply even the best of laws. He that would make his own liberty secure, must guard even his enemy from oppression; for if he violates this duty, he establishes a precedent that will reach to himself.

9   JEREMY BENTHAM

Two revolutions occurred in 1789—the one in France, of which almost everyone knows (or should know), and the second in England, in the form of Jeremy Bentham's (1748-1832) *Principles of Morals and Legislation*. And Bentham's ideas were indeed revolutionary, even though their immediate political impact was slight. Do not follow tradition, argued Bentham, in deciding how to employ the power of government. Do not trust the common law, or the uncommon law of religion, or the dictates of conscience. Decide issues such as whether and how people convicted of a particular crime should be punished by asking whether the proposed solutions or remedies add to the utility of a majority of citizens.

A striking yet familiar notion is utility, and Bentham's genius was his recognition that, as government ceased to be the preserve of an hereditary caste and became a *public* enterprise, there was need of such a standard. As the number of people who could influence government increased, the number and range of "public" issues also increased, and liberalism needed some standard of value— besides majority rule or natural rights—to guide this changed government through the thicket of new issues. And how simple it all would be. The pain and pleasure which government policies produced could be measured, and changes could then be made in such policies to increase the level of public pleasure and reduce the level of public pain.

Law was not the sacred expression of the "people's will" or the wisdom of learned judges. Instead, law was merely a device, a tool by which to maximize the public utility. Nothing was sacred. On the other hand, nothing was impossible. If a graduated income tax increased the general happiness (while, obviously, reducing some individuals' pleasures), allowing stores to stay open on Sunday might well do the same (while perhaps aiding the same people that the tax had "hurt"). Bentham's ideas, so new in 1789, are given at least lip service today, especially in the United States. But many of those who define the public's "interest" as the public's "pleasure" have not thought through the implications of Bentham's position. He himself never had the time to work it all out, but he remained confident to the end of his life that the concept of utility would be a sure guide to competent and just liberal government.

AN INTRODUCTION TO THE PRINCIPLES OF MORALS AND LEGISLATION*

Nature has placed mankind under the governance of two sovereign masters, *pain* and *pleasure*. It is for them alone to point out what we ought to do, as well as to determine what we shall do. On the one hand the standard of right and wrong, on the other the chain of causes and effects, are fastened to their throne. They govern us in all we do, in all we say, in all we think: every effort we can make to throw off our subjection, will serve but to demonstrate and confirm it. In words a man may pretend to abjure their empire: but in reality he will remain subject to it all the while. The *principle of utility*[1] recognises this subjection, and assumes it for the foundation of that system, the object of which is to rear the fabric of felicity by the hands of reason and of law. Systems which attempt to question it, deal in sounds instead of sense, in caprice instead of reason, in darkness instead of light.

But enough of metaphor and declamation: it is not by such means that moral science is to be improved.

An Introduction to the Principles of Morals and Legislation, Vols. 1 and 2 (London: W. Pickering and E. Wilson, 1823), chapters 1, 3, 4, 13, and 17.

The principle of utility is the foundation of the present work: it will be proper therefore at the outset to give an explicit and determinate account of what is meant by it. By the principle of utility is meant that principle which approves or disapproves of every action whatsoever, according to the tendency which it appears to have to augment or diminish the happiness of the party whose interest is in question: or, what is the same thing in other words, to promote or to oppose that happiness. I say of every action whatsoever; and therefore not only of every action of a private individual, but of every measure of government.

By utility is meant that property in any object, whereby it tends to produce benefit, advantage, pleasure, good, or happiness, (all this in the present case comes to the same thing) or (what comes again to the same thing) to prevent the happening of mischief, pain, evil, or unhappiness to the party whose interest is considered: if that party be the community in general, then the happiness of the community: if a particular individual, then the happiness of that individual. . . .

The interest of the community is one of the most general expressions that can occur in the phraseology of morals: no wonder that the meaning of it is lost. When it has a meaning, it is this: The community is a fictitious *body*, composed of the individual persons who are considered as constituting as it were its *members*. The interest of the community then is, what?—the sum of the interests of the several members who compose it.

It is in vain to talk of the interest of the community, without understanding what is the interest of the individual. A thing is said to promote the interest, or to be *for* the interest, of an individual, when it tends to add to the sum total of his pleasures: or, what comes to the same thing, to diminish the sum total of his pains.

An action then may be said to be conformable to the principle of utility, or, for shortness sake, to utility, (meaning with respect to the community at large) when the tendency it has to augment the happiness of the community is greater than any it has to diminish it.

When an action, or in particular a measure of government, is supposed by a man to be conformable to the principle of utility, it may be convenient, for the purposes of discourse, to imagine a kind of law or dictate, called a law or dictate of utility: and to speak of the action in question, as being conformable to such a law or dictate. . . .

Of an action that is conformable to the principle of utility, one may always say either that it is one that ought to be done, or at least that it is not one that ought not to be done. One may say also, that it is right it should be done; at least that it is not wrong it should be done: that it is a right action; at least that it is not a wrong action. When thus interpreted, the words *ought*, and *right* and *wrong*, and others of that stamp, have a meaning: when otherwise, they have none.

Has the rectitude of this principle been ever formally contested? It should seem that it had, by those who have not known what they have been meaning. Is it susceptible of any direct proof? It should seem not: for that which is used to prove every thing else, cannot itself be proved: a chain of proofs must have their commencement somewhere. To give such proof is as impossible as it is needless.

Not that there is or ever has been that human creature breathing, however stupid or perverse, who has not on many, perhaps on most occasions of his life, deferred to it. By the natural constitution of the human frame, on most occasions of their lives men in general embrace this principle, without thinking of it: if not for the ordering of their own actions, yet for the trying of their own actions, as well as of those of other men. There have been, at the same time, not many, perhaps, even of the most intelligent, who have been disposed to embrace it purely and without reserve. There are even few who have not taken some occasion or other to quarrel with it, either on account of their not understanding always how to apply it, or on account of some prejudice or other which they were afraid to examine into, or could not bear to part with. For such is the stuff that man is made of: in principle and in practice, in a right track and in a wrong one, the rarest of all human qualities is consistency.

When a man attempts to combat the principle of utility, it is with reasons drawn, without his being aware of it, from that very principle itself. His arguments, if they prove anything, prove not that the principle is *wrong*, but that, according to the applications he supposes to be made of it, it is *misapplied*. Is it possible for a man to move the earth? Yes; but he must first find out another earth to stand upon.

It has been shown that the happiness of the individuals, of whom a community is composed, that is their pleasures and their security, is the end and the sole end which the legislator ought to have in view: the sole standard, in conformity to which each individual ought, as far as depends upon the legislator, to be *made* to fashion his behaviour. But whether it be this or any thing else that is to be *done*, there is nothing by which a man can ultimately be *made* to do it, but either pain or pleasure. . . .

Pleasures then, and the avoidance of pains, are the *ends* which the legislator has in view: it behoves him therefore to understand their *value*. Pleasures and pains are the *instruments* he has to work with: it behoves him therefore to understand their force, which is again, in other words, their value.

To a person considered *by himself*, the value of a pleasure or pain considered *by itself*, will be greater or less, according to the four following circumstances:[2]

1. Its *intensity*.
2. Its *duration*.
3. Its *certainty* or *uncertainty*.
4. Its *propinquity* or *remoteness*.

These are the circumstances which are to be considered in estimating a pleasure or a pain considered each of them by itself. But when the value of any pleasure or pain is considered for the purpose of estimating the tendency of any *act* by which it is produced, there are two other circumstances to be taken into the account; these are,

5. Its *fecundity*, or the chance it has to being followed by sensations of the *same* kind: that is, pleasures, if it be a pleasure: pains, if it be a pain.

6. Its *purity*, or the chance it has of *not* being followed by sensations of the *opposite* kind: that is, pains, if it be a pleasure: pleasures, if it be a pain.

These two last, however, are in strictness scarcely to be deemed properties of the pleasure or the pain itself; they are not, therefore, in strictness to be taken into the account of the value of that pleasure or that pain. They are in strictness to be deemed properties only of the act, or other event, by which such pleasure or pain has been produced; and accordingly are only to be taken into the account of the tendency of such act or such event.

To a *number* of persons, with reference to each of whom the value of a pleasure or a pain is considered, it will be greater or less, according to seven circumstances: to wit, the six preceding ones; *viz.*

1. Its *intensity*.

2. Its *duration*.

3. Its *certainty* or *uncertainty*.

4. Its *propinquity* or *remoteness*.

5. Its *fecundity*.

6. Its *purity*.

And one other; to wit:

7. Its *extent*; that is, the number of persons to whom it *extends*; or (in other words) who are affected by it.

To take an exact account then of the general tendency of any act, by which the interests of a community are affected, proceed as follows. Begin with any one person of those whose interests seem most immediately to be affected by it: and take an account,

1. Of the value of each distinguishable *pleasure* which appears to be produced by it in the *first* instance.

2. Of the value of each *pain* which appears to be produced by it in the *first* instance.

3. Of the value of each pleasure which appears to be produced by it *after* the first. This constitutes the *fecundity* of the first *pleasure* and the *impurity* of the first *pain*.

4. Of the value of each *pain* which appears to be produced by it after the first. This constitutes the *fecundity* of the first *pain*, and the *impurity* of the first pleasure.

5. Sum up all the values of all the *pleasures* on the one side, and those of all the pains on the other. The balance, if it be on the side of pleasure, will give the *good* tendency of the act upon the whole, with respect to the interests of that *individual* person; if on the side of pain, the *bad* tendency of it upon the whole.

6. Take an account of the *number* of persons whose interests appear to be concerned; and repeat the above process with respect to each. *Sum up* the numbers expressive of the degrees of *good* tendency, which the act has, with respect to each individual, in regard to whom the tendency of it is *good* upon the whole: do this again with respect to each individual, in regard to whom the tendency of it is *bad* upon the whole. Take the *balance*; which, if on the side of *pleasure*, will give the general *good tendency* of the act, with respect to the total number or community of individuals concerned; if on the side of pain, the general *evil tendency*, with respect to the same community.

It is not to be expected that this process should be strictly pursued previously to every moral judgment, or to every legislative or judicial operation. It may, however, be always kept in view: and as near as the process actually pursued on these occasions approaches to it, so near will such process approach to the character of an exact one.

The same process is alike applicable to pleasure and pain, in whatever shape they appear: and by whatever denomination they are distinguished: to pleasure, whether it be called *good* (which is properly the cause or instrument of pleasure) or *profit* (which is distant pleasure, or the cause or instrument of distant pleasure,) or *convenience*, or *advantage, benefit, emolument, happiness*, and so forth: to pain, whether it be called *evil*, (which corresponds to *good)* or *mischief*, or *inconvenience*, or *disadvantage*, or *loss*, or *unhappiness*, and so forth.

Nor is this a novel and unwarranted, any more than it is a useless theory. In all this there is nothing but what the practice of mankind, wheresoever they have a clear view of their own interest, is perfectly conformable to. An article of property, an estate in land, for instance, is valuable, on what account? On account of the pleasures of all kinds which it enables a man to produce, and what comes to the same thing the pains of all kinds which it enables him to avert. But the value of such an article of property is universally understood to rise or fall according to the length or shortness of the time which a man has in it: the certainty or uncertainty of its coming into possession: and the nearness or remoteness of the time at which, if at all, it is to come into possession. . . .

The general object which all laws have, or ought to have, in common, is to augment the total happiness of the community; and therefore, in the first place, to exclude, as far as may be, every thing that tends to subtract from that happiness: in other words, to exclude mischief.

But all punishment is mischief: all punishment in itself is evil. Upon the principle of utility, if it ought at all to be admitted, it ought only to be admitted in as far as it promises to exclude some greater evil.

It is plain, therefore, that in the following cases punishment ought not to be inflicted.

1. Where it is *groundless*; where there is no mischief for it to prevent; the act not being mischievous upon the whole.

2. Where it must be *inefficacious*: where it cannot act so as to prevent the mischief.

3. Where it is *unprofitable*, or too *expensive*; where the mischief it would produce would be greater than what it prevented.

4. Where it is *needless*: where the mischief may be prevented, or cease of itself, without it: that is, at a cheaper rate. . . .

Now an offence is an act prohibited, or (what comes to the same thing) an act of which the contrary is commanded by the law: and what is it that the law can be employed in doing, besides prohibiting and commanding? It should seem then, according to this view of the matter, that were we to have settled what may be proper to be done with relation to offences, we should thereby have settled every thing that may be proper to be done in the way of law. Yet that branch which concerns the method of dealing with offences, and which is termed sometimes the *criminal*, sometimes the *penal*, branch, is universally understood to be but one out of two branches which compose the whole subject of the art of legislation; that which is termed the *civil* being the other. Between these two branches then, it is evident enough, there cannot but be a very intimate connection; so intimate is it indeed, that the limits between them are by no means easy to mark out. The case is the same in some degree between the whole business of legislation (civil and penal branches taken together) and that of private ethics. . . .

In the course of this enquiry, that part of it I mean which concerns the limits between the civil and the penal branch of law, it will be necessary to settle a number of points, of which the connection with the main question might not at first sight be suspected. To ascertain what sort of a thing *a* law is; what the *parts* are that are to be found in it; what it must contain in order to be *complete*; what the connection is between that part of a body of laws which belongs to the subject of *procedure*; and the rest of the law at large:—All these, it will be seen, are so many problems, which must be solved before any satisfactory answer can be given to the main question above mentioned.

Nor is this their only use: for it is evident enough, that the notion of a complete law must first be fixed, before the legislator can in any case know what it is he has to do, or when his work is done.

Ethics at large may be defined, the art of directing men's actions to the production of the greatest possible quantity of happiness, on the part of those whose interest is in view. . . .

Ethics, in as far as it is the art of directing a man's own actions, may be stiled the *art of self-government*, or *private ethics*.

What other agents then are there, which, at the same time that they are under the influence of man's direction, are susceptible of happiness? They are of two sorts: 1. Other human beings who are stiled persons. 2. Other animals, which on account of their interests having been neglected by the insensibility of the ancient jurists, stand degraded into the class of *things*. As to other human beings, the art of directing their actions to the above end is what we mean, or at least the only thing which, upon the principle of utility, we *ought* to mean, by the art of government: which, in as far as the measures it displays itself in are of a permanent nature, is generally distinguished by the name of *legislation*: as it is by that of *administration*, when they are of a temporary nature, determined by the occurrences of the day. . . .

. . .Ethics then, in as far as it is the art of directing a man's actions in this respect, may be termed the art of discharging one's duty to one's self: and the quality which a man manifests by the discharge of this branch of duty (if duty it is to be called) is that of *prudence*. In as far as his happiness, and that of any other person or persons whose interests are considered, depends upon such parts of his behaviour as may affect the interests of those about him, it may be said to depend upon his *duty to others*; or, to use a phrase now somewhat antiquated, his *duty to his neighbour*. Ethics then, in as far as it is the art of directing a man's actions in this respect, may be termed the art of discharging one's duty to one's neighbour. Now the happiness of one's neighbour may be consulted in two ways: 1. In a negative way, by forbearing to diminish it. 2. In a positive way, by studying to increase it. A man's duty to his neighbour is accordingly partly negative and partly positive: to discharge the negative branch of it, is *probity*: to discharge the positive branch, *beneficence*.

It may here be asked, How it is that upon the principle of private ethics, legislation and religion out of the question, a man's happiness depends upon such parts of his conduct as affect, immediately at least, the happiness of no one but himself: this is as much as to ask, What motives (independent of such as legislation and religion may chance to furnish) can one man have to consult the happiness of another? by what motives, or, which comes to the same thing, by what obligations, can he be bound to obey the dictates of *probity* and *beneficence*? In answer to this, it cannot but be admitted, that the only interests which a man at all times and upon all occasions is sure to find *adequate* motives for consulting, are his own. Notwithstanding this, there are no occasions in which a man has not some motives for consulting the happiness of other men. In the first place, he has, on all occasions, the purely social motive of sympathy or benevolence: in the next place, he has on most occasions, the semi-social motives of love of amity and love of reputation. The motive of sympathy will act upon him with more or less effect, according to the *bias* of his sensibility: the two other motives, according to a variety of circumstances, principally according to the strength of his intellectual powers, the firmness and steadiness of his mind, the quantum of his moral sensibility, and the characters of the people he has to deal with.

Now private ethics has happiness for its end: and legislation can have no other. Private ethics concerns every member, that is, the happiness and the actions of every member of any community that can be proposed; and legislation can concern no more. Thus far, then, private ethics and the art of legislation go hand in hand. The end they have, or ought to have, in view, is of the same nature. The persons whose happiness they ought to have in view, as also the persons whose conduct they ought to be occupied in directing, are precisely the same. The very acts they ought to be conversant about, are even in a *great measure* the same. Where then lies the difference? In that the acts which they ought to be conversant about, though in a great measure, are not *perfectly and throughout* the same. There is no case in which a private man ought not to direct his own conduct to the production of his own happiness, and of that of his fellow-creatures: but there are cases in which the legislator ought not (in a direct way at least, and by means of punishment applied immediately to particular *individual* acts) to attempt to direct the conduct of the several other members of the community. Every act which promises to be beneficial upon the whole to the community (himself included) each individual ought to perform of himself: but it is not every such act that the legislator ought to compel him to perform. Every act which promises to be pernicious upon the whole to the community (himself included) each individual ought to abstain from of himself: but it is not every such act that the legislator ought to compel him to abstain from.

Where then is the line to be drawn?—We shall not have far to seek for it. The business is to give an idea of the cases in which ethics ought, and in which legislation ought not (in a direct manner at least) to interfere. If legislation interferes in a direct manner, it must be by punishment. Now the cases in which punishment, meaning the punishment of the political sanction, ought not to be inflicted, have been already stated. If then there be any of these cases in which, although legislation ought not, private ethics does or ought to interfere, these cases will serve to point out the limits between the two arts or branches of science. These cases, it may be remembered, are of four sorts: 1. Where punishment would be groundless. 2. Where it would be inefficacious. 3. Where it would be unprofitable. 4. Where it would be needless. . . .

Constitutional Code, Its Connexion With the Two Others

Besides the civil and penal, every complete body of law must contain a third branch, the *constitutional*.

The constitutional branch is chiefly employed in conferring, on particular classes of persons, *powers*, to be exercised for the good of the whole society, or of considerable parts of it, and prescribing *duties* to the persons invested with those powers.

The powers are principally constituted, in the first instance, by discoercive or permissive laws, operating as exceptions to certain laws of the coercive or imperative kind. Instance: *A tax-gatherer, as such, may, on such and such an occasion, take such and such things, without any other TITLE*.

The duties are created by imperative laws, addressed to the persons on whom the powers are conferred. Instance: *On such and such an occasion, such and such a tax-gatherer shall take such and such things. Such and such a judge shall, in such and such a case, cause persons so and so offending to be hanged.*

The parts which perform the function of indicating who the individuals are, who, in every case, shall be considered as belonging to those classes, have neither a permissive complexion, nor an imperative.

They are so many masses of expository matter, appertaining in common to all laws, into the texture of which, the names of those classes of persons have occasion to be inserted. Instance; imperative matter:—*Let the judge cause whoever, in due course of law, is convicted of stealing, to be hanged.* Nature of the expository matter:—Who is the person meant by the word *judge*? He who has been *invested* with that office in such a manner: and in respect of whom no *event* has happened, of the number of those, to which the effect is given, of reducing him to the condition of one *divested* of that office.

Thus it is, that one and the same law, one and the same command, will have its matter divided, not only between two great codes, or main branches of the whole body of the laws, the civil and the penal; but amongst three such branches, the civil, the penal, and the constitutional.

In countries, where a great part of the law exists in no other shape, than that of what in England is called *common* law but might be more expressively termed *judiciary*, there must be a great multitude of laws, the import of which cannot be sufficiently made out for practice, without referring to this common law, for more or less of the expository matter belonging to them. Thus in England the exposition of the word *title*, that basis of the whole fabrick of the laws of property is no where else to be found. And, as uncertainty is the very essence of every particle of law so denominated (for the instant it is clothed in a certain authoritative form of words it changes its nature, and passes over to the other denomination) hence it is that a great part of the laws in being in such countries remain uncertain and incomplete. What are those countries? To this hour, every one on the surface of the globe.

Had the science of architecture no fixed nomenclature belonging to it—were there no settled names, for distinguishing the different sorts of buildings, nor the different parts of the same building from each other—what would it be? It would be what the science of legislation, considered with respect to its *form*, remains at present.

Were there no architects who could distinguish a dwelling-house from a barn, or a side-wall from a ceiling, what would architects be? They would be what all legislators are at present. . . .

Take, for instance, so many well meant endeavours on the part of popular bodies, and so many well meant recommendations in ingenious books, to restrain supreme representative assemblies, from making laws in such and such cases, or to such and such an effect. Such laws, to answer the intended purpose, require a perfect mastery in the science of law, considered in respect of its form— . . . but a perfect, or even a moderate insight into that science, would prevent their being couched in those loose and inadequate terms, in which they may be observed so frequently to be conceived; as a perfect acquaintance with the dictates of utility on that head would, in many, if not in most, of those instances, discounsel the attempt. Keep to the letter, and in attempting to prevent the making of bad laws, you will find them prohibiting the making of the most necessary laws, perhaps even of all laws: quit the letter, and they express no more then if each man were to say, *Your laws shall become ipso facto void, as often as they contain any thing which is not to my mind.*

Of such unhappy attempts, examples may be met with in the legislation of many nations: but in none more frequently than in that newly-created nation, one of the most enlightened, if not the most enlightened, at this day on the globe.

Take for instance, the *Declaration of Rights*, enacted by the state of North Carolina, in convention, in or about the month of September, 1788, and said to be copied, with a small exception, from one in like manner enacted by the state of Virginia.

The following, to go no farther, is the first and fundamental article.

"That there are certain natural rights, of which men, when they form a social compact, cannot deprive or divest their posterity, among which are the enjoyment of life and liberty, with the means of acquiring, possessing, and protecting property, and pursuing and obtaining happiness and safety."

Not to dwell on the oversight of confining to posterity the benefit of the rights thus declared, what follows? That—as against those whom the protection, thus meant to be afforded, includes—every law, or other order, *divesting* a man of *the enjoyment of life or liberty*, is void.

Therefore this is the case, amongst others, with every coercive law.

Therefore, as against the persons thus protected, every order, for example, to pay money on the score of taxation, or of debt from individual to individual, or otherwise, is void; for the effect of it, if complied with, is "to *deprive* and *divest him*," *pro tanto*, of the enjoyment of liberty, viz. the liberty of paying or not paying as he thinks proper: not to mention the species opposed to imprisonment, in the event of such a mode of coercion's being resorted to: likewise, of property, which is itself, a *"means of acquiring, possessing, and protecting property, and of pursuing and obtaining happiness and safety."*

Therefore also, as against such persons, every order to attack an armed enemy, in time of war, is also void: for, the necessary effect of such an order is, "to *deprive* some of them of *the enjoyment of life.*" . . .

Individualism and Tolerance

Individualism and tolerance are perhaps the two topics most central to liberalism, and each is the reverse image of the other. If we are to allow (and even encourage) individuals to hold ideas which are peculiarly their own (and sometimes just plain peculiar), then they must be willing to render the same respect to us. That doctrine seems correct enough now, but it was and always will be heresy to those who *know* some ideas are right and others are wrong. Indeed, even in liberal societies the belief in tolerance is always being tested. The temptation to silence those who disagree or criticize or ridicule must always be strong.

Individualism, however, has meant more to liberals than the individual's right to think and say what he pleases about community affairs. Individualism has also meant, for example, the freedom to travel, to own, to buy and to sell, and to live with and even love people of one's own choosing. Individualism has also had a positive side for liberal thinkers and activists. It has not always been enough simply to tolerate individual differences of opinion or of ways of living. Liberals have struggled to *promote* individual differences of talent and ability. American liberals, especially, have changed the very nature of education on the *faith* that there is some talent out there just waiting for the chance to express itself, to bloom to the benefit of particular persons and of society generally. This faith in the social, as well as personal, benefits of individualism has been stronger among some liberals than among others, but it persists as a central element of liberal thought (see, for example, the Rawls selection).

There is yet another side to the liberal ideal of individualism, a side which is less faith than fun. It is, perhaps, best represented here in the selection by Voltaire, although we do not wish readers to believe that Voltaire was anything but a serious student of politics and society. Nevertheless, liberals such as Voltaire often catch our attention by holding our foolish ideas or practices up for well-deserved ridicule, and liberal societies have—at their best—been communities full of people and politicians able to laugh at themselves and at one another. Political humor and caricature may be liberalism's saving grace. As Voltaire might have said, the liberalism which cannot laugh at itself must become a religion, and "true" religions are the enemies of tolerance and individuality.

---

10 JOHN LOCKE

John Locke wrote *A Letter Concerning Toleration* in 1685 while in exile in Holland. It was anonymously published in 1689, first in Latin and then in English. He wrote two other, longer letters and died while working on a fourth one defending tolerance. In this letter, which summarizes his thinking, Locke makes a plea for religious tolerance based on the ideas that Christianity requires tolerance, that the truth will be discovered if people are free to seek it, that people are fallible, that rulers have limited powers which reach only external behavior not beliefs, that no one can invade the religious rights of others, and that there is a separation between church and state. As can be seen below, however, Locke denied tolerance to some groups. These included those who held opinions contrary to what was necessary to maintain civil society, those who denied the existence of God, those who owed allegiance to a foreign prince and, by implication, to the intolerant.

A LETTER CONCERNING TOLERATION*

The toleration of those that differ from others in matters of religion, is so agreeable to the Gospel of Jesus Christ, and to the genuine reason of mankind, that it seems monstrous for men to be so blind, as not to perceive the necessity and advantage of it. . . .that some may not colour their spirit of persecution and unchristian cruelty, with a pretence of care of the publick weal, and observation of the laws; and that others, under pretence of religion, may not seek impunity for their libertinism and licentiousness; in a word, that none may impose either upon himself or others, by the pretences of loyalty and obedience to the prince, or of tenderness and sincerity in the worship of God; I esteem it above all things necessary to distinguish exactly the business of civil government from that of religion, and to settle the just bounds that lie between the one and the other. . . .

Four Letters on Toleration (London, 1870).

The commonwealth seems to me to be a society of men constituted only for the procuring, the preserving, and the advancing their own civil interests.

Civil interests I call life, liberty, health, and indolency of body; and the possession of outward things, such as money, lands, houses, furniture, and the like.

It is the duty of the civil magistrate, by the impartial execution of equal laws, to secure unto all the people in general, and to every one of his subjects in particular, the just possession of these things belonging to this life. If any one presume to violate the laws of publick justice and equity, established for the preservation of these things, his presumption is to be checked by the fear of punishment, consisting in the deprivation or diminution of those civil interests, or goods, which otherwise he might and ought to enjoy. . . .

Now that the whole jurisdiction of the magistrate reaches only to these civil concernments; and that all civil power, right, and dominion, is bounded and confined to the only care of promoting these things; and that it neither can nor ought in any manner to be extended to the salvation of souls; these following considerations seem unto me abundantly to demonstrate.

First, because the care of souls is not committed to the civil magistrate, any more than to other men. It is not committed unto him, I say, by God; because it appears not that God has ever given any such authority to one man over another, as to compel any one to his religion. Nor can such power be vested in the magistrate by the consent of the people; because no man can so far abandon the care of his own salvation, as blindly to leave it to the choice of any other, whether prince or subject, to prescribe to him what faith or worship he shall embrace. For no man can, if he would, conform his faith to the dictates of another. All the life and power of true religion consists in the outward and full persuasion of the mind; and faith is not faith without believing. Whatever profession we make, to whatever outward worship we conform, if we are not fully satisfied in our own mind that the one is true, and the other well pleasing unto God, such profession and such practice, far from being any furtherance, are indeed great obstacles to our salvation. . . .

In the second place. The care of souls cannot belong to the civil magistrate, because his power consists only in outward force: but true and saving religion consists in the inward persuasion of the mind, without which nothing can be acceptable to God. And such is the nature of the understanding, that it cannot be compelled to the belief of any thing by outward force. Confiscation of estate, imprisonment, torments, nothing of that nature can have any such efficacy as to make men change the inward judgment that they have framed of things.

It may indeed be alleged, that the magistrate may make use of arguments, and thereby draw the heterodox into the way of truth, and procure their salvation. I grant it; but this is common to him with other men. In teaching, instructing, and redressing the erroneous by reason, he may certainly do what becomes any good man to do. Magistracy does not oblige him to put off either humanity or Christianity. But it is one thing to persuade, another to command; one thing to press with arguments, another with penalties. . . . For laws are of no force at all without penalties, and penalties in this case are absolutely impertinent; because they are not proper to convince the mind. . . . It is only light and evidence that can work a change in men's opinions; and that light can in no manner proceed from corporal sufferings, or any other outward penalties.

In the third place, the care of the salvation of men's souls cannot belong to the magistrate; because, though the rigour of laws and the force of penalties were capable to convince and change men's minds, yet would not that help at all to the salvation of their souls. For, there being but one truth, one way to heaven; what hope is there that more men would be led into it, if they had no other rule to follow but the religion of the court, and were put under a necessity to quit the light of their own reason, to oppose the dictates of their own consciences, and blindly to resign up themselves to the will of their governors, and to the religion, which either ignorance, ambition, or superstition had chanced to establish in the countries where they were born? In the variety and contradiction of opinions in religion, wherein the princes of the world are as much divided as in their secular interests, the narrow way would be much straitened; one country alone would be in the right, and all the rest of the world put under an obligation of following their princes in the ways that lead to destruction: and that which heightens the absurdity, and very ill suits the notion of a deity, men would owe their eternal happiness or their eternal misery to the places of their nativity.

These considerations, to omit many others that might have been urged to the same purpose, seem unto me sufficient to conclude, that all the power of civil government relates only to men's civil interests, is confined to the care of the things of this world, and has nothing to do with the world to come.

Let us now consider what a church is. A church then I take to be a voluntary society of men, joining themselves together of their own accord, in order to the publick worshipping of God, in such a manner as they may judge acceptable to him, and effectual to the salvation of their souls.

I say, it is a free and voluntary society. Nobody is born a member of any church; otherwise the religion of parents would descend unto children, by the same right of inheritance as their temporal estates, and every one would hold his faith by the same tenure he does his lands; than which nothing can be imagined more absurd. . . . No man by nature is bound unto any particular church or sect, but every one joins himself voluntarily to that society in which he believes he has found that profession and worship which is truly acceptable to God. The hopes of salvation, as it was the only cause of his entrance into that communion, so it can be the only reason of his stay there. . . .

It follows now that we consider what is the power of this church, and unto what laws it is subject.

Forasmuch as no society, how free soever, or upon whatsoever slight occasion instituted (whether of philosophers for learning, of merchants for commerce, or of men of leisure for mutual conversation and discourse), no church or company, I say, can in the least subsist and hold together, but will presently dissolve and break to pieces, unless it be regulated by some laws, and the members all consent to observe some order. Place, and time of meeting must be agreed on; rules for admitting and excluding members must be established; distinction of officers, and putting things into a regular course, and such like, cannot be omitted. But since the joining together of several members into this church-society, as has already been demonstrated, is absolutely free and spontaneous, it necessarily follows, that the right of making its laws can belong to none but the society itself, or at least, which is the same thing, to those whom the society by common consent has authorised thereunto.

But it may to asked, by what means then shall ecclesiastical laws be established, if they must be thus destitute of all compulsive power? I answer, they must be established by means suitable to the nature of such things, whereof the external profession and observation, if not proceeding from a thorough conviction and approbation of the mind, is altogether useless and unprofitable. The arms by which the members of this society are to be kept within their duty, are exhortations, admonitions, and advice. If by these means the offenders will not be reclaimed, and the erroneous convinced, there remains nothing further to be done, but that such stubborn and obstinate persons, who give no ground to hope for their reformation, should be cast out and separated from the society. This is the last and utmost force of ecclesiastical authority: no other punishment can thereby be inflicted, than that the relation ceasing between the body and the member which is cut off, the person so condemned ceases to be a part of that church.

These things being thus determined, let us inquire in the next place, how far the duty of Toleration extends, and what is required from every one by it.

And first: I hold, that no church is bound by the duty of Toleration to retain any such person in her bosom, as after admonition continues obstinately to offend against the laws of the society. For these being the condition of communion, and the bond of the society, if the breach of them were permitted without any animadversion, the society would immediately be thereby dissolved. But nevertheless, in all such cases care is to be taken that the sentence of excommunication, and the execution thereof, carry with it no rough usage, of word or action, whereby the ejected person may any ways be damnified in body or estate. For all force . . . belongs only to the magistrate, nor ought any private persons, at any time, to use force; unless it be in self-defence against unjust violence. Excommunication neither does nor can deprive the excommunicated person of any of those civil goods that he formerly possessed. All those things belong to the civil government, and are under the magistrate's protection. The whole force of excommunication.consists only in this, that the resolution of the society in that respect being declared, the union that was between the body and some member, comes thereby to be dissolved. . . .

Secondly: No private person has any right, in any manner to prejudice another person in his civil enjoyments, because he is of another church or religion. All the rights and franchises that belong to him as a man, or as a denison, are inviolably to be preserved to him. These are not the business of religion. . . . If any man err from the right way, it is his own misfortune, no injury to thee: nor therefore art thou to punish him in the things of this life, because thou supposest he will be miserable in that which is to come.

What I say concerning the mutual Toleration of private persons differing from one another in religion, I understand also of particular churches; which stand as it were in the same relation to each other as private persons among themselves, nor has any one of them any manner of jurisdiction over any other, no not even when the civil magistrate, as it sometimes happens, comes to be of this or the other communion. For the civil government can give no new right to the church, nor the church to the civil government. . . . This is the fundamental and immutable right of a spontaneous society, that it has power to remove any of its members who transgress the rules of its institution: but it cannot, by the accession of any new members, acquire any right of jurisdiction over those that are not joined with it. And therefore peace, equity and friendship, are always mutually to be observed by particular churches, in the same manner as by private persons, without any pretence of superiority or jurisdiction over one another.

No body . . . neither single persons, nor churches, nay, nor even common-wealths, have any just title to invade the civil rights and worldly goods of each other, upon pretence of religion. Those that are of another opinion, would do well to consider with themselves how pernicious a seed of discord and war, how powerful a provocation to endless hatreds, rapines, and slaughters, they thereby furnish unto mankind. No peace and security, no not so much as common friendship, can ever be established or preserved amongst men, so long as this opinion prevails, that dominion is founded in grace, and that religion is to be propagated by force of arms.

In the third place: Let us see what the duty of Toleration requires from those who are distinguished from the rest of mankind, from the laity, as they please to call us, by some ecclesiastical character and office; whether they be bishops, priests, presbyters, ministers, or however else dignified or distinguished . . . whencesoever their authority be sprung, since it is ecclesiastical, it ought to be confined within the bounds of the church, nor can it in any manner be extended to civil affairs; because the church itself is a thing absolutely separate and distinct from the commonwealth. The boundaries on both sides are fixed and immoveable. He jumbles heaven and earth together, the things most remote and opposite, who mixes these societies; which are in their original, end, business, and in every thing, perfectly distinct, and infinitely different from each other. No man therefore, with whatsoever ecclesiastical office he be dignified, can deprive another man that is not of his church and faith, either of liberty, or of any part of his worldly goods, upon the account of that difference which is between them in religion. For whatsoever is not lawful to the whole church, cannot, by any ecclesiastical right, become lawful to any of its members.

But this is not all. It is not enough that ecclesiastical men abstain from violence and rapine, and all manner of persecution. He that pretends to be a successor of the apostles, and takes upon him the office of teaching, is obliged also to admonish his hearers of the duties of peace, and good-will towards all men; as well towards the erroneous as the orthodox; towards those that differ from them in faith and worship, as well as towards those that agree with them therein: and he ought industriously to exhort all men, whether private persons or magistrates, if any such there be in his church, to charity, meekness, and toleration; and diligently endeavour to allay and temper all that heat, and unreasonable averseness of mind, which either any man's fiery zeal for his own sect, or the craft of others, has kindled against dissenters. . . . For it will be very difficult to persuade men of sense, that he, who with dry eyes, and satisfaction of mind, can deliver his brother unto the executioner, to be burnt alive, does sincerely and heartily concern himself to save that brother from the flames of hell in the world to come.

In the last place. Let us now consider what is the magistrate's duty in the business of toleration: which we think is very certainly considerable.

We have already proved, that the care of souls does not belong to the magistrate. . . . The care therefore of every man's soul belongs unto himself, and is to be left unto himself. But what if he neglect the care of his soul? I answer, what if he neglect the care of his health, or of his estate, which things are nearlier related to the government of the magistrate than the other? Will the magistrate provide by an express law, that such a one shall not become poor or sick? Laws provide, as much as is possible, that the goods and health of subjects be not injured by the fraud or violence of others; they do not guard them from the negligence or illhusbandry of the possessors themselves. No man can be forced to be rich or healthful, whether he will nor no. Nay, God himself will not save men against their wills. Let us suppose, however, that some prince were desirous to force his subjects to accumulate riches, or to preserve the health and strength of their bodies. Shall it be provided by law, that they must consult none but Roman physicians, and shall every one be bound to live according to their prescriptions! What, shall no potion, no broth be taken, but what is prepared either in the Vatican, suppose or in a Geneva shop? Or, to make these subjects rich, shall they all be obliged by law to become merchants, or musicians? Or, shall every one turn victualler, or smith, because there are some that maintain their families plentifully, and grow rich in those professions? But it may be said, there are a thousand ways to wealth, but one only way to heaven. It is well said indeed, especially by those that plead for compelling men into this or the other way. For if there were several ways that lead thither, there would not be so much as a pretence left to compulsion. But now, if I be marching on with my utmost vigour, in that way which, according to the sacred geography, leads strait to Jerusalem; why am I beaten and ill used by others, because, perhaps, I wear not buskins; because my hair is not of the right cut; because, perhaps, I have not been dipt in the right fashion; because I eat flesh upon the road, or some other food which agrees with my stomach; because I avoid certain by-ways, which seem unto me to lead into briars or precipices; because amongst the several paths that are in the same road, I choose that to walk in which seems to be the straightest and cleanest; because I avoid to keep company with some travellers that are less grave, and others that are more sour than they ought to be; or in fine, because I follow a guide that either is, or is not, clothed in white, and crowned with a mitre? Certainly, if we consider right, we shall find that for the most part they are such frivolous things as these, that, without any prejudice to religion or the salvation of souls, if not accompanied with superstition or hypocrisy, might either be observed or omitted; I say, they are such like things as these, which breed implacable enmities amongst Christian brethren, who are all agreed in the substantial and truly fundamental part of religion.

But let us grant unto these zealots, who condemn all things that are not of their mode, that from these circumstances arise different ends. What shall we conclude from thence? There is only one of these which is the true way to eternal happiness. But in this great variety of ways that men follow, it is still doubted which is this right one. Now neither the care of the commonwealth, nor the right of enacting laws, does discover this way that leads to heaven more certainly to the magistrate, than every private man's search and study discovers it unto himself. . . . For if it were so, how could it come to pass that the lords of the earth should differ so vastly as they do in religious matters? But let us grant that it is probable the way to eternal life may be better known by a prince than by his subjects; or at least, that in this incertitude of things, the safest and most commodious way for private persons is to follow his dictates. You will say, what then? If he should bid you follow merchandize for your livelihood, would you decline that course for fear it should not succeed? I answer: I would turn merchant upon the prince's command, because in case I should have ill success in trade, he is abundantly able to make up my loss some other way. If it be true, as he pretends, that he desires I should thrive and grow rich, he can set me up again when unsuccessful voyages have broken me. But this is not the case, in the things that regard the life to come. If there I take wrong course, if in that respect I am once undone, it is not in the magistrate's power to repair my loss, to ease my suffering, or to restore me in any measure, much less entirely, to a good estate. What security can be given for the kingdom of heaven?

Perhaps some will say, that they do not suppose this infallible judgment, that all men are bound to follow in the affairs of religion, to be in the civil magistrate, but in the church. What the church has determined, that the civil magistrate orders to be observed; and he provides by his authority that no body shall either act or believe, in the business of religion, otherwise than the church teaches. So that the judgment of those things is in the church. The magistrate himself yields obedience thereunto, and requires the like obedience from others. I answer. . . . The one only narrow way which leads to heaven is not better known to the magistrate than to private persons, and therefore I cannot safely take him for my guide, who may probably be as ignorant of the way as myself, and who certainly is less concerned for my salvation than I myself am. Amongst so many kings of the Jews, how many of them were there whom any Israelite, thus blindly following, had not fallen into idolatry, and thereby into destruction? Yet nevertheless, you bid me be of good courage, and tell me that all is now safe and secure, because the magistrate does not now enjoin the observance, of his own decrees in matters of religion, but only the decrees of the church. Of what church I beseech you? Of that certainly which likes him best. . . .

But after all, the principal consideration, and which absolutely determines this controversy, is this. Although the magistrate's opinion in religion be sound, and the way that he appoints be truly evangelical, yet if I be not thoroughly persuaded thereof in my own mind, there will be no safety for me in following it. No way whatsoever that I shall walk in against the dictates of my conscience, will ever bring me to the mansions of the blessed. I may grow rich by an art that I take not delight in; I may be cured of some disease by remedies that I have not faith in; but I cannot be saved by a religion that I distrust, and by a worship that I abhor. . . . In a word: Whatsoever may be doubtful in religion, yet this at least is certain, that no religion which I believe not to be true, can be either true, or profitable unto me. In vain therefore do princes compel their subjects to come into their church-communion, under pretence of saving their souls. If they believe, they will come of their own accord; if they believe not, their coming will nothing avail them. How great soever, in fine, may be the pretence of good-will and charity, and concern for the salvation of men's souls, men cannot be forced to be saved whether they will or no. And therefore, when all is done, they must be left to their own consciences.

Concerning outward worship, I say, in the first place, that the magistrate has no power to enforce by law, either in his own church, or much less in another, the use of any rites or ceremonies whatsoever in the worship of God. And this, not only because these churches are free societies, but because whatsoever is prac-tised in the worship of God, is only so far justifiable as it is believed by those that practise it to be acceptable unto him. . . .

In the next place: As the magistrate has no power to impose by his laws, the use of any rites and ceremonies in any church, so neither has he any power to forbid the use of such rites and ceremonies as are already received, approved, and prac-tised by any church: because if he did so, he would destroy the church itself; the end of whose institution is only to worship God with freedom, after its own manner.

You will say: By this rule, if some congregations should have a mind to sacri-fice infants, or, as the primitive Christians were falsely accused, lustfully pollute themselves in promiscuous uncleanness; or practise any other such heinous enormities; is the magistrate obliged to tolerate them, because they are committed in a religious assembly? I answer, No. These things are not lawful in the ordi ary course of life, nor in any private house; and therefore neither are they so in the worship of God; or in any religious meeting. . . . The part of the magistrate is only to take care that the commonwealth receive no prejudice, and that there be no injury done to any man, either in life or estate. . . .

By this we see what difference there is between the church and the commonwealth. Whatsoever is lawful in the commonwealth, cannot be prohibited by the magistrate in the church. Whatsoever is permitted unto any of his subjects for their ordinary use, neither can nor ought to be forbidden by him to any sect of people for their religious uses. If any man may lawfully take bread or wine, either sitting or kneeling in his own house, the law ought not to abridge him of the same liberty in his religious worship; though in the church the use of bread and wine be very different, and be there applied to the mysteries of faith, and rites of divine worship. But those things that are prejudicial to the commonweal of a people in their ordinary use, and are therefore forbidden by laws, those things ought not be permitted to churches in their sacred rites. Only the magistrate ought always to be very careful that he do not misuse his authority, to the oppression of any church, under pretence of publick good.

It may be said: What if a church be idolatrous, is that also to be tolerated by the magistrate? In answer, I ask: What power can be given to the magistrate for the suppression of an idolatrous church, which may not, in time and place, be made use of to the ruin of an orthodox one? For it must be remembered, that the civil power is the same every where, and the religion of every prince is orthodox to himself. If therefore such a power be granted unto the civil magistrate . . . he may extirpate, by violence and blood, the religion which is there reputed idolatrous: by the same rule, another magistrate, in some neighbouring country, may oppress the reformed religion; and, in India, the Christian. The civil power can either change every thing in religion, according to the prince's pleasure, or it can change nothing. If it be once permitted to introduce any thing into religion, by the means of laws and penalties, there can be no bounds put to it; but it will in the same manner be lawful to alter every thing, according to that rule of truth which the magistrate has framed unto himself. No man whatsoever ought therefore to be deprived of his terrestrial enjoyments, upon account of his religion. Not even Americans [Indians] subjected unto a Christian prince, are to be punished either in body or goods, for not embracing our faith and worship. If they are persuaded that they please God in observing the rites of their own country, and that they shall obtain happiness by that means, they are to be left unto God and themselves. Let us trace this matter to the bottom. Thus it is: An inconsiderable and weak number of Christians, destitute of every thing, arrive in a pagan country; these foreigners beseech the inhabitants, by the bowels of humanity, that they would succour them with the necessaries of life; those necessaries are given them, habitations are granted, and they all join together, and grow up into one body of people. The Christian religion by this means takes root in that country, and spreads itself; but does not suddenly grow the strongest. While things are in this condition, peace, friendship, faith, and equal justice, are preserved amongst them. At length the magistrate becomes a Christian, and by that means their party becomes the most powerful. Then immediately all compacts are to be broken, all civil rights to be violated, that idolatry may be extirpated; and unless these innocent pagans, strict observers of the rules of equity and the law of nature, and no ways offending against the laws of the society, I say unless they will forsake their ancient religion, and embrace a new and strange one, they are to be turned out of the lands and possessions of their forefathers, and perhaps deprived of life itself. Then at last it appears what zeal for the church, joined with the desire of dominion, is capable to produce; and how easily the pretence of religion, and of the care of souls, serves for a cloak to covetousness, rapine, and ambition.

Now whosoever maintains that idolatry is to be rooted out of any place by laws, punishments, fire and sword, may apply this story to himself. For the reason of the thing is equal, both in America and Europe. . . .

But idolatry, say some, is a sin, and therefore not to be tolerated. If they said it were therefore to be avoided, the inference were good. But it does not follow, that because it is a sin it ought therefore to be punished by the magistrate. For it does not belong unto the magistrate to make use of his sword in punishing every thing, indifferently, that he takes to be a sin against God. Covetousness, uncharitableness, idleness, and many other things are sins, by the consent of all men, which yet no man ever said were to be punished by the magistrate. The reason is, because they are not prejudicial to other men's rights, nor do they break the publick peace of societies. Nay, even the sins of lying and perjury are no where punishable by laws; unless in certain cases, in which the real turpitude of the thing, and the offence against God, are not considered, but only the injury done unto men's neighbours, and to the commonwealth. And what if in another country, to a Mahometan or a pagan prince, the Christian religion seem false and offensive to God; may not the Christians for the same reason, and after the same manner, be extirpated there?

Thus far concerning outward worship. Let us now consider the articles of faith.

The articles of religion are some of them practical, and some speculative. Now, though both sorts consist in the knowledge of truth, yet these terminate simply in the understanding, those influence the will and manners. Speculative opinions, therefore, and articles of faith, as they are called, which are required only to be believed, cannot be imposed on any church by the law of the land. For it is absurd that things should be enjoined by laws, which are not in men's power to perform. And to believe this or that to be true, does not depend upon our will. . . . But . . . some say, let men at least profess that they believe. A sweet religion indeed, that obliges men to dissemble, and tell lies both to God and man, for the salvation of their souls! If the magistrate thinks to save men thus, he seems to understand little of the way of salvation. And if he does it not in order to save them, why is he so solicitous about the articles of faith as to enact them by a law?

Further: The magistrate ought not to forbid the preaching or professing of any speculative opinions in any church, because they have no manner of relation to the civil rights of the subjects. If a Roman Catholick believe that to be really the body of Christ, which another man calls bread, he does no injury thereby to his neighbour. If a Jew does not believe the New Testament to be the word of God, he does not thereby alter any thing in men's civil rights. If a heathen doubt of both Testaments, he is not therefore to be punished as a pernicious citizen. The power of the magistrate, and the estates of the people, may be equally secure, whether any man believe these things or no. I readily grant, that these opinions are false and absurd. But the business of laws is not to provide for the truth of opinions, but for the safety and security of the commonwealth, and of every particular man's goods and person. And so it ought to be. For truth certainly would do well enough, if she were once left to shift for herself. She seldom has received, and I fear never will receive, much assistance from the power of great men, to whom she is but rarely known, and more rarely welcome. She is not taught by laws, nor has she any need of force to procure her entrance into the minds of men. Errors indeed prevail by the assistance of foreign and borrowed succours. But if truth makes not her way into the understanding by her own light, she will be but the weaker for any borrowed force violence can add to her. . . .

A good life, in which consists not the least part of religion and true piety, concerns also the civil government: and in it lies the safety both of men's souls, and of the commonwealth. Moral actions belong therefore to the jurisdiction both of the outward and inward court; both of the civil and domestick governor; I mean, both of the magistrate and conscience. Here therefore is great danger, lest one of these jurisdictions intrench upon the other, and discord arise between the keeper of the publick peace and the overseers of souls. But if what has been already said concerning the limits of both these governments be rightly considered, it will easily remove all difficulty in this matter.

. . . [I]t is easy to understand to what end the legislative power ought to be directed, and by what measures regulated; and that is the temporal good and outward prosperity of the society; which is the sole reason of men's entering into society, and the only thing they seek and aim at in it. And it is also evident what liberty remains to men in reference to their eternal salvation, and that is, that every one should do what he in his conscience is persuaded to be acceptable to the Almighty, on whose good pleasure and acceptance depends his eternal happiness. For obedience is due in the first place to God, and afterwards to the laws.

But some may ask: What if the magistrate should enjoin any thing by his authority, that appears unlawful to the conscience of a private person? I answer: That if government be faithfully administered, and the counsels of the magistrate be indeed directed to the publick good, this will seldom happen. But if perhaps it do so fall out, I say, that such a private person is to abstain from the action that he judges unlawful; and he is to undergo the punishment, which it is not unlawful for him to bear. For the private judgment of any person concerning a law enacted in political matters, for the publick good, does not take away the obligation of that law, nor deserve a dispensation. But if the law indeed be concerning things that lie not within the verge of the magistrate's authority; as for example, that the people, or any party amongst them, should be compelled to embrace a strange religion, and join in the worship and ceremonies of another church; men are not in these cases obliged by that law, against their consciences. For the political society is instituted for no other end, but only to secure every man's possession of the things of this life. The care of each man's soul, and of the things of heaven, which neither does belong to the commonwealth, nor can be subjected to it, is left entirely to every man's self. . . .

But what if the magistrate believe such a law as this to be for the publick good? I answer: As the private judgment of any particular person, if erroneous, does not exempt him from the obligation of law, so the private judgment, as I may call it, of the magistrate, does not give him any new right of imposing laws upon his subjects, which neither was in the constitution of the government granted him, nor ever was in the power of the people to grant: and least of all, if he make it his business to enrich and advance his followers and fellow sectaries, with the spoils of others. But what if the magistrate believe that he has a right to make such laws, and that they are for the publick good; and his subjects believe the contrary? Who shall be judge between them? I answer: God alone. For there is no judge upon earth between the supreme magistrate and the people. God, I say, is the only judge in this case, who will retribute unto every one at the last day according to his deserts; that is, according to his sincerity and uprightness in endeavouring to promote piety, and the publick weal and peace of mankind. But what shall be done in the mean while? I answer: The principal and chief care of every one ought to be of his own soul first, and in the next place, of the publick peace: though yet there are very few will think it is peace there, where they see all laid waste. There are two sorts of contests amongst men: the one managed by law, the other by force: and they are of that nature, that where the one ends, the other always begins. . . . You will say then the magistrate being the stronger will have his will, and carry his point. Without doubt. But the question is not here concerning the doubtfulness of the event, but the rule of right.

But to come to particulars. I say, First, no opinions contrary to human society, or to those moral rules which are necessary to the preservation of civil society, are to be tolerated by the magistrate. But of those indeed examples in any church are rare. For no sect can easily arrive to such a degree of madness, as that it should think fit to teach, for doctrines of religion, such things as manifestly undermine the foundations of society, and are therefore condemned by the judgment of all mankind: because their own interest, peace, reputation, every thing would be thereby endangered.

Another more secret evil, but more dangerous to the commonwealth, is when men arrogate to themselves, and to those of their own sect, some peculiar prerogative covered over with a specious shew of deceitful words, but in effect opposite to the civil right of the community. For example. We cannot find any sect that teaches expressly and openly, that men are not obliged to keep their promise; that princes may be dethroned by those that differ from them in religion; or that the dominion of all things belongs only to themselves. For these things, proposed thus nakedly and plainly, would soon draw on them the eye and hand of the magistrate, and awaken all the care of the commonwealth to a watchfulness against the spreading of so dangerous an evil. But nevertheless, we find those that say the same things, in other words. What else do they mean, who teach that faith is not to be kept with hereticks? Their meaning, forsooth, is that the privilege of breaking faith belongs unto themselves: for they declare all that are not of their communion to be hereticks, or at least may declare them so whensoever they think fit. . . . These therefore, and the like, who attribute unto the faithful, religious, and orthodox, that is, in plain terms, unto themselves, any peculiar privilege or power above other mortals, in civil concernments; or who, upon pretence of religion, do challenge any manner of authority over such, as are not associated with them in their ecclesiastical communion; I say these have no right to be tolerated by the magistrate; as neither those that will not own and teach the duty of tolerating all men in matters of mere religion. For what do all these and the like doctrines signify; but that they may, and are ready upon any occasion to seize the government, and possess themselves of the estates and fortunes of their fellow-subjects; and that they only ask leave to be tolerated by the magistrate so long, until they may find themselves strong enough to effect it.

Again: That church can have no right to be tolerated by the magistrate, which is constituted upon such a bottom, that all those who enter into it, do thereby *ipso facto*, deliver themselves up to the protection and service of another prince. For by this means the magistrate would give way to the settling of a foreign jurisdiction in his own country, and suffer his own people to be listed, as it were, for soldiers against his own government. Nor does the frivolous and fallacious distinction between the court and the church afford any remedy to this inconvenience; especially when both the one and the other are equally subject to the absolute authority of the same person; who has not only power to persuade the members of his church to whatsoever he lists, either as purely religious, or as in order thereunto; but can also enjoin it them on pain of eternal fire. . . .

Lastly, those are not at all to be tolerated who deny the being of God. Promises, convenants, and oaths, which are the bonds of human society, can have no hold upon an atheist. The taking away of God, though but even in thought, dissolves all. Besides also, those that by their atheism undermine and destroy all religion, can have no pretence of religion whereupon to challenge the privilege of a Toleration. As for other practical opinions, though not absolutely free from all error, yet if they do not tend to establish domination over others, or civil impunity to the church in which they are taught, there can be no reason why they should not be tolerated.

. . . [I]f men enter into seditious conspiracies, it is not religion inspires them to it in their meetings, but their sufferings and oppressions that make them willing to ease themselves. Just and moderate governments are every where quiet, every where safe. But oppression raises ferments, and makes men struggle to cast off an uneasy and tyrannical yoke. I know that seditions are very frequently raised upon pretence of religion. But it is as true, that, for religion, subjects are frequently ill treated, and live miserably. Believe me, the stirs that are made, proceed not from any peculiar temper of this or that church or religious society; but from the common disposition of all mankind, who when they groan under an heavy burthen, endeavour naturally to shake off the yoke that galls their necks. Suppose this business of religion were let alone, and that there were some other distinction made between men and men, upon account of their different complexions, shapes, and features, so that those who have black hair, for example, or grey eyes, should not enjoy the same privileges as other citizens; that they should not be permitted either to buy or sell, or live by their callings; that parents should not have the government and education of their own children; that they should either be excluded from the benefit of the laws, or meet with partial judges; can it be doubted but these persons, thus distinguished from others by the colour of their hair and eyes, and united together by one common persecution, would be as dangerous to the magistrate, as any others that had associated themselves merely upon the account of religion?. . . There is one only thing which gathers people into seditious commotions, and that is oppression.

That we may draw towards a conclusion. The sum of all we drive at is, that every man enjoy the same rights that are granted to others. Is it permitted to worship God in the Roman manner? Let it be permitted to do it in the Geneva form also. Is it permitted to speak Latin in the market-place? Let those that have a mind to it, be permitted to do it also in the church. Is it lawful for any man in his own house to kneel, stand, sit, or use any other posture; and to cloath himself in white or black, in short or in long garments? Let it not be made unlawful to eat bread, drink wine, or wash with water in the church. In a word: whatsoever things are left free by law in the common occasions of life, let them remain free unto every church in divine worship. . . .

Ecclesiastical assemblies, and sermons, are justified by daily experience, and publick allowance. These are allowed to people of some one persuasion: why not to all?. . . Thus if solemn assemblies, observations of festivals, publick worship, be permitted to any one sort of professors; all these things ought to be permitted to the Presbyterians, Independents, Anabaptists, Arminians, Quakers, and others, with the same liberty. Nay, if we may openly speak the truth, and as becomes one man to another, neither Pagan nor Mahometan, nor Jew, ought to be excluded from the civil rights of the commonwealth, because of his religion. The Gospel commands no such thing. . . . And the commonwealth, which embraces indifferently all men that are honest, peaceable, and industrious, requires it not. Shall we suffer a Pagan to deal and trade with us, and shall we not suffer him to pray unto and worship God? If we allow the Jews to have private houses and dwellings amongst us, why should we not allow them to have synagogues? Is their doctrine more false, their worship more abominable, or is the civil peace more endangered, by their meeting in publick than in their private houses? But if these things may be granted to Jews and Pagans, surely the condition of any Christians ought not to be worse than theirs, in a Christian commonwealth.

. . . It is not the diversity of opinons, which cannot be avoided, but the refusal of toleration to those that are of different opinions, which might have been granted, that has produced all the bustles and wars, that have been in the Christian world, upon account of religion. The heads and leaders of the church, moved by avarice and insatiable desire of dominion, making use of the immoderate ambition of magistrates, and the credulous superstition of the giddy multitude, have incensed and animated them against those that dissent from themselves; by preaching unto them, contrary to the laws of the Gospel, and to the precepts of charity, that schismatics and heretics are to be outed of their possessions, and destroyed. And thus have they mixed together, and confounded two things, that are in themselves most different, the church and the commonwealth. . . . This is the unhappy agreement that we see between the church and state. Whereas if each of them would contain itself within its own bounds, the one attending to the worldly welfare of the commonwealth, the other to the salvation of souls, it is impossible that any discord should ever have happened between them.

11 VOLTAIRE

Voltaire (François-Marie Arouet, 1694-1778) may seem out of place in a collection devoted to the works of Anglo-American liberal thinkers, but he assuredly is not. As perhaps the most visible, certainly the most productive, and easily the most appealing of the *philosophes*, Voltaire came to epitomize the clever and skeptical Enlightenment intellectual. For his part, Voltaire was quite aware of his eminence and notoriety, and he cultivated his image accordingly. As a result, it is often difficult to separate the "real" Voltaire from the Voltaire of myth and legend (some of which he created himself). He did not, for example, ever say, "I disagree with everything you say, but I shall fight to the death for your right to say it." That was too drastic a step for the man to take. Voltaire was indeed impulsive and melodramatic, but he was no fool or martyr. (Those of you who have read *Candide* know that.) Yet his was the kind of life from which legends are easily made, and, as often as not, the image of Voltaire as the clever but superficial cynic triumphs over the reality of Voltaire the shrewd and serious political intellectual.

As a political thinker, Voltaire was clearly a liberal, though because he came along before the English liberals had invented market economics, he might well have been uneasy in the company of nineteenth-century advocates of laissez-faire. Voltaire took his ideas from Locke, but Voltaire's passion for justice, free thought, and toleration was stronger and more vocal than Locke's. Voltaire turned his wit and intelligence against prejudice, ignorance, and superstition and adroitly buried them all under a mountain of penetrating and funny essays, plays, stories, and poems. He did not believe that reason was infallible or that social equality was necessary in a just society. But he was one of the leading proponents of free thought and religious toleration in the eighteenth century (or any century, for that matter), and his work affected the whole of intelligent Europe.

A TREATISE ON TOLERATION*

Chapter 10
Whether It Is of Service to Indulge the People in Superstition

Such is the weakness and perversity of the human race that it is undoubtedly more eligible for them to be subject to every possible kind of superstition, provided it is not of a bloody nature, than to live without religion. Man has always stood in need of a curb; and though it was certainly very ridiculous to sacrifice to fauns, satyrs, and naiads, yet it was more reasonable and advantageous to adore even those fantastic images of the deity than to be given up to atheism. An atheist of any capacity, and invested with power, would be as dreadful a scourge to the rest of mankind as the most bloody enthusiast.

When men have not true notions of the Deity, false ideas must supply their place, like as in troublesome and calamitous times we are obliged to trade with base money when good is not to be procured. . . . Wherever there is a fixed com-

---

*John Morley, ed., *The Works of Voltaire* Vol.2 (New York: E.R. DuMont, 1901), part 2, pp. 264-76.

munity, religion is necessary; the laws are a curb upon open crimes, and religion upon private ones.

But when once men have embraced a pure and holy religion, superstition then becomes not only needless, but very hurtful. Those whom God has been pleased to nourish with bread ought not to be fed upon acorns.

Superstition is to religion what astrology is to astronomy, the foolish daughter of a wise mother. These two daughters, however, have for a long time governed this world with uncontrollable sway.

In those dark and barbarous times amongst us, when there were hardly two feudal lords who had a New Testament in their houses, it might be pardonable to present the common people with fables; I mean those feudal lords, their ignorant wives, and brutish vassals. . . .

Reason is every day making her way into the tradesman's counting house, as well as into the palaces of our nobility. It behooves us then to cultivate the fruits of this reason, more especially as it is impossible to prevent them from sprouting forth. . . .

If the masters of error, I mean the great masters who were so long a time prayed to and reverenced for brutalizing the human species, were at present to enjoin us to believe that the seed must rot in the earth before it can sprout; that this earth continues immovable on its basis without revolving about the sun; that the tides are not the natural effect of gravitation; that the rainbow is not formed by the refraction and reflection of the rays of light, etc., and were they to bring certain passages of Scripture badly understood and worse interpreted to authenticate their ordinances, how would they be looked upon by every person of common capacity? Would fools be thought too harsh a name to be imposed on them? But if they should have recourse to compulsion and persecution to establish their insolent ignorance, would not madmen and butchers be deemed a proper appellation?

The more that monkish superstition becomes contemptible, the more bishops are respected and the clergy in general esteemed. They do good in their professions, whereas the monkish superstition of foreign climates occasioned a great deal of mischief. But of all superstitions, that of hating our neighbor on account of his opinion is surely the most dangerous! And will it not be granted me that there would be more sense and reason in adoring the holy navel, the holy prepuce, and the milk and the robe of the Blessed Virgin, than to detest and persecute our brother?

Chapter 21
Virtue Is Better Than Learning

The fewer dogmas, the fewer disputes; and the fewer disputes, the fewer calamities: if this is not true I am much mistaken.

Religion is instituted to make us happy in this life and the next. But what is required to make us happy in the life to come? To be just. And in this? To be merciful and forbearing.

It would be the height of madness to pretend to bring all mankind to think exactly in the same manner in regard to metaphysics. We might, with much greater ease, subject the whole universe by force of arms than subject the minds of all the inhabitants of one single village.

But Euclid found no difficulty in persuading every one of the truths of geometry. And why? Because there is not one of them which is not a self-evident corollary on this simple axiom: "Two and two make four." But is it not altogether the same with relation to the complicated maxims in metaphysics and divinity.

Eusebius and Socrates tell us that when Bishop Alexander and Arius the priest began first to dispute in what manner the Logos or word proceeded from the Father, the Emperor Constantine wrote to them in the following terms: "You are great fools to dispute about things you do not understand."

If the two contending parties had been wise enough to acknowledge that the emperor was in the right Christendom would not have been drenched in blood for upwards of three centuries.

And, indeed, what can be more ridiculous, or rather detestable, than to address mankind in this manner: "My friends, it is not sufficient that you are faithful subjects, dutiful children, tender parents, and upright neighbors; that you live in the continual practice of virtue; that you are grateful, benevolent, and generous, and worship the Saviour of the world in peace; it is furthermore required of you that you should know how a thing may be begotten from all eternity, without being made from all eternity; and if you cannot distinguish the homoousian in the hypostasis, we declare to you that you are damned to all eternity; and in the meantime we shall begin by cutting your throats"? . . .

Constantine, however, did not persevere in silencing the two parties; he might easily have summoned the chiefs of the disputes before him, and have demanded of them by what authority they disturbed the peace of mankind. "Are you," he might have said, "possessed of the genealogy of the heavenly family? What is it to you whether the Son was made or begotten, provided that you are faithful to Him; that you preach a sound doctrine, and practise that doctrine if you can? I have committed many faults in my lifetime, and so have you; I have been ambitious, so have you; it has cost me many falsehoods and cruelties to attain to the empire; I have murdered my nearest relative that stood in my way; but I now repent, and am willing to make atonement for my crime by restoring peace to the Roman Empire; do not you prevent me from doing the only good action which can possibly make my former cruel ones forgotten; but rather assist me to end my days in peace." Perhaps Constantine might not, by this speech, have prevailed over the minds of the disputants, and perhaps he might rather be pleased with presiding in a council in a long crimson robe, and his forehead glittering with jewels.

This, however, opened a passage to all those dreadful calamities which overran the West from Asia. Out of every contested verse there issued a fury armed with a quibble and a poniard, who inspired mankind at once with folly and cruelty. The Huns, the Heruli, the Goths, and Vandals, who came afterwards, did infinitely less mischief: and the greatest they did was that of afterwards engaging in the same fatal disputes.

Chapter 22
Of Universal Toleration

It does not require any great art or studied elocution to prove that Christians ought to tolerate one another. Nay, I shall go still farther and say that we ought to look upon all men as our brethren. How! call a Turk, a Jew, and a Siamese, my brother? Yes, doubtless; for are we not all children of the same parent, and the creatures of the same Creator?

But these people hold us in contempt, and call us idolaters! Well, then, I should tell them that they were to blame. And I fancy that I could stagger the headstrong pride of an imaum, or a talapoin, were I to address them in the following manner:

"This little globe, which is no more than a point, rolls, together with many other globes, in that immensity of space in which we are all alike confounded. Man, who is an animal, about five feet high, is certainly a very inconsiderable part of the creation; but one of those hardly visible beings says to others of the same kind inhabiting another spot of the globe: Hearken to me, for the God of all these worlds has enlightened me. There are about nine hundred millions of us little insects who inhabit the earth, but my ant-hill is alone cherished by God, who holds all the rest in horror and detestation; those who live with me upon my spot will alone be happy and all the rest eternally wretched."

They would here stop me short and ask, "What madman could have made so ridiculous a speech?" I should then be obliged to answer them, "It is yourselves." After which I should endeavor to pacify them, but perhaps that would not be very easy.

I might next address myself to the Christians and venture to say, for example, to a Dominican, one of the judges of the inquisition: "Brother, you know that every province in Italy has a jargon of its own and that they do not speak in Venice and Bergamo as they do in Florence. The Academy della Crusca has fixed the standard of the Italian language; its dictionary is an unerring rule, and Buon Matei's grammar is an infallible guide, from neither of which we ought to depart; but do you think that the president of the academy, or in his absence Buon Matei, could in conscience order the tongues of all the Venetians and Bergamese, who persisted in their own country dialect, to be cut out?"

The inquisitor would, perhaps, make me this reply: "There is a very wide difference; here the salvation of your soul is concerned; and it is entirely for your good that the directory of the inquisition ordains that you shall be seized, upon the deposition of a single person, though of the most infamous character; that you shall have no person to plead for you, nor even be acquainted with the name of your accuser; that the inquisitor shall promise you favor, and afterwards condemn you; that he shall make you undergo five different kinds of torture, and that at length you shall be either whipped, sent to the galleys, or burned at the stake, . . ."

To all which I should take the liberty of making the following reply: "Dear brother, you may perhaps be in the right, and I am perfectly well convinced of the great benefit you intend me; but may I not be saved without all this?". . .

O ye different worshippers of a God of mercy! if ye have cruel hearts, if, while you adore that Deity who has placed the whole of His law in these few words, "Love God and your neighbor," you have loaded that pure and holy law with sophistical and unintelligible disputes, if you have lighted the flames of discord sometimes for a new word, and at others for a single letter only; if you have annexed eternal punishment to the omission of some few words, or of certain ceremonies which other people cannot comprehend, I must say to you with tears of compassion for mankind: "Transport yourselves with me to that great instant in which all men are to receive judgment from the hand of God, who will then do unto every one according to their works, and with me behold all the dead of past ages appearing in His presence. Are you very sure that our heavenly Father and Creator will say to the wise and virtuous Confucius, to the great legislator Solon, to Pythagoras, Zaleucus, Socrates, Plato, the divine Antoninus, the good Trajan, to Titus, the delight of human kind, and to many others who have been the models of human kind: 'Depart from me, wretches! into torments that know neither alleviation nor end; but are, like Himself, everlasting. But you, my well-beloved servants, John Chatel, Ravaillac, Cartouche, Damiens, etc., who have died according to the rules prescribed by the Church, enter into the joy of your Lord, and sit forever at my right hand in majesty and glory.'"

Methinks I see you start with horror at these words; however, as they have escaped me, let them pass; I shall say nothing more to you.

A Philosophical Dictionary*

Liberty of Opinion

Towards the year 1707, the time at which the English gained the battle of Sara-gossa, protected Portugal, and for some time gave a king to Spain, Lord Boldmind, a general officer who had been wounded, was at the waters of Bareges. He there met with Count Medroso, who having fallen from his horse behind the baggage, at a league and a half from the field of battle, also came to take the waters. He was a familiar of the Inquisition, while Lord Boldmind was only familiar in conversation. One day after their wine, he held this dialogue with Medroso:

BOLDMIND.—You are then the sergeant of the Dominicans? You exercise a villainous trade.

MEDROSO.—It is true; but I would rather be their servant than their victim, and I have preferred the unhappiness of burning my neighbor to that of being roasted myself.

BOLDMIND.—What a horrible alternative! You were a hundred times happier under the yoke of the Moors, who freely suffered you to abide in all your supersti-tions, and conquerors as they were, arrogated not to themselves the strange right of sending souls to hell.

MEDROSO.—What would you have? It is not permitted us either to write, speak, or even to think. If we speak, it is easy to misinterpret our words, and still more our writings; and as we cannot be condemned in an *auto-da-fe* for our secret thoughts, we are menaced with being burned eternally by the order of God him-self, if we think not like the Jacobins. They have persuaded the government that if we had common sense the entire state would be in combustion, and the nation become the most miserable upon earth.

BOLDMIND.—Do you believe that we English who cover the seas with ves-sels, and who go to gain battles for you in the south of Europe, can be so unhappy? Do you perceive that the Dutch, who have ravished from you almost all your discoveries in India, and who at present are ranked as your protectors, are cursed of God for having given entire liberty to the press, and for making com-merce of the thoughts of men? Has the Roman Empire been less powerful because Tullius Cicero has written with freedom?

MEDROSO.—Who is this Tullius Cicero? I have never heard his name pro-nounced at St. Hermandad.

BOLDMIND.—He was a bachelor of the university of Rome, who wrote that

---

*John Morley, ed., *The Works of Voltaire,* Vol. II (New York: E.R. DuMont, 1901), part 1, pp. 126-30.

which he thought, like Julius Caesar, Marcus Aurelius, Titus Lucretius Carus, Plinius, Seneca, and other sages.

MEDROSO.—I know none of them; but I am told that the Catholic religion, Biscayan and Roman, is lost if we begin to think.

BOLDMIND.—It is not for you to believe it; for you are sure that your religion is divine, and that the gates of hell cannot prevail against it. If that is the case, nothing will ever destroy it.

MEDROSO.—No; but it may be reduced to very little; and it is through having thought, that Sweden, Denmark, all your island, and the half of Germany groan under the frightful misfortune of not being subjects of the pope. It is even said that, if men continue to follow their false lights, they will soon have merely the simple adoration of God and of virtue. If the gates of hell ever prevail so far, what will become of the holy office?

BOLDMIND.—If the first Christians had not the liberty of thought, does it not follow that there would have been no Christianity?

MEDROSO.—I understand you not.

BOLDMIND.—I readily believe it. I would say, that if Tiberius and the first emperors had fostered Jacobins, they would have hindered the first Christians from having pens and ink; and had it not been a long time permitted in the Roman Empire to think freely, it would be impossible for the Christians to establish their dogmas. If, therefore, Christianity was only formed by liberty of opinion, by what contradiction, by what injustice, would you now destroy the liberty on which alone it is founded?

When some affair of interest is proposed to us, do we not examine it for a long time before we conclude upon it? What interest in the world is so great as our eternal happiness or misery? There are a hundred religions on earth which all condemn us if we believe your dogmas, which *they* call impious and absurd; why, therefore, not examine these dogmas?

MEDROSO.—How can I examine them? I am not a Jacobin.

BOLDMIND.—You are a man, and that is [enough].

MEDROSO.—Alas! you are more of a man than I am.

BOLDMIND.—You have only to teach yourself to think; you are born with a mind, you are a bird in the cage of the Inquisition, the holy office has clipped your wings, but they will grow again. He who knows not geometry can learn it: all men can instruct themselves. Is it not shameful to put your soul into the hands of those to whom you would not intrust your money? Dare to think for yourself.

MEDROSO.—It is said that if the world thought for itself, it would produce strange confusion.

BOLDMIND.—Quite the contrary. When we assist at a spectacle, every one freely tells his opinion of it, and the public peace is not thereby disturbed; but if some insolent protector of a poet would force all people of taste to proclaim that to be good which appears to them bad, blows would follow, and the two parties would throw apples of discord at one another's heads, as once happened at London. Tyrants over mind have caused a part of the misfortunes of the world. We are happy in England only because every one freely enjoys the right of speaking his opinion.

MEDROSO.—We are all very tranquil at Lisbon, where no person dares speak his.

BOLDMIND.—You are tranquil, but you are not happy: it is the tranquility of galley-slaves, who row in cadence and in silence.

MEDROSO.—You believe, then, that my soul is at the galleys?

BOLDMIND—Yes, and I would deliver it.

MEDROSO.—But if I find myself well at the galleys?

BOLDMIND.—Why, then, you deserve to be there. . . .

THE IGNORANT PHILOSOPHER*

A Short Digression

In the beginning of the foundation of the hospital of the *Quinze Vingt*, we know that the inmates were all equal, and that their little transactions were decided by the majority of votes.

By the sense of feeling they distinguished perfectly well brass from silver coin; none of them ever took the money of Brie for that of Burgundy. Their smell was more refined than that of their neighbors who possessed two eyes.

They reasoned perfectly well upon the four senses, that is to say, they knew everything that the blind are allowed to know, and they lived as peaceably and as happily as could be expected.

Unfortunately, one of their professors pretended to have clear ideas with regard to sight. He made himself heard; he intrigued; he persuaded enthusiasts, and at length he was acknowledged as the chief of the community. He set himself up as a perfect judge of colors, and all was lost.

The first dictator of the *Quinze Vingt* formed at first a little council, with whose assistance he made himself master of all the alms. By acquiring this control nobody dared to oppose him. He declared that all the inhabitants of the *Quinze Vingt* were dressed in white. The blind believed him. They spoke of nothing but their fine white clothes, though there was not a single vestment of that color. All their neighbors laughed at them.

They went and complained to the dictator, who gave them a very cool reception. He treated them as innovators, free-thinkers, rebels, who had been seduced

*John Morley, ed., *The Works of Voltaire*, Vol. 18 (New York: E. R. DuMont, 1901), part 2, pp. 292-93.

by the erroneous opinions of those who had eyes, and who dared to doubt the absolute infallibility of their master. This quarrel produced two contending parties.

The dictator, to appease them, issued an arret, affirming that all their clothes were red, although there was not a single garment in the *Quinze Vingt* of that color. Fresh complaints soon arose in the community. The dictator lost all patience and became enraged. The other blind inmates were equally irritated. A battle ensued which lasted a long time, and peace was not restored until all the members of the *Quinze Vingt* were allowed to use their own judgments with respect to the color of their dress.

A deaf man reading this short history, acknowledged that these blind people were quite wrong in pretending to judge of colors; but he continued firmly of the opinion that deaf people were the only proper judges of music.

12 JOHN STUART MILL

On Liberty, by John Stuart Mill, is the most persuasive liberal defense of freedom of speech and inquiry, and its author the most renowned of liberal philosophers. Indeed, Mill's work has had such an impact upon liberalism that many people are unaware of the great diversity within nineteenth-century liberal thought. Mill's defense of free speech and free thought has also had a strong impact on American political and legal thinking. For example, much of the work of the Supreme Court in the twentieth century in the area of free speech rests on positions first explored by Mill in *On Liberty*.

ON LIBERTY*

Introduction

. . . The object of this Essay is to assert one very simple principle, as entitled to govern absolutely the dealings of society with the individual in the way of compulsion and control, whether the means used be physical force in the form of legal penalties, or the moral coercion of public opinion. That principle is, that the sole

---

On Liberty, in *On Liberty* and *The Subjugation of Women* (New York: Henry Holt and Co., 1885), pp. 33-96.

end for which mankind are warranted, individually or collectively, in interfering with the liberty of action of any of their number, is self-protection. That the only purpose for which power can be rightfully exercised over any member of a civilized community, against his will, is to prevent harm to others. His own good, either physical or moral, is not a sufficient warrant. He cannot rightfully be compelled to do or forbear because it will be better for him to do so, because it will make him happier, because, in the opinions of others, to do so would be wise, or even right. There are good reasons for remonstrating with him, or reasoning with him, or persuading him, or entreating him, but not for compelling him, or visiting him with any evil, in case he do otherwise. To justify that, the conduct from which it is desired to deter him must be calculated to produce evil to some one else. The only part of the conduct of any one, for which he is amenable to society, is that which concerns others. In the part which merely concerns himself, his independence is, of right, absolute. Over himself, over his own body and mind, the individual is sovereign.

It is, perhaps, hardly necessary to say that this doctrine is meant to apply only to human beings in the maturity of their faculties. We are not speaking of children, or of young persons below the age which the law may fix as that of manhood or womanhood. Those who are still in a state to require being taken care of by others, must be protected against their own actions as well as against external injury. For the same reason, we may leave out of consideration those backward states of society in which the race itself may be considered as in its nonage. . . .

It is proper to state that I forego any advantage which could be derived to my argument from the idea of abstract right, as a thing independent of utility. I regard utility as the ultimate appeal on all ethical questions; but it must be utility in the largest sense, grounded on the permanent interests of man as a progressive being. Those interests, I contend, authorize the subjection of individual spontaneity to external control, only in respect to those actions of each, which concern the interest of other people. If any one does an act hurtful to others, there is a *prima facie* case for punishing him, by law, or, where legal penalties are not safely applicable, by general disapprobation. There are also many positive acts for the benefit of others, which he may rightfully be compelled to perform; such as, to give evidence in a court of justice; to bear his fair share in the common defense, or in any other joint work necessary to the interest of the society of which he enjoys the protection; and to perform certain acts of individual beneficence, such as saving a fellow creature's life, or interposing to protect the defenceless against ill-usage, things which whenever it is obviously a man's duty to do, he may rightfully be made responsible to society for not doing. A person may cause evil to others not only by his actions but by his inaction, and in either case he is justly accountable to them for the injury. The latter case, it is true, requires a much more cautious exercise of compulsion than the former. To make any one answerable for doing evil to others, is the rule; to make him answerable for not preventing evil, is, comparatively speaking, the exception. Yet there are many cases clear enough and grave enough to justify that exception. . . .

But there is a sphere of action in which society, as distinguished from the individual, has, if any, only an indirect interest; comprehending all that portion of a person's life and conduct which affects only himself, or, if it also affects others, only with their free, voluntary, and undeceived consent and participation. When I say only himself, I mean directly, and in the first instance: for whatever affects himself, may affect others *through* himself; and the objection which may be grounded on this contingency, will receive consideration in the sequel. This, then, is the appropriate region of human liberty. It comprises, first, the inward domain of consciousness; demanding liberty of conscience, in the most comprehensive sense; liberty of thought and feeling; absolute freedom of opinion and sentiment on all subjects, practical or speculative, scientific, moral, or theological. The liberty of expressing and publishing opinions may seem to fall under a different principle, since it belongs to that part of the conduct of an individual which concerns other people; but being almost of as much importance as the liberty of thought itself, and resting in great part on the same reasons, is practically inseparable from it. Secondly, the principle requires liberty of tastes and pursuits; of framing the plan of our life to suit our own character; of doing as we like, subject to such consequences as may follow; without impediment from our fellow-creatures, so long as what we do does not harm them, even though they should think our conduct foolish, perverse, or wrong. Thirdly, from this liberty of each individual, follows the liberty, within the same limits, of combination among individuals; freedom to unite, for any purpose not involving harm to others: the persons combining being supposed to be of full age, and not forced or deceived.

No society in which these liberties are not, on the whole, respected, is free, whatever may be its form of government; and none is completely free in which they do not exist absolute and unqualified. The only freedom which deserves the name, is that of pursuing our own good in our own way, so long as we do not attempt to deprive others of theirs, or impede their efforts to obtain it. Each is the proper guardian of his own health, whether bodily, or mental and spiritual. Mankind are greater gainers by suffering each other to live as seems good to themselves, than by compelling each to live as seems good to the rest.

Though this doctrine is anything but new, and, to some persons, may have the air of a truism, there is no doctrine which stands more directly opposed to the general tendency of existing opinion and practice. Society has expended fully as much effort in the attempt (according to its lights) to compel people to conform to its notions of personal, as of social excellence. . . .

On the Liberty of Thought and Discussion

The time, it is to be hoped, is gone by when any defence would be necessary of the "liberty of the press" as one of the securities against corrupt or tyrannical government. No argument, we may suppose, can now be needed, against permitting a legislature or an executive, not identified in interest with the people, to prescribe opinions to them, and determine what doctrines or what arguments they shall be allowed to hear. . . . Let us suppose, therefore, that the government is entirely at one with the people, and never thinks of exerting any power of coercion unless in agreement with what it conceives to be their voice. But I deny the right of the people to exercise such coercion, either by themselves, or by their government. The power itself is illegitimate. The best government has no more title to it than the worst. It is as noxious, or more noxious, when exerted in accordance with public opinion, than when in opposition to it. If all mankind minus one, were of one opinion, and only one person were of the contrary opinion, mankind would be no more justified in silencing that one person, then he, if he had the power, would be justified in silencing mankind. Were an opinion a personal possession of no value except to the owner; if to be obstructed in the enjoyment of it were simply a private injury, it would make some difference whether the injury was inflicted only on a few persons or on many. But the peculiar evil of silencing the expression of an opinion is, that it is robbing the human race; posterity as well as the existing generation; those who dissent from the opinion, still more than those who hold it. If the opinion is right, they are deprived of the opportunity of exchanging error for truth: if wrong, they lose, what is almost as great a benefit, the clearer perception and livelier impression of truth, produced by its collision with error.

It is necessary to consider separately these two hypotheses, each of which has a distinct branch of the argument corresponding to it. We can never be sure that the opinion we are endeavoring to stifle is a false opinion; and if we are sure, stifling it would be an evil still.

First: the opinion which it is attempted to suppress by authority may possibly be true. Those who desire to suppress it, of course deny its truth; but they are not infallible. . . . To refuse a hearing to an opinion, because they are sure that it is false, is to assume that *their* certainty is the same thing as *absolute* certainty. All silencing of discussion is an assumption of infallibility. . . .

Unfortunately for the good sense of mankind, the fact of their fallibility is far from carrying the weight in their practical judgment, which is always allowed to it in theory; for while every one well knows himself to be fallible, few think it necessary to take any precautions against their own fallibility, or admit the supposition that any opinion, of which they feel very certain, may be one of the examples of the error to which they acknowledge themselves to be liable. . . .

The objection likely to be made to this argument, would probably take some such form as the following. There is no greater assumption of infallibility in forbidding the propagation of error, than in any other thing which is done by public authority on its own judgment and responsibility. Judgment is given to men that they may use it. Because it may be used erroneously, are men to be told that they ought not to use it at all? To prohibit what they think pernicious, is not claiming exemption from error, but fulfilling the duty incumbent on them, although fallible, of acting on their conscientious conviction. If we were never to act on our opinions, because those opinions may be wrong, we should leave all our interests uncared for, and all our duties unperformed. . . . It is the duty of governments, and of individuals, to form the truest opinions they can; to form them carefully, and never impose them upon others unless they are quite sure of being right. But when they are sure (such reasoners may say), it is not conscientiousness but cowardice to shrink from acting on their opinions, and allow doctrines which they honestly think dangerous to the welfare of mankind, either in this life or in another, to be scattered abroad without restraint, because other people, in less enlightened times, have persecuted opinions now believed to be true. Let us take care, it may be said, not to make the same mistake: but governments and nations have made mistakes in other things, which are not denied to be fit subjects for the exercise of authority: they have laid on bad taxes, made unjust wars. Ought we therefore to lay on no taxes, and, under whatever provocation, make no wars? Men, and governments, must act to the best of their ability. There is no such thing as absolute certainty, but there is assurance sufficient for the purposes of human life. We may, and must, assume our opinion to be true for the guidance of our own conduct: and it is assuming no more when we forbid bad men to pervert society by the propagation of opinions which we regard as false and pernicious.

I answer, that it is assuming very much more. There is the greatest difference between presuming an opinion to be true, because, with every opportunity for contesting it, it has not been refuted, and assuming its truth for the purpose of not permitting its refutation. Complete liberty of contradicting and disproving our opinion, is the very condition which justifies us in assuming its truth for purposes of action; and on no other terms can a being with human faculties have any rational assurance of being right. . . .

. . . The whole strength and value, then, of human judgment, depending on the one property, that it can be set right when it is wrong, reliance can be placed on it only when the means of setting it right are kept constantly at hand. In the case of any person whose judgment is really deserving of confidence, how has it become so? Because he has kept his mind open to criticism of his opinions and conduct. Because it has been his practice to listen to all that could be said against him. . . .

. . . If even the Newtonian philosophy were not permitted to be questioned, mankind could not feel as complete assurance of its truth as they now do. The beliefs which we have most warrant for, have no safeguard to rest on, but a standing invitation to the whole world to prove them unfounded. If the challenge is not accepted, or is accepted and the attempt fails, we are far enough from certainty still; but we have done the best that the existing state of human reason admits of; we have neglected nothing that could give the truth a chance of reaching us: if the lists are kept open, we may hope that if there be a better truth, it will be found when the human mind is capable of receiving it; and in the meantime we may rely on having attained such approach to truth, as is possible in our own day. This is the amount of certainty attainable by a fallible being, and this the sole way of attaining it.

Strange it is, that men should admit the validity of the arguments for free discussion, but object to their being "pushed to an extreme;" not seeing that unless the reasons are good for an extreme case, they are not good for any case. Strange that they should imagine that they are not assuming infallibility when they acknowledge that there should be free discussion on all subjects which can possibly be *doubtful*, but think that some particular principle or doctrine should be forbidden to be questioned because it is *so certain*, that is, because *they are certain* that it is certain. To call any proposition certain, while there is any one who would deny its certainty if permitted, but who is not permitted, is to assume that we ourselves, and those who agree with us, are the judges of certainty, and judges without hearing the other side. . . .

. . . Mankind can hardly be too often reminded, that there was once a man named Socrates, between whom and the legal authorities and public opinion of his time, there took place a memorable collision. Born in an age and country abounding in individual greatness, this man has been handed down to us by those who best knew both him and the age, as the most virtuous man in it; while *we* know him as the head and prototype of all subsequent teachers of virtue, the source equally of the lofty inspiration of Plato and the judicious utilitarianism of Aristotle, "*i maestri di color che sanno,*" the two headsprings of ethical as of all other philosophy. This acknowledged master of all the eminent thinkers who have since lived—whose fame, still growing after more than two thousand years, all but outweighs the whole remainder of the names which make his native city illustrious—was put to death by his countrymen, after a judicial conviction, for impiety and immorality. Impiety, in denying the gods recognized by the State; indeed his accuser asserted that he believed in no gods at all. Immorality, in being, by his doctrines and instructions, a "corruptor of youth." Of these charges the tribunal, there is every ground for believing, honestly found him guilty, and condemned the man who probably of all then born had deserved best of mankind, to be put to death as a criminal. . . .

. . . Let us add one more example, the most striking of all if the impressiveness of an error is measured by the wisdom and virtue of him who falls into it. If ever any one, possessed of power, had grounds for thinking himself the best and most enlightened among his contemporaries, it was the Emperor Marcus Aurelius. Absolute monarch of the whole civilized world, he preserved through life not only the most unblemished justice, but what was less to be expected from his Stoical breeding, the tenderest heart. The few failings which are attributed to him, were all on the side of indulgence: while his writings, the highest ethical product of the ancient mind, differ scarcely perceptibly, if they differ at all, from the most characteristic teachings of Christ. This man, a better Christian in all but the dogmatic sense of the word, than almost any of the ostensibly Christian sovereigns who have since reigned, persecuted Christianity. Placed at the summit of all the previous attainments of humanity, with an open, unfettered intellect, and a character which led him of himself to embody in his moral writings the Christian ideal, he yet failed to see that Christianity was to be a good and not an evil to the world, with his duties to which he was so deeply penetrated. Existing society he knew to be in a deplorable state. But such as it was, he saw or thought he saw, that it was held together and prevented from being worse, by belief and reverence of the received divinities. As a ruler of mankind, he deemed it his duty not to suffer society to fall in pieces; and saw not how, if its existing ties were removed, any others could be formed which could again knit it together. The new religion openly aimed at dissolving these ties: unless, therefore, it was his duty to adopt that religion, it seemed to be his duty to put it down. . . . Unless any one who approves of punishment for the promulgation of opinions, flatters himself that he is a wiser and better man than Marcus Aurelius—more deeply versed in the wisdom of his time, more elevated in his intellect above it—more earnest in his search for truth, or more single-minded in his devotion to it when found;—let him abstain from that assumption of the joint infallibility of himself and the multitude, which the great Antoninus made with so unfortunate a result. . . .

. . . No one can be a great thinker who does not recognize, that as a thinker it is his first duty to follow his intellect to whatever conclusions it may lead. Truth gains more even by the errors of one who, with due study and preparation, thinks for himself, than by the true opinions of those who only hold them because they do not suffer themselves to think. Not that it is solely, or chiefly, to form great thinkers, that freedom of thinking is required. On the contrary, it is as much, and even more indispensable, to enable average human beings to attain the mental stature which they are capable of. There have been, and may again be, great individual thinkers, in a general atmosphere of mental slavery. But there never has been, nor ever will be, in that atmosphere, an intellectually active people. . . .

Let us now pass to the second division of the argument, and dismissing the supposition that any of the received opinions may be false, let us assume them to be true, and examine into the worth of the manner in which they are likely to be held, when their truth is not freely and openly canvassed. However unwillingly a person who has a strong opinion may admit the possibility that his opinion may be false, he ought to be moved by the consideration that however true it may be, if it is not fully, frequently, and fearlessly discussed, it will be held as a dead dogma, not a living truth.

There is a class of persons (happily not quite so numerous as formerly) who think it enough if a person assents undoubtingly to what they think true, though he has no knowledge whatever of the grounds of the opinion, and could not make a tenable defence of it against the most superficial objections. Such persons, if they can once get their creed taught from authority, naturally think that no good, and some harm, comes of its being allowed to be questioned. Where their influence prevails, they make it nearly impossible for the received opinion to be rejected wisely and considerately though it may still be rejected rashly and ignorantly; for to shut out discussion entirely is seldom possible, and when it once gets in, beliefs not grounded on conviction are apt to give way before the slightest semblance of an argument. Waiving, however, this possibility—assuming that the true opinion abides in the mind, but abides as a prejudice, a belief independent of, and proof against, argument—this is not the way in which truth ought to be held by a rational being. This is not knowing the truth. Truth, thus held, is but one superstition the more, accidentally clinging to the words which enunciate a truth. . . .

. . . The greatest orator, save one, of antiquity, has left it on record that he always studied his adversary's case with as great, if not with still greater, intensity than even his own. What Cicero practised as the means of forensic success, requires to be imitated by all who study any subject in order to arrive at the truth. He who knows only his own side of the case, knows little of that. His reasons may be good, and no one may have been able to refute them. But if he is equally unable to refute the reasons on the opposite side; if he does not so much as know what they are, he has no ground for preferring either opinion. The rational position for him would be suspension of judgment, and unless he contents himself with that, he is either led by authority, or adopts, like the generality of the world, the side to which he feels most inclination. Nor is it enough that he should hear the arguments of adversaries from his own teachers, presented as they state them, and accompanied by what they offer as refutations. That is not the way to do justice to the arguments, or bring them into real contact with his own mind. He must be able to hear them from persons who actually believe them; who defend them in earnest, and do their very utmost for them. He must know them in their most plausible and persuasive form; he must feel the whole force of the difficulty which the true view of the subject has to encounter and dispose of, else he will never really possess himself of the portion of truth which meets and removes that difficulty. Ninety-nine in a hundred of what are called educated men are in this condition, even of those who can argue fluently for their opinions. Their conclusion may be true, but it might be false for anything they know: they have never thrown themselves into the mental position of those who think differently from them, and considered what such persons may have to say; and consequently they do not, in any proper sense of the word, know the doctrine which they themselves profess. They do not know those parts of it which explain and justify the remainder; the considerations which show that a fact which seemingly conflicts with another is reconcilable with it, or that, of two apparently strong reasons, one and not the other ought to be preferred. All that part of the truth which turns the scale, and decides the judgment of a completely informed mind, they are strangers to;

nor is it ever really known, but to those who have attended equally and impartially to both sides, and endeavored to see the reasons of both in the strongest light. So essential is this discipline to a real understanding of moral and human subjects, that if opponents of all important truths do not exist, it is indispensable to imagine them, and supply them with the strongest arguments which the most skilful devil's advocate can conjure up. . . .

. . . The fact, however, is, that not only the grounds of the opinion are forgotten in the absence of discussion, but too often the meaning of the opinion itself. The words which convey it, cease to suggest ideas, or suggest only a small portion of those they were originally employed to communicate. Instead of a vivid conception and a living belief, there remain only a few phrases retained by rote; or, if any part, the shell and husk only of the meaning is retained the finer essence being lost. . . .

. . . We have hitherto considered only two possibilities: that the received opinion may be false, and some other opinion, consequently, true; or that, the received opinion being true, a conflict with the opposite error is essential to a clear apprehension and deep feeling of its truth. But there is a commoner case than either of these; when the conflicting doctrines, instead of being one true and the other false, share the truth between them; and the nonconforming opinion is needed to supply the remainder of the truth, of which the received doctrine embodies only a part. Popular opinions, on subjects not palpable to sense, are often true, but seldom or never the whole truth. They are a part of the truth; sometimes a greater, sometimes a smaller part, but exaggerated, distorted, and disjoined from the truths by which they ought to be accompanied and limited. Heretical opinions, on the other hand, are generally some of these suppressed and neglected truths, bursting the bonds which kept them down, and either seeking reconciliation with the truth contained in the common opinion, or fronting it as enemies, and setting themselves up, with similar exclusiveness, as the whole truth. . . .

In politics, again, it is almost a commonplace, that a party of order or stability, and a party of progress or reform, are both necessary elements of a healthy state of political life; until the one or the other shall have so enlarged its mental grasp as to be a party equally of order and of progress, knowing and distinguishing what is fit to be preserved from what ought to be swept away. Each of these modes of thinking derives its utility from the deficiencies of the other; but it is in a great measure the opposition of the other that keeps each within the limits of reason and sanity. Unless opinions favorable to democracy and to aristocracy, to property and to equality, to cooperation and to competition, to luxury and to abstinence, to sociality and individuality, to liberty and discipline, and all the other standing antagonisms of practical life, are expressed with equal freedom, and enforced and defended with equal talent and energy, there is no chance of both elements obtaining their due; one scale is sure to go up, and the other down. . . . On any of the great open questions just enumerated, if either of the two opinions has a better claim than the other, not merely to be tolerated, but to be encouraged and countenanced, it is the one which happens at the particular time and place to be in a minority. That is the opinion which, for the time being, represents the neglected interests, the side of human well-being which is in danger of obtaining less than its share. . . .

We have now recognized the necessity to the mental well-being of mankind (on which all their other well-being depends) of freedom of opinion, and freedom of the expression of opinion, on four distinct grounds; which we will now briefly recapitulate.

First, if any opinion is compelled to silence, that opinion may, for aught we can certainly know, be true. To deny this is to assume our own infallibility.

Secondly, though the silenced opinion be an error, it may, and very commonly does, contain a portion of truth; and since the general or prevailing opinion on any subject is rarely or never the whole truth, it is only by the collision of adverse opinions that the remainder of the truth has any chance of being supplied.

Thirdly, even if the received opinion be not only true, but the whole truth; unless it is suffered to be, and actually is, vigorously and earnestly contested, it will, by most of those who receive it, be held in the manner of a prejudice, with little comprehension or feeling of its rational grounds. And not only this, but, fourthly, the meaning of the doctrine itself will be in danger of being lost, or enfeebled, and deprived of its vital effect on the character and conduct; the dogma becoming a mere formal profession, inefficacious for good, but cumbering the ground, and preventing the growth of any real and heartfelt conviction from reason or personal experience. . . .

13　DAVID SPITZ

As a scholar (*The Liberal Idea of Freedom, Patterns of Anti-Democratic Thought, Democracy and the Challenge of Power*), essayist, and lecturer, David Spitz (1916-1979) developed and defended liberal ideals and institutions for over three decades. He was especially effective at attacking the contemporary opponents of liberalism, as he does in this selection. At the same time, however, he offers a succinct defense of liberal ideas and modern liberal government, restating in the process positions central to the traditions of liberal thought.

A LIBERAL PERSPECTIVE ON LIBERALISM AND CONSERVATISM*

In the political sphere, the unity or tradition of liberalism is unambiguous. Its preeminent principle is political equality. Whatever the form of state, whatever the historical situation or national character, the liberal has associated himself with the battle against entrenched privilege. Always the liberal has denied that power and station are the appropriate perquisites of lineage, or of the exercise of force, or of something called History or God. Always the liberal has looked to that which is common to men, not to that which divides them. This does not mean that the liberal is oblivious to the fact that men are not identical, that there are indeed differences of religion and race, wealth and power, talent and intelligence. What it does mean is that for the liberal such differences, important though they may be for certain purposes, are politically irrelevant. Each man has a life to live, the poorest as well as the richest man. Each man requires freedom—to exercise his reason, to discover and develop his talents, to achieve his full growth and stature as an individual. And each man suffers the consequences of deprivation and injustice, the oppressor no less than the oppressed. Hence each man has a common stake in the conditions, and in the determination of the conditions, under which he lives.

Liberals have no faith in human infallibility, or in the capacity of an allegedly superior few to respect the principle of equality or to withstand the corrupting temptations of power. Hence, while liberals recognize that political decisions taken by the people may be wrong, decisions taken by a self-proclaimed aristocracy are not necessarily right. Indeed, their wrongs have been far more numerous! What is crucial, then, is a political arrangement that makes possible the peaceful and effective correction of error. This dictates democracy, for only democracy provides a constitutional mechanism for the removal of the rulers by the ruled. Whatever its limitations or defects, democracy commends itself to liberals by this one overriding virtue—the principle of responsibility, by which the governed can protect themselves from misgovernment. This is why liberalism has consistently opposed authoritarianism in politics, why it has fought against all forms of oligarchical rule.

Conservatism, in contrast, has traditionally been identified with the impulse to hierarchy, a hierarchy based on the inequality of men. What is impressive to the conservative is that societies are made up of men, not Man, and that men are different. Some men (it is held) are wiser, more intelligent, more talented, better

---

Left, Right, and Center: Essays on Liberalism and Conservatism in the United States (Gambier, Ohio: Public Affairs Conference Cen er, 1965), pp. 26-37. Reprinted by permission of the Public Affairs Conference Center of Kenyon College.

informed, than others. And if some men are superior and others average or inferior, it is the height of folly, conservatives argue, to let the unwise, through their numerical superiority, govern the wise or even themselves. For if they are unwise, they will make wrong decisions and thus defeat the very purposes they seek to accomplish. Indeed, because they are unwise, they cannot, save by accident, know what the right purposes are. It is true that conservatives are not always in agreement as to the character of the superior few. Some believe this superiority derives from race or blood; others, that it is an attribute of wealth or strength; still others, that it is associated with intelligence or virtue. But that there are a superior few, whether determined by nature or nurture, conservatives do not doubt. Hence the right political order is in the conservative view that which in one way or another institutionalizes this crucial fact.

Moreover, when the conservative speaks of order, he has in mind an order that is given, not contrived. Its laws are to be discovered, not created, to be adhered to, not defied. Just as the heavenly bodies have their accustomed place, just as the waters fall and the trees rise, so there is pattern and degree in human communities. . . . Hence those who are qualified to rule must rule; those who are fit but to obey must obey. And if, at a particular moment, the few who actually occupy the seats of power are not those fitted by reason and nature to rule . . . still it is better to have order than disorder. This is why conservatives, despite internal disagreements, have throughout history defended the prevailing aristocratic order, resisted the encroachments of egalitarianism, and associated themselves with the upper or dominant class.

In the economic sphere, this distinction between liberalism as representative of the interests of the lower class and conservatism as spokesman for the interests of the upper classes is even more clear. . . .

. . . As a conservative like Alexander Hamilton fully understood, economic power divorced from and antagonistic to political power makes for an unhealthy, perhaps an impossible, situation. For economic power will not stand idly by and permit itself to be destroyed. On the contrary, because it perceives its interests, because it has the knowledge and skills appropriate to the promotion of those interests, and because, above all, it possesses the means and the will to act in defense of those interests, it will destroy the forces antagonistic to it. If, then, order is to be maintained, it must be an order which unites economic power with political power. And this, in the conservative view, inexorably means an attachment of political power to the interests of the dominant economic class. This is why conservatives defend not simply wealth, but inherited wealth. This is why conservatives oppose tax policies and measures that seek to regulate the conduct of businessmen, that is, to reduce their power and position. This is why conservatives speak little of human or civil rights, but much of property and vested rights.

Liberalism, on the other hand, has always been identified with the interests of the lower classes—not because the lower classes have by some mystery of incarnation been blessed with a monopoly of virtue but because wealth, especially inherited wealth, is not a sufficient test of function or capacity. In the liberal view, all men are equal. Insofar as distinctions of place and power must be admitted, they properly derive only from the free recorded and continuing consent of the people, not from such arbitrary factors as ancestry or ruthless force. It is hoped, and by some believed, that the people will choose wisely, that they will recognize men on the basis of merit, or demonstrated competence. To discover merit, equality of opportunity is essential. This requires the elimination of hereditary privilege and of unwarranted discriminatory practices, such as those based on race or religion or sex. It requires, even more, the reduction of great inequalities of wealth which make equality of opportunity impossible. It requires, from a positive standpoint, the creation of those conditions which assure access to all positions to those who, whatever their origins, demonstrate by their individual qualities and achievements that they merit them. It is thoroughly false and misleading to assert, as some critics of liberalism do, that liberals seek absolute equality of condition, that liberals recognize and respect no differences. On the contrary, what liberals contend is that equality of opportunity is the necessary condition for the rational determination of those qualities in which men are different and truly unequal, and hence in what respects power and position may properly be apportioned. Anything other than this is a defense of artificial and false inequalities.

Liberalism is concerned not only with equality of this sort in the economic sphere; it is concerned also with liberty. Now what is crucial about private ownership of property in the real world is that such ownership confers power without responsibility; those who own property have the legal right to use it to promote their own interests, whatever the consequences of their decisions on the welfare of others. Such ownership divides men into independent and dependent men; by denying some men equal access to the use of the earth—though we have not, curiously, sought to deny them equal access to air and to water, perhaps because this presents certain practical difficulties—such ownership forces some men to become the slaves or servants of others. This enables those who possess property to use, to exploit, other men for their advantage. And it is this fact, that some men can use other men, can treat them as a means to their purposes rather than as ends in themselves, that constitutes in the liberal view a debasement of man.

For this reason, liberals have traditionally supported the efforts of the lower classes, through legislation by government and through the countervailing pressures of economic organizations, e.g., the labor unions, to curb the great economic powers of the owners and managers and to give workers a voice in determining the conditions under which they labor. Liberals have sought to restrain and curtail the growth of corporate monopoly, which destroys individual enterprise and penalizes the consumer. They have sought to introduce into the operation of the giant large-scale enterprises that today constitute the economic-technological system a pattern of controls that mitigate the depersonalizing and dehumanizing effects of a master-servant relationship. They have even urged government to move directly into the economic sphere through the public ownership and operation of certain services and industries, where private ownership either has served the public interest inadequately or has diverted natural and social resources away from this public interest to the promotion of private gain. In diverse ways, including schemes that look to the transformation of the entire system of economic power, liberals have sought to lessen the harsh impact of oligarchical rule in economic life, to introduce a measure of democracy within or democratic controls over the industrial-technological process, to assure freedom from arbitrary command within the economic no less than within the political sphere. For how can a man be equal and free when he is a dependent and servile man? Not the rights of property, then, however these may be defined, but the rights of man are for liberalism the guiding principle of economic organization and action.

We come, finally, to the distinction between liberalism and conservatism in the intellectual or cultural sphere. Here the issue that divides these camps, while not unrelated to social classes, turns primarily on their respective attitudes toward freedom of inquiry and expression.

Conservatism, it is claimed, seeks to conserve not everything but only the Good. But the Good is not self-evident; hence conservatism requires a standard or body of principles by which we can distinguish the good from the bad. It requires, even more, a demonstration that this standard or set of principles is both applicable and right. Conservatives agree that there is, indeed there must be, such a standard or body of principles. It exists because it is inherent in the very nature of things. It needs, then, only to be discovered and, when discovered, to be obeyed. What defines and accounts for the present malaise, the malpractices and discontents of our time, is from this standpoint the fact that men no longer seek or abide by these true principles. They look to opinion rather than to knowledge, and opinion, precisely because it is not knowledge, is an uncertain and puny guide. More than that, opinion in democratic states is formed by average, which means inferior, men. Hence policies based upon public opinion are likely to be wrong. Only if we recapture and adhere to the true principles of political life, conservatives argue, can we hope to achieve right and good government.

It is true that conservatives are in no sense agreed as to what these true principles are, or why they are warranted. Some conservatives believe that these principles are revealed by God, or, in some constructions, by His teachings as these are mediated by and through His One True Church, whichever it might be—for not all conservatives agree as to which God is God and what it is that God says. Others derive these correct principles from history or tradition, but since there are, alas, conflicting traditions or at least diverse readings of the same tradition, this leads to multiple and not always consistent principles. Still others look to nature, to the doctrines of natural law or natural right, but here again there seems to be considerable disagreement as to what it is that nature teaches. And some, finally, appeal to intuition, to a subjective but nonetheless (it is said) correct apprehension of what is right as distinct from what is wrong; though here again, since men do not all palpitate in the same way, intuitive judgments do not always coincide. Despite these differences and conflicts, which often divide conservatives into congeries of warring sects, they are all, in one crucial respect at least, still conservatives; for they all believe in the existence of an absolute truth, of an objective moral order, and hence of a political system and body of policies deriving from and corresponding to the principles of this true morality. . . .

This is why, finally, conservatives are so partial to religion, though it is curious to note that their defense of religion is often couched not in terms of its truth but in terms of its utility. For conservatives generally, as even for men otherwise so diverse in their outlooks as Hobbes and Rousseau, concerned as they are with stability, it is far more important to have a single religion than to have the ''right'' religion. A universal or general commitment to the same religion—in contemporary America, according to some conservatives, *any* religion—not only precludes religious, i.e., civil, wars; it also makes for piety, which makes for obedience, which makes for stability and peace.

Whatever the specific formulation of the conservative creed, the fact that it does build throughout on a claimed objective truth produces the same practical consequences. Above all, these include the disparagement of freedom of inquiry and a readiness to limit and control freedom of expression. Since the truth is already known, freedom of inquiry rests in the conservative view on a false premise: that it is proper seriously to entertain error. In fact, because error may appear in attractive and plausible guise, unsophisticated minds may well mistake it for truth. To permit the unrestrained expression of such falsehoods may lead to their widespread acceptance. Then error, not truth, will govern mankind. Since it is the business of government, according to conservatives, to apply justice and achieve virtue, not speech but ''good'' speech, not conflicting ideas but ''right'' ideas, should alone be tolerated. The idea of an open society, in which men are free to utter and debate diverse opinions, including the wrong opinions, is from this standpoint both evil and absurd. What is vital is the inculcation of right attitudes, right habits, right conduct; and this can only be achieved if men who know what is right teach and control those who would not otherwise understand or do what is right. Thus conservatism moves towards an authoritarian, conformist society, based upon the rule of allegedly aristocratic minds. This has been its traditional pattern. This is, on the whole, its present practice.

Liberalism differs from conservatism most sharply in its insistence on the value of individual liberty, and concomitantly on the value of freedom of inquiry and of expression. It may, though it need not, deny that absolute truths, at least with respect to the ''right'' political principles, are known; but whether these truths are known or not, liberalism insists nonetheless on the freedom to examine them, to subject them to empirical and logical criticism, and to expose them to the challenge of conflicting ideas. Skepticism about ultimate values, that is to say, is often associated with the liberal creed; but while it is appropriate to that creed it is not necessary to it. Individual liberty, however, with all that this implies in the way of cultural diversity or nonconformity in cultural and intellectual life, is indispensable to the liberal idea.

Insofar as liberalism repudiates the conservative claim to absolute and infallible truth, it rests on the assumption that man is born not stupid but infinitely ignorant, and that however much he may learn in his very short span of life, the things he learns amount to but a small portion of what there is to be be known. Always the things he does not know are greater than the things he does know. Consequently, the beliefs he holds to be true may prove, on the basis of later knowledge, to be erroneous or only partially true. Awareness of this fact makes for a certain measure of humility; it also leads to a commitment to the methods of rational inquiry, rather than to the specific results that may at any one time emerge from such inquiry. The basic value of the liberal is, from this standpoint, the value of free inquiry; his basic attitude, the skeptical, or at least the inquiring, mind. . . .

Liberalism need not, however, be identified only with this skeptical approach to knowledge. It is altogether possible for one to believe that the truth is known and still hold to a liberal defense of toleration. In part, this rests on . . . one's confidence in the validity of his position, along with a conviction that opinion should be countered only by opinion, not by force. . . . In part, however, it rests on the recognition that in a society constituted of diverse men and groups many may claim to know the truth. Though all cannot be right, the political problem is to deal with a situation in which all believe they are right. Authoritarians provide a simple method of resolving this difficulty: The ''right,'' that is, the most powerful, group suppresses the others. But since force is irrelevant to truth, the most powerful group may not in fact be the group that is right. Hence reason dictates a solution other than force. This solution, for the liberal, is twofold. On the one hand, he would have the state leave these different groups alone. Where it is possible for each group to pursue its own truths, its own values, without infringing upon or denying the values of the other, there is a *prima facie* case for freedom. To this extent, at least, the state is a limited state. On the other hand, where such differences produce conflicts, the liberal would seek to negotiate these conflicts through free debate and free criticism in the marketplace of opinion. This does not, of course, assure the victory of the ''right'' view, but it gives the ''right'' view its maximum opportunity to prevail. And unless one is prepared to maintain that evidence and logic generally lead men to the wrong conclusions, it is difficult for the liberal to understand why so rational and peaceful a method of resolving differences is inappropriate, why it is better, say, to resort to mutual slaughter. Even if the "wrong" view should carry the day, there remains, through this method, full opportunity to continue to criticize and to show, with the added knowledge of experience, that it requires correction.

The ultimate argument of the liberal in this context, however, is his belief that individual liberty is a good in itself. What defines a man, according to an ancient teaching, is his reason. Now for reason to be exercised, a choice must exist. There can be no choices without alternatives, and there can be no alternatives without liberty. To deny individual liberty, either in the presentation of alternatives or the making of choices, is to deny an individual that which constitutes his humanity. Instead of his right to exercise his reason, someone else's reason is exercised for him. He is then not a man but a child. If he is to be a man, he must be free—to inquire, to consider diverse possibilities, to choose among them, and to pursue, so far as he can, his own way or style of life. From these conflicting ideas and practices, liberalism believes, men can learn and mutually aid one another to grow. Without these, there can be only a deadening uniformity. Individual liberty, and its consequent diversities, becomes then a cardinal principle of liberalism.

It is not to be denied that equality and liberty, both central tenets of liberalism, stand at times in a state of tension. Equality of opportunity, for example, may well run into conflict with the liberty of a parent to raise his child with the benefit of whatever advantages he may be able to give him. Then men must choose between equally ultimate values, and this is admittedly not an easy choice. But this is not a problem unique to liberals, and what liberals can well argue is that through freedom of inquiry and expression men can more rationally and peacefully negotiate these conflicts.

In sum, then, what distinguishes liberalism from conservatism is that, politically, liberalism stands for democracy and the equality of men, while conservatism inclines toward oligarchy based on certain alleged inequalities of men; economically, liberalism represents the interests of the lower classes and argues for equality of opportunity and the protection of human rights, while conservatism is associated with the interests of the upper classes and defends vested property rights; intellectually, liberalism is committed to individual liberty and the freedoms of inquiry and expression, while conservatism is far more concerned with the applications of an already existing objective Truth and the consequent curbing of erroneous and pernicious doctrines. It would be misleading to imply that all liberals, much less all so-called liberal states, affirm and consistently practice all these aspects of the liberal creed, or that conservatives do so with respect to their doctrines. But as categories of analysis rather than as descriptions of actual men or groups, the elements that make up this multidimensional understanding of liberalism and conservatism may enable us more easily to comprehend and to identify what it is that men and groups actually do.

14 JOHN RAWLS

With the publication of *A Theory of Justice* in 1971, John Rawls revived the concept of the social contract as a major intellectual component of liberalism. The social contract was an important element in the thinking of John Locke and other early liberals. Locke needed a *social* contract in order to bolster his claim that *political* ideas and institutions were human products and so under human control. The concept of a society-wide agreement was also the basis of early liberal justifications of political obligation. People could be called upon to obey those institutions or laws to which they had consented. But before people could consent to be governed, there had to be a "people," and the social contract idea both explained how a "people" could exist separate from government and how they could act together to commit themselves morally to the decisions which the institutions of such a government would make. In addition, a social contract was impossible except among responsible persons, and the early liberals had need of a doctrine of government which would build upon the notion of individual responsibility.

Beginning with the philosopher David Hume (1711-1776), critics of the social contract idea attacked its historical validity and its moral adequacy. The second criticism was the more serious. If one generation of Americans had consented to the Constitution, for example, what about those generations who weren't alive when the Constitution was ratified but who nevertheless have been expected (or forced) to obey the law? And why should a contract, *simply because it is a contract*, be binding? If contracts determine what is right and what is not, then how could a "contract" between a mob leader and a hired killer be wrong? Wrong such contracts most certainly are, but to explain finally why they are wrong you must go beyond the act of contracting itself. Locke's social contract formed around some values (such as private property) and ignored others. Why? The critics of Locke said the answer—if indeed there were an answer—could not be found in the idea of contract alone.

Liberals abandoned the social contract idea in the late nineteenth century because they had no satisfactory answers to such criticisms. *A Theory of Justice* attempts to provide those answers. Rawls wants to *demonstrate*, to prove, that the right type of contractual setting will produce a contract with basic rules that are ethically sound. His goal is to show that a people can freely choose principles which are right and that a government can be established upon such principles. Rawls denies that liberal ideas of justice must be either utilitarian or the product of majority sentiment. He has, in so doing, broken new ground for liberal political philosophy.

A THEORY OF JUSTICE*

The Main Idea of the Theory of Justice

My aim is to present a conception of justice which generalizes and carries to a higher level of abstraction the familiar theory of the social contract as found, say, in Locke, Rousseau, and Kant.[1] In order to do this we are not to think of the original contract as one to enter a particular society or to set up a particular form of government. Rather, the guiding idea is that the principles of justice for the basic structure of society are the object of the original agreement. They are the principles that free and rational persons concerned to further their own interests would accept in an initial position of equality as defining the fundamental terms of their association. These principles are to regulate all further agreements; they specify the kinds of social cooperation that can be entered into and the forms of government that can be established. This way of regarding the principles of justice I shall call justice as fairness.

Thus we are to imagine that those who engage in social cooperation choose together, in one joint act, the principles which are to assign basic rights and duties and to determine the division of social benefits. Men are to decide in advance how they are to regulate their claims against one another and what is to be the foundation charter of their society. Just as each person must decide by rational reflection what constitutes his good, that is, the system of ends which it is rational for him to pursue, so a group of persons must decide once and for all what is to count among them as just and unjust. The choice which rational men would make in this hypothetical situation of equal liberty, assuming for the present that this choice problem has a solution, determines the principles of justice.

In justice as fairness the original position of equality corresponds to the state of nature in the traditional theory of the social contract. This original position is not, of course, thought of as an actual historical state of affairs, much less as a primitive condition of culture. It is understood as a purely hypothetical situation characterized so as to lead to a certain conception of justice. Among the essential features of this situation is that no one knows his place in society, his class position or social status, nor does any one know his fortune in the distribution of natural assets and abilities, his intelligence, strength, and the like. I shall even assume that the parties do not know their conceptions of the good or their special psychological propensities. The principles of justice are chosen behind a veil of ignorance. This ensures that no one is advantaged or disadvantaged in the choice of principles by the outcome of natural chance or the contingency of social cir-

---

A Theory of Justice (Cambridge, Mass.: Harvard University Press, 1971), pp. 11-22, 60-61, 206-8. Reprinted by Permission of The Belknap Press of Harvard University Press and The Clarendon Press (Oxford), Copyright © 1971 by the President and Fellows of Harvard College.

cumstances. Since all are similarly situated and no one is able to design principles to favor his particular condition, the principles of justice are the result of a fair agreement or bargain. For given the circumstances of the original position, the symmetry of everyone's relations to each other, this initial situation is fair between individuals as moral persons, that is, as rational beings with their own ends and capable, I shall assume, of a sense of justice. The original position is, one might say, the appropriate initial status quo, and thus the fundamental agreements reached in it are fair. This explains the propriety of the name "justice as fairness": it conveys the idea that the principles of justice are agreed to in an initial situation that is fair. The name does not mean that the concepts of justice and fairness are the same, any more than the phrase "poetry as metaphor" means that the concepts of poetry and metaphor are the same.

Justice as fairness begins, as I have said, with one of the most general of all choices which persons might make together, namely, with the choice of the first principles of a conception of justice which is to regulate all subsequent criticism and reform of institutions. Then, having chosen a conception of justice, we can suppose that they are to choose a constitution and a legislature to enact laws, and so on, all in accordance with the principles of justice initially agreed upon. Our social situation is just if it is such that by this sequence of hypothetical agreements we would have contracted into the general system of rules which defines it. Moreover, assuming that the original position does determine a set of principles (that is, that a particular conception of justice would be chosen), it will then be true that whenever social institutions satisfy these principles those engaged in them can say to one another that they are cooperating on terms to which they would agree if they were free and equal persons whose relations with respect to one another were fair. They could all view their arrangements as meeting the stipulations which they would acknowledge in an initial situation that embodies widely accepted and reasonable constraints on the choice of principles. The general recognition of this fact would provide the basis for a public acceptance of the corresponding principles of justice. No society can, of course, be a scheme of cooperation which men enter voluntarily in a literal sense; each person finds himself placed at birth in some particular position in some particular society, and the nature of this position materially affects his life prospects. Yet a society satisfying the principles of justice as fairness comes as close as a society can to being a voluntary scheme, for it meets the principles which free and equal persons would assent to under circumstances that are fair. In this sense its members are autonomous and the obligations they recognize self-imposed.

One feature of justice as fairness is to think of the parties in the initial situation as rational and mutually disinterested. This does not mean that the parties are egoists, that is, individuals with only certain kinds of interests, say in wealth, prestige, and domination. But they are conceived as not taking an interest in one another's interests. They are to presume that even their spiritual aims may be opposed, in the way that the aims of those of different religions may be opposed.

Moreover, the concept of rationality must be interpreted as far as possible in the narrow sense, standard in economic theory, of taking the most effective means to given ends. . . .

In working out the conception of justice as fairness one main task clearly is to determine which principles of justice would be chosen in the original position. To do this we must describe this situation in some detail and formulate with care the problem of choice which it presents. These matters I shall take up in the immediately succeeding chapters. It may be observed, however, that once the principles of justice are thought of as arising from an original agreement in a situation of equality, it is an open question whether the principle of utility would be acknowledged. Offhand it hardly seems likely that persons who view themselves as equals, entitled to press their claims upon one another, would agree to a principle which may require lesser life prospects for some simply for the sake of a greater sum of advantages enjoyed by others. Since each desires to protect his interests, his capacity to advance his conception of the good, no one has a reason to acquiesce in an enduring loss for himself in order to bring about a greater net balance of satisfaction. In the absence of strong and lasting benevolent impulses, a rational man would not accept a basic structure merely because it maximized the algebraic sum of advantages irrespective of its permanent effects on his own basic rights and interests. Thus it seems that the principle of utility is incompatible with the conception of social cooperation among equals for mutual advantage. It appears to be inconsistent with the idea of reciprocity implicit in the notion of a well-ordered society. . . .

I shall maintain instead that the persons in the initial situation would choose two rather different principles: the first requires equality in the assignment of basic rights and duties, while the second holds that social and economic inequalities, for example inequalities of wealth and authority, are just only if they result in compensating benefits for everyone, and in particular for the least advantaged members of society. These principles rule out justifying institutions on the grounds that the hardships of some are offset by a greater good in the aggregate. It may be expedient but it is not just that some should have less in order that others may prosper. But there is no injustice in the greater benefits earned by a few provided that the situation of persons not so fortunate is thereby improved. The intuitive idea is that since everyone's well-being depends upon a scheme of cooperation without which no one could have a satisfactory life, the division of advantages should be such as to draw forth the willing cooperation of everyone taking part in it, including those less well situated. Yet this can be expected only if reasonable terms are proposed. The two principles mentioned seem to be a fair agreement on the basis of which those better endowed, or more fortunate in their social position, neither of which we can be said to deserve, could expect the willing cooperation of others when some workable scheme is a necessary condition of the welfare of all. Once we decide to look for a conception of justice that nullifies the accidents of natural endowment and the contingencies of social cir-

cumstance as counters in quest for political and economic advantage, we are led
to these principles. They express the result of leaving aside those aspects of the
social world that seem arbitrary from a moral point of view.

The problem of the choice of principles, however, is extremely difficult. I do
not expect the answer I shall suggest to be convincing to everyone. It is, therefore, worth noting from the outset that justice as fairness, like other contract
views, consists of two parts: (1) an interpretation of the initial situation and of the
problem of choice posed there, and (2) a set of principles which, it is argued,
would be agreed to. One may accept the first part of the theory (or some variant
thereof), but not the other, and conversely. The concept of the initial contractual
situation may seem reasonable although the particular principles proposed are
rejected. To be sure, I want to maintain that the most appropriate conception of
this situation does lead to principles of justice contrary to utilitarianism and
perfectionism, and therefore that the contract doctrine provides an alternative to
these views. Still, one may dispute this contention even though one grants that the
contractarian method is a useful way of studying ethical theories and of setting
forth their underlying assumptions.

Justice as fairness is an example of what I have called a contract theory. . . . As
I have mentioned, to understand it one has to keep in mind that it implies a certain
level of abstraction. In particular, the content of the relevant agreement is not to
enter a given society or to adopt a given form of government, but to accept certain
moral principles. Moreover, the undertakings referred to are purely hypothetical:
a contract view holds that certain principles would be accepted in a well-defined
initial situation.

The merit of the contract terminology is that it conveys the idea that principles
of justice may be conceived as principles that would be chosen by rational persons, and that in this way conceptions of justice may be explained and justified.
The theory of justice is a part, perhaps the most significant part, of the theory of
rational choice. Furthermore, principles of justice deal with conflicting claims
upon the advantages won by social cooperation; they apply to the relations among
several persons or groups. The word "contract" suggests this plurality as well as
the condition that the appropriate division of advantages must be in accordance
with principles acceptable to all parties. The condition of publicity for principles
of justice is also connoted by the contract phraseology. Thus, if these principles
are the outcome of an agreement, citizens have a knowledge of the principles that
others follow. It is characteristic of contract theories to stress the public nature of
political principles. . . .

4. The Original Position and Justification

I have said that the original position is the appropriate initial status quo which
insures that the fundamental agreements reached in it are fair. This fact yields the

name "justice as fairness." It is clear, then, that I want to say that one conception of justice is more reasonable than another, or justifiable with respect to it, if rational persons in the initial situation would choose its principles over those of the other for the role of justice. Conceptions of justice are to be ranked by their acceptability to persons so circumstanced. Understood in this way the question of justification is settled by working out a problem of deliberation: we have to ascertain which principles it would be rational to adopt given the contractual situation. This connects the theory of justice with the theory of rational choice. . . .

. . . The aim is to rule out those principles that it would be rational to propose for acceptance, however little the chance of success, only if one knew certain things that are irrelevant from the standpoint of justice. For example, if a man knew that he was wealthy, he might find it rational to advance the principle that various taxes for welfare measures be counted unjust; if he knew that he was poor, he would most likely propose the contrary principle. To represent the desired restrictions one imagines a situation in which everyone is deprived of this sort of information. One excludes the knowledge of those contingencies which sets men at odds and allows them to be guided by their prejudices. In this manner the veil of ignorance is arrived at in a natural way. This concept should cause no difficulty if we keep in mind the constraints on arguments that it is meant to express. At any time we can enter the original position, so to speak, simply by following a certain procedure, namely, by arguing for principles of justice in accordance with these restrictions.

It seems reasonable to suppose that the parties in the original position are equal. That is, all have the same rights in the procedure for choosing principles; each can make proposals, submit reasons for their acceptance, and so on. Obviously the purpose of these conditions is to represent equality between human beings as moral persons, as creatures having a conception of their good and capable of a sense of justice. The basis of equality is taken to be similarity in these two respects. Systems of ends are not ranked in value; and each man is presumed to have the requisite ability to understand and to act upon whatever principles are adopted. Together with the veil of ignorance, these conditions define the principles of justice as those which rational persons concerned to advance their interests would consent to as equals when none are known to be advantaged or disadvantaged by social and natural contingencies.

There is, however, another side to justifying a particular description of the original position. This is to see if the principles which would be chosen match our considered convictions of justice or extend them in an acceptable way. We can note whether applying these principles would lead us to make the same judgments about the basic structure of society which we now make intuitively and in which we have the greatest confidence; or whether, in cases where our present judgments are in doubt and given with hesitation, these principles offer a resolution which we can affirm on reflection. There are questions which we feel sure must be answered in a certain way. For example, we are confident that religious intolerance and racial discrimination are unjust. We think that we have examined these things with care and have reached what we believe is an impartial judgment not likely to be distorted by an excessive attention to our own interests. These convictions are provisional fixed points which we presume any conception of justice must fit. But we have much less assurance as to what is the correct distribution of wealth and authority. Here we may be looking for a way to remove our doubts. We can check an interpretation of the initial situation, then, by the capacity of its principles to accommodate our firmest convictions and to provide guidance where guidance is needed. . . .

I do not claim for the principles of justice proposed that they are necessary truths or derivable from such truths. A conception of justice cannot be deduced from self-evident premises or conditions on principles; instead, its justification is a matter of the mutual support of many considerations, of everything fitting together into one coherent view.

A final comment. We shall want to say that certain principles of justice are justified because they would be agreed to in an initial situation of equality. I have emphasized that this original position is purely hypothetical. It is natural to ask why, if this agreement is never actually entered into, we should take any interest in these principles, moral or otherwise. The answer is that the conditions embodied in the description of the original position are ones that we do in fact accept. Or if we do not, then perhaps we can be persuaded to do so by philosophical reflection. Each aspect of the contractual situation can be given supporting grounds. Thus what we shall do is to collect together into one conception a number of conditions on principles that we are ready upon due consideration to recognize as reasonable. These constraints express what we are prepared to regard as limits on fair terms of social cooperation. One way to look at the idea of the original position, therefore, is to see it as an expository device which sums up the meaning of these conditions and helps us to extract their consequences. On the other hand, this conception is also an intuitive notion that suggests its own elaboration, so that led on by it we are drawn to define more clearly the standpoint from which we can best interpret moral relationships. We need a conception that enables us to envision our objective from afar: the intuitive notion of the original position is to do this for us. . . .

II. Two Principles of Justice

I shall now state in a provisional form the two principles of justice that I believe would be chosen in the original position. . . .

The first statement of the two principles reads as follows:

First: each person is to have an equal right to the most extensive basic liberty compatible with a similar liberty for others.

Second: social and economic inequalities are to be arranged so that they are both (a) reasonably expected to be to everyone's advantage, and (b) attached to positions and offices open to all. . . .

By the way of general comment, these principles primarily apply, as I have said, to the basic structure of society. They are to govern the assignment of rights and duties and to regulate the distribution of social and economic advantages. As their formulation suggests, these principles presuppose that the social structure can be divided into two more or less distinct parts, the first principle applying to the one, the second to the other. They distinguish between those aspects of the social system that define and secure the equal liberties of citizenship and those that specify and establish social and economic inequalities. The basic liberties of citizens are, roughly speaking, political liberty (the right to vote and to be eligible for public office) together with freedom of speech and assembly; liberty of conscience and freedom of thought; freedom of the person along with the right to hold (personal) property; and freedom from arbitrary arrest and seizure as defined by the concept of the rule of law. These liberties are all required to be equal by the first principle, since citizens of a just society are to have the same basic rights.

The second principle applies, in the first approximation, to the distribution of income and wealth and to the design of organizations that make use of differences in authority and responsibility, or chains of command. While the distribution of wealth and income need not be equal, it must be to everyone's advantage, and at the same time, positions of authority and offices of command must be accessible to all. One applies the second principle by holding positions open, and then, subject to this constraint, arranges social and economic inequalities so that everyone benefits.

These principles are to be arranged in a serial order with the first principle prior to the second. This ordering means that a departure from the institutions of equal liberty required by the first principle cannot be justified by, or compensated for, by greater social and economic advantages. The distribution of wealth and income, and the hierarchies of authority, must be consistent with both the liberties of equal citizenship and equality of opportunity. . . .

The question of equal liberty of conscience is settled. It is one of the fixed points of our considered judgments of justice. But precisely because of this fact it illustrates the nature of the argument for the principle of equal liberty. The reasoning in this case can be generalized to apply to other freedoms, although not always with the same force. Turning then to liberty of conscience, it seems evident that the parties must choose principles that secure the integrity of their religious and moral freedom. They do not know, of course, what their religious or moral convictions are, or what is the particular content of their moral or religious obligations as they interpret them. Indeed, they do not know that they think of themselves as having such obligations. The possibility that they do suffices for the argument, although I shall make the stronger assumption. Further, the parties do not know how their religious or moral view fares in their society, whether, for example, it is in the majority or the minority. All they know is that they have obligations which they interpret in this way. The question they are to decide is which principle they should adopt to regulate the liberties of citizens in regard to their fundamental religious, moral, and philosophical interests.

Now it seems that equal liberty of conscience is the only principle that the persons in the original position can acknowledge. They cannot take chances with their liberty by permitting the dominant religious or moral doctrine to persecute or to suppress others if it wishes. Even granting (what may be questioned) that it is more probable than not that one will turn out to belong to the majority (if a majority exists), to gamble in this way would show that one did not take one's religious or moral convictions seriously, or highly value the liberty to examine one's beliefs. Nor on the other hand, could the parties consent to the principle of utility. In this case their freedom would be subject to the calculus of social interests and they would be authorizing its restriction if this would lead to a greater net balance of satisfaction. . . .

Moreover, the initial agreement on the principle of equal liberty is final. An individual recognizing religious and moral obligations regards them as binding absolutely in the sense that he cannot qualify his fulfillment of them for the sake of greater means for promoting his other interests. Greater economic and social benefits are not a sufficient reason for accepting less than equal liberty. It seems possible to consent to an unequal liberty only if there is a threat of coercion which it is unwise to resist from the standpoint of liberty itself. For example, the situation may be one in which a person's religion or his moral view will be tolerated provided that he does not protest, whereas claiming an equal liberty will bring greater repression that cannot be effectively opposed. But from the perspective of the original position there is no way of ascertaining the relative strength of various doctrines and so these considerations do not arise. The veil of ignorance leads to an agreement on the principle of equal liberty; and the strength of religious and moral obligations as men interpret them seems to require that the two principles be put in serial order, at least when applied to freedom of conscience.

It may be said against the principle of equal liberty that religious sects, say, cannot acknowledge any principle at all for limiting their claims on one another. The duty to religious and divine law being absolute, no understanding among persons of different faiths is permissible from a religious point of view. Certainly men have often acted as if they held this doctrine. It is unnecessary, however, to argue against it. It suffices that if any principle can be agreed to, it must be that of equal liberty. A person may indeed think that others ought to recognize the same beliefs and first principles that he does, and that by not doing so they are grievously in error and miss the way to their salvation. But an understanding of religious obligation and of philosophical and moral first principles shows that we cannot expect others to acquiesce in an inferior liberty. Much less can we ask them to recognize us as the proper interpreter of their religious duties or moral obligations.

SECTION FOUR

Liberalism and Laissez-Faire Economics

Laissez-faire is a theory of economics and a theory of politics. It argues that freedom to pursue your self-interest is natural and the necessary condition for individual and social good, development, and advancement. This economic argument has a significant political content. Political components include the political-social assumptions and preferences of authors, the conditions necessary to achieve the policy or system reflected in the economic theory, and the political-social results of attempts to implement the theory.

The authors in this section accepted the basic values of liberalism: liberty, individualism, tolerance, and the notion that people have the potential to achieve their own ends. They assumed that the market was the major arena of freedom, that it was in fact free, that no one could (or should) control it and that government and governmental interference in the free market were the major sources of coercion and inefficiency. In more extreme statements, such as those by Spencer and his American disciple William Graham Sumner, they sometimes saw the market and economic activity as the primary arena and focus for liberty. Though they did not agree on the exact area within which the market best functioned, they agreed on the principle that governmental interference would upset both freedom and efficiency. Thus the theory of a free market carried with it a strong statement of what government may and may not do. Government was generally limited to protecting people from crime, enforcing contracts, providing a limited range of public works or services, and national defense. Individuals and small groups could not do these things profitably for themselves. More extensive involvement in the economy would upset individual freedom and the natural operation of the market. Laissez-faire economics became political in its effort to eliminate politics, incorporate much political activity into the economy, or at least reduce the role and place of government.

Laissez-faire theorists assumed that there is a natural order which tends toward harmony. They agreed the economy is self-regulating, requiring little or no outside intervention to make it work. Freedom is a natural law of economic advancement, leading to natural results. Thus the division of labor, competition, free markets, trade, and economic activity in general were natural. In this they also assumed a specific picture of human nature. It was based on individualism, the assumption that people are naturally eager to promote their self-interest and that they are naturally competitive. Being natural, these drives should be allowed free expression. People entered society not for a great common enterprise but to provide a framework within which to pursue their own interest. Free pursuit of self-interest would tend toward producing natural harmony, order, justice, and a distribution of rewards based solely on what each person contributed to a natural, competitive economic process. The wages, dividends, profits, and rents which people received depended, therefore, under a system of liberty, on the supply and demand for whatever each person had to offer. Nothing could artificially raise or successfully lower this reward. Arbitrary efforts to do so would only rob some people of their liberty and property while reducing production, employment, and competition. Not only does this lead to the conclusion that a limited government is normal and natural but also that a person's position and rewards are due to his or her contribution to a free, natural, and impersonal economic process. Thus each individual is responsible for whatever rewards he or she receives. Barring accidents, which private charity may alleviate, wealth and poverty are completely natural. Again, the need for strong government is removed.

Such doctrines had important results. Initially they were extremely liberating, helping to upset the remnants of medieval and mercantilist control which retarded growth of individual and community wealth. Laissez-faire ideas changed traditional relations, freeing some individuals from group limitations. They also led to greater emphasis on private wealth and enjoyment of wealth, with little or no sense of obligation to others. Laissez-faire thinking encouraged the investment and risk-taking which characterized the industrial revolution. But the doctrine, which demanded that freedom lies in pursuing your self-interest above all else, encouraged extremes of wealth and poverty, huge concentrations of wealth, massive and unprecedented social transformation, destruction of freedom for some, ignoring the common interest and, some charged, inefficiency.

Laissez-faire thinkers did not accept the same policies. The writers in this section were much more subtle and aware of politics than were the people who popularized their doctrine. They were not merely apologists for big business. Laissez-faire is not a single theory of political economy but many related theories sharing common assumptions. There are significant differences between writers. Thus Adam Smith allowed government a larger role than did Herbert Spencer. All agreed, however, that there are natural economic rules or laws which we cannot safely ignore. These selections examine both laissez-faire assumptions and the political-social results of following natural economic laws and relations.

15 JOHN LOCKE

John Locke wrote extensively about economics as well as philosophy and politics. In this selection he discusses the origins of private property, providing one of the intellectual bases for later laissez-faire theory. His general emphasis on rights, freedom, and the dangers of government to freedom also supported laissez-faire conclusions and policies.

OF PROPERTY*

27. Though the Earth, and all inferior Creatures be common to all Men, yet every Man has a *Property* in his own *Person*: This no Body has any right to but himself. The *Labour* of his Body, and the *Work* of his Hands, we may say, are properly his. Whatsoever then he removes out of the State that Nature hath provided, and left it in, he hath mixed his *Labour* with, and joyned to it something that is his own, and thereby makes it his *Property*. It being by him removed from the common State Nature hath placed it in, it hath by this *Labour* something annexed to it, that excludes the common Right of other Men. For this *Labour* being the unquestionable Property of the Labourer, no Man but he can have a Right to what that is once joyned to, at least where there is enough, and as good left in common for others.

28. He that is nourished by the Acorns he pickt up under an Oak, or the Apples he gathered from the Trees in the Wood, has certainly appropriated them to himself. No body can deny but the Nourishment is his. I ask then, When did they begin to be his? When he digested? Or when he eat? Or when he boiled? Or when he brought them home? Or when he pickt them up? And 'tis plain, if the first gathering made them not his, nothing else could. That *Labour* put a Distinction between them and common: That added something to them more than Nature, the common Mother of all, had done, and so they became his private Right. . . . Thus the Grass my Horse has bit; the Turfs my Servant has cut; and the Ore I have digg'd in any Place, where I have a Right to them in common with others, become my *Property,* without the Assignation or Consent of any body. The *Labour* that was mine, removing them out of that common State they were in, hath *fixed* my *Property* in them.

---

*Second Treatise of Government, chapter 5.

30. Thus this Law of Reason makes the Deer that *Indian's* who hath killed it; 'tis allowed to be his Goods, who hath bestowed his Labour upon it, though before it was the common Right of every one. And amongst those who are counted the civiliz'd part of Mankind, who have made and multiplied positive Laws to determine *Property,* this original Law of Nature, for the *beginning of Property,* in what was before common, still takes place; and by vertue thereof, what Fish any one catches in the Ocean, that great and still remaining Common of Mankind; or what Ambergreise any one takes up here, is *by* the *Labour* that removes it out of that common State Nature left it in, *made* his *Property,* who takes that Pains about it. And even amongst us, the Hare that any one is hunting, is thought his who pursues her during the Chase. For being a Beast that is still looked upon as common, and no Man's private Possession; whoever has employ'd so much *Labour* about any of that kind, as to find and pursue her, has thereby removed her from the State of Nature, wherein she was common, and hath *begun a Property.*

31. It will perhaps be objected to this, That if gathering the Acorns, or other Fruits of the Earth, etc. makes a Right to them, then any one may *ingross* as much as he will. To which I answer, Not so. The same Law of Nature, that does by this means give us Property, does also *bound* that *Property* too. *God has given us all things richly,* 1 Tim. vi. 12. is the Voice of Reason confirmed by Inspiration. But how far has he given it us? *To enjoy.* As much as any one can make use of to any Advantage of Life before it spoils; so much he may by his Labour fix a Property in: Whatever is beyond this, is more than his Share, and belongs to others. Nothing was made by God for Man to spoil or destroy. And thus considering the Plenty of natural Provisions there was a long time in the World, and the few Spenders; and to how small a Part of that Provision the Industry of one Man could extend it self, and ingross it to the Prejudice of others; especially keeping within the *Bounds,* set by Reason, *of* what might serve for his *Use;* there could be then little room for Quarrels or Contentions about Property so establish'd.

32. But the *chief Matter of Property* being now not the Fruits of the Earth, and the Beasts that subsist on it, but *the Earth it Self;* as that which takes in and carries with it all the rest: I think it is plain, that *Property* in that too is acquir'd as the former. *As much Land* as a Man Tills, Plants, Improves, Cultivates, and can use the Product of, so much is his *Property.* He by his Labour does, as it were, inclose it from the Common. Nor will it invalidate his Right to say, Every body else has an equal Title to it, and therefore he cannot appropriate, he cannot inclose, without the Consent of all his Fellow-Commoners, all Mankind. God, when he gave the World in common to all Mankind, commanded Man also to labour, and the Penury of his Condition required it of him. God and his Reason commanded him to subdue the Earth, i.e. improve it for the Benefit of Life, and therein lay out something upon it that was his own, his Labour. He that in Obedience to this Command of God, subdued, tilled and sowed any part of it, thereby

annexed to it something that was his *Property,* which another had no Title to, nor could without Injury take from him.

46. The greatest part of *things really useful* to the life of Man, and such as the necessity of subsisting made the first Commoners of the World look after, as it doth the *Americans* now, *are* generally things of *Short Duration*; such as, if they are not consumed by use, will decay and perish of themselves: Gold, Silver and Diamonds, are things, that Fancy or Agreement hath put the Value on, more than real Use, and the necessary support of Life. Now of those good things which Nature hath provided in common, every one had a Right as hath been said to as much as he could use, and *Property* in all he could affect with his Labour; all that his *Industry* could extend to, to alter from the state Nature had put it in, was his. He that *gathered* a hundred Bushels of Acorns or Apples, had thereby a *Property* in them, they were his Goods as soon as gathered. He was only to look, that he used them before they spoiled, else he took more than his share, and robb'd others. And indeed it was a foolish thing, as well as dishonest, to hoard up more, than he could make use of. If he gave away a part to any body else, so that it perished not uselessly in his Possession, these he also made use of. And if he also bartered away Plumbs, that would have rotted in a Week, for Nuts that would last good for his eating a whole Year he did no injury, he wasted not the common stock; destroyed no part of the portion of Goods that belonged to others, so long as nothing perished uselessly in his hands. Again, If he would give his Nuts for a piece of Metal, pleased with its Colour; or exchange his Sheep for Shells, or Wooll for a Sparkling Peble or a Diamond, and keep those by him all his Life, he invaded not the Right of others, he might heap up as much of these durable things as he pleased; the *exceeding of the bounds of his just Property* not lying in the largeness of his Possession, but the perishing of any thing uselessly in it.

47. And thus *came in the use of Money,* some lasting thing that Men might keep without spoiling, and that by mutual Consent Men would take in exchange for the truly useful, but perishable supports of Life.

48. And as different degrees of Industry were apt to give Men Possessions in different Proportions, so this *Invention of Money* gave them the Opportunity to continue and enlarge them. . . . Where there is not something, both lasting and scarce, and so valuable, to be hoarded up, there Men will not be apt to enlarge their *Possessions of Land,* were it never so rich, never so free for them to take. For I ask, what would a Man value Ten thousand, or an Hundred thousand Acres of excellent *Land,* ready cultivated, and well stocked too with Cattle in the middle of the In-land Parts of *America,* where he had no hopes of Commerce with other parts of the World, to draw *Money* to him by the sale of the Product? It would not be worth the inclosing, and we should see him give up again to the wild Common of Nature, whatever was more than would supply the conveniencies of Life to be had there for him and his Family.

49. Thus in the Beginning all the World was *America,* and more so than that is

now; for no such thing as *Money* was any where known. Find out something that hath the *Use and Value of Money* amongst his Neighbours, you shall see the same Man will begin presently to *enlarge* his Possessions.

50. But since Gold and Silver, being little useful to the Life of Man in proportion to Food, Rayment, and Carriage, has its *Value* only from the consent of Men, whereof *Labour* yet *makes,* in great part, *the Measure,* it is plain, that Men have agreed to a disproportionate and unequal *Possession of the Earth,* they having by a tacit and voluntary Consent, found out a Way how a Man may fairly possess more Land, than he himself can use the Product of, by receiving in Exchange for the overplus Gold and Silver, which may be hoarded up without Injury to any one; these Metals not spoiling or decaying in the hands of the Possessor. This Partage of things in an inequality of private Possessions, Men have made practicable out of the bounds of Society, and without Compact only by putting a Value on Gold and Silver, and tacitly agreeing in the use of Money. For in Governments, the Laws regulate the right of Property, and the possession of Land is determined by positive Constitutions.

16 ADAM SMITH

Adam Smith (1723-1790) was the synthesizer and founder of laissez-faire political economy. Passionately concerned with economic and political freedom, he opposed all forms of arbitrary restraints. Smith considered liberty to be the essential condition to improve individual and public welfare. In *The Wealth of Nations,* first published in 1776, Smith argued that there is a tendency toward harmony between people, that everyone will benefit if each is allowed to pursue his own interest. He emphasized "natural liberty"—negative freedom—freedom from restraint and freedom to seek one's own interest, though he considered education to be essential to allow people to take advantage of their freedom. Self-interest, if honestly pursued, could benefit all—his famous "invisible hand"—because there is a natural order in human affairs which can produce harmony. Government interference and excessive spending (Book 2, Ch. 3) "retarded the natural progress of England towards wealth and improvement," wasted wealth, interfered with the natural working of the economy, and destroyed liberty. Though Smith wanted to get government out of economic relations he also realized that good government was necessary. It provides the framework for a free economy: justice, personal security, some public works, and protection from foreign enemies.

The Wealth of Nations has broad political and social significance. Smith considered pursuit of self-interest, individualism, competition, and a free market to be completely natural. Restraints of any kind produced waste. As with laissez-faire theory in general, Smith's economic theory is also political theory because it defines the area of legitimate governmental activity. The free market reduces the role and scope of government by claiming that many activities involving production, distribution, wealth, and class relations are subject to natural laws. Government becomes the realm of coercion and compulsion, both enemies of natural liberty. In the end, this leaves open the possibility for the growth of private power. Smith, however, is not an apologist for twentieth-century multinational corporations or other large concentrations of economic power. He wanted limited government because he thought that government intervention would cause monopoly, upsetting competition between many small producers and consumers, but he also warned that each producer's natural self-interest was to achieve monopoly.

In the selection that follows, Smith discusses the naturalness of the economy and the political-social requirements for a successful economy. This is one which allows each person freely to pursue his own self-interest—a laissez-faire economy.

THE WEALTH OF NATIONS*

Of the Division of Labour

It is the great multiplication of the productions of all the different arts, in consequence of the division of labour, which occasions, in a well-governed society, that universal opulence which extends itself to the lowest ranks of the people. Every workman has a great quantity of his own work to dispose of beyond what he himself has occasion for; and every other workman being exactly in the same situation, he is enabled to exchange a great quantity of his own goods for a great quantity, or, what comes to the same thing, for the price of a great quantity of theirs. He supplies them abundantly with what they have occasion for, and they accommodate him as amply with what he has occasion for, and a general plenty diffuses itself through all the different ranks of the society.

The Wealth of Nations in *The Works of Adam Smith, LL. D.* (London: 1812), Book 1, chapters 1, 2, 10; Book 4, chapters 2, 9; Book 5, chapter 1.

Observe the accommodation of the most common artificer or day-labourer in a civilized and thriving country, and you will perceive that the number of people of whose industry a part, though but a small part, has been employed in procuring him this accommodation, exceeds all computation. . . .

Of the Principle which gives Occasion to the Division of Labour

This division of labour, from which so many advantages are derived, is not originally the effect of any human wisdom, which foresees and intends that general opulence to which it gives occasion. It is the necessary, though very slow and gradual, consequence of a certain propensity in human nature which has in view no such extensive utility; the propensity to truck, barter, and exchange one thing for another.

Whether this propensity be one of those original principles in human nature, of which no further account can be given; or whether, as seems more probable, it be the necessary consequence of the faculties of reason and speech, it belongs not to our present subject to enquire. It is common to all men, and to be found in no other race of animals, which seem to know neither this nor any other species of contracts. . . . In civilized society he [man] stands at all times in need of the co-operation and assistance of great multitudes, while his whole life is scarce sufficient to gain the friendship of a few persons. In almost every other race of animals each individual, when it is grown up to maturity, is intirely independent, and in its natural state has occasion for the assistance of no other living creature. But man has almost constant occasion for the help of his brethren, and it is in vain for him to expect it from their benevolence only. He will be more likely to prevail if he can interest their self-love in his favour, and shew them that it is for their own advantage to do for him what he requires of them. Whoever offers to another a bargain of any kind, proposes to do this: Give me that which I want, and you shall have this which you want, is the meaning of every such offer; and it is in this manner that we obtain from one another the far greater part of those good offices which we stand in need of. It is not from the benevolence of the butcher, the brewer, or the baker, that we expect our dinner, but from their regard to their own interest. We address ourselves, not to their humanity but to their self-love, and never talk to them of our own necessities but of their advantages. Nobody but a beggar chuses to depend chiefly upon the benevolence of his fellow-citizens. Even a beggar does not depend upon it entirely. The charity of well-disposed people, indeed, supplies him with the whole fund of his subsistence. But though this principle ultimately provides him with all the necessaries of life which he has occasion for, it neither does nor can provide him with them as he has occasion for them. The greater part of his occasional wants are supplied in the same manner as those of other people, by treaty, by barter, and by purchase. With the money which one man gives him he purchases food. The old cloaths which another bestows upon him he exchanges for other old cloaths which suit him better, or for lodging, or for food, or for money, with which he can buy either food, cloaths, or lodging, as he has occasion.

As it is by treaty, by barter, and by purchase, that we obtain from one another the greater part of those mutual good offices which we stand in need of, so it is this same trucking disposition which originally gives occasion to the division of labour. In a tribe of hunters or shepherds a particular person makes bows and arrows, for example, with more readiness and dexterity than any other. He frequently exchanges them for cattle or for venison with his companions; and he finds at last that he can in this manner get more cattle and venison, than if he himself went to the field to catch them. From a regard to his own interest, therefore, the making of bows and arrows grows to be his chief business, and he becomes a sort of armourer. Another excels in making the frames and covers of their little huts or moveable houses. He is accustomed to be of use in this way to his neighbours, who reward him in the same manner with cattle and with venison, till at last he finds it his interest to dedicate himself entirely to this employment, and to become a sort of house-carpenter. In the same manner a third becomes a smith or a brazier; a fourth a tanner or dresser of hides or skins, the principal part of the clothing of savages. And thus the certainty of being able to exchange all that surplus part of the produce of his own labour, which is over and above his own consumption, for such parts of the produce of other men's labour as he may have occasion for, encourages every man to apply himself to a particular occupation, and to cultivate and bring to perfection whatever talent or genius he may possess for that particular species of business.

The difference of natural talents in different men is, in reality, much less than we are aware of; and the very different genius which appears to distinguish men of different professions, when grown up to maturity, is not upon many occasions so much the cause, as the effect of the division of labour. The difference between the most dissimilar characters, between a philosopher and a common street porter, for example, seems to arise not so much from nature, as from habit, custom, and education. When they came into the world, and for the first six or eight years of their existence, they were, perhaps, very much alike, and neither their parents nor playfellows could perceive any remarkable difference. About that age, or soon after, they come to be employed in very different occupations. The difference of talents comes then to be taken notice of, and widens by degrees, till at last the vanity of the philosopher is willing to acknowledge scarce any resemblance. But without the disposition to truck, barter, and exchange, every man must have procured to himself every necessary and conveniency of life which he wanted. All must have had the same duties to perform, and the same work to do, and there could have been no such difference of employment as could alone give occasion to any great difference of talent.

As it is this disposition which forms that difference of talents, so remarkable among men of different professions, so it is this same disposition which renders that difference useful. . . . [T]he most dissimilar geniuses are of use to one another; the different produces of their respective talents, by the general disposition to truck, barter, and exchange, being brought, as it were, into a common stock, where every man may purchase whatever part of the produce of other men's talents he has occasion for.

Wages and Profit in the different Employments of Labour and Stock

The whole of the advantages and disadvantages of the different employments of labour and stock must, in the same neighbourhood, be either perfectly equal or continually tending to equality. If in the same neighbourhood, there was any employment evidently either more or less advantageous than the rest, so many people would crowd into it in the one case, and so many would desert it in the other, that its advantages would soon return to the level of other employments. This at least would be the case in a society where things were left to follow their natural course, where there was perfect liberty, and where every man was perfectly free both to chuse what occupation he thought proper, and to change it as often as he thought proper. Every man's interest would prompt him to seek the advantageous, and to shun the disadvantageous employment.

Pecuniary wages and profit, indeed, are everywhere in Europe extremely different according to the different employments of labour and stock. But this difference arises partly from certain circumstances in the employments themselves . . . and partly from the policy of Europe, which no-where leaves things at perfect liberty.

Inequalities arising from the Nature of the Employment themselves

The five following are the principal circumstances which, so far as I have been able to observe, make up for a small pecuniary gain in some employments, and counter-balance a great one in others: first, the agreeableness or disagreeableness of the employments themselves; secondly, the easiness and cheapness, or the difficulty and expence of learning them; thirdly, the constancy or inconstancy of employment in them; fourthly, the small or great trust which must be reposed in those who exercise them; and fifthly, the probability or improbability of success in them.

Inequalities occasioned by the Policy of Europe

. . . But the policy of Europe, by not leaving things at perfect liberty, occasions other inequalities of much greater importance.

It does this chiefly in the three following ways. First, by restraining the competition in some employments to a smaller number than would otherwise be disposed to enter into them; secondly, by increasing it in others beyond what it naturally would be; and, thirdly, by obstructing the free circulation of labour and stock, both from employment to employment and from place to place.

First, The policy of Europe occasions a very important inequality in the whole of the advantages and disadvantages of the different employments of labour and stock, by restraining the competition in some employments to a smaller number than might otherwise be disposed to enter into them.

The exclusive privileges of corporations are the principal means it makes use of for this purpose.

The exclusive privilege of an incorporated trade necessarily restrains the competition, in the town where it is established, to those who are free of the trade. To have served an apprenticeship in the town, under a master properly qualified, is commonly the necessary requisite for obtaining this freedom. The bye-laws of the corporation regulate sometimes the number of apprentices which any master is allowed to have, and almost always the number of years which each apprentice is obliged to serve. The intention of both regulations is to restrain the competition to a much smaller number than might otherwise be disposed to enter into the trade. The limitation of the number of apprentices restrains it directly. A long term of apprenticeship restrains it more indirectly, but as effectually, by increasing the expence of education.

The pretence that corporations are necessary for the better government of the trade, is without any foundation. The real and effectual discipline which is exercised over a workman, is not that of his corporation, but that of his customers. It is the fear of losing their employment which restrains his frauds and corrects his negligence. An exclusive corporation necessarily weakens the force of this discipline. A particular set of workmen must then be employed, let them behave well or ill. . . .

Secondly, The policy of Europe, by increasing the competition in some employments beyond what it naturally would be, occasions another inequality of an opposite kind in the whole of the advantages and disadvantages of the different employments of labour and stock.

It has been considered as of so much importance that a proper number of young people should be educated for certain professions, that sometimes the public, and sometimes the piety of private founders have established many pensions, scholarships, exhibitions, bursaries, etc. for this purpose, which draw many more people into those trades than could otherwise pretend to follow them. In all christian countries, I believe the education of the greater part of churchmen is paid for in this manner. Very few of them are educated altogether at their own expence. The long, tedious and expensive education, therefore, of those who are, will not always procure them a suitable reward, the church being crowded with people who, in order to get employment, are willing to accept of a much smaller recompence than what such an education would otherwise have entitled them to. . . .

Thirdly, The policy of Europe, by obstructing the free circulation of labour and stock both from employment to employment, and from place to place, occasions in some cases a very inconvenient inequality in the whole of the advantages and disadvantages of their different employments.

The statute of apprenticeship obstructs the free circulation of labour from one employment to another, even in the same place. The exclusive privileges of corporations obstruct it from one place to another, even in the same employment.

It frequently happens that while high wages are given to the workmen in one manufacture, those in another are obliged to content themselves with bare subsistence. The one is in an advancing state, and has therefore a continual demand for new hands: the other is in a declining state, and the superabundance of hands is continually increasing. Those two manufactures may sometimes be in the same town, and sometimes in the same neighbourhood, without being able to lend the least assistance to one another. The statute of apprenticeship may oppose it in the one case, and both that and an exclusive corporation in the other. In many different manufactures, however, the operations are so much alike, that the workmen could easily change trades with one another, if those absurd laws did not hinder them. The arts of weaving plain linen and plain silk, for example, are almost entirely the same. That of weaving plain woollen is somewhat different; but the difference is so insignificant, that either a linen or a silk weaver might become a tolerable workman in a very few days. If any of those three capital manufactures, therefore, were decaying, the workmen might find a resource in one of the other two which was in a more prosperous condition; and their wages would neither rise too high in the thriving, nor sink too low in the decaying manufacture . . . wherever the statute of apprenticeship takes place, [workers] have no other choice but either to come upon the parish, or to work as common labourers, for which, by their habits, they are much worse qualified than for any sort of manufacture that bears any resemblance to their own. They generally, therefore, chuse to come upon the parish.

[Limits placed upon Government]

The general industry of the society never can exceed what the capital of the society can employ. As the number of workmen that can be kept in employment by any particular person must bear a certain proportion to his capital, so the number of those that can be continually employed by all the members of a great society, must bear a certain proportion to the whole capital of that society, and never can exceed that proportion. No regulation of commerce can increase the quantity of industry in any society beyond what its capital can maintain. It can only divert a part of it into a direction into which it might not otherwise have gone; and it is by no means certain that this artificial direction is likely to be more advantageous to the society than that into which it would have gone of its own accord.

Every individual is continually exerting himself to find out the most advantageous employment for whatever capital he can command. It is his own advantage, indeed, and not that of the society, which he has in view. But the study of his own advantage naturally, or rather necessarily leads him to prefer that employment which is most advantageous to the society.

First, every individual endeavours to employ his capital as near home as he can, and consequently as much as he can in the support of domestic industry; provided always that he can thereby obtain the ordinary, or not a great deal less than the ordinary profits of stocks.

Secondly, every individual who employs his capital in the support of domestic industry, necessarily endeavours so to direct that industry, that its produce may be of the greatest possible value.

The produce of industry is what it adds to the subject or materials upon which it is employed. In proportion as the value of this produce is great or small, so will likewise be the profits of the employer. But it is only for the sake of profit that any man employs a capital in the support of industry; and he will always, therefore, endeavour to employ it in the support of that industry of which the produce is likely to be of the greatest value, or to exchange for the greatest quantity either of money or of other goods.

But the annual revenue of every society is always precisely equal to the exchangeable value of the whole annual produce of its industry, or rather is precisely the same thing with that exchangeable value. As every individual, therefore, endeavours as much as he can both to employ his capital in the support of domestic industry, and so to direct that industry that its produce may be of the greatest value; every individual necessarily labours to render the annual revenue of the society as great as he can. He generally, indeed, neither intends to promote the public interest, nor knows how much he is promoting it. By preferring the support of domestic to that of foreign industry, he intends only his own security; and by directing that industry in such a manner as its produce may be of the greatest value, he intends only his own gain, and he is in this, as in many other cases, led by an invisible hand to promote an end which was no part of his intention. Nor is it always the worse for the society that it was no part of it. By pursuing his own interest he frequently promotes that of the society more effectually than when he really intends to promote it. I have never known much good done by those who affected to trade for the public good. It is an affectation, indeed, not very common among merchants, and very few words need be employed in dissuading them from it.

What is the species of domestic industry which his capital can employ, and of which the produce is likely to be of the greatest value, every individual, it is evident, can, in his local situation, judge much better than any statesman or lawgiver can do for him. The statesman, who should attempt to direct private people in what manner they ought to employ their capital would not only load himself with a most unnecessary attention, but assume an authority which could safely be trusted, not only to no single person, but to no council or senate whatever, and which would no-where be so dangerous as in the hands of a man who had folly and presumption enough to fancy himself fit to exercise it.

. . . [E]very system which endeavours, either, by extraordinary encouragements, to draw towards a particular species of industry a greater share of the capital of the society than what would naturally go to it; or, by extraordinary restraints, to force from a particular species of industry some share of the capital which would otherwise be employed in it; is in reality subversive of the great purpose which it means to promote. It retards, instead of accelerating, the progress of the society towards real wealth and greatness; and diminishes, instead of increasing, the real value of the annual produce of its land and labour.

All systems either of preference or of restraint, therefore, being thus completely taken away, the obvious and simple system of natural liberty establishes itself of its own accord. Every man, as long as he does not violate the laws of justice, is left perfectly free to pursue his own interest his own way, and to bring both his industry and capital into competition with those of any other man, or order of men. The Sovereign is completely discharged from a duty, in the attempting to perform which he must always be exposed to innumerable delusions, and for the proper performance of which no human wisdom or knowledge could ever be sufficient; the duty of superintending the industry of private people, and of directing it towards the employments most suitable to the interest of the society. According to the system of natural liberty, the Sovereign has only three duties to attend to; three duties of great importance, indeed, but plain and intelligible to common understandings: first, the duty of protecting the society from the violence and invasion of other independent societies; secondly, the duty of protecting, as far as possible, every member of the society from the injustice or oppression of every other member of it, or the duty of establishing an exact administration of justice; and, thirdly, the duty of erecting and maintaining certain public works and certain public institutions, which it can never be for the interest of any individual, or small number of individuals, to erect and maintain; because the profit could never repay the expence to any individual or small number of individuals, though it may frequently do much more than repay it to a great society.

The expence of defending the society, and that of supporting the dignity of the chief magistrate, are both laid out for the general benefit of the whole society. It is reasonable, therefore, that they should be defrayed by the general contribution of the whole society, all the different members contributing, as nearly as possible, in proportion to their respective abilities.

The expence of the administration of justice too, may, no doubt, be considered as laid out for the benefit of the whole society. There is no impropriety, therefore, in its being defrayed by the general contribution of the whole society. The persons, however, who give occasion to this expence are those who, by their injustice in one way or another, make it necessary to seek redress or protection from the courts of justice. The persons again most immediately benefited by this expence, are those whom the courts of justice either restore to their rights, or maintain in their rights. The expence of the administration of justice, therefore, may very properly be defrayed by the particular contribution of one or other, or both of those two different sets of persons, according as different occasions may require, that is, by the fees of court. It cannot be necessary to have recourse to the general contribution of the whole society, except for the conviction of those criminals who have not themselves any estate or fund sufficient for paying those fees.

Those local or provincial expences of which the benefit is local or provincial (what is laid out, for example, upon the police of a particular town or district) ought to be defrayed by a local or provincial revenue, and ought to be no burden upon the general revenue of the society. It is unjust that the whole society should contribute towards an expence of which the benefit is confined to a part of the society.

The expence of maintaining good roads and communications is, no doubt, beneficial to the whole society, and may, therefore, without any injustice, be defrayed by the general contribution of the whole society. This expence, however, is most immediately and directly beneficial to those who travel or carry goods from one place to another, and to those who consume such goods. The turnpike tolls in England, and the duties called peages in other countries, lay it altogether upon those two different sets of people, and thereby discharge the general revenue of the society from a very considerable burden.

The expence of the institutions for education and religious instruction, is likewise, no doubt, beneficial to the whole society, and may, therefore, without injustice, be defrayed by the general contribution of the whole society. This expence, however, might perhaps with equal propriety, and even with some advantage, be defrayed altogether by those who receive the immediate benefit of such education and instruction, or by the voluntary contribution of those who think they have occasion for either the one or the other.

When the institutions or public works which are beneficial to the whole society, either cannot be maintained altogether, or are not maintained altogether by the contribution of such particular members of the society as are most immediately benefited by them, the deficiency must, in most cases, be made up by the general contribution of the whole society. . . .

[Education]

In the progress of the division of labour, the employment of the far greater part of those who live by labour, that is, of the great body of the people, comes to be confined to a few very simple operations; frequently to one or two. But the understandings of the greater part of men are necessarily formed by their ordinary employments. The man whose whole life is spent in performing a few simple operations, of which the effects too are, perhaps, always the same, or very nearly the same, has no occasion to exert his understanding, or to exercise his invention in finding out expedients for removing difficulties which never occur. He naturally loses, therefore, the habit of such exertion, and generally becomes as stupid and ignorant as it is possible for a human creature to become. The torpor of his mind renders him, not only incapable of relishing or bearing a part in any rational conversation, but of conceiving any generous, noble, or tender sentiment, and consequently of forming any just judgment concerning many even of the ordinary duties of private life. Of the great and extensive interests of his country he is altogether incapable of judging; and unless very particular pains have been taken to render him otherwise, he is equally incapable of defending his country in war. The uniformity of his stationary life naturally corrupts the courage of his mind, and makes him regard with abhorrence the irregular, uncertain, and adventurous life of a soldier. It corrupts even the activity of his body, and renders him incapable of exerting his strength with vigour and perseverance, in any other employment than that to which he has been bred. His dexterity at his own particular trade seems, in this manner, to be acquired at the expence of his intellectual, social, and martial virtues. But in every improved and civilized society this is the state into which the labouring poor, that is, the great body of the people, must necessarily fall, unless government takes some pains to prevent it.

The education of the common people requires, perhaps, in a civilized and commercial society, the attention of the public more than that of people of some rank and fortune. People of some rank and fortune are generally eighteen or nineteen years of age before they enter upon that particular business, profession, or trade, by which they propose to distinguish themselves in the world. They have before that full time to acquire, or at least to fit themselves for afterwards acquiring, every accomplishment which can recommend them to the public esteem, or render them worthy of it. . . . If they are not always properly educated, it is seldom from the want of expence laid out upon their education; but from the improper application of that expence. . . . The employments too in which people of some rank or fortune spend the greater part of their lives, are not, like those of the common people, simple and uniform. They are almost all of them extremely complicated, and such as exercise the head more than the hands. The understandings of those who are engaged in such employments can seldom grow torpid from want of exercise. The employments of people of some rank and fortune, besides, are seldom such as harass them from morning to night. They generally have a good deal of leisure, during which they may perfect themselves in every branch either of useful or ornamental knowledge of which they may have laid the foundation, or for which they may have acquired some taste in the earlier part of life.

It is otherwise with the common people. They have little time to spare for education. Their parents can scarce afford to maintain them even in infancy. As soon as they are able to work, they must apply to some trade by which they can earn their subsistence. That trade too is generally so simple and uniform as to give little exercise to the understanding; while, at the same time, their labour is both so constant and so severe, that it leaves them little leisure and less inclination to apply to, or even to think of any thing else.

But though the common people cannot, in any civilized society, be so well instructed as people of some rank and fortune, the most essential parts of education, however, to read, write, and account, can be acquired at so early a period of life, that the greater part even of those who are to be bred to the lowest occupations, have time to acquire them before they can be employed in those occupations. For a very small expence the public can facilitate, can encourage, and can even impose upon almost the whole body of the people, the necessity of acquiring those most essential parts of education.

The public can facilitate this acquisition, by establishing in every parish or district a little school, where children may be taught for a reward so moderate, that even a common labourer may afford it; the master being partly, but not wholly paid by the public; because, if he was wholly, or even principally paid by it, he would soon learn to neglect his business. . . . If in those little schools the books, by which the children are taught to read, were a little more instructive than they commonly are; and if, instead of a little smattering of Latin . . . they were instructed in the elementary parts of geometry and mechanics, the literary education of this rank of people would perhaps be as complete as it can be. . . .

. . . A man without the proper use of the intellectual faculties of a man, is, if possible, more contemptible than even a coward, and seems to be mutilated and deformed in a still more essential part of the character of human nature. Though the state was to derive no advantage from the instruction of the inferior ranks of people, it would still deserve its attention that they should not be altogether uninstructed. The state, however, derives no inconsiderable advantage from their instruction. The more they are instructed, the less liable they are to the delusions of enthusiasm and superstition, which, among ignorant nations, frequently occasion the most dreadful disorders. An instructed and intelligent people, besides, are always more decent and orderly than an ignorant and stupid one. They feel themselves, each individually, more respectable, and more likely to obtain the respect of their lawful superiors, and they are therefore more disposed to respect those superiors. They are more disposed to examine, and more capable of seeing through the interested complaints of faction and sedition, and they are, upon that account, less apt to be misled into any wanton or unnecessary opposition to the measures of government. In free countries, where the safety of government depends very much upon the favourable judgment which the people may form of its conduct, it must surely be of the highest importance that they should not be disposed to judge rashly or capriciously concerning it.

17 THOMAS MALTHUS

In 1798, Thomas Robert Malthus (1766–1834) anonymously published the first edition of his *Essay on the Principle of Population as it Affects the Future Improvement of Society*. In it he denied the contention of people such as his father Daniel Malthus, the Marquis de Condorcet, and William Godwin that man and society are capable of perfection and population growth. Malthus stated that the food supply grows at a slower rate than population. Food shortages will limit population growth through starvation, vice, and misery, making perfection or even significant improvement impossible.

As with many people today who are concerned with the impact of resource depletion and population growth on the quality of life, Malthus drew definite political and social conclusions from his population ideas. He is an early advocate of political and economic laissez-faire. He believed that there are natural economic laws of production and distribution. One of these laws is that nature limited population growth through limiting the increase in food production. Though in his later editions Malthus stated that there are preventive checks to population growth—late marriage and chastity—which might improve individual welfare and society, still the positive checks of vice and misery would apply in most cases.

Because economic laws are natural, Malthus asserted, there is nothing government can do to aid the poor. Interference would only rob some people of their goods and liberty and worsen the situation by increasing the number to be fed without increasing the amount of food. Therefore we must allow natural economic relations to work themselves out. Poverty is due to overpopulation among the poor and can be eliminated only when the poor voluntarily limit their numbers. The rich and government were not responsible for poverty, could do nothing to improve the situation, and had no obligation to attempt to do so. Distribution was therefore natural. The selection below illustrates some of Malthus's political and social conclusions. His ideas were influential in the passage of a poor law reform bill in 1834, which overturned the traditional belief that the poor have a right to food and support.

An Essay on the Principle of Population*

Statement of the Subject.
Ratios of the Increase of Population and Food.

In an inquiry concerning the improvement of society, the mode of conducting the subject which naturally presents itself, is—

1. To investigate the causes that have hitherto impeded the progress of mankind towards happiness; an ,

2. To examine the probability of the total or partial removal of these causes in future.

. . . The principal object of the present essay is to examine the effects of one great cause intimately united with the very nature of man. . . .

The cause to which I allude, is the constant tendency in all animated life to increase beyond the nourishment prepared for it.

In the northern states of America, where the means of subsistence have been more ample, the manners of the people more pure, and the checks to early marriages fewer, than in any of the modern states of Europe, the population has been found to double itself, for above a century and a half successively, in less than twenty-five years. . . .

It may safely be pronounced, therefore, that population, when unchecked, goes on doubling itself every twenty-five years, or increases in a geometrical ratio.

The rate according to which the productions of the earth may be supposed to increase, will not be so easy to determine. Of this, however, we may be perfectly certain, that the ratio of their increase in a limited territory must be of a totally different nature from the ratio of the increase of population. . . . Man is necessarily confined in room. When acre has been added to acre till all the fertile land is occupied, the yearly increase of food must depend upon the melioration of the land already in possession. This is a fund, which, from the nature of all soils, instead of increasing, must be gradually diminishing. But population, could it be supplied with food, would go on with unexhausted vigour; and the increase of one period would furnish the power of a greater increase the next, and this without any limit.

If it be allowed that by the best possible policy, and great encouragements to agriculture, the average produce of the island [Britain] could be doubled in the first twenty-five years, it will be allowing, probably, a greater increase than could with reason be expected.

An Essay on the Principle of Population, 7th ed. (London, 1872), book 1, chapters 1, 2; book 3, chapters 5, 6; book 4, chapters 3, 6.

In the next twenty-five years, it is impossible to suppose that the produce could be quadrupled. It would be contrary to all our knowledge of the properties of land. The improvement of the barren parts would be a work of time and labour; and it must be evident to those who have the slightest acquaintance with agricultural subjects, that in proportion as cultivation extended, the additions that could yearly be made to the former average produce must be gradually and regularly diminishing. That we may be the better able to compare the increase of population and food, let us make a supposition, which, without pretending to accuracy, is clearly more favourable to the power of production in the earth than any experience we have had of its qualities will warrant.

Let us suppose that the yearly additions which might be made to the former average produce, instead of decreasing, which they certainly would do, were to remain the same; and that the produce of this island might be increased every twenty-five years, by a quantity equal to what it at present produces. The most enthusiastic speculator cannot suppose a greater increase than this. In a few centuries it would make every acre of land in the island like a garden.

If this supposition be applied to the whole earth, and if it be allowed that the subsistence for man which the earth affords might be increased every twenty-five years by a quantity equal to what it at present produces, this will be supposing a rate of increase much greater than we can imagine that any possible exertions of mankind could make it.

It may be fairly pronounced, therefore, that, considering the present average state of the earth, the means of subsistence, under circumstances the most favourable to human industry, could not possibly be made to increase faster than in an arithmetical ratio.

The necessary effects of these two different rates of increase, when brought together, will be very striking. Let us call the population of this island eleven millions; and suppose the present produce equal to the easy support of such a number. In the first twenty-five years the population would be twenty-two millions, and the food being also doubled, the means of subsistence would be equal to this increase. In the next twenty-five years, the population would be forty-four millions, and the means of subsistence only equal to the support of thirty-three millions. In the next period the population would be eighty-eight millions, and the means of subsistence just equal to the support of half that number. And, at the conclusion of the first century, the population would be a hundred and seventy-six millions, and the means of subsistence only equal to the support of fifty-five millions, leaving a population of a hundred and twenty-one millions totally unprovided for.

Taking the whole earth, instead of this island, emigration would of course be excluded; and, supposing the present population equal to a thousand millions, the human species would increase as the numbers 1, 2, 4, 8, 16, 32, 64, 128, 256; and subsistence as 1, 2, 3, 4, 5, 6, 7, 8, 9. In two centuries the population would be to the means of subsistence as 256 to 9; in three centuries as 4096 to 13, and in two thousand years the difference would be almost incalculable.

In this supposition no limits whatever are placed to the produce of the earth. It may increase for ever, and be greater than any assignable quantity; yet still the power of population being in every period so much superior, the increase of the human species can only be kept down to the level of the means of subsistence by the constant operation of the strong law of necessity, acting as a check upon the greater power.

Of the General Checks to Population, and the Mode of Their Operation

. . . [T]he following propositions are intended to be proved:—

1. Population is necessarily limited by the means of subsistence.

2. Population invariably increases where the means of subsistence increase, unless prevented by some very powerful and obvious checks.

3. These checks, and the checks which repress the superior power of population, and keep its effects on a level with the means of subsistence, are all resolvable into moral restraint, vice, and misery.

Of Poor-Laws

To remedy the frequent distresses of the poor, laws to enforce their relief have been instituted; and in the establishment of a general system of this kind England has particularly distinguished herself. But it is to be feared that though it may have alleviated a little the intensity of individual misfortune, it has spread the evil over a much larger surface.

It is a subject often started in conversation, and mentioned always as a matter of great surprise, that notwithstanding the immense sum which is annually collected for the poor in this country, there is still so much distress among them. . . . But a man who looks a little below the surface of things would be much more astonished if the fact were otherwise than it is observed to be, or even if a collection universally of eighteen shillings in the pound instead of four were materially to alter it. [A pound contained 20 shillings.]

Suppose that by a subscription of the rich, the eighteenpence or two shillings which men earn now were made up to five shillings, it might be imagined perhaps that they would then be able to live comfortably, and have a piece of meat every day for their dinner. But this would be a very false conclusion. The transfer of three additional shillings a day to each labourer would not increase the quantity of meat in the country. There is not at present enough for all to have a moderate share. What would then be the consequence? The competition among the buyers in the market of meat would rapidly raise the price from eightpence or ninepence to two or three shillings in the pound, and the commodity would not be divided among many more than it is at present. When an article is scarce, and cannot be distributed to all, he that can show the most valid patent, that is, he that offers the most money, becomes the possessor. If we can suppose the competition among the buyers of meat to continue long enough for a greater number of cattle to be reared annually, this could only be done at the expense of the corn, which would be a very disadvantageous exchange; for it is well known that the country could not then support the same population, and when subsistence is scarce in proportion to the number of people, it is of little consequence whether the lowest members of the society possess two shillings or five. They must at all events be reduced to live upon the hardest fare, and in the smallest quantity.

It might be said perhaps that the increased number of purchasers in every article would give a spur to productive industry, and that the whole produce of the island would be increased. But the spur that these fancied riches would give to population would more than counterbalance it; and the increased produce would be to be divided among a more than proportionably increased number of people.

. . . [N]o possible sacrifices of the rich, particularly in money, could for any time prevent the recurrence of distress among the lower members of society whoever they were. Great changes might indeed be made. The rich might become poor, and some of the poor rich; but while the present proportion between population and food continues, a part of the society must necessarily find it difficult to support a family, and this difficulty will naturally fall on the least fortunate members.

. . . But if I only give him money, supposing the produce of the country to remain the same, I give him a title to a larger share of that produce than formerly, which share he cannot receive without diminishing the shares of others. . . .

. . . At the same time we must not forget that both humanity and true policy imperiously require that we should give every assistance to the poor on these occasions that the nature of the case will admit. If provisions were to continue at the price of scarcity, the wages of labour must necessarily rise, or sickness and famine would quickly diminish the number of labourers; and the supply of labour being unequal to the demand, its price would soon rise in a still greater proportion than the price of provisions. But even one or two years of scarcity, if the poor were left entirely to shift for themselves, might produce some effect of this kind, and consequently it is our interest as well as our duty to give them temporary aid in such seasons of distress. It is on such occasions that every cheap substitute for bread and every mode of economising food should be resorted to. Nor should we be too ready to complain of that high price of corn which by encouraging importation increases the supply.

The poor-laws of England tend to depress the general condition of the poor in these two ways. Their first obvious tendency is to increase population without increasing the food for its support. A poor man may marry with little or no prospect of being able to support a family without parish assistance. They may be said therefore to create the poor which they maintain; and as the provisions of the country must in consequence of the increased population be distributed to every man in smaller proportions, it is evident that the labour of those who are not supported by parish assistance will purchase a smaller quantity of provisions than before, and consequently more of them must be driven to apply for assistance.

Secondly, the quantity of provisions consumed in workhouses, upon a part of the society that cannot in general be considered as the most valuable part, diminishes the shares that would otherwise belong to more industrious and more worthy members, and thus in the same manner forces more to become dependent. If the poor in the workhouses were to live better than they do now, this new distribution of the money of the society would tend more conspicuously to depress the condition of those out of the workhouses by occasioning an advance in the price of provisions.

Fortunately for England a spirit of independence still remains among the peasantry. The poor-laws are strongly calculated to eradicate this spirit. They have succeeded in part; but had they succeeded as completely as might have been expected, their pernicious tendency would not have been so long concealed.

Hard as it may appear in individual instances, dependent poverty ought to be held disgraceful. Such a stimulus seems to be absolutely necessary to promote the happiness of the great mass of mankind; and every general attempt to weaken this stimulus, however benevolent its intention, will always defeat its own purpose. If men be induced to marry from the mere prospect of parish provision, they are not only unjustly tempted to bring unhappiness and dependence upon themselves and children, but they are tempted without knowing it to injure all in the same class with themselves.

The poor-laws of England appear to have contributed to raise the price of provisions and to lower the real price of labour. They have therefore contributed to impoverish that class of people whose only possession is their labour. It is also difficult to suppose that they have not powerfully contributed to generate that carelessness and want of frugality observable among the poor, so contrary to the disposition generally to be remarked among petty tradesmen and small farmers. The labouring poor, to use a vulgar expression, seem always to live from hand to mouth. Their present wants employ their whole attention, and they seldom think of the future. . . . The poor-laws may therefore be said to diminish both the power and the will to save among the common people, and thus to weaken one of the strongest incentives to sobriety and industry, and consequently to happiness.

The poor-laws of England were undoubtedly instituted for the most benevolent purpose; but it is evident they have failed in attaining it. They certainly mitigate some cases of severe distress which might otherwise occur; though the state of the poor who are supported by parishes, considered in all its circumstances, is very miserable. But one of the principal objections to the system is that for the assistance which some of the poor receive, in itself almost a doubtful blessing, the whole class of the common people of England is subjected to a set of grating, inconvenient and tyrannical laws, totally inconsistent with the genuine spirit of the constitution. . . . And the obstructions continually occasioned in the market of labour by these laws have a constant tendency to add to the difficulties of those who are struggling to support themselves without assistance.

These evils attendant on the poor-laws seem to be irremediable. If assistance be to be distributed to a certain class of people, a power must be lodged somewhere of discriminating the proper objects and of managing the concerns of the institutions that are necessary; but any great interference with the affairs of other people is a species of tyranny, and in the common course of things the exercise of this power may be expected to become grating to those who are driven to ask for support. The tyranny of churchwardens and overseers is a common complaint among the poor; but the fault does not lie so much in these persons who probably before they were in power were not worse than other people, but in the nature of all such institutions.

. . . [W]e have practised an unpardonable deceit upon the poor, and have promised what we have been very far from performing.

The attempts to employ the poor on any great scale in manufactures have almost invariably failed, and the stock and materials have been wasted. In those few parishes which, by better management or larger funds, have been enabled to persevere in this system, the effect of these new manufactures in the market must have been to throw out of employment many independent workmen who were before engaged in fabrications of a similar nature. . . .

Of the Only Effectual Mode of Improving
the Condition of the Poor

. . . I do not see how it is possible for any person who acknowledges the principle of utility as the great criterion of moral rules, to escape the conclusion that moral restraint, or the abstaining from marriage till we are in a condition to support a family, with a perfectly moral conduct during that period, is the strict line of duty, and when revelation is taken into the question, this duty undoubtedly receives very powerful confirmation. At the same time I believe that few of my readers can be less sanguine than I am in their expectations of any sudden and great change in the general conduct of men on this subject. . . .

. . . The happiness of the whole is to be the result of the happiness of individuals, and to begin first with them. No co-operation is required. Every step tells. He who performs his duty faithfully will reap the full fruits of it, whatever may be the number of others who fail. This duty is intelligible to the humblest capacity. It is merely that he is not to bring beings into the world for whom he cannot find the means of support. When once this subject is cleared from the obscurity thrown over it by parochial laws and private benevolence, every man must feel the strongest conviction of such an obligation. If he cannot support his children, they must starve; and if he marry in the face of a fair probability that he shall not be able to support his children, he is guilty of all the evils which he thus brings upon himself, his wife, and his offspring. It is clearly his interest, and will tend greatly to promote his happiness, to defer marrying, till by industry and economy he is in a capacity to support the children that he may reasonably expect from his marriage; and as he cannot in the meantime gratify his passions without violating an express command of God, and running a great risk of injuring himself or some of his fellow-creatures, considerations of his own interest and happiness will dictate to him the strong obligation to a moral conduct while he remains unmarried.

However powerful may be the impulses of passion, they are generally in some degree modified by reason. And it does not seem entirely visionary to suppose that, if the true and permanent cause of poverty were clearly explained and forcibly brought home to each man's bosom, it would have some and perhaps not an inconsiderable influence on his conduct; at least the experiment has never yet been fairly tried. Almost everything that has been hitherto done for the poor has tended, as if with solicitous care, to throw a veil of obscurity over this subject and to hide from them the true cause of their poverty. When the wages of labour are hardly sufficient to maintain two children, a man marries and has five or six; he of course finds himself miserably distressed. He accuses the insufficiency of the price of labour to maintain a family. . . . He accuses the partial and unjust institutions of society which have awarded him an inadequate share of the produce of the earth. . . . The last person that he would think of accusing is himself, on whom in fact the principal blame lies except so far as he has been deceived by the higher classes of society. . . .

Till these erroneous ideas have been corrected, and the language of nature and reason has been generally heard on the subject of population, instead of the language of error and prejudice, it cannot be said that any fair experiment has been made with the understandings of the common people; and we cannot justly accuse them of improvidence and want of industry, till they act as they do now, after it has been brought home to their comprehensions, that they are themselves the cause of their own poverty; that the means of redress are in their own hands, and in the hands of no other persons whatever; that the society in which they live and the government which presides over it, are without any *direct* power in this respect; and that however ardently they may desire to relieve them, and whatever attempts they may make to do so, they are really and truly unable to execute what they benevolently wish, but unjustly promise; that when the wages of labour will not maintain a family, it is an incontrovertible sign that their king and country do not want more subjects, or at least that they cannot support them; that, if they marry in this case, so far from fulfilling a duty to society, they are throwing an useless burden on it, at the same time that they are plunging themselves into distress, and that they are acting directly contrary to the will of God, and bringing down upon themselves various diseases, which might all, or the greater part, have been avoided if they had attended to the repeated admonitions which he gives by the general laws of nature to every being capable of reason.

In all old and fully-peopled states it is from this method and this alone that we can rationally expect any essential and permanent melioration in the condition of the labouring classes of the people.

In an endeavour to raise the proportion of the quantity of provisions to the number of consumers in any country, our attention would naturally be first directed to the increasing of the absolute quantity of provisions; but finding that as fast as we did this the number of consumers more than kept pace with it, and that with all our exertions we were still as far as ever behind, we should be convinced that our efforts directed only in this way would never succeed. It would appear to be setting the tortoise to catch the hare. Finding therefore that from the laws of nature we could not proportion the food to the population, our next attempt should naturally be to proportion the population to the food. If we can persuade the hare to go to sleep the tortoise may have some chance of overtaking her.

We are not however to relax our efforts in increasing the quantity of provisions, but to combine another effort with it, that of keeping the population, when once it has been overtaken, at such a distance behind as to effect the relative proportion which we desire, and thus unite the two grand *desiderata* a great actual population and a state of society in which abject poverty and dependence are comparatively but little known, two objects which are far from being incompatible.

Effects of the Knowledge of the Principal Cause of Poverty on Civil Liberty

It may appear perhaps that a doctrine which attributes the greatest part of the sufferings of the lower classes of society exclusively to themselves is unfavourable to the cause of liberty, as affording a tempting opportunity to governments of oppressing their subjects at pleasure and laying the whole blame on the laws of nature and the imprudence of the poor. We are not however to trust to first appearances . . . nothing would so powerfully contribute to the advancement of rational freedom as a thorough knowledge generally circulated of the principal cause of poverty, and that the ignorance of this cause, and the natural consequences of this ignorance, form at present one of the chief obstacles to its progress.

The pressure of distress on the lower classes of people, together with the habit of attributing this distress to their rulers, appears to me to be the rock of defence, the castle, the guardian spirit of despotism. It affords to the tyrant the fatal and unanswerable plea of necessity. It is the reason why every free government tends constantly to destruction, and that its appointed guardians become daily less jealous of the encroachments of power. It is the reason why so many noble efforts in the cause of freedom have failed, and why almost every revolution after long and painful sacrifices has terminated in a military despotism. While any dissatisfied man of talents has power to persuade the lower classes of people that all their poverty and distress arise solely from the iniquity of the government, though perhaps the greatest part of what they suffer is unconnected with this cause, it is evident that the seeds of fresh discontents and fresh revolutions are continually sowing. When an established government has been destroyed, finding that their poverty is not removed, their resentment naturally falls upon the successors to power; and when these have been immolated without producing the desired effect, other sacrifices are called for, and so on without end. Are we to be surprised that under such circumstances the majority of well-disposed people, finding that a government with proper restrictions is unable to support itself against the revolutionary spirit, and weary and exhausted with perpetual change to which they can see no end, should give up the struggle in despair, and throw themselves into the arms of the first power which can afford them protection against the horrors of anarchy?

A mob, which is generally the growth of a redundant population goaded by resentment for real sufferings, but totally ignorant of the quarter from which they originate, is of all monsters the most fatal to freedom. It fosters a prevailing tyranny, and engenders one where it was not. . . . If political discontents were blended with the cries of hunger, and a revolution were to take place by the instrumentality of a mob clamouring for want of food, the consequences would be unceasing change and unceasing carnage, the bloody career of which nothing but the establishment of some complete despotism could arrest.

. . . In this case it is more the ignorance and delusion of the lower classes of the people that occasions the oppression, than the actual disposition of the government to tyranny. . . .

If the great truths on these subjects were more generally circulated, and the lower classes of people could be convinced that by the laws of nature, independently of any particular institutions except the great one of property, which is absolutely necessary in order to attain any considerable produce, no person has any claim or *right* on society for subsistence if his labour will not purchase it, the greatest part of the mischievous declamation on the unjust institutions of society would fall powerless to the ground. The poor are by no means inclined to be visionary. Their distresses are always real, though they are not attributed to the real causes. If these causes were properly explained to them, and they were taught to know what part of their present distress was attributable to government, and what part to causes totally unconnected with it, discontent and irritation among the lower classes of people would shew themselves much less frequently than at present; and when they did shew themselves would be much less to be dreaded. . . .

. . . Could we but take away this fear, reform and improvement would proceed with as much facility as the removal of nuisances or the paving and lighting of the streets. . . .

The most successful supporters of tyranny are without doubt those general declaimers who attribute the distresses of the poor, and almost all the evils to which society is subject, to human institutions and the iniquity of governments. The falsity of these accusations and the dreadful consequences that would result from their being generally admitted and acted upon, make it absolutely necessary that they should at all events be resisted, not only on account of the immediate revolutionary horrors to be expected from a movement of the people acting under such impressions (a consideration which must at all time have very great weight), but also on account of the extreme probability that such a revolution would terminate in a much worse despotism than that which it had destroyed. On these grounds a genuine friend of freedom, a zealous advocate for the real rights of man, might be found among the defenders of a considerable degree of tyranny. A cause bad in itself might be supported by the good and the virtuous, merely because that which was opposed to it was much worse; and because it was absolutely necessary at the moment to make a choice between the two. Whatever therefore may be the intention of those indiscriminate accusations against governments their real effect undoubtedly is to add a weight of talents and principles to the prevailing power which it never would have received otherwise.

It is a truth which I trust has been sufficiently proved in the course of this work, that under a government constructed upon the best and purest principles and executed by men of the highest talents and integrity, the most squalid poverty and wretchedness might universally prevail from an inattention to the prudential check to population. And as this cause of unhappiness has hitherto been so little understood that the efforts of society have always tended rather to aggravate than to lessen it, we have the strongest reasons for supposing that in all the governments with which we are acquainted a great part of the misery to be observed among the lower classes of the people arises from this cause.

The inference therefore which Mr. Paine and others have drawn against governments from the unhappiness of the people is palpably unfair; and before we give a sanction to such accusations it is a debt we owe to truth and justice to ascertain how much of this unhappiness arises from the principle of population, and how much is fairly to be attributed to government. When this distinction has been properly made, and all the vague, indefinite, and false accusations removed, government would remain, as it ought to be, clearly responsible for the rest; and the amount of this would still be such as to make the responsibility very considerable. Though government has but little power in the direct and immediate relief of poverty yet its indirect influence on the prosperity of its subjects is striking and incontestable. And the reason is, that though it is comparatively impotent in its efforts to make the food of a country keep pace with an unrestricted increase of population, yet its influence is great in giving the best direction to those checks which in some form or other must necessarily take place. . . .

The first grand requisite to the growth of prudential habits is the perfect security of property, and the next perhaps is that respectability and importance which are given to the lower classes by equal laws and the possession of some influence in the framing of them. The more excellent therefore is the government the more does it tend to generate that prudence and elevation of sentiment by which alone in the present state of our being poverty can be avoided.

It has been sometimes asserted that the only reason why it is advantageous that the people should have some share in the government is that a representation of the people tends best to secure the framing of good and equal laws, but that if the same object could be attained under a despotism the same advantage would accrue to the community. If however the representative system, by securing to the lower classes of society a more equal and liberal mode of treatment from their superiors, gives to each individual a greater personal respectability and a greater fear of personal degradation, it is evident that it will powerfully co-operate with the security of property in animating the exertions of industry and in generating habits of prudence, and thus more powerfully tend to increase the riches and prosperity of the lower classes of the community than if the same laws had existed under a despotism.

But though the tendency of a free constitution and a good government to diminish poverty be certain, yet their effect in this way must necessarily be indirect and slow, and very different from the direct and immediate relief which the lower classes of people are too frequently in the habit of looking forward to as the consequence of a revolution. This habit of expecting too much, and the irritation occasioned by disappointment, continually give a wrong direction to their efforts in favour of liberty, and constantly tend to defeat the accomplishment of those gradual reforms in government and that slow melioration of the condition of the lower classes of society which are really attainable. It is of the very highest importance therefore to know distinctly what government cannot do as well as what it can. If I were called upon to name the cause which in my conception had more than any other contributed to the very slow progress of freedom, so disheartening to every liberal mind, I should say that it was the confusion that had existed respecting the causes of the unhappiness and discontents which prevail in society, and the advantage which governments had been able to take and indeed had been compelled to take of this confusion to confirm and strengthen their power. I cannot help thinking therefore that a knowledge generally circulated that the principal cause of want and unhappiness is only indirectly connected with government and totally beyond its power directly to remove, and that it depends upon the conduct of the poor themselves, would instead of giving any advantage to governments, give a great additional weight to the popular side of the question by removing the dangers with which from ignorance it is at present accompanied, and thus tend in a very powerful manner to promote the cause of rational freedom.

18 HERBERT SPENCER

Herbert Spencer (1820-1903) has suffered from a bad press in the twentieth century. His ideas have been attacked as unscientific, simplistic, and dangerous. He has been portrayed (and with some reason) as the foremost Anglo-American defender of laissez-faire and as the major intellectual champion of social darwinism, which, in its crudest form, was used to justify vicious forms of social and racial discrimination. Yet Spencer was not the ideologue of the status quo, certainly not at the beginning of his long career as a social philosopher.

In Victoria's heyday (the 1850s), the status quo meant a society dominated by privilege and custom, and the privileged had a history of using the powers of king and Parliament to protect their dominant social position. In the selection which follows, Spencer describes a few of the foolish, frustrating, and often harmful consequences of state action under such circumstances. Like so many other liberals, Spencer did not believe such interference in human affairs was necessary or justified. He argued that state regulation was a remnant of the Middle Ages, when society was "static" and only the fortunate few were free. Yet English society was anything but static in the middle of the nineteenth century, and Spencer could see no reason why the state should be used to inhibit or stop the inevitable (and good) social changes which were altering English society to its roots. It is this emphasis upon the need for and the desirability of change (and the personal freedom and responsibility which would spring from it) which makes Spencer a liberal.

SOCIAL STATICS*

The Constitution of the State

It is a tolerably well-ascertained fact that men are still selfish. And that beings answering to this epithet will employ the power placed in their hands for their

---

Social Statics (New York: D. Appleton and Co., 1892).

own advantage is self-evident. Directly or indirectly, either by hook or by crook, if not openly then in secret, their private ends will be served. Granting the proposition that men are selfish, we cannot avoid the corollary that those who possess authority will, if permitted, use it for selfish purposes.

Should any one need facts in proof of this, he may find them at every page in the nearest volume of history. . . .

Why ask whether those in power *have* sought their own advantage in preference to that of others? With human nature as we know it, they must have done so. It is this same tendency in men to pursue gratification at the expense of their neighbours which renders government needful. Were we not selfish, legislative restraint would be unnecessary. Evidently, then, the very existence of a State-authority proves that irresponsible rulers will sacrifice the public good to their personal benefit: all solemn promises, specious professions, and carefully-arranged checks and safeguards, notwithstanding.

It is a pity that those who speak disparagingly of the masses have not wisdom enough, or candour enough, to make due allowance for the unfavourable circumstances in which the masses are placed. Suppose that, after carefully weighing the evidence, it should turn out the the working men *do* exhibit greater vices than those more comfortably off; does it therefore follow that they are morally worse? Are the additional temptations under which they labour to be left out of the estimate? Shall as much be expected at their hands as from those born into a more fortunate position? Ought the same demands to be made upon the possessors of five talents as upon the possessors of ten? Surely the lot of the hard-handed labourer is pitiable enough without having harsh judgments passed upon him. Consider well these endowments of his—these capacities, affections, tastes, and the vague yearnings to which they give birth. Think of him now with his caged-up desires doomed to a daily, weekly, yearly round of painful toil, with very little remission save for food and sleep. Observe how he is tantalized by the pleasures he sees his richer brethren partaking of, but from which he must be for ever debarred. Note the humiliation he suffers from being looked down upon as of no account among men. And then remember that he has nothing to look forward to but a monotonous continuance of this till death. Is this a salutary state of things to live under?

It is very easy for you, O respectable citizen, seated in your easy chair with your feet on the fender, to hold forth on the misconduct of the people;—very easy for you to censure their extravagant and vicious habits;—very easy for you to be a pattern of frugality, of rectitude, of sobriety. What else should you be? Here are you surrounded by comforts, possessing multiplied sources of lawful happiness, with a reputation to maintain, an ambition to fulfil, and the prospect of a competency for your old age. A shame indeed would it be if with these advantages you were not well regulated in your behaviour. You have a cheerful home, are warmly and cleanly clad, and fare, if not sumptuously every day, at any rate abundantly. For your hours of relaxation there are amusements. A newspaper arrives regularly to satisfy your curiosity; if your tastes are literary, books may be had in plenty; and there is a piano if you like music. You can afford to entertain your friends, and are entertained in return. There are lectures, and concerts, and exhibitions, accessible if you incline to them. You may have a holiday when you choose to take one, and can spare money for an annual trip to the sea-side. And enjoying all these privileges you take credit to yourself for being a well-conducted man! Small praise to you for it! If *you* do not contract dissipated habits where is the merit? You have few incentives to do so. It is no honour to *you* that you do not spend your savings in sensual gratification; you have pleasures enough without. But what would you do if placed in the position of the labourer? How would these virtues of yours stand the wear and tear of poverty? . . . Let us see you tied to an irksome employment from dawn till dusk; fed on meagre food, and scarcely enough of that; married to a factory girl ignorant of domestic management; deprived of the enjoyments which education opens up; with no place of recreation but the pot-house; and then let us see whether you would be as steady as you are. Suppose your savings had to be made, not as now, out of surplus income, but out of wages already insufficient for necessaries; and then consider whether to be provident would be as easy as you at present find it. Conceive yourself one of a class contemptuously termed "the great unwashed;" stigmatized as brutish, stolid, vicious; suspected of harbouring wicked designs; and then say whether the desire to be respectable would be as practically operative on you as now. Lastly, imagine that seeing your capacities were but ordinary, and your competitors innumerable, you despaired of ever attaining to a higher station; and then think whether the incentives to perseverance and forethought would be as strong as your existing ones.

After all it is a pitiful controversy, this about the relative vices of rich and poor. Two school-boys taunting each other with faults of which they were equally guilty, would best parody it. While indignant Radicalism denounces "the vile aristocrats," these in their turn enlarge with horror on the brutality of the mob. Neither party sees its own sins. Neither party recognizes in the other, itself in a different dress. Neither party can believe that it would do all the other does if placed in like circumstances. Yet a cool by-stander finds nothing to choose between them—knows that these class-recriminations are but the inflammatory symptoms of a uniformly-diffused immorality. Label men how you please with titles of "upper," and "middle," and "lower," you cannot prevent them being units of the same society, acted upon by the same spirit of the age, moulded after the same type of character. . . . Whoso is placed among the savage will in process of time grow savage too; let his companions be treacherous and he will become treacherous in self-defence; surround him with the kind-hearted and he will soften; amid the refined he will acquire polish; and the same influences which thus rapidly adapt the individual to his society, ensure, though by a slower process, the general uniformity of a national character. This is no unsupported the-

ory. Look when or where we please, thickly-strewn proofs may be gathered. . . .
In the present day dishonesty shows itself not less in the falsification of dockyard
accounts, or the "cooking" of railway-reports, than in burglary or sheepstealing;
while those who see heartlessness in the dealings of slop-tailors and their sweat-
ers, may also find it in the conduct of rich landlords who get double rent from
poor allotment holders, and in that of responsible ladies who underpay half-
starved seamstresses . . . a reference to the sporting papers will show that the
lingering instincts of the savage are at this moment exhibited by about an equal
percentage of all classes.

If by ignorance is meant want of information on matters which, for the due
performance of his function, the citizen should understand (and no other definition is to the point), then it is a great error to suppose that ignorance is peculiar to
the unenfranchised. Were there no other illustrations, sufficient proof that this
ignorance is shared by those on the register, might be gathered from their conduct
at elections. Much might be inferred from the tuft-hunting spirit exhibited in the
choice of aristocratic representatives. Some doubts might be cast on the penetra-
tion of men who, while they complain of the pressure of taxation, send to parliament hordes of military and naval officers, who have an interest in making that
taxation still greater. Or the pretensions of the present holders of political power
to superior knowledge, might be tested by quotations from the debates of a farmers' market-ordinary, and from those of the assembly into which electoral wisdom is distilled. . . .

A democracy, properly so called, is a political organization modelled in accordance with the law of equal freedom. . . .

In speaking of it we use such terms as *free* institutions, *self*-government, civil
liberty, all implying this. But the diminution of external restraint can take place
only at the same rate as the increase of internal restraint. Conduct has to be ruled
either from without or from within. If the rule from within is not efficient, there
must exist a supplementary rule from without. If, on the other hand, all men are
properly ruled from within, government becomes needless, and all men are perfectly free. Now the chief faculty of self-rule being the moral sense, the degree of
freedom in their institutions which any given people can bear, will be proportion-
ate to the diffusion of this moral sense among them. And only when its influence
greatly predominates can so large an instalment of freedom as a democracy
implies become possible.

Lastly, the supremacy of this same faculty affords the only guarantee for the
stability of a democracy. On the part of the ruled it gives rise to what we call a
jealousy of their liberties—a watchful determination to resist anything like
encroachment upon their rights; while it generates among the rulers such respect
for these rights as checks any desire they may have to agress. Conversely, let the
ruled be deficient in the instinct of freedom, and they will be indifferent to the
gradual usurpation of their privileges so long as it entails no immediate inconve-

nience upon them; and the rulers, in such case, being deficient in sympathetic regard for these privileges, will be, to a like extent, unscrupulous in usurping. Let us observe, in detail, the different modes in which men thus contra-distinguished comport themselves under a representative form of government. Among a people not yet fitted for such a form, citizens, lacking the impulse to claim equal powers, become careless in the exercise of their franchise, and even pride themselves on not interfering in public affairs. Provided their liberties are but indirectly affected, they will watch the passing of the most insidious measures with vacant unconcern. It is only barefaced aggressions that they can perceive to be aggressions at all. Placing, as they do, but little value on their privileges, they are readily bribed. When threatened, instead of assuming that attitude of dogged resistance which the instinct of freedom dictates, they truckle. If tricked out of a right of citizenship, they are quite indifferent about getting it again; and, indeed, when the exercise of it conflicts with any immediate interest, are glad to give it up,— will even petition, as in times past did many of the corporate towns, both in England and Spain, that they may be excused from electing representatives. Meanwhile, in accordance with that law of social homogeneity lately dwelt upon, those in authority are in a like ratio ready to encroach. They intimidate, they bribe, they plot; and by degrees establish a comparatively coercive government. On the other hand, among a people sufficiently endowed with the faculty responding to the law of equal freedom, no such retrograde process is possible. The man of genuinely democratic feeling loves liberty as a miser loves gold, for its own sake and quite irrespective of its apparent advantages. What he thus highly values he sleeplessly watches; and he opposes aggression the moment it commences. Should any assume undue prerogatives, he straightway steps up to them and demands their authority for so doing. Transactions that seem in the remotest degree underhand awaken his suspicions, which are not to be laid so long as anything remains unexplained. If in any proposed arrangement there be a latent danger to the liberties of himself and others, he instantly discovers it and refuses his consent. He is alarmed by such a proposal as the disfranchisement of a constituency by the legislature; for it at once occurs to him that the measure thus levelled against one may be levelled against many. To call that responsible government under which a cabinet-minister can entangle the nation in a quarrel about some paltry territory before they know anything of it, he sees to be absurd. It needs no chain of reasoning to show him that the assumption, by a delegated assembly, of the power to lengthen its own existence from three years to seven, is an infraction of the representative principle; and no plausible professions of honourable intentions can check his opposition to the setting up of so dangerous a precedent. Still more excited is he when applied to for grants of public money, with the understanding that on a future occasion he shall be told how they have been spent. Flimsy excuses about "exigencies of the State," and the like, cannot entrap him into so glaring an act of self-stultification. Thus is he ever on the watch to stop encroachment. And when a community consists of men animated by the spirit thus exemplified, the continuance of liberal institutions is certain. . . .

The Limit of State-Duty

Observe . . . the government and the dissentient citizen. Says the citizen:—

"What is it that you, as the ruling agency, have been appointed for? Is it not to maintain the rights of those who employ you; or, in other words, to guarantee to each the fullest freedom for the exercise of his faculties compatible with the equal freedom of all others?"

"It has been so decided."

"And it has been also decided that you are justified in diminishing this freedom only to such an extent as may be needful for preserving the remainder, has it not?"

"That is evidently a corollary."

"Exactly. And now let me ask what is this property, this money, of which, in the shape of taxes, you are demanding from me an additional amount for a further purpose? Is it not that which enables me to get food, clothing, shelter, recreation, or to repeat the original expression—that on which I depend for the exercise of most of my faculties?"

"It is."

"Therefore to decrease my property is to decrease my freedom to exercise my faculties, is it not?"

"Clearly."

"Then this new impost of yours will practically decrease my freedom to exercise my faculties?"

"Yes."

"Well, do you not now perceive the contradiction? Instead of acting the part of a protector you are acting the part of an aggressor. What you were appointed to guarantee me and others, you are now taking away. To see that the liberty of each man to pursue the objects of his desires is unrestricted, save by the like liberty of all, is your special function. To diminish this liberty by means of taxes, or civil restraints, more than is needful for performing such function, is wrong, because adverse to the function itself. Now your new impost does so diminish this liberty more than is needful, and is consequently unjustifiable."

I will perhaps be urged, however, that the evil done by a government, when it thus oversteps its original duty, is only an apparent one; seeing that although it diminishes men's spheres of action in one direction, it adds to them in another. All such supplementary functions, an objector may say, subserve in some way or other the wants of society; that is, they facilitate the satisfaction of men's desires;

that is, they afford to men greater freedom for the exercise of their faculties. For if you argue that taking away a man's property diminishes his *means* of exercising them, then you must in fairness admit that, by procuring for him certain of the objects he desires, or by taking away the obstacles that lie between him and those objects, or by otherwise helping him to his ends, the State is increasing his power to exercise his faculties, and hence is practically increasing his freedom.

To all which the answer is, that cutting away men's opportunities on one side, to add to them on another, is at best accompanied by a loss. Let us remember that the force by which a society, through its government, works out certain results, is not increased by administrative mechanisms but that part of it escapes in friction. Government evidently cannot create any facilities for the exercise of faculties; all it can do is to re-distribute them. Set down the amount of power to satisfy his wants, which it takes from a citizen in extra taxes; deduct the serious waste occurring under official manipulations; and the remainder, transformed into some new shape, is all that can be returned to him. The transaction is consequently a losing one. So that while, in attempting to serve the public by undertaking supplementary functions, a government fails in its duty towards all who dissent; it does not really compensate for this by additional advantages afforded to the rest; to whom it merely gives with one hand, less than it takes away with the other.

But in truth the transaction is a yet more detrimental one than it thus appears, for even the gift is a delusion. The expediency-philosophy, of which this general State-superintendence is a practical expression, embodies the belief that government ought not only to guarantee men the unmolested pursuit of happiness, but should provide the happiness for them. Now no scheme could be more self-defeating. Man . . . consists of a congeries of faculties qualifying him for surrounding conditions. Each of these faculties, if normally developed, yields to him, when exercised, a gratification constituting part of his happiness; while in the act of exercising it, some deed is done subserving the wants of the man as a whole, and affording to the faculties the opportunities of performing in turn their respective functions, and of producing every one its peculiar pleasure: so that, when healthily balanced, each subserves all and all subserve each. We cannot live at all unless this mechanism works with some efficiency; and we can live entirely only when the reciprocity between capacities and requirements is perfect. Evidently, then, one who is thus rightly constituted cannot be helped. To do anything for him by some artificial agency, is to supersede certain of his powers—is to leave them unexercised, and therefore to diminish his happiness.

"But men are *not* complete; they are *not* healthily developed; they have *not* capacities in harmony with their wants; and therefore, as matters stand, a government does *not* by its interpositions pre-occupy offices which there are faculties to fill." Very true; but next to being what we ought to be, the most desirable thing is that we should become what we ought to be as fast as possible. We have to lose the characteristics which fitted us for our original state, and to gain those which will fit us for our present state; and the question to be asked, respecting these mechanical remedies for our deficiencies, is—do they facilitate the change? A moment's thought will convince us that they retard it. Demand and supply is the law of life as well as the law of trade. Would you draw out and increase some feeble sentiment? Then you must set it to do, as well as it can, the work required of it. It must be kept ever active, ever strained, ever inconvenienced by its incompetence. Under this treatment it will, in the slow course of generations, attain to efficiency; and what was once its impossible task will become the source of a healthy, pleasurable, and desired excitement. But let a State-instrumentality be thrust between such faculty and its work, and the process of adaptation is at once suspended. The embryo agency now superseded by some commission—some board and staff of officers, straightway dwindles; for power is as inevitably lost by inactivity as it is gained by activity. Hence, humanity no longer goes on moulding itself into harmony with the natural requirements of the social state; but begins, instead, to assume a form fitting these artificial requirements. And thus, as before said, not only does a government reverse its function by taking away more property than is needful for protective purposes, but even what it gives, in return for the excess so taken, is in essence a loss.

There is indeed one faculty, or rather combination of faculties, for whose shortcomings the State, as far as in it lies, may advantageously compensate—that, namely, by which society is made possible. It is clear that any being whose constitution is to be moulded into fitness for new conditions of existence, must be placed under those conditions. This granted, it follows that as man has been, and is still, deficient in those feelings which prevent the recurring antagonisms of individuals and their consequent disunion, some artifical agency is required by which their union may be maintained; Only by the process of adaptation itself, can be produced that character which makes social equilibrium spontaneous. And hence, while this process is going on, an instrumentality must be employed, firstly, to bind men into the social state, and secondly to check all conduct endangering the existence of that state. Such an instrumentality we have in a government.

And now mark that whether we consider government from this point of view, or from that previously occupied, our conclusions respecting it are in essence identical. For when government fulfils the function here assigned it, of retaining men in the circumstances to which they are to be adapted, it fulfils the function which we on other grounds assigned it—that of protector. To administer justice,—to mount guard over men's rights,—is simply to render society possible. And seeing that the two definitions are thus at root the same, we shall be prepared for the fact that, in whichever way we specify its duty, the State cannot exceed that duty without defeating itself. For, if regarded as a protector, we find that the moment it does anything more than protect, it becomes an aggressor instead of a protector; and, if regarded as a help to adaptation, we find that when it does anything more than sustain the social state, it retards adaptation instead of hastening it.

To the assertion that the boundary line of State-duty as above drawn is at the wrong place, the obvious rejoinder is—show us where it should be drawn. This appeal expediency-philosophers have never yet been able to answer. Their alleged definitions are no definitions at all. As was proved at the outset, to say that government ought to do that which is "expedient," or to do that which will tend to produce the "greatest happiness," or to do that which will subserve the "general good," is to say just nothing; for there are countless disagreements respecting the natures of these desiderata. A definition of which the terms are indefinite is an absurdity. Whilst the practical interpretation of "expediency" remains a matter of opinion, to say that a government should do that which is "expedient," is to say that it should do, what we think it should do!

Still then our demand is—a definition. Between the two extremes of its possible action, where lies the proper limitation? Shall it extend its interference to the fixing of creeds, as the old times; or to overlooking modes of manufacture, farming operations, and domestic affairs, as it once did; or to commerce, as of late—to popular education, as now—to public health, as already—to dress, as in China— to literature, as in Austria—to charity, to manners, to amusements? If not to all of them, to which of them? Should the perplexed inquirer seek refuge in authority, he will find precedents not only for these but for many more such interferences. If, like those who disapprove of master-tailors having their work done off the premises, or like those who want to prevent the produce of industrial prisons displacing that of the artizans, or like those who would restrain charity-school children from competing with seamstresses, he thinks it desirable to meddle with trade-arrangements, there are plenty of exemplars for him. There is the law of Henry VII., which directed people at what fairs they should sell their goods; and that of Edward VI., which enacted a fine of £100 for a usurious bargain; and that of James I., which prescribed the quantity of ale to be sold for a penny; and that of Henry VIII., which made it penal to sell any pins but such as are "double headed, and their head soldered fast to the shank, and well smoothed; the shank well shaven; the point well and round-filed and sharpened." . . . And if work is to be regulated, is it not proper that work should be provided, and the idle compelled to perform a due amount of it? In which case how shall we deal with our vagrant population? Shall we take a hint from Fletcher of Saltoun, who warmly advocated the establishment of slavery in Scotland as a boon to "so many thousands of our people who are at this day dying for want of bread"? or shall we adopt the analogous suggestion of Mr. Carlyle, who would remedy the distresses of Ireland by organizing its people into drilled regiments of diggers? The hours of labour too— what must be done about these? Having acceded to the petition of the factory-workers, ought we not to entertain that of the journeyman-bakers? and if that of the journeyman-bakers, why not, as Mr. Cobden asks, consider the cases of the glass-blowers, the nightmen, the iron-founders, the Sheffield knife-grinders, and indeed all other classes, including the hardworked M.P.'s themselves? And when employment has been provided, and the hours of labour fixed, and trade-regulations settled, we must decide how far the State ought to look after people's minds, and morals, and health. There is this education question: having satisfied the prevalent wish for government schools with tax-paid teachers, and adopted Mr. Ewart's plan for town-libraries and museums, should we not canvass the supplementary proposal to have national lecturers? . . . And when it had been agreed to put the sick under the care of public officials, consistency would of course demand the adoption of Mr. G. A. Walker's system of government funerals, under which "those in authority" are "to take especial care" that "the poorest of our brethren" shall have "an appropriate and solemn transmission" to the grave, and are to grant in certain cases "gratuitous means of interment." Having carried out thus far the communist plan of doing everything for everybody, should we not consider the peoples' amusements, and, taking example from the opera-subsidy in France, establish public ball-rooms, and *gratis* concerts, and cheap theatres, with State-paid actors, musicians, and masters of the ceremonies: using care at the same time duly to regulate the popular taste, as indeed, in the case of the Art-Union subscribers, our present Government proposed to do? Speaking of taste naturally reminds us of dress, in which sundry improvements might be enforced; . . . The matter of health, too, would need attending to; and, in dealing with this, might we not profitably reconsider those ancient statutes which protected peoples' stomachs by restricting the expenses of their tables; or, remembering how injurious are our fashionable late hours, might we not advantageously take a hint from the old Norman practice, and (otherwise prompted) fix the time at which people should put out their fires and go to bed. . . . And then, by way of making the superintendence complete, would it not be well to follow the example of the Danish king who gave directions to his subjects how they should scour their floors, and polish their furniture?

Multiply these questions; add to them the endless subordinate ones to which they must give rise; and some idea may be formed of the maze through which the expediency-philosopher has to find his way. Where now is his clue? If he would escape the charge of political empiricism, he must show us some test by which he can in each case ascertain whether or not State-superintendence is desirable. Between the one extreme of entire non-interference, and the other extreme in which every citizen is to be transformed into a grown-up baby, there lie innumerable stopping places; and he who would have the State do more than protect, is required to say where he means to draw the line, and to give us reasons why it must be just there and nowhere else.

After the difficulty of finding out the thing to be done, comes the other difficulty of finding out the way to do it. Let us excuse the expediency-philosopher one half of his task—let us assume something to be unanimously agreed to as a proper undertaking; and now suppose we enquire of him—How about your means of accomplishing it? Are you quite sure that your apparatus will not break down under its work? quite sure that it will produce the result you wish? quite sure that it will not produce some very different result? There is no lack of warnings. "Let us put down usury," said to themselves the rulers of the middle ages. They tried, and did just the reverse of what they intended; for it turned out that "all regulations interfering with the interest of money render its terms more rigorous and burdensome." "We will exterminate Protestantism," whispered the Continental Catholics to one another. They tried, and instead of doing this they planted in England the germs of a manufacturing organization which has to a great extent superseded their own. "It will be well to give the labouring classes fixed settlements," thought the Poor-Law legislators; and, having acted out this thought, there eventually grew up the clearance system, with its overcrowded cottages and nonresident labour-gangs. "We must suppress these brothels," decided the authorities of Berlin in 1845. They did suppress them; and in 1848, the registrar's books and the hospital returns proved matters to be considerably worse than before. . . . Are not such warnings worthy of attention?

Then as to his administrative mechanisms—can he answer for the satisfactory working of them? The common remark that public business is worse managed than all other business, is not altogether unfounded. To-day he will find it illustrated in the doings of a department which makes a valuable estate like the New Forest, a loss to the country of £3000 a year; which allowed Salcey Forest to be wholly cut down and made away with by a dishonest agent; and which, in 1848, had its accounts made up to March, 1839, only. To-morrow he may read of Admiralty bunglings—of ships ill-built, pulled to pieces, rebuilt, and patched; and of a sluggishness which puts the national dockyards "about seven years" behind all others. . . . Official delay is seen in the snail-paced progress of the Museum Catalogue; official mismanagement in the building of Houses of Parliament not fit for speaking in; and official perversity in the opposition always made to improvements by the Excise, the Customs, and the Post-Office authorities. Does the expediency-philosopher feel no apprehensions on contemplating such evidence? Or, as one specially professing to be guided by experience, does he think that on the whole experience is in his favour?

"It is a gross delusion to believe in the sovereign power of political machinery," says M. Guizot. True: and it is not only a gross delusion but a very dangerous one. Let a people believe in government-omnipotence, and they will be pretty certain to get up revolutions to achieve impossibilities. Between their exorbitant ideas of what the State ought to do for them on the one side, and its miserable performances on the other, there will surely be generated feelings extremely inimical to social order.

But this belief in "the sovereign power of political machinery" is not born with men; they are taught it. And how are they taught it? Evidently by these preachers of universal legislative superintendence, and by having seen, from their childhood, all kinds of functions undertaken by government officials. . . . Was it not natural that men living under the regulation of legions of prefects, sub-prefects, inspectors, controllers, intendants, commissaries, and other civil employes to the number of 535,000—men who were educated by the government, and taught religion by it—who had to ask its consent before they could stir from home—who could not publish a handbill without a permit from the authorities, nor circulate a newspaper after the censor's veto—who daily saw it dictating regulations for railways, inspecting and managing mines, building bridges, making roads, and erecting monuments—who were led to regard it as the patron of science, literature, and the fine arts, and as the dispenser of honours and rewards—who found it undertaking the manufacture of gunpowder, superintending the breeding of horses and sheep, playing the part of public pawnbroker, and monopolizing the sale of tobacco and snuff—who saw it attending to everything, from the execution of public works down to the sanitary inspection of prostitutes; was it not natural that men so circumstanced should acquire exalted ideas of State power? And, having acquired such ideas, were they not likely to desire the State to compass for them unattainable benefits; to get angry because it did not do this; and to attempt by violent means the enforcement of their wishes? Evidently the reply must be affirmative. . . .

There are other modes, too, in which social stability is endangered by this interference system. It is a very expensive system. The further it is carried the larger become the revenues required; and we all know that heavy taxation is inseparable from discontent. Moreover, it is in its nature essentially despotic. In governing everything it unavoidably cramps men; and, by diminishing their liberty of action, angers them. It galls by its infinity of ordinances and restrictions; it offends by profession to help those whom it will not allow to help themselves; and it vexes by its swarms of dictatorial officials, who are for ever stepping in between men and their pursuits. . . .

Thus, if we regard government as a means of upholding the social state, we find that, besides suffering a *direct* loss of power to perform its duty on attempting anything else, there are several subsidiary ways in which the assumption of additional functions endangers the fulfillment of its original function.

The Regulation of Commerce

In putting a veto upon any commercial intercourse, or in putting obstacles in the way of any such intercourse, a government trenches upon men's liberties of action; and by so doing directly reverses its function. To secure for each man the fullest freedom to exercise his faculties compatible with the like freedom of all others, we find to be the State's duty. Now trade-prohibitions and trade-restric-

tions not only do not secure this freedom, but they take it away. So that in enforcing them the State is transformed from a maintainer of rights into a violator of
rights. If it be criminal in a civil power commissioned to shield us from murder to
turn murderer itself; if it be criminal in it to play the thief, though set to keep off
thieves; then must it be criminal in it to deprive men, in any way, of liberty to
pursue the objects they desire, when it was appointed to insure them that
liberty. . . .

Fortunately it is now needless to enforce the doctrine of commercial freedom
by any considerations of policy. After making continual attempts to improve
upon the laws of trade, from the time of Solon downwards, men are at length
beginning to see that such attempts are worse than useless. Political economy has
shown us in this matter—what indeed it is its chief mission to show—that our
wisest plan is to let things take their own course. An increasing sense of justice,
too, has assisted in convincing us. We have here learned, what our forefathers
learned in some cases, and what, alas! we have yet to learn in many more, that
nothing but evil can arise from inequitable regulations. The necessity of respecting the principles of abstract rectitude—this it is that we have had another lesson
upon. Look at it rightly and we shall find that all the Anti-Corn-Law League did,
with its lectures, its newspapers, its bazaars, its monster meetings, and its ton of
tracts, was to teach people—what should have been very clear to them without
any such teaching—that no good can come of violating men's rights. By bitter
experience and a world of talk we have at length been made partially to believe as
much. Be it true or not in other cases, we are now quite certain that it is true in
trade. In respect to this at least we have declared that, for the future, we will obey
the law of equal freedom.

The Response to Laissez-Faire Within Liberalism

In this section we examine efforts to develop alternatives to laissez-faire from within the liberal tradition. The popular image of modern liberals often holds that liberals favor an expansive, interventionist state. This is in marked contrast to the minimal laissez-faire state of many nineteenth-century liberals. Though the popular image is wrong in holding that liberals sometimes favor greater governmental power for its own sake, it is correct to say that most contemporary liberals are willing to employ governmental power to protect what they consider to be basic liberal values in a changing political, social, and economic milieu. This development represents a growing belief that intervention in some social and economic relations, especially those where it is possible to exercise arbitrary power or discrimination, may be necessary to protect both economic efficiency and political-economic liberty. It does not reject the laissez-faire ideals of voluntarism and competition between self-sufficient individuals, but argues that in conditions of large-scale industry and massive concentrations of private economic power the assumptions of laissez-faire political economy do not always exist. As Keynes states below, the economy is not always self-regulating. There is not always free or real competition. Doing nothing does not necessarily produce the best results. People can be deprived of their individualism and freedom by private as well as governmental power. Liberalism requires that both tendencies be opposed.

In a significant sense this group of liberals, which represents the dominant tendency among contemporary Anglo-American liberals, rejects the laissez-faire assumption that the economy is self-regulating and that only a self-regulating economy can be efficient and just. Rather it argues that an unregulated economy, even if such a thing were possible, would produce gross inefficiency and massive injustice. It would prepare the ground for violence and revolution, which would destroy freedom as well as what is valuable in capitalism and private enterprise. They point to the frequent depressions, massive poverty, unemployment, and

217

revolutionary dangers in the nineteenth and early twentieth centuries as support for their idea that a completely unregulated economy produces political, social, moral, and economic disaster. They argue that what was once a genuinely liberal policy, such as laissez-faire, may no longer protect liberal values in a significantly different environment. Rather than adhering to old policies, liberal democratic government is capable of successfully intervening in the economy. Such intervention helps reduce depressions, economic waste, unemployment, inflation, and economic oppression while preserving freedom and choice.

These liberals also argue that pursuit of pure self-interest need not always lead to the common good. For example, freely allowing people to dump poisonous wastes wherever they wish or allowing parents to send their children to work rather than school interferes with other persons' individual freedoms and the common good. Political, social, and economic justice may require that government regulation limit the economic "freedom" of some to protect and increase the freedom and choices of all. This aid and protection may also promote the conditions for positive freedom. Thus the authors in this section accepted and defended private property and capitalism, but denied they are inevitably linked to laissez-faire and the distribution that it produces. In varying degrees they agreed that successful intervention is possible, even necessary, to maintain a capitalist society as well as the freedom and individualism that laissez-faire claimed to create and protect. These liberals do not see the issue as either liberty or government, but liberty and government to save and incorporate the values and fundamental elements of traditional liberalism into changed circumstances. This includes recognizing the community and common interest while admitting the importance and even primacy of individuals; that individual freedom may be destroyed by the abuse of freedom which tramples on the rights of others; that liberalism requires that we balance claims in order to protect as wide a range as possible of basic principles and values.

John Maynard Keynes stated this issue as well as anyone else: "The political problem of mankind is to combine three things: economic efficiency, social justice, and individual liberty. The first needs criticism, precaution, and technical knowledge; the second, an unselfish and enthusiastic spirit, which loves the ordinary man; the third, tolerance, breadth, appreciation of the excellencies of variety and independence, which prefers, above everything, to give unhindered opportunity to the exceptional and to the aspiring. The second ingredient is the best possession of the great party of the proletariat. [Labour] But the first and third require the qualities of the party [Liberal] which, by its traditions and ancient sympathies, has been the home of economic individualism and social liberty.''*

---

*"Liberalism and Labour," in *The Collected Writings of John Maynard Keynes*, Vol. 9: *Essays in Persuasion* (London: Macmillan, 1972), p. 311.

19 JOHN STUART MILL

In addition to being a philosopher and political theorist, John Stuart Mill (1806-1873) wrote about economics. He published seven editions of his influential *Principles of Political Economy With Some of Their Applications to Social Philosophy*. Mill accepted many of the assumptions and arguments of laissez-faire economics, but not all of its political and social conclusions. He denied that distribution of the economic product is determined by natural laws. Rather, he said, it is determined by the kinds of social and political institutions which we construct. This means that patterns of economic distribution are not fixed but can be changed.

The selection reprinted below represents the beginning of the development of an important branch of liberalism which argues that government can successfully intervene to reform or change the economy. In wanting to give a chance to socialism and communism Mill refers to nineteenth-century versions, many of which emphasized cooperative and communal ventures, not our contemporary authoritarian states which claim to be socialist or communist. As with Keynes later, however, Mill believed (*Principles*, Book 2, ch. 1, section 4) "the object to be principally aimed at in the present stage of human development, is not the subversion of the system of individual property, but the improvement of it, and the full participation of every member of the community in its benefits."

PRINCIPLES OF POLITICAL ECONOMY*

. . . The laws and conditions of the production of wealth, partake of the character of physical truths. There is nothing optional or arbitrary in them. Whatever mankind produce, must be produced in the modes, and under the conditions, imposed by the constitution of external things, and by the inherent properties of their own bodily and mental structure. Whether they like it or not, their productions will be limited by the amount of their previous accumulation, and, that being given, it will be proportional to their energy, their skill, the perfection of their machinery, and their judicious use of the advantages of combined labour. Whether they like it or not, a double quantity of labour will not raise, on the same land, a double quantity of food, unless some improvement takes place in the processes of culti-

---

*Principles of Political Economy (New York, 1897), Book 2, chapter 1; Book 4, chapters 6, 7.

vation. Whether they like it or not, the unproductive expenditure of individuals will *pro tanto* tend to impoverish the community, and only their productive expenditure will enrich it. The opinions, or the wishes, which may exist on these different matters, do not control the things themselves. We cannot, indeed, foresee to what extent the modes of production may be altered, or the productiveness of labour increased, by future extensions of our knowledge of the laws of nature suggesting new processes of industry of which we have at present no conception. But howsoever we may succeed in making for ourselves more space within the limits set by the constitution of things, we know that there must be limits. We cannot alter the ultimate properties either of matter or mind, but can only employ those properties more or less successfully, to bring about the events in which we are interested.

It is not so with the Distribution of Wealth. That is a matter of human institution solely. The things once there, mankind, individually or collectively, can do with them as they like. They can place them at the disposal of whomsoever they please, and on whatever terms. Further, in the social state, in every state except total solitude, any disposal whatever of them can only take place by the consent of society, or rather of those who dispose of its active force. Even what a person has produced by his individual toil, unaided by any one, he cannot keep, unless by the permission of society. Not only can society take it from him, but individuals could and would take it from him, if society only remained passive; if it did not either interfere *en masse*, or employ and pay people for the purpose of preventing him from being disturbed in the possession. The distribution of wealth, therefore, depends on the laws and customs of society. The rules by which it is determined, are what the opinions and feelings of the ruling portion of the community make them, and are very different in different ages and countries; and might be still more different, if mankind so chose.

. . . Society can subject the distribution of wealth to whatever rules it thinks best; but what practical results will flow from the operation of those rules, must be discovered, like any other physical or mental truths, by observation and reasoning.

We proceed, then, to the consideration of the different modes of distributing the produce of land and labour, which have been adopted in practice, or may be conceived in theory. Among these, our attention is first claimed by that primary and fundamental institution, on which, unless in some exceptional and very limited cases, the economical arrangements of society have always rested, though in its secondary features it has varied, and is liable to vary. I mean, of course, the institution of individual property.

Private property, as an institution, did not owe its origin to any of those considerations of utility, which plead for the maintenance of it when established. Enough is known of rude ages, both from history and from analogous states of society in our own time, to show, that tribunals (which always precede laws) were originally established, not to determine rights, but to repress violence and terminate quarrels. With this object chiefly in view, they naturally enough gave legal effect to first occupancy, by treating as the aggressor the person who first commenced violence, by turning, or attempting to turn, another out of possession. The preservation of the peace, which was the original object of civil government, was thus attained; while by confirming, to those who already possessed it, even what was not the fruit of personal exertion, a guarantee was incidentally given to them and others that they would be protected in what was so.

In considering the institution of property as a question in social philosophy, we must leave out of consideration its actual origin in any of the existing nations of Europe. We may suppose a community unhampered by any previous possession; a body of colonists, occupying for the first time an uninhabited country; bringing nothing with them but what belonged to them in common, and having a clear field for the adoption of the institutions and polity which they judged most expedient; required, therefore, to choose whether they would conduct the work of production on the principle of individual property, or on some system of common ownership and collective agency.

If private property were adopted, we must presume that it would be accompanied by none of the initial inequalities and injustice which obstruct the beneficial operation of the principle in old society. Every full-grown man or woman, we must suppose, would be secured in the unfettered use and disposal of his or her bodily and mental faculties; and the instruments of production, the land and tools, would be divided fairly among them, so that all might start, in respect to outward appliances, on equal terms. It is possible also to conceive that in this original apportionment, compensation might be made for the injuries of nature, and the balance redressed by assigning to the less robust members of the community advantages in the distribution, sufficient to put them on a par with the rest. But the division, once made, would not again be interfered with; individuals would be left to their own exertions and to the ordinary chances, for making an advantageous use of what was assigned to them. If individual property, on the contrary, were excluded, the plan which must be adopted would be to hold the land and all instruments of production as the joint property of the community, and to carry on the operations of industry on the common account. The direction of the labour of the community would devolve upon a magistrate or magistrates, whom we may suppose elected by the suffrages of the community, and whom we must assume to be voluntarily obeyed by them. The division of the produce would in like manner be a public act. The principle might either be that of complete equality, or of apportionment to the necessities or deserts of individuals, in whatever manner might be conformable to the ideas of justice or policy prevailing in the community.

The assailants of the principle of individual property may be divided into two classes: those whose scheme implies absolute equality in the distribution of the physical means of life and enjoyment, and those who admit inequality, but grounded on some principle, or supposed principle, of justice or general expediency, and not, like so many of the existing social inequalities, dependent on accident alone. At the head of the first class . . . is Communism, a word of continental origin, only of late introduced into this country. The word Socialism, which originated among the English Communists, and was assumed by them as a name to designate their own doctrine, is now, on the Continent, employed in a larger sense; not necessarily implying Communism, or the entire abolition of private property, but applied to any system which requires that the land and the instruments of production should be the property, not of individuals, but of communities or associations, or of the government. . . .

If, therefore, the choice were to be made between Communism with all its chances, and the present state of society with all its sufferings and injustices; if the institution of private property necessarily carried with it as a consequence, that the produce of labour should be apportioned as we now see it, almost in an inverse ratio to the labour—the largest portions to those who have never worked at all, the next largest to those whose work is almost nominal, and so in a descending scale, the remuneration dwindles as the work grows harder and more disagreeable, until the most fatiguing and exhausting bodily labour cannot count with certainty on being able to earn even the necessaries of life; if this, or Communism, were the alternative, all the difficulties, great or small, of Communism, would be but as dust in the balance. But to make the comparison applicable, we must compare Communism at its best, with the régime of individual property, not as it is, but as it might be made. The principle of private property has never yet had a fair trial in any country; and less so, perhaps, in this country than in some others. The social arrangements of modern Europe commenced from a distribution of property which was the result, not of just partition, or acquisition by industry, but of conquest and violence: and notwithstanding what industry has been doing for many centuries to modify the work of force, the system still retains many and large traces of its origin. The laws of property have never yet conformed to the principles on which the justification of private property rests. They have made property of things which never ought to be property, and absolute property where only a qualified property ought to exist. They have not held the balance fairly between human beings, but have heaped impediments upon some, to give advantage to others; they have purposely fostered inequalities, and prevented all from starting fair in the race. That all should indeed start on perfectly equal terms, is inconsistent with any law of private property: but if as much pains as has been taken to aggravate the inequality of chances arising from the natural working of the principle, had been taken to temper that inequality by every means not subversive of the principle itself; if the tendency of legislation had been to favour the diffusion, instead of the concentration of wealth—to encourage the subdivision of the large masses, instead of striving to keep them together; the principle of individual property would have been found to have no necessary connexion with the physical and social evils which almost all Socialist writers assume to be inseparable from it.

Private property, in every defence made of it, is supposed to mean, the guarantee to individuals of the fruits of their own labour and abstinence. The guarantee to them of the fruits of the labour and abstinence of others, transmitted to them without any merit or exertion of their own, is not of the essence of the institution, but a mere incidental consequence, which when it reaches a certain height, does not promote, but conflicts with the ends which render private property legitimate. To judge of the final destination of the institution of property, we must suppose everything rectified, which causes the institution to work in a manner opposed to that equitable principle, of proportion between remuneration and exertion, on which in every vindication of it that will bear the light, it is assumed to be grounded. We must also suppose two conditions realized, without which neither Communism nor any other laws or institutions could make the condition of the mass of mankind other than degraded and miserable. One of these conditions is, universal education; the other, a due limitation of the numbers of the community. With these, there could be no poverty even under the present social institutions: and these being supposed, the question of socialism is not, as generally stated by Socialists, a question of flying to the sole refuge against the evils which now bear down humanity; but a mere question of comparative advantages which futurity must determine. We are too ignorant either of what individual agency in its best form, or Socialism in its best form, can accomplish, to be qualified to decide which of the two will be the ultimate form of human society.

If a conjecture may be hazarded, the decision will probably depend mainly on one consideration, viz. which of the two systems is consistent with the greatest amount of human liberty and spontaneity. After the means of subsistence are assured, the next in strength of the personal wants of human beings is liberty; and (unlike the physical wants, which as civilization advances become more moderate and more amenable to control) it increases instead of diminishing in intensity, as the intelligence and the moral faculties are more developed. The perfection both of social arrangements and of practical morality would be, to secure to all persons complete independence and freedom of action, subject to no restriction but that of not doing injury to others: and the education which taught or the social institutions which required them to exchange the control of their own actions for any amount of comfort or affluence, or to renounce liberty for the sake of equality, would deprive them of one of the most elevated characteristics of human nature. It remains to be discovered how far the preservation of this characteristic would be found compatible with the Communistic organization of society. No doubt, this, like all other objections to the Socialist schemes, is vastly exaggerated. The members of the association need not be required to live together more than they do now, nor need they be controlled in the disposal of their individual share of the produce, and of the probably large amount of leisure which, if they limited their production to things really worth producing, they would possess. Individuals need not be chained to an occupation, or to a particular locality. The restraints of Communism would be freedom in comparison with the present condition of the majority of the human race. The generality of labourers in this and most other countries, have as little choice of occupation or freedom of locomotion, are practically as dependent on fixed rules and on the will of others, as they could be on any system short of actual slavery; to say nothing of the entire domestic subjection of one half the species, to which it is the signal honour of Owenism and most other forms of Socialism that they assign equal rights, in all respects, with those of the hitherto dominant sex. But it is not by comparison with the present bad state of society that the claims of Communism can be estimated; nor is it sufficient that it should promise greater personal and mental freedom than is now enjoyed by those who have not enough of either to deserve the name. The question is, whether there would be any asylum left for individuality of character; whether public opinion would not be a tyrannical yoke; whether the absolute dependence of each on all, and surveillance of each by all, would not grind all down into a tame uniformity of thoughts, feelings, and actions. This is already one of the glaring evils of the existing state of society, notwithstanding a much greater diversity of education and pursuits, and a much less absolute dependence of the individual on the mass, than would exist in the Communistic régime. No society in which eccentricity is a matter of reproach, can be in a wholesome state. It is yet to be ascertained whether the Communistic scheme would be consistent with that multiform development of human nature, those manifold unlikenesses, that diversity of tastes and talents, and variety of intellectual points of view, which not only form a great part of the interest of human life, but by bringing intellects into stimulating collision, and by presenting to each innumerable notions that he would not have conceived of himself, are the mainspring of mental and moral progression.

. . . But while I agree and sympathize with Socialists in this practical portion of their aims, I utterly dissent from the most conspicuous and vehement part of their teaching, their declamations against competition. With moral conceptions in many respects far ahead of the existing arrangements of society, they have in general very confused and erroneous notions of its actual working; and one of their greatest errors, as I conceive, is to charge upon competition all the economical evils which at present exist. They forget that wherever competition is not, monopoly is; and that monopoly, in all its forms, is the taxation of the industrious for the support of indolence, if not of plunder. They forget, too, that with the exception of competition among labourers, all other competition is for the benefit of the labourers, by cheapening the articles they consume; that competition even in the labour market is a source not of low but of high wages, wherever the competition *for* labour exceeds the competition *of* labour, as in America, in the colonies, and in the skilled trades; and never could be a cause of low wages, save by the overstocking of the labour market through the too great numbers of the labourers' families; while, if the supply of labourers is excessive, not even Socialism can prevent their remuneration from being low. Besides, if association were universal, there would be no competition between labourer and labourer; and that between association and association would be for the benefit of the consumers, that is, of the associations; of the industrious classes generally.

I do not pretend that there are no inconveniences in competition, or that the moral objections urged against it by Socialist writers, as a source of jealousy and hostility among those engaged in the same occupation, are altogether groundless. But if competition has its evils, it prevents greater evils. . . . It is the common error of Socialists to overlook the natural indolence of mankind; their tendency to be passive, to be the slaves of habit, to persist indefinitely in a course once chosen. Let them once attain any state of existence which they consider tolerable, and the danger to be apprehended is that they will thenceforth stagnate; will not exert themselves to improve, and by letting their faculties rust, will lose even the energy required to preserve them from deterioration. Competition may not be the best conceivable stimulus, but it is at present a necessary one, and no one can foresee the time when it will not be indispensable to progress. . . .

Instead of looking upon competition as the baneful and anti-social principle which it is held to be by the generality of Socialists, I conceive that, even in the present state of society and industry, every restriction of it is an evil, and every extension of it, even if for the time injuriously affecting some class of labourers, is always an ultimate good. To be protected against competition is to be protected in idleness, in mental dulness; to be saved the necessity of being as active and as intelligent as other people; and if it is also to be protected against being underbid for employment by a less highly paid class of labourers, this is only where old custom or local and partial monopoly has placed some particular class of artisans in a privileged position as compared with the rest; and the time has come when the interest of universal improvement is no longer promoted by prolonging the privileges of a few. . . . What is now required is not to bolster up old customs, whereby limited classes of labouring people obtain partial gains which interest them in keeping up the present organization of society, but to introduce new general practices beneficial to all; and there is reason to rejoice at whatever makes the privileged classes of skilled artisans feel, that they have the same interests, and depend for their remuneration on the same general causes, and must resort for the improvement of their condition to the same remedies, as the less fortunately circumstanced and comparatively helpless multitude.

. . . [I]n contemplating any progressive movement, not in its nature unlimited, the mind is not satisfied with merely tracing the laws of the movement: it cannot but ask the further question, to what goal? Towards what ultimate point is society tending by its industrial progress? When the progress ceases, in what condition are we to expect that it will leave mankind?

It must always have been seen, more or less distinctly, by political economists, that the increase of wealth is not boundless: that at the end of what they term the progressive state lies the stationary state, that all progress in wealth is but a postponement of this, and that each step in advance is an approach to it. We have now been led to recognize that this ultimate goal is at all times near enough to be fully in view; that we are always on the verge of it, and that if we have not reached it long ago, it is because the goal itself flies before us. The richest and most prosperous countries would very soon attain the stationary state, if no further improvements were made in the productive arts, and if there were a suspension of the overflow of capital from those countries into the uncultivated or illcultivated regions of the earth.

This impossibility of ultimately avoiding the stationary state . . . must have been, to the political economists of the last two generations, an unpleasing and discouraging prospect; for the tone and tendency of their speculations goes completely to identify all that is economically desirable with the progressive state, and with that alone. With Mr. M'Culloch, for example, prosperity does not mean a large production and a good distribution of wealth, but a rapid increase of it. . . .

Even in a progressive state of capital, in old countries, a conscientious or prudential restraint on population is indispensable, to prevent the increase of numbers from outstripping the increase of capital, and the condition of the classes who are at the bottom of society from being deteriorated. Where there is not, in the people, or in some very large proportion of them, a resolute resistance to this deterioration—a determination to preserve an established standard of comfort—the condition of the poorest class sinks, even in a progressive state, to the lowest point which they will consent to endure. The same determination would be equally effectual to keep up their condition in the stationary state, and would be quite as likely to exist. Indeed, even now, the countries in which the greatest prudence is manifested in the regulating of population, are often those in which capital increases least rapidly. Where there is an indefinite prospect of employment for increased numbers, there is apt to appear less necessity for prudential restraint. If it were evident that a new hand could not obtain employment but by displacing, or succeeding to, one already employed, the combined influences of prudence and public opinion might in some measure be relied on for restricting the coming generation within the numbers necessary for replacing the present.

I cannot, therefore, regard the stationary state of capital and wealth with the unaffected aversion so generally manifested towards it by political economists of the old school. I am inclined to believe that it would be, on the whole, a very considerable improvement on our present condition. I confess I am not charmed with the ideal of life held out by those who think that the normal state of human beings is that of struggling to get on; that the trampling, crushing, elbowing, and treading on each other's heels, which form the existing type of social life, are the most desirable lot of human kind, or anything but the disagreeable symptoms of one of the phases of industrial progress. The northern and middle states of America are a specimen of this stage of civilization in very favourable circumstances; having, apparently, got rid of all social injustices and inequalities that affect persons of Caucasian race and of the male sex, while the proportion of population to capital and land is such as to ensure abundance to every able-bodied member of the community who does not forfeit it by misconduct. They have the six points of Chartism,[1] and they have no poverty: and all that these advantages seem to have yet done for them (notwithstanding some incipient signs of a better tendency) is that the life of the whole of one sex is devoted to dollar-hunting, and of the other to breeding dollar-hunters. This is not a kind of social perfection which philanthropists to come will feel any very eager desire to assist in realizing. Most fitting, indeed, is it, that while riches are power, and to grow as rich as possible the universal object of ambition, the path to its attainment should be open to all, without favour or partiality. But the best state for human nature is that in which, while no one is poor, no one desires to be richer, nor has any reason to fear being thrust back, by the efforts of others to push themselves forward.

That the energies of mankind should be kept in employment by the struggle for riches, as they were formerly by the struggle of war, until the better minds succeed in educating the others into better things, is undoubtedly more desirable than that they should rust and stagnate. While minds are coarse they require coarse stimuli, and let them have them. In the meantime, those who do not accept the present very early stage of human improvement as its ultimate type, may be excused for being comparatively indifferent to the kind of economical progress which excites the congratulations of ordinary politicians; the mere increase of production and accumulation. For the safety of national independence it is essential that a country should not fall much behind its neighbours in these things. But in themselves they are of little importance, so long as either the increase of population or anything else prevents the mass of the people from reaping any part of the benefit of them. . . . It is only in the backward countries of the world that increased production is still an important object: in those most advanced, what is economically needed is a better distribution, of which one indispensable means is a stricter restraint on population. Levelling institutions, either of a just or of an unjust kind, cannot alone accomplish it; they may lower the heights of society, but they cannot, of themselves, permanently raise the depths.

On the other hand, we may suppose this better distribution of property attained by the joint effect of the prudence and frugality of individuals, and of a system of legislation favouring equality of fortunes, so far as is consistent with the just claim of the individual to the fruits, whether great or small, of his or her own industry. We may suppose, for instance . . . a limitation of the sum which any one person may acquire by gift or inheritance, to the amount sufficient to constitute a moderate independence. Under this twofold influence, society would exhibit these leading features: a well-paid and affluent body of labourers; no enormous fortunes, except what were earned and accumulated during a single lifetime; but a much larger body of persons than at present, not only exempt from the coarser toils, but with sufficient leisure, both physical and mental, from mechanical details, to cultivate freely the graces of life, and afford examples of them to the classes less favourably circumstanced for their growth. This condition of society, so greatly preferable to the present, is not only perfectly compatible with the stationary state, but, it would seem, more naturally allied with that state than with any other.

There is room in the world, no doubt, and even in old countries, for a great increase of population, supposing the arts of life to go on improving, and capital to increase. But even if innocuous, I confess I see very little reason for desiring it. The density of population necessary to enable mankind to obtain, in the greatest degree, all the advantages both of co-operation and of social intercourse, has, in all the most populous countries, been attained. A population may be too crowded, though all be amply supplied with food and raiment. It is not good for man to be kept perforce at all times in the presence of his species. A world from which solitude is extirpated, is a very poor ideal. Solitude, in the sense of being often alone, is essential to any depth of meditation or of character; and solitude in the presence of natural beauty and grandeur, is the cradle of thoughts and aspirations which are not only good for the individual, but which society could ill do without. Nor is there much satisfaction in contemplating the world with nothing left to the spontaneous activity of nature; with every rood of land brought into cultivation, which is capable of growing food for human beings; every flowery waste or natural pasture ploughed up, all quadrupeds or birds which are not domesticated for man's use exterminated as his rivals for food, every hedgerow or superfluous tree rooted out, and scarcely a place left where a wild shrub or flower could grow without being eradicated as a weed in the name of improved agriculture. If the earth must lose that great portion of its pleasantness which it owes to things that the unlimited increase of wealth and population would extirpate from it, for the mere purpose of enabling it to support a larger, but not a better or a happier population, I sincerely hope, for the sake of posterity, that they will be content to be stationary, long before necessity compels them to it.

It is scarcely necessary to remark that a stationary condition of capital and population implies no stationary state of human improvement. There would be as much scope as ever for all kinds of mental culture, and moral and social progress; as much room for improving the Art of Living, and much more likelihood of its being improved, when minds ceased to be engrossed by the art of getting on. Even the industrial arts might be as earnestly and as successfully cultivated, with this sole difference, that instead of serving no purpose but the increase of wealth, industrial improvements would produce their legitimate effect, that of abridging labour. Hitherto it is questionable if all the mechanical inventions yet made have lightened the day's toil of any human being. They have enabled a greater population to live the same life of drudgery and imprisonment, and an increased number of manufacturers and others to make fortunes. They have increased the comforts of the middle classes. But they have not yet begun to effect those great changes in human destiny, which it is in their nature and in their futurity to accomplish. Only when, in addition to just institutions, the increase of mankind shall be under the deliberate guidance of judicious foresight, can the conquests made from the powers of nature by the intellect and energy of scientific discoverers, become the common property of the species, and the means of improving and elevating the universal lot.

20 THOMAS HILL GREEN

In the writings and lectures of the Oxford philosopher and political reformer T. H. Green (1836-1882), one finds again and again an argument which runs about like this: (1) The goal of liberal government is to allow men to become morally responsible. (2) For men to become responsible, they must be free to choose among alternative forms of action. (3) This freedom must be real in order for it to be effective; where alternatives are arbitrarily defined or restrained, choice cannot be meaningful. (4) Inequalities of income or education which have nothing to do with an individual's *native* talents will impair his ability to choose and arbitrarily restrict the range of alternatives from which he may pick. (5) The state should act to reduce such inequalities because they are an obstacle to the fundamental goal of a liberal society. This argument, that the liberal idea of freedom consists of much more than merely being left alone, is the foundation of the contemporary *liberal* welfare state.

"Liberal Legislation and Freedom of Contract" is an important part of this argument. Green was reacting to the way in which defenders of laissez-faire had turned the institution of contract into an absolute. Indirectly, he also attacked the English utilitarians for allowing this to happen. Most importantly, "Liberal Legislation and Freedom of Contract" marks a line of departure: the years immediately after Green's death would see the Liberal party officially adopt many of his ideas and then turn them into concrete reforms. This would undoubtedly have pleased the retiring, sensitive Green because he meant his reform proposals and his philosophical critiques of the utilitarians and the "evolutionists" like Spencer to have practical effects.

LIBERAL LEGISLATION AND
FREEDOM OF CONTRACT*

. . . We shall probably all agree that freedom, rightly understood, is the greatest of blessings; that its attainment is the true end of all our effort as citizens. But when we thus speak of freedom, we should consider carefully what we mean by it. We do not mean merely freedom from restraint or compulsion. We do not mean merely freedom to do as we like irrespectively of what it is that we like. We do not mean a freedom that can be enjoyed by one man or one set of men at the cost of a loss of freedom to others. When we speak of freedom as something to be so highly prized, we mean a positive power or capacity of doing or enjoying something worth doing or enjoying, and that, too, something that we do or enjoy in common with others. We mean by it a power which each man exercises through the help or security given him by his fellow-men, and which he in turn helps to secure for them. When we measure the progress of a society by its growth in freedom, we measure it by the increasing development and exercise on the whole of those powers of contributing to social good with which we believe the members of the society to be endowed; in short, by the greater power on the part of the citizens as a body to make the most and best of themselves. Thus, though of course there can be no freedom among men who act not willingly but under compulsion, yet on the other hand the mere removal of compulsion, the mere enabling a man to do as he likes, is in itself no contribution to true freedom. In one sense no man is so well able to do as he likes as the wandering savage. He has no master. There is no one to say him nay. Yet we do not count him really free, because the freedom of savagery is not strength, but weakness. The actual powers of the noblest savage do not admit of comparison with those of the humblest citizen of a law-abiding state. He is not the slave of man, but he is the slave of nature. Of compulsion by natural necessity he has plenty of experience, though of restraint by society none at all. Nor can he deliver himself from that compulsion except by submitting to this restraint. So to submit is the first step in true freedom, because the first step towards the full exercise of the faculties with which man is endowed. But we rightly refuse to recognise the highest development on the part of an

*R. L. Nettleship, ed., *Works of Thomas Hill Green*, 3d edition, vol. 3 (London: Longmans, Green and Co., 1891), pp. 370-86.

exceptional individual or exceptional class, as an advance towards the true freedom of man, if it is founded on a refusal of the same opportunity to other men. The powers of the human mind have probably never attained such force and keenness, the proof of what society can do for the individual has never been so strikingly exhibited, as among the small groups of men who possessed civil privileges in the small republics of antiquity. The whole framework of our political ideas, to say nothing of our philosophy, is derived from them. But in them this extraordinary efflorescence of the privileged class was accompanied by the slavery of the multitude. That slavery was the condition on which it depended, and for that reason it was doomed to decay. There is no clearer ordinance of that supreme reason, often dark to us, which governs the course of man's affairs, than that no body of men should in the long run be able to strengthen itself at the cost of others' weakness. The civilisation and freedom of the ancient world were short-lived because they were partial and exceptional. If the ideal of true freedom is the maximum of power for all members of human society alike to make the best of themselves, we are right in refusing to ascribe the glory of freedom to a state in which the apparent elevation of the few is founded on the degradation of the many, and in ranking modern society, founded as it is on free industry, with all its confusion and ignorant licence and waste of effort, above the most splendid of ancient republics.

If I have given a true account of that freedom which forms the goal of social effort, we shall see that freedom of contract, freedom in all the forms of doing what one will with one's own, is valuable only as a means to an end. That end is what I call freedom in the positive sense: in other words, the liberation of the powers of all men equally for contributions to a common good. No one has a right to do what he will with his own in such a way as to contravene this end. It is only through the guarantee which society gives him that he has property at all, or, strictly speaking, any right to his possessions. This guarantee is founded on a sense of common interest. Every one has an interest in securing to every one else the free use and enjoyment and disposal of his possessions, so long as that freedom on the part of one does not interfere with a like freedom on the part of others, because such freedom contributes to that equal development of the faculties of all which is the highest good for all. This is the true and the only justification of rights of property. Rights of property, however, have been and are claimed which cannot be thus justified. We are all now agreed that men cannot rightly be the property of men. The institution of property being only justifiable as a means to the free exercise of the social capabilities of all, there can be no true right to property of a kind which debars one class of men from such free exercise altogether. We condemn slavery no less when it arises out of a voluntary agreement on the part of the enslaved person. A contract by which any one agreed for a certain consideration to become the slave of another we should reckon a void contract. Here, then, is a limitation upon freedom of contract which we all recognise as rightful. No contract is valid in which human persons, willingly or unwillingly, are dealt with as commodities, because such contracts of necessity defeat the end for which alone society enforces contracts at all.

Are there no other contracts which, less obviously perhaps but really, are open to the same objection? In the first place, let us consider contracts affecting labour. Labour, the economist tells us, is a commodity exchangeable like other commodities. This is in a certain sense true, but it is a commodity which attaches in a peculiar manner to the person of man. Hence restrictions may need to be placed on the sale of this commodity which would be unnecessary in other cases, in order to prevent labour from being sold under conditions which make it impossible for the person selling it ever to become a free contributor to social good in any form. This is most plainly the case when a man bargains to work under conditions fatal to health, e.g. in an unventilated factory. Every injury to the health of the individual is, so far as it goes, a public injury. It is an impediment to the general freedom; so much deduction from our power, as members of society, to make the best of ourselves. Society is, therefore, plainly within its right when it limits freedom of contract for the sale of labour, so far as is done by our laws for the sanitary regulations of factories, workshops, and mines. It is equally within its right in prohibiting the labour of women and young persons beyond certain hours. If they work beyond those hours, the result is demonstrably physical deterioration; which, as demonstrably, carries with it a lowering of the moral forces of society. For the sake of that general freedom of its members to make the best of themselves, which it is the object of civil society to secure, a prohibition should be put by law, which is the deliberate voice of society, on all such contracts of service as in a general way yield such a result. The purchase or hire of unwholesome dwellings is properly forbidden on the same principle. Its application to compulsory education may not be quite so obvious, but it will appear on a little reflection. Without a command of certain elementary arts and knowledge, the individual in modern society is as effectually crippled as by the loss of a limb or a broken constitution. He is not free to develop his faculties. With a view to securing such freedom among its members it is as certainly within the province of the state to prevent children from growing up in that kind of ignorance which practically excludes them from a free career in life, as it is within its province to require the sort of building and drainage necessary for public health.

Our modern legislation then with reference to labour, and education, and health, involving as it does manifold interference with freedom of contract, is justified on the ground that it is the business of the state, not indeed directly to promote moral goodness, for that, from the very nature of moral goodness, it cannot do, but to maintain the conditions without which a free exercise of the human faculties is impossible. It does not indeed follow that it is advisable for the state to do all which it is justified in doing. . . . It is one question whether of late the central government has been unduly trenching on local government, and another question whether the law of the state, either as administered by central or by provincial authorities, has been unduly interfering with the discretion of individuals. We may object most strongly to advancing centralisation, and yet wish that the law should put rather more than less restraint on those liberties of the individual which are a social nuisance. But there are some political speculators whose objection is not merely to centralisation, but to the extended action of law altogether. They think that the individual ought to be left much more to himself than has of late been the case. Might not our people, they ask, have been trusted to learn in time for themselves to eschew unhealthy dwellings, to refuse dangerous and degrading employment, to get their children the schooling necessary for making their way in the world? Would they not for their own comfort, if not from more chivalrous feeling, keep their wives and daughters from overwork? Or, failing this, ought not women, like men, to learn to protect themselves? Might not all the rules, in short, which legislation of the kind we have been discussing is intended to attain, have been attained without it; not so quickly, perhaps, but without tampering so dangerously with the independence and self-reliance of the people?

Now, we shall probably all agree that a society in which the public health was duly protected, and necessary education duly provided for, by the spontaneous action of individuals, was in a higher condition than one in which the compulsion of law was needed to secure these ends. But we must take men as we find them. Until such a condition of society is reached, it is the business of the state to take the best security it can for the young citizens' growing up in such health and with so much knowledge as is necessary for their real freedom. In so doing it need not at all interfere with the independence and self-reliance of those whom it requires to do what they would otherwise do for themselves. The man who, of his own right feeling, saves his wife from overwork and sends his children to school, suffers no moral degradation from a law which, if he did not do this for himself, would seek to make him do it. Such a man does not feel the law as constraint at all. To him it is simply a powerful friend. It gives him security for that being done efficiently which, with the best wishes, he might have much trouble in getting done efficiently if left to himself. No doubt it relieves him from some of the responsibility which would otherwise fall to him as head of a family, but, if he is what we are supposing him to be, in proportion as he is relieved of responsibilities in one direction he will assume them in another. The security which the state gives him for the safe housing and sufficient schooling of his family will only make him the more careful for their well-being in other respects, which he is left to look after for himself. We need have no fear, then, of such legislation having an ill effect on those who, without the law, would have seen to that being done, though probably less efficiently, which the law requires to be done. But it was not their case that the laws we are considering were especially meant to meet. It was the overworked women, the ill-housed and untaught families, for whose benefit they were intended. And the question is whether without these laws the suffering classes could have been delivered quickly or slowly from the condition they were in. Could the enlightened self-interest or benevolence of individuals, working under a system of unlimited freedom of contract, have ever brought them into a state compatible with the free development of the human faculties? No one considering the facts can have any doubt as to the answer to this question. Left to itself, or to the operation of casual benevolence, a degraded population perpetuates and increases itself. Read any of the authorised accounts, given before royal or parliamentary commissions, of the state of the labourers, especially of the women and children, as they were in our great industries before the law was first brought to bear on them, and before freedom of contract was first interfered with in them. Ask yourself what chance there was of a generation, born and bred under such conditions, ever contracting itself out of them. Given a certain standard of moral and material well-being, people may be trusted not to sell their labour, or the labour of their children, on terms which would not allow that standard to be maintained. But with large masses of our population, until the laws we have been considering took effect, there was no such standard. There was nothing on their part, in the way either of self-respect or established demand for comforts, to prevent them from working and living, or from putting their children to work and live, in a way in which no one who is to be a healthy and free citizen can work and live. No doubt there were many high-minded employers who did their best for their workpeople before the days of state-interference, but they could not prevent less scrupulous hirers of labour from hiring it on the cheapest terms. It is true that cheap labour is in the long run dear labour, but it is so only in the long run, and eager traders do not think of the long run. If labour is to be had under conditions incompatible with the health or decent housing or education of the labourer, there will always be plenty of people to buy it under those conditions, careless of the burden in the shape of rates and taxes which they may be laying up for posterity. Either the standard of well-being on the part of the sellers of labour must prevent them from selling their labour under these conditions, or the law must prevent it. With a population such as ours was forty years ago, and still largely is, the law must prevent it and continue the prevention for some generations, before the sellers will be in a state to prevent it for themselves. . . .

. . . The peasant farmer is scarcely more free to contract with his landlord than is a starving labourer to bargain for good wages with a master who offers him work. When many contracts between landlord and tenant are made under such pressure, reverence for contract, which is the safeguard of society, is sure to disappear, and this I believe to be the chief reason why the farmers of southern and western Ireland have been so easily led astray by the agitation of the land league. That agitation strikes at the roots of all contract, and therefore at the very foundation of modern society; but if we would effectually withstand it, we must cease to insist on maintaining the forms of free contract where the reality is impossible. We must in some way give the farmers of Ireland by law that protection which, as a rule, they have been too weak to obtain for themselves singly by contract, protection against the confiscation of the fruits of the labour and money they have spent on the soil, whether that confiscation take the form of actual eviction or of a constant enhancement of rent. To uphold the sanctity of contracts is doubtless a prime business of government, but it is no less its business to provide against contracts being made, which, from the helplessness of one of the parties to them, instead of being a security for freedom, become an instrument of disguised oppression.

I have left myself little time to speak of the principles on which some of us hold that, in the matter of intoxicating drinks, a further limitation of freedom of contract is needed in the interest of general freedom. I say a further limitation, because there is no such thing as a free sale of these drinks at present. Men are not at liberty to buy and sell them when they will, where they will, and as they will. But our present licensing system, while it creates a class of monopolists especially interested in resisting any effectual restraint of the liquor traffic, does little to lessen the facilities for obtaining strong drink. Indeed the principle upon which licenses have been generally given has been avowedly to make it easy to get drink. The restriction of the hours of sale is no doubt a real check so far as it goes, but it remains the case that every one who has a weakness for drink has the temptation staring him in the face during all hours but those when he ought to be in bed. The effect of the present system, in short, is to prevent the drink-shops from coming unpleasantly near the houses of well-to-do people, and to crowd them upon the quarters occupied by the poorer classes, who have practically no power of keeping the nuisance from them. Now it is clear that the only remedy which the law can afford for this state of things must take the form either of more stringent rules of licensing, or of a power entrusted to the householders in each district of excluding the sale of intoxicants altogether from among them.

I do not propose to discuss the comparative merits of these methods of procedure. One does not exclude the other. They may very well be combined. One may be best suited for one kind of population, the other for another kind. But either, to be effectual, must involve a large interference with the liberty of the individual to do as he likes in the matter of buying and selling alcohol. It is the justifiability of that interference that I wish briefly to consider.

We justify it on the simple ground of the recognised right on the part of society to prevent men from doing as they like, if, in the exercise of their peculiar tastes in doing as they like, they create a social nuisance. There is no right to freedom in the purchase and sale of a particular commodity, if the general result of allowing such freedom is to detract from freedom in the higher sense, from the general power of men to make the best of themselves. Now with anyone who looks calmly at the facts, there can be no doubt that the present habits of drinking in England do lay a heavy burden on the free development of man's powers for social good, a heavier burden probably than arises from all other preventible causes put together. It used to be the fashion to look on drunkenness as a vice which was the concern only of the person who fell into it so long as it did not lead him to commit assault on his neighbours. No thoughtful man any longer looks on it in this way. We know that, however decently carried on, the excessive drinking of one man means an injury to others in health, purse, and capability, to which no limits can be placed. Drunkenness in the head of a family means, as a rule, the impoverishment and degradation of all members of the family; and the presence of a drink-shop at the corner of a street means, as a rule, the drunkenness of a certain number of heads of families in that street. Remove the drink-shops, and, as the experience of many happy communities sufficiently shows, you almost, perhaps in time altogether, remove the drunkenness. Here, then, is a wide-spreading social evil, of which society may, if it will, by a restraining law, to a great extent, rid itself, to the infinite enhancement of the positive freedom enjoyed by its members. All that is required for the attainment of so blessed a result is so much effort and self-sacrifice on the part of the majority of citizens as is necessary for the enactment and enforcement of the restraining law. The major-ity of citizens may still be far from prepared for such an effort. That is a point on which I express no opinion. To attempt a restraining law in advance of the social sentiment necessary to give real effect to it, is always a mistake. But to argue that an effectual law in restraint of the drink-traffic would be a wrongful interference with individual liberty, is to ignore the essential condition under which alone every particular liberty can rightly be allowed to the individual, the condition, namely, that the allowance of that liberty is not, as a rule, and on the whole, an impediment to social good.

The more reasonable opponents of the restraint for which I plead, would proba-bly argue not so much that it was necessarily wrong in principle, as that it was one of those short cuts to a good end which ultimately defeat their own object. They would take the same line that has been taken by the opponents of state-interfer-ence in all its forms. "Leave the people to themselves," they would say; "as their standard of self-respect rises, as they become better housed and better edu-cated, they will gradually shake off the evil habit. The cure so effected may not be so rapid as that brought by a repressive law, but it will be more lasting. Better that it should come more slowly through the spontaneous action of individuals, than more quickly through compulsion."

But here again we reply that it is dangerous to wait. The slower remedy might be preferable if we were sure that it was a remedy at all, but we have no such assurance. There is strong reason to think the contrary. Every year that the evil is left to itself, it becomes greater. The vested interest in the encouragement of the vice becomes larger, and the persons affected by it more numerous. . . . Better education, better housing, more healthy rules of labour, no doubt lessen the temptations to drink for those who have the benefit of these advantages, but meanwhile drunkenness is constantly recruiting the ranks of those who cannot be really educated, who will not be better housed, who make their employments dangerous and unhealthy. An effectual liquor law in short is the necessary complement of our factory acts, our education acts, our public health acts. Without it the full measure of their usefulness will never be attained. They were all opposed in their turn by the same arguments that are now used against a restraint of the facilities for drinking. Sometimes it was the argument that the state had no business to interfere with the liberties of the individual. Sometimes it was the dilatory plea that the better nature of man would in time assert itself, and that meanwhile it would be lowered by compulsion. Happily a sense of the facts and necessities of the case got the better of the delusive cry of liberty. Act after act was passed preventing master and workman, parent and child, house-builder and house-holder, from doing as they pleased, with the result of a great addition to the real freedom of society. The spirit of self-reliance and independence was not weakened by those acts. Rather it received a new development. The dead weight of ignorance and unhealthy surroundings, with which it would otherwise have had to struggle, being partially removed by law, it was more free to exert itself for higher objects. When we ask for a stringent liquor law, which should even go to the length of allowing the householders of a district to exclude the drink traffic altogether, we are only asking for a continuation of the same work, a continuation necessary to its complete success. . . . The danger of legislation, either in the interests of a privileged class or for the promotion of particular religious opinions, we may fairly assume to be over. The popular jealousy of law, once justifiable enough, is therefore out of date. The citizens of England now make its law. We ask them by law to put a restraint on themselves in the matter of strong drink. We ask them further to limit, or even altogether to give up, the not very precious liberty of buying and selling alcohol, in order that they become more free to exercise the faculties and improve the talents which God has given them.

21 JOHN MAYNARD KEYNES

John Maynard Keynes (1883-1946) provided the intellectual justification for much of the contemporary political economy. This includes the modern, liberal, interven ionist, welfare state, and international cooperation through organizations such as the International Monetary Fund. His *General Theory of Employment, Interest and Money* (1936) revolutionized economic theory and the governmental and social policies based on it. Keynes argued that the older laissez-faire theory applied only in a limited, special case, that of full employment. However, full employment was the exception, not the rule; therefore it was necessary to create new economic theory and new public policies that would reflect the change in theory.

Unlike laissez-faire theorists who saw government intervention as upsetting the natural equilibrium of the economy, Keynes argued that such intervention is necessary to ensure that the economy will function properly. Keynes' economics are associated with his view that society has a communal responsibility to create the conditions for a better, civilized life, and the state must take the lead. However, in both his economics and in his political values Keynes doubted that there is a natural harmony which can be discovered or produced by noninterventionist policies. Governments, therefore, have to plan consciously for and direct society and the economy.

Planning involves uncertainty, difficult choices, and conscious interventions in the economy to prevent or correct both economic and social-political instability. He felt that such intervention is necessary to cure unemployment, save the essential features of capitalism, and protect individualism. The political and economic aspects of any problem cannot be easily separated. Without intervention, Keynes felt, capitalism and individualism would be overwhelmed and destroyed by the forces set loose by massive unemployment and human misery between the two world wars.

The selections below sample Keynes' political and social ideas. "The Means to Prosperity" illustrates reform liberalism's economic justification of job creation.

THE END OF LAISSEZ-FAIRE (1926)*

Economists, like other scientists, have chosen the hypothesis from which they set out, and which they offer to beginners, because it is the simplest, and not because it is the nearest to the facts. Partly for this reason, but partly, I admit, because they have been biased by the traditions of the subject, they have begun by assuming a state of affairs where the ideal distribution of productive resources can be

---

* "The End of Laissez-Faire," in *The Collected Writings of John Maynard Keynes*, Vol. 9: *Essays in Persuasion* (London: Macmillan, 1972), pp. 282-94. Reprinted by permission of Macmillan, Cambridge University Press, and Lord Kahn.

brought about through individuals acting independently by the method of trial and error in such a way that those individuals who move in the right direction will destroy by competition those who move in the wrong direction. This implies that there must be no mercy or protection for those who embark their capital or their labour in the wrong direction. It is a method of bringing the most successful profit-makers to the top by a ruthless struggle for survival, which selects the most efficient by the bankruptcy of the less efficient. It does not count the cost of the struggle, but looks only to the benefits of the final result which are assumed to be permanent. The object of life being to crop the leaves off the branches up to the greatest possible height, the likeliest way of achieving this end is to leave the giraffes with the longest necks to starve out those whose necks are shorter.

Corresponding to this method of attaining the ideal distribution of the instruments of production between different purposes, there is a similar assumption as to how to attain the ideal distribution of what is available for consumption. In the first place, each individual will discover what amongst the possible objects of consumption *he* wants most by the method of trial and error "at the margin," and in this way not only will each consumer come to distribute his consumption most advantageously, but each object of consumption will find its way into the mouth of the consumer whose relish for it is greatest compared with that of the others, because that consumer will outbid the rest. Thus, if only we leave the giraffes to themselves, (1) the maximum quantity of leaves will be cropped because the giraffes with the longest necks will, by dint of starving out the others, get nearest to the trees; (2) each giraffe will make for the leaves which he finds most succulent amongst those in reach; and (3) the giraffes whose relish for a given leaf is greatest will crane most to reach it. In this way more and juicier leaves will be swallowed, and each individual leaf will reach the throat which thinks it deserves most effort.

This assumption, however, of conditions where unhindered natural selection leads to progress, is only one of the two provisional assumptions which, taken as literal truth, have become the twin buttresses of *laissez-faire*. The other one is the efficacy, and indeed the necessity, of the opportunity for unlimited private money-making as an *incentive* to maximum effort. Profit accrues, under *laissez-faire*, to the individual who, whether by skill or good fortune, is found with his productive resources in the right place at the right time. A system which allows the skilful or fortunate individual to reap the whole fruits of this conjuncture evidently offers an immense incentive to the practice of the art of being in the right place at the right time. Thus one of the most powerful of human motives, namely, the love of money, is harnessed to the task of distributing economic resources in the way best calculated to increase wealth.

The parallelism between economic *laissez-faire* and Darwinianism . . . is now seen, as Herbert Spencer was foremost to recognise, to be very close indeed. Just as Darwin invoked sexual love, acting through sexual selection, as an adjutant to natural selection by competition, to direct evolution along lines which should be desirable as well as effective, so the individualist invokes the love of money, acting through the pursuit of profit, as an adjutant to natural selection, to bring about the production of the greatest possible scale of what is most strongly desired as measured by exchange value.

The beauty and the simplicity of such a theory are so great that it is easy to forget that it follows not from the actual facts, but from an incomplete hypothesis introduced for the sake of simplicity. Apart from other objections to be mentioned later, the conclusion that individuals acting independently for their own advantage will produce the greatest aggregate of wealth, depends on a variety of unreal assumptions to the effect that the processes of production and consumption are in no way organic, that there exists a sufficient foreknowledge of conditions and requirements, and that there are adequate opportunities of obtaining this foreknowledge. For economists generally reserve for a later stage of their argument the complications which arise—(1) when the efficient units of production are large relatively to the units of consumption, (2) when overhead costs or joint costs are present, (3) when internal economies tend to the aggregation of production, (4) when the time required for adjustments is long, (5) when ignorance prevails over knowledge, and (6) when monopolies and combinations interfere with equality in bargaining—they reserve, that is to say, for a later stage their analysis of the actual facts. Moreover, many of those who recognise that the simplified hypothesis does not accurately correspond to fact conclude nevertheless that it does represent what is "natural" and therefore ideal. They regard the simplified hypothesis as health, and the further complications as disease.

Yet besides this question of fact there are other considerations, familiar enough, which rightly bring into the calculation the cost and character of the competitive struggle itself, and the tendency for wealth to be distributed where it is not appreciated most. If we have the welfare of the giraffes at heart, we must not overlook the sufferings of the shorter necks who are starved out, or the sweet leaves which fall to the ground and are trampled underfoot in the struggle, or the overfeeding of the long-necked ones, or the evil look of anxiety or struggling greediness which overcasts the mild faces of the herd.

Let us clear from the ground the metaphysical or general principles upon which, from time to time, *laissez-faire* has been founded. It is *not* true that individuals possess a prescriptive 'natural liberty' in their economic activities. There is *no* 'compact' conferring perpetual rights on those who Have or on those who Acquire. The world is *not* so governed from above that private and social interest always coincide. It is *not* so managed here below that in practice they coincide. It is *not* a correct deduction from the principles of economics that enlightened self-interest always operates in the public interest. Nor is it true that self-interest generally *is* enlightened; more often individuals acting separately to promote their own ends are too ignorant or too weak to attain even these. Experience does *not* show that individuals, when they make up a social unit, are always less clear-sighted than when they act separately.

We cannot therefore settle on abstract grounds, but must handle on its merits in detail what Burke termed "one of the finest problems in legislation, namely, to determine what the State ought to take upon itself to direct by the public wisdom, and what it ought to leave, with as little interference as possible, to individual exertion." We have to discriminate between what Bentham, in his forgotten but useful nomenclature, used to term *Agenda* and *Non-Agenda*, and to do this without Bentham's prior presumption that interference is, at the same time, "generally needless" and "generally pernicious." Perhaps the chief task of economists at this hour is to distinguish afresh the *Agenda* of government from the *Non-Agenda*; and the companion task of politics is to devise forms of government within a democracy which shall be capable of accomplishing the *Agenda*. . . .

I criticise doctrinaire State Socialism, not because it seeks to engage men's altruistic impulses in the service of society, or because it departs from *laissez-faire*, or because it takes away from man's natural liberty to make a million, or because it has courage for bold experiments. All these things I applaud. I criticise it because it misses the significance of what is actually happening; because it is, in fact, little better than a dusty survival of a plan to meet the problems of fifty years ago, based on a misunderstanding of what someone said a hundred years ago. Nineteenth-century State Socialism sprang from Bentham, free competition, etc., and is in some respects a clearer, in some respects a more muddled version of just the same philosophy as underlies nineteenth-century individualism. Both equally laid all their stress on freedom, the one negatively to avoid limitations on existing freedom, the other positively to destroy natural or acquired monopolies. They are different reactions to the same intellectual atmosphere.

. . . The important thing for government is not to do things which individuals are doing already, and to do them a little better or a little worse; but to do those things which at present are not done at all.

Many of the greatest economic evils of our time are the fruits of risk, uncertainty, and ignorance. It is because particular individuals, fortunate in situation or in abilities, are able to take advantage of uncertainty and ignorance, and also because for the same reason big business is often a lottery, that great inequalities of wealth come about; and these same factors are also the cause of the unemployment of labour, or the disappointment of reasonable business expectations, and of the impairment of efficiency and production. Yet the cure lies outside the operations of individuals; it may even be to the interest of individuals to aggravate the disease. I believe that the cure for these things is partly to be sought in the deliberate control of the currency and of credit by a central institution, and partly in the collection and dissemination on a great scale of data relating to the business situation, including the full publicity, by law if necessary, of all business facts which it is useful to know. These measures would involve society in exercising directive intelligence through some appropriate organ of action over many of the inner intricacies of private business, yet it would leave private initiative and enterprise unhindered. Even if these measures prove insufficient, nevertheless, they will furnish us with better knowledge than we have now for taking the next step.

. . . I believe that some coordinated act of intelligent judgement is required as to the scale on which it is desirable that the community as a whole should save, the scale on which these savings should go abroad in the form of foreign investments, and whether the present organisation of the investment market distributes savings along the most nationally productive channels. I do not think that these matters should be left entirely to the chances of private judgement and private profits, as they are at present.

. . . The time has already come when each country needs a considered national policy about what size of population, whether larger or smaller than at present or the same, is most expedient. And having settled this policy, we must take steps to carry it into operation. The time may arrive a little later when the community as a whole must pay attention to the innate quality as well as to the mere numbers of its future members.

These reflections have been directed towards possible improvements in the technique of modern capitalism by the agency of collective action. There is nothing in them which is seriously incompatible with what seems to me to be the essential characteristic of capitalism, namely the dependence upon an intense appeal to the money-making and money-loving instincts of individuals as the main motive force of the economic machine. . . . I may do well to remind you, in conclusion, that the fiercest contests and the most deeply felt divisions of opinion are likely to be waged in the coming years not round technical questions, where the arguments on either side are mainly economic, but round those which, for want of better words, may be called psychological or, perhaps, moral.

Many people, who are really objecting to capitalism as a way of life, argue as though they were objecting to it on the ground of its inefficiency in attaining its own objects. Contrariwise, devotees of capitalism are often unduly conservative, and reject reforms in its technique, which might really strengthen and preserve it, for fear that they may prove to be first steps away from capitalism itself. Nevertheless, a time may be coming when we shall get clearer than at present as to when we are talking about capitalism as an efficient or inefficient technique, and when we are talking about it as desirable or objectionable in itself. For my part I think that capitalism, wisely managed, can probably be made more efficient for attaining economic ends than any alternative system yet in sight, but that in itself it is in many ways extremely objectionable. Our problem is to work out a social organisation which shall be as efficient as possible without offending our notions of a satisfactory way of life.

The next step forward must come, not from political agitation or premature experiments, but from thought. We need by an effort of the mind to elucidate our own feelings. At present our sympathy and our judgement are liable to be on different sides, which is a painful and paralysing state of mind. In the field of action reformers will not be successful until they can steadily pursue a clear and definite object with their intellects and their feelings in tune. There is no party in the world at present which appears to me to be pursuing right aims by right methods. Material poverty provides the incentive to change precisely in situations where there is very little margin for experiments. Material prosperity removes the incentive just when it might be safe to take a chance. Europe lacks the means, America the will, to make a move. We need a new set of convictions which spring naturally from a candid examination of our own inner feelings in relation to the outside facts.

ART AND THE STATE (1936)*

The ancient world knew that the public needed circuses as well as bread. And, policy apart, its rulers for their own glory and satisfaction expended an important proportion of the national wealth on ceremony, works of art and magnificent buildings. These policies, habits and traditions were not confined to the Greek and Roman world. They began as early as man working with his bare hands has left records behind him. . . . But there commenced in the eighteenth century and reached a climax in the nineteenth a new view of the functions of the State and of Society, which still governs us today.

This view was the utilitarian and economic—one might almost say financial—ideal, as the sole, respectable purpose of the community as a whole; the most dreadful heresy, perhaps, which has ever gained the ear of a civilised people. Bread and nothing but bread, and not even bread, and bread accumulating at compound interest until it has turned into a stone. Poets and artists have lifted occasional weak voices against the heresy. I fancy that the Prince Consort was the last protester to be found in high places. But the Treasury view has prevailed. Not only in practice. The theory is equally powerful. We have persuaded ourselves that it is positively wicked for the State to spend a halfpenny on non-economic purposes. Even education and public health only creep in under an economic alias

---

*"Art and the State," *The Listener*, Aug. 26, 1936, pp. 371-72. Reprinted by permission of Lord Kahn.

on the ground that they "pay." We still apply some frantic perversion of business arithmetic in order to settle the problem whether it pays better to pour milk down the drains or to feed it to school children. One form alone of uncalculated expenditure survives from the heroic age—War. And even that must sometimes pretend to be economic. If there arises some occasion of non-economic expenditure which it would be a manifest public scandal to forgo, it is thought suitable to hand round the hat to solicit the charity of private persons.

This expedient is sometimes applied in cases which would be incredible if we were not so well accustomed to them. An outstanding example is to be found where the preservation of the countryside from exploitation is required for reasons of health, recreation, amenity or natural beauty. This is a particularly good example of the way in which we are hag-ridden by a perverted theory of the State, not only because no expenditure of the national resources is involved but, at the most, only a transfer from one pocket into another, but because there is perhaps no current matter about the importance and urgency of which there is such national unanimity in every quarter. When a stretch of cliff, a reach of the Thames, a slope of down is scheduled for destruction, it does not occur to the Prime Minister that the obvious remedy is for the State to prohibit the outrage and pay just compensation, if any; that would be uneconomic. There is probably no man who minds the outrage more than he. But he is the thrall of the sub-human denizens of the Treasury. There is nothing for it but a letter to *The Times* and to hand round the hat. He even helps to administer a private charity fund, nobly provided by a foreigner, to make such donations as may be required from time to time to prevent such things as Shakespeare's cliff from being converted into cement. So low have we fallen today in our conception of the duty and purpose, the honour and glory of the State.

We regard the preservation of the national monuments bequeathed to us from earlier times as properly dependent on precarious and insufficient donations from individuals more public-spirited than the community itself. Since Lincoln Cathedral, crowning the height which has been for two thousand years one of the capital centres of England, can collapse to the ground before the Treasury will regard so uneconomic a purpose as deserving of public money, it is no matter for wonder that the high authorities build no more hanging gardens of Babylon, no more Pyramids, Parthenons, Coliseums, Cathedrals, Palaces, not even Opera Houses, Theatres, Colonnades, Boulevards and Public Places. Our grandest exercises today in the arts of public construction are the arterial roads, which, however, creep into existence under a cloak of economic necessity and by the accident that a special tax ear-marked for them brings in returns of unexpected size, not all of which can be decently diverted to other purposes.

Even more important than the permanent monuments of dignity and beauty in which each generation should express its spirit to stand for it in the procession of time are the ephemeral ceremonies, shows and entertainments in which the common man can take his delight and recreation after his work is done, and which can make him feel, as nothing else can, that he is one with, and part of, a community, finer, more gifted, more splendid, more care-free than he can be by himself. Our experience has demonstrated plainly that these things cannot be successfully carried on if they depend on the motive of profit and financial success. The exploitation and incidental destruction of the divine gift of the public entertainer by prostituting it to the purposes of financial gain is one of the worser crimes of present-day capitalism. How the State could best play its proper part it is hard to say. We must learn by trial and error. But anything would be better than the present system. . . .

THE MEANS TO PROSPERITY (1933)*

If our poverty were due to famine or earthquake or war—if we lacked material things and the resources to produce them, we could not expect to find the means to prosperity except in hard work, abstinence, and invention. In fact, our predicament is notoriously of another kind. It comes from some failure in the immaterial devices of the mind, in the working of the motives which should lead to the decisions and acts of will, necessary to put in movement the resources and technical means we already have. It is as though two motor-drivers, meeting in the middle of a highway, were unable to pass one another because neither knows the rule of the road. Their own muscles are no use; a motor engineer cannot help them; a better road would not serve. Nothing is required and nothing will avail, except a little clear thinking.

So, too, our problem is not a human problem of muscles and endurance. It is not an engineering problem or an agricultural problem. It is not even a business problem, if we mean by business those calculations and dispositions and organising acts by which individual entrepreneurs can better themselves. Nor is it a banking problem, if we mean by banking those principles and methods of shrewd judgement by which lasting connections are fostered and unfortunate commitments avoided. On the contrary, it is, in the strictest sense, an economic problem or, to express it better, as suggesting a blend of economic theory with the art of statesmanship, a problem of political economy.

I call attention to the nature of the problem, because it points us to the nature of the remedy. . . . There are still people who believe that the way out can only be found by hard work, endurance, frugality, improved business methods, more

_____

*"The Means to Prosperity," in *Collected Works of John Maynard Keynes*, Vol. 9: *Essays in Persuasion* (London: Macmillan, 1972), pp. 335-47; 354-55. Reprinted by permission of Macmillan, Cambridge University Press, and Lord Kahn.

cautious banking and, above all, the avoidance of devices. . . . These people will never, I fear, get by. . . .

It is the existing situation which we should find paradoxical. There is nothing paradoxical in the suggestion that some immaterial adjustment—some change, so to speak "on paper"—should be capable of working wonders. The paradox is to be found in 250,000 building operatives out of work in Great Britain, when more houses are our greatest material need. It is the man who tells us that there is no means, consistent with sound finance and political wisdom, of getting the one to work at the other, whose judgement we should instinctively doubt. The calculations which we ought to suspect are those of the statesman who, being already burdened with the support of the unemployed, tells us that it would involve him in heavy liabilities, present and to come, which the country cannot afford, if he were to set the men to build the houses; and the sanity to be questioned is his, who thinks it more economical and better calculated to increase the national wealth to maintain unemployed shipbuilders, than to spend a fraction of what their maintenance is costing him, in setting them to construct one of the greatest works of man.

When, on the contrary, I show, a little elaborately, as in the ensuing chapter, that to create wealth will increase the national income and that a large proportion of any increase in the national income will accrue to an Exchequer, amongst whose largest outgoings is the payment of incomes to those who are unemployed and whose receipts are a proportion of the incomes of those who are occupied, I hope the reader will feel, whether or not he thinks himself competent to criticise the argument in detail, that the answer is just what he would expect—that it agrees with the instinctive promptings of his common sense.

Nor should the argument seem strange that taxation may be so high as to defeat its object, and that, given sufficient time to gather the fruits, a reduction of taxation will run a better chance than an increase of balancing the budget. For to take the opposite view today is to resemble a manufacturer who, running at a loss, decides to raise his price, and when his declining sales increase the loss, wrapping himself in the rectitude of plain arithmetic, decides that prudence requires him to raise the price still more—and who, when at last his account is balanced with nought on both sides, is still found righteously declaring that it would have been the act of a gambler to reduce the price when you were already making a loss.

The reluctance to support schemes of capital development at home as a means to restore prosperity is generally based on two grounds—the meagreness of the employment created by the expenditure of a given sum, and the strain on national and local budgets of the subsidies which such schemes usually require. These are quantitative questions not easily answered with precision. But I will endeavour to give reasons for the belief that the answers to both of them are much more favourable than is commonly supposed.

It is often said that in Great Britain it costs £500 capital expenditure on public works to give one man employment for a year. This is based on the amount of labour directly employed on the spot. But it is easy to see that the materials used and the transport required also give employment. If we allow for this as we should, the capital expenditure per man-year of additional employment is usually estimated, in the case of building for example, at £200.

But if the new expenditure is additional and not merely in substitution for other expenditure, the increase of employment does not stop there. The additional wages and other incomes paid out are spent on additional purchases, which in turn lead to further employment. If the resources of the country were already fully employed, these additional purchases would be mainly reflected in higher prices and increased imports. But in present circumstances this would be true of only a small proportion of the additional consumption, since the greater part of it could be provided without much change of price by home resources which are at present unemployed. Moreover, in so far as the increased demand for food, resulting from the increased purchasing power of the working classes, served either to raise the prices or to increase the sales of the output of primary producers at home and abroad, we should today positively welcome it. It would be much better to raise the price of farm products by increasing the demand for them than by artificially restricting their supply.

Nor have we yet reached the end. The newly employed who supply the increased purchases of those employed on the new capital works will, in their turn, spend more, thus adding to the employment of others; and so on. Some enthusiasts, perceiving the fact of these repercussions, have greatly exaggerated the total result. . . . For at each stage there is, so to speak, a certain proportion of leakage. At each stage a certain proportion of the increased income is not passed on in increased employment. Some part will be saved by the recipient; some part raises prices and so diminishes consumption elsewhere, except in so far as producers spend their increased profits; some part will be spent on imports; some part is merely a substitution for expenditure previously made out of the dole or private charity or personal savings; and some part may reach the Exchequer without relieving the taxpayer to an equal extent. Thus in order to sum the net effect on employment of the series of repercussions, it is necessary to make reasonable assumptions as to the proportion lost in each of these ways. . . .

It is obvious that the appropriate assumptions vary greatly according to circumstances. If there were little or no margin of unemployed resources, then, as I have said above, the increased expenditure would largely waste itself in higher prices and increased imports (which is, indeed, a regular feature of the later stages of a boom in new construction). If the dole was as great as a man's earnings when in work and was paid for by borrowing, there would be scarcely any repercussions at all. On the other hand, now that the dole is paid for by taxes and not by borrowing (so that a reduction in the dole may be expected to increase the spending power of the taxpayer), we no longer have to make so large a deduction on this head. . . .

We are now ready to estimate the total relief to the budget. For purposes of broad calculation the average cost of a man on the dole is usually taken at £50 a year. Hence a loan expenditure of £100, by affording two-thirds of a man-year of employment for workers previously supported by the dole, reduces the cost of unemployment relief by £33.

But there is a further benefit to the budget, due to the fact that our loan expenditure of £100 will increase the national income by £200. For the yield of the taxes rises and falls more or less in proportion to the national income. Our budgetary difficulties today are mainly due to the decline in the national income. Now for the nation as a whole, leaving on one side transactions with foreigners, its income is exactly equal to its expenditure (including in expenditure both consumption-expenditure and new capital-expenditure, but excluding intermediate exchanges from one hand to another);—the two being simply different names for the same thing, my expenditure being your income.

Now on the average about 20 per cent of the national income is paid to the Exchequer in taxes. The exact proportion depends on how the new income is distributed between the higher ranges of income subject to direct taxation, and the lower ranges which are touched by indirect taxes; also the yield of some taxes is not closely correlated with changes in national income. To allow for these doubts, let us take the proportion of the new income accruing to the Exchequer at 10 per cent, i.e. £20 of new revenue from £200 increase of income. . . .

Thus the total benefit to the Exchequer of an additional loan-expenditure of £100 is at least £33 *plus* £20, or £53 altogether, i.e. a little more than a half of the loan-expenditure. We need see nothing paradoxical in this. We have reached a point where a considerable proportion of every further decline in the national income is visited on the Exchequer through the agency of the dole and the decline in the yield of the taxes. It is natural, therefore, that the benefit of measures to increase the national income should largely accrue to the Exchequer.

If we apply this reasoning to the projects for loan-expenditure which are receiving support today in responsible quarters, we see that it is a complete mistake to believe that there is a dilemma between schemes for increasing employment and schemes for balancing the budget—that we must go slowly and cautiously with the former for fear of injuring the latter. Quite the contrary. There is no possibility of balancing the budget except by increasing the national income, which is much the same thing as increasing employment.

Some cynics, who have followed the argument thus far, conclude that nothing except a war can bring a major slump to its conclusion. For hitherto war has been the only object of governmental loan-expenditure on a large scale which governments have considered respectable. In all the issues of peace they are timid, over-cautious, half-hearted, without perseverance or determination, thinking of a loan as a liability and not as a link in the transformation of the community's surplus resources, which will otherwise be wasted, into useful capital assets.

I hope that her government will show that Great Britain can be energetic even in the tasks of peace. It should not be difficult to perceive that 100,000 houses are a national asset and 1 million unemployed men a national liability.

CONCLUDING NOTES ON THE SOCIAL PHILOSOPHY TOWARDS WHICH THE GENERAL THEORY [OF EMPLOYMENT] MIGHT LEAD (1936)*

The outstanding faults of the economic society in which we live are its failure to provide for full employment and its arbitrary and inequitable distribution of wealth and incomes. . . .

Since the end of the nineteenth century significant progress towards the removal of very great disparities of wealth and income has been achieved through the instrument of direct taxation—income tax and surtax and death duties—especially in Great Britain. Many people would wish to see this process carried much further, but they are deterred by two considerations; partly by the fear of making skilful evasions too much worth while and also of diminishing unduly the motive towards risk-taking, but mainly, I think, by the belief that the growth of capital depends upon the strength of the motive towards individual saving and that for a large proportion of this growth we are dependent on the savings of the rich out of their superfluity. Our argument does not affect the first of these considerations. But it may considerably modify our attitude towards the second. For we have seen that, up to the point where full employment prevails, the growth of capital depends not at all on a low propensity to consume but is, on the contrary, held back by it; and only in conditions of full employment is a low propensity to consume conducive to the growth of capital. Moreover, experience suggests that in existing conditions saving by institutions and through sinking funds is more than adequate, and that measures for the redistribution of incomes in a way likely to raise the propensity to consume may prove positively favourable to the growth of capital.

The existing confusion of the public mind on the matter is well illustrated by the very common belief that the death duties are responsible for a reduction in the capital wealth of the country. Assuming that the State applies the proceeds of

*"Concluding Notes . . .," in *The General Theory of Employment, Interest and Money* (London: Macmillan, 1973), Vol. 7, pp. 372-84. Reprinted by permission of Macmillan, Cambridge University Press, and Lord Kahn.

these duties to its ordinary outgoings so that taxes on incomes and consumption are correspondingly reduced or avoided, it is, of course, true that a fiscal policy of heavy death duties has the effect of increasing the community's propensity to consume. But inasmuch as an increase in the habitual propensity to consume will in general (i.e. except in conditions of full employment) serve to increase at the same time the inducement to invest, the inference commonly drawn is the exact opposite of the truth.

Thus our argument leads towards the conclusion that in contemporary conditions the growth of wealth, so far from being dependent on the abstinence of the rich, as is commonly supposed, is more likely to be impeded by it. One of the chief social justifications of great inequality of wealth is, therefore, removed. I am not saying that there are no other reasons, unaffected by our theory, capable of justifying some measure of inequality in some circumstances. But it does dispose of the most important of the reasons why hitherto we have thought it prudent to move carefully. This particularly affects our attitude towards death duties: for there are certain justifications for inequality of incomes which do not apply equally to inequality of inheritances.

For my own part, I believe that there is social and psychological justification for significant inequalities of incomes and wealth, but not for such large disparities as exist to-day. There are valuable human activities which require the motive of money-making and the environment of private wealth-ownership for their full fruition. Moreover, dangerous human proclivities can be canalised into comparatively harmless channels by the existence of opportunities for money-making and private wealth, which, if they cannot be satisfied in this way, may find their outlet in cruelty, the reckless pursuit of personal power and authority, and other forms of self-aggrandisement. It is better that a man should tyrannise over his bank balance than over his fellow-citizens; and whilst the former is sometimes denounced as being but a means to the latter, sometimes at least it is an alternative. But it is not necessary for the stimulation of these activities and the satisfaction of these proclivities that the game should be played for such high stakes as at present. Much lower stakes will serve the purpose equally well, as soon as the players are accustomed to them. The task of transmuting human nature must not be confused with the task of managing it. Though in the ideal commonwealth men may have been taught or inspired or bred to take no interest in the stakes, it may still be wise and prudent statemanship to allow the game to be played, subject to rules and limitations, so long as the average man, or even a significant section of the community, is in fact strongly addicted to the money-making passion.

In some other respects the foregoing theory is moderately conservative in its implications. For whilst it indicates the vital importance of establishing certain central controls in matters which are now left in the main to individual initiative, there are wide fields of activity which are unaffected. The State will have to exercise a guiding influence on the propensity to consume partly through its scheme of taxation, partly by fixing the rate of interest, and partly, perhaps, in other ways. Furthermore, it seems unlikely that the influence of banking policy on the rate of interest will be sufficient by itself to determine an optimum rate of investment. I conceive, therefore, that a somewhat comprehensive socialisation of investment will prove the only means of securing an approximation to full employment; though this need not exclude all manner of compromises and of devices by which public authority will co-operate with private initiative. But beyond this no obvious case is made out for a system of State Socialism which would embrace most of the economic life of the community. It is not the ownership of the instruments of production which it is important for the State to assume. If the State is able to determine the aggregate amount of resources devoted to augmenting the instruments and the basic rate of reward to those who own them, it will have accomplished all that is necessary. Moreover, the necessary measures of socialisation can be introduced gradually and without a break in the general traditions of society.

Our criticism of the accepted classicial [i.e. laissez-faire] theory of economics has consisted not so much in finding logical flaws in its analysis as in pointing out that its tacit assumptions are seldom or never satisfied, with the result that it cannot solve the economic problems of the actual world. But if our central controls succeed in establishing an aggregate volume of output corresponding to full employment as nearly as is practicable, the classical theory comes into its own again from this point onwards. If we suppose the volume of output to be given, i.e. to be determined by forces outside the classical scheme of thought, then there is no objection to be raised against the classical analysis of the manner in which private self-interest will determine what in particular is produced, in what proportions the factors of production will be combined to produce it, and how the value of the final product will be distributed between them. . . . Thus, apart from the necessity of central controls to bring about an adjustment between the propensity to consume and the inducement to invest, there is no more reason to socialise economic life than there was before.

To put the point concretely, I see no reason to suppose that the existing system seriously misemploys the factors of production which are in use. There are, of course, errors of foresight; but these would not be avoided by centralising decisions. When 9,000,000 men are employed out of 10,000,000 willing and able to work, there is no evidence that the labour of these 9,000,000 men is misdirected. The complaint against the present system is not that these 9,000,000 men ought to be employed on different tasks, but that tasks should be available for the remaining 1,000,000 men. It is in determining the volume, not the direction, of actual employment that the existing system has broken down.

Thus . . . the result of filling in the gaps in the classical theory is not to dispose of the "Manchester System," but to indicate the nature of the environment which the free play of economic forces requires if it is to realise the full potentialities of production. The central controls necessary to ensure full employment will, of course, involve a large extension of the traditional functions of government. Furthermore, the modern classical theory has itself called attention to various conditions in which the free play of economic forces may need to be curbed or guided. But there will still remain a wide field for the exercise of private initiative and responsibility. Within this field the traditional advantages of individualism will still hold good.

Let us stop for a moment to remind ourselves what these advantages are. They are partly advantages of efficiency—the advantages of decentralisation and of the play of self-interest. The advantage to efficiency of the decentralisation of decisions and of individual responsibility is even greater, perhaps, than the nineteenth century supposed; and the reaction against the appeal to self-interest may have gone too far. But, above all, individualism, if it can be purged of its defects and its abuses, is the best safeguard of personal liberty in the sense that, compared with any other system, it greatly widens the field for the exercise of personal choice. It is also the best safeguard of the variety of life, which emerges precisely from this extended field of personal choice, and the loss of which is the greatest of all the losses of the homogeneous or totalitarian state. For this variety preserves the traditions which embody the most secure and successful choices of former generations; it colours the present with the diversification of its fancy; and, being the handmaid of experiment as well as of tradition and of fancy, it is the most powerful instrument to better the future.

Whilst, therefore, the enlargement of the functions of government, involved in the task of adjusting to one another the propensity to consume and the inducement to invest, would seem to a nineteenth-century publicist or to a contemporary American financier to be a terrific encroachment on individualism, I defend it, on the contrary, both as the only practicable means of avoiding the destruction of existing economic forms in their entirety and as the condition of the successful functioning of individual initiative.

For if effective demand is deficient, not only is the public scandal of wasted resources intolerable, but the individual enterpriser who seeks to bring these resources into action is operating with the odds loaded against him. The game of hazard which he plays is furnished with many zeros, so that the players *as a whole* will lose if they have the energy and hope to deal all the cards. Hitherto the increment of the world's wealth has fallen short of the aggregate of positive individual savings; and the difference has been made up by the losses of those whose courage and initiative have not been supplemented by exceptional skill or unusual good fortune. But if effective demand is adequate, average skill and average good fortune will be enough.

The authoritarian state systems of to-day seem to solve the problem of unemployment at the expense of efficiency and of freedom. It is certain that the world will not much longer tolerate the unemployment which, apart from brief intervals of excitement, is associated—and, in my opinion, inevitably associated—with present-day capitalistic individualism. But it may be possible by a right analysis of the problem to cure the disease whilst preserving efficiency and freedom.

Is the fulfillment of these ideas a visionary hope? Have they insufficient roots in the motives which govern the evolution of political society? Are the interests which they will thwart stronger and more obvious than those which they will serve?

I do not attempt an answer in this place. . . . But if the ideas are correct—an hypothesis on which the author himself must necessarily base what he writes—it would be a mistake, I predict, to dispute their potency over a period of time. At the present moment people are unusually expectant of a more fundamental diagnosis; more particularly ready to receive it; eager to try it out, if it should be even plausible. But apart from this contemporary mood, the ideas of economists and political philosophers, both when they are right and when they are wrong, are more powerful than is commonly understood. Indeed the world is ruled by little else. Practical men, who believe themselves to be quite exempt from any intellectual influences, are usually the slaves of some defunct economist. Madmen in authority, who hear voices in the air, are distilling their frenzy from some academic scribbler of a few years back. I am sure that the power of vested interests is vastly exaggerated compared with the gradual encroachment of ideas. Not, indeed, immediately, but after a certain interval; for in the field of economic and political philosophy there are not many who are influenced by new theories after they are twenty-five or thirty years of age, so that the ideas which civil servants and politicians and even agitators apply to current events are not likely to be the newest. But, soon or late, it is ideas, not vested interests, which are dangerous for good or evil.

Liberalism Confronts the Authoritarianism and Value Confusion of the Twentieth Century

Liberalism and liberal governments have taken a beating in the twentieth century. At the beginning of the century, Anglo-American liberals, from Lloyd George to Woodrow Wilson, shared visions of a future where liberal beliefs and institutions would eliminate war, poverty, tyranny, and ignorance. Instead, the leaders of the Liberal party in England and the Progressives in America found their dreams and hard-won reforms challenged and thwarted by a veritable host of disasters: wars, national rivalries, revolution, economic collapse, fear, apathy, and senseless discrimination. Such terrible events shook deeply the confidence liberals had had in themselves, their ideas, and in the institutions they had endorsed or accepted. Even worse for the liberals was the growth of authoritarianism in countries such as Germany. Liberalism, which had appeared poised to sweep the world in 1900, seemed on the decline as early as the 1930s.

Matters have not improved much since. Politics in England and in the Scandinavian countries is, as often as not, class politics, with class-based political parties contesting issues which are fundamentally economic. This is not what the great liberal thinkers of the nineteenth century had in mind. America liberals have been divided into two hostile camps ever since the New Deal. The *laissez-faire*-liberals, who now call themselves "conservatives," struggle with the "new" liberals, who advocate state intervention in community affairs in order to reduce inequalities of individual income and status. Internationally there is no liberal position. Where once liberals had advocated free trade and self-determination, they are now believers in everything from "human rights" to international stability through the economic suzerainty of the United States.

Intellectual challenges to liberalism have also been severe in the twentieth century. It is not clear even now that liberalism can deal effectively with the problem

of social and economic inequality which a capitalistic economy creates. Nor is it
certain that liberalism is still a public philosophy. In the United States, for example, the growing economic responsibilities of the federal government have
encouraged the development of a form of interest group pluralism that threatens
the very idea of a *public* interest. There may, in effect, be no *public* anymore. If
so, then the future of liberalism in America (and hence in the world) is bleak.

Finally, the notion of a political doctrine worth believing in has faded in this
century. Too many people have been disappointed too often by political ideologies which have produced little but frustration and suffering. Liberalism has suffered in consequence. Yet, as the selections in this section show, liberal ideals
still raise the hopes and stir the thoughts of citizens in societies with liberal institutions. For many of these people, liberal values and goals still seem worthwhile.
The issue, then, is less whether liberal values are good values than whether liberals have a political doctrine which they can promote and practice.

22   C.B. MACPHERSON

C.B. Macpherson is one of the most influential critics of modern liberal ideas and
values. Yet his has not been a destructive enterprise. He has worked and written
to "establish the need and possibility of a theory of democracy which will get
clear of the disabling central defect of current liberal-democratic theory, while
holding on to, or recovering, the humanistic values which liberal democracy has
always claimed" (Macpherson, *Democratic Theory,* 1973, Preface).

Macpherson has been quite critical of those who would use the terms "liberalism" and "democracy" as synonyms. Indeed, if he is correct, the term "liberal
democracy" is rather a contradiction because it unites two sets of values and
ideals which must conflict. Precisely why they must conflict is the subject of the
following selection.

THE MAXIMIZATION OF DEMOCRACY*

. . . I shall argue that the justifying theory of our Western democracies rests on
two maximizing claims—a claim to maximize individual utilities and a claim to

---

*"The Maximization of Democracy," in *Democratic Theory: Essays in Retrieval* (New York: Oxford
University Press, 1973). Reprinted by permission of Oxford University Press.

maximize individual powers; that neither of these claims can be made good, partly because of inherent defects, partly because of changed circumstances: and that the changed circumstances both permit and require a change in some of the theory's assumptions.

Changed circumstances have created new difficulties for democratic theory because of the very breadth of its claims. One of the central values of our democratic theory has been the surpassing importance of freedom of choice. We have claimed a sort of political consumers' sovereignty which ensures that the society will respond to changes in consumer preference, just as the market economy on which our Western democracies are based responds to changes in effective demand. But what is not often noticed in this connection is that, in what might be called the world-wide political market, consumers' preferences are rapidly changing. We in the West have still the same predominant preference for a 'free society,' but the other two-thirds of the world—the communist nations and the newly independent, under-developed countries which are neither communist nor liberal-democratic—have now become global effective demanders, and are demanding something different. If we believe in consumers' sovereignty we must be prepared to let the new effective demand take its course and to admit that it has moral claims. To grant this is not to demonstrate that we should abandon our cherished theory: it is at most an argument for coexistence of theories.

But our situation is both worse and better than this suggests. Worse, in that the appearance of serious competitors to liberal-democratic society has stiffened the requirements of a justifying theory. Better, in that certain twentieth-century developments have opened a possibility of avoiding the main fault in the justifying theory we inherited from the nineteenth century. Whether twentieth-century developments also make possible a sufficiently fundamental change in our institutions this paper does not attempt to explore.

The main elements of the justifying theory of our Western or liberal democracies—I use the terms interchangeably, for reasons that will be apparent[1]—can, I suggest, be stated as two maximizing claims: the claim to maximize individual utilities, and the claim to maximize individual powers. The first claim is familiar to students of political theory in its nineteenth-century Utilitarian form. The second, less immediately familiar, is I suggest a useful and revealing way of formulating the extra-Utilitarian claims that were built into the liberal theory as soon as it became liberal-democratic, say from John Stuart Mill on. Both claims are made in the name of individual personality. The argument in both cases is that the liberal society provides for the greatest measure of realization of human personality, though in the two cases the essential character of that personality is seen differently, and the different views have different historical roots. Before examining the two claims it may be useful to place them, provisionally at least, in the Western intellectual tradition.

The first claim is that the liberal-democratic society, by instituting a wider freedom of individual choice than does any non-liberal society, maximizes individual satisfactions or utilities. The claim is not only that it maximizes the aggregate of satisfactions, but that it does so equitably: that it maximizes the satisfactions to which, on some concept of equity, each individual is entitled. This claim implies a particular concept of man's essence. To treat the maximization of utilities as the ultimate justification of a society, is to view man as essentially a consumer of utilities. It is only when man is seen as essentially a bundle of appetites demanding satisfaction that the good society is the one which maximizes satisfactions. This view of man, dominant in Benthamism, goes back beyond the classical political economists. It is firmly embedded in the liberal tradition and has remained a considerable part of the case for the liberal-democratic society today.

The second claim is that the liberal-democratic society maximizes men's human powers, that is, their potential for using and developing their uniquely human capacities. This claim is based on a view of man's essence not as a consumer of utilities but as a doer, a creator, an enjoyer of his human attributes. These attributes may be variously listed and assessed: they may be taken to include the capacity for rational understanding, for moral judgement and action, for aesthetic creation or contemplation, for the emotional activities of friendship and love, and, sometimes, for religious experience. Whatever the uniquely human attributes are taken to be, in this view of man their exertion and development are seen as ends in themselves, a satisfaction in themselves, not simply a means to consumer satisfactions. It is better to travel than to arrive. Man is not a bundle of appetites seeking satisfaction but a bundle of conscious energies seeking to be exerted.

This is almost an opposite view of the essence of man from that of the Utilitarians. It came, indeed, as a reaction against the crude Benthamite view of man as consumer. Benthamism provoked in the nineteenth century a variety of reactions, conservative, radical, and middle of the road, ranging from Carlyle and Nietzsche, through John Stuart Mill, to Ruskin and Marx. All these thinkers brought back, in one way or another, the idea of the essence of man as activity rather than consumption. I say brought back, because it is an old idea in the Western humanist tradition. From Aristotle until the seventeenth century it was more usual to see the essence of man as purposeful activity, as exercise of one's energies in accordance with some rational purpose, than as the consumption of satisfactions. It was only with the emergence of the modern market society, which we may put as early as the seventeenth century in England, that this concept of man was narrowed and turned into almost its opposite. Man was still held to be essentially a purposive, rational creature, but the essence of rational behaviour was increasingly held to lie in unlimited individual appropriation, as a means of satisfying unlimited desire for utilities. Man became an infinite appropriator and an infinite consumer; an infinite appropriator because an infinite desirer. From Locke to James Mill this concept of man became increasingly prevalent. The nineteenth-century reaction against it, radical, moderate, and conservative, was an attempt o reclaim and restate the much older tradition. But the Utilitarian concept was by then too deeply rooted in the market society to be driven out of the liberal tradition, while too clearly inadequate to be allowed any longer to dominate it. The result can be seen in John Stuart Mill and T.H. Green and the whole subsequent liberal-democratic tradition: an uneasy compromise between the two views of man's essence, and, correspondingly, an unsure mixture of the two maximizing claims made for the liberal-democratic society.

It is not surprising that the two concepts of man, and the two maximizing claims, were brought together. For the problem which the first liberal-*democratic* thinkers faced, in the nineteenth century, was to find a way of accommodating the pre-democratic liberal tradition of the previous two centuries to the new moral climate of democracy. The liberal tradition had been built in a market society, whose ethos was competitive maximization of utilities. The liberal thinkers of the seventeenth and eighteenth centuries had assumed, quite correctly, that the society they were talking about was a market society operating by contractual relations between free individuals who offered their powers, natural and acquired, in the market with a view to getting the greatest return they could. A man's powers, in this view, were not of his essence but were merely instrumental: they were, in Hobbes's classic phrase, "his present means to obtain some future apparent good." Powers were a way of getting utilities.[2] The society was permeated with utility-maximizing behaviour. Liberal thinkers could not abandon the implicit concept of man as a maximizer of utilities without abandoning all the advantages they found in the liberal society.

Why, then, was it necessary for liberal-democratic thinkers to add the other concept of man and the other maximizing claim? Two reasons are fairly evident. One was the repugnance of men like John Stuart Mill to the crass materialism of the market society, which had by then had time to show what it could do. It clearly had not brought that higher quality of life which the earlier liberals had counted on its bringing. A second reason may be seen in the belief of mid-nineteenth-century liberals that the democratic franchise could not be withheld much longer. Given this conviction, it seemed urgent to moralize the society before the mass took control. It was thus necessary to present an image of liberal-democratic society which could be justified by something more morally appealing (to the liberal thinker and, hopefully, to the new democratic mass) than the old utilitarianism. This could be done, consonantly with the liberal commitment to individual freedom, by offering as the rationale of liberal-democratic society its provision of freedom to make the most of oneself. Thus individual freedom to maximize one's powers could be added to the freedom to maximize utilities. A newly moralized, liberal-democratic society could claim, as a market society, to maximize individuals' chosen utilities, and, as a free society, to maximize their powers. Neither claim has stood up very well.

The claim that the liberal-democratic society maximizes individual utilities (and does so equitably) may be reduced to an economic claim. It is in substance a claim that the market economy of individual enterprise and individual rights of unlimited appropriation, i.e. the capitalist market economy, with the requisite social and political institutions, maximizes individual utilities and does so equitably. To reduce the utility-maximizing claim to economic terms is not to exclude from liberal-democratic claims the value attached to other liberal institutions. Civil and political liberties are certainly held to have a value apart from their instrumental economic value. But they are less often thought of as *utilities* than as prerequisite conditions for the exertion and development of individual *powers*. We may therefore exclude them here and consider them under the other maximizing heading.

The claim that the capitalist market economy maximizes individual utilities has already been pretty well destroyed by twentieth-century economists, although few political theorists seem to realize this. For one thing, the claim to maximize the aggregate of individual utilities involves an insuperable logical difficulty. The satisfactions that different individuals get from particular things cannot be compared on a single measuring scale. Therefore they cannot be added together. Therefore it cannot be shown that the set of utilities which the market actually produces is greater than some other set that might have been produced by some other system. Therefore it cannot be shown that the market maximizes aggregate utility.

The claim that the market maximizes utilities equitably runs into even greater difficulties. Equity here refers to the distribution of the aggregate among the individual members of the society. Equity has, in the liberal tradition, generally been held to require distribution in proportion to the contributions made by each to the aggregate product. How is it claimed that the market does this? Economists can demonstrate that, assuming some specific distribution of resources or income, the operation of the perfectly free competitive market will give each the maximum satisfaction to which his contribution entitles him. But unless it can be shown that the given distribution of resources or income is just, the claim of equitable maximization is not sustained. The most that can be shown by the economists' model is that the pure competitive market gives everyone a reward proportional to what he contributes by way of any resources he owns, whether his energy and skill, his capital, or his land, or other resources. But this leaves open the question whether the actual pattern of ownership of all these resources is equitable. If equity is held to require rewards proportional to the individual energy and skill expended— which was John Stuart Mill's "equitable principle" of property—the market model can be demonstrated to be inequitable. For it distributes rewards proportionally to other owned resources, as well as energy and skill, however the ownership of the other resources was acquired, and no one argues that the ownership of the other resources is in proportion to the energy and skill exerted by their owners.

The market, then, does not maximize utilities equitably accc̃ːding to work. Nor does it maximize equitably according to need, on any egalitarian concept of need. Bentham, indeed, had made the egalitarian assumption that individuals have equal capacities for pleasure, and hence have equal need, and had argued that in calculating aggregate utility each individual should count as one and no one as more than one. He then demonstrated that, by the law of diminishing utility, utility would be maximized by an absolutely equal distribution of wealth. He then pointed out that equal distribution would be totally incompatible with security of property, including profit, which he saw as the indispensable incentive to productivity. He concluded that the claims of equality must yield to the claims of security, in order to maximize the aggregate production of utilities. What Bentham showed with admirable clarity was that, as soon as you make the market assumption about profit incentives, you must abandon the possibility of weighting each individual equally in calculating the maximum utility. Bentham did not claim that the market maximizes utilities equitably according to his concept of equity; he demonstrated, rather, that the market cannot do so.

Other concepts of equity than the two we have just examined—distribution according to work, and distribution according to assumed equal need—are possible, but none that is consistent with the minimum egalitarian assumptions of a democratic theory provides a demonstration that the market maximizes utilities equitably.

Thus the claim to maximize utilities, and the claim to do so equitably, both fail, even on the assumption of perfect competition. There is the further difficulty that the capitalist market economy moves steadily away from perfect competition towards oligopoly, monopoly, and managed prices and production. In the measure that it does so, its claim to maximize utilities fails on yet another ground.

The claim that the liberal-democratic society maximizes men's powers is more complex, though the basic conception is clear enough. To collect into this one principle—maximization of individual powers—all the main claims of liberal democracy other than the utility-maximizing one is no doubt a considerable simplification, but it has the merit of drawing attention to fundamental factors which are often overlooked. The power-maximizing principle is offered here as a reformulation of the extra-Utilitarian principles that were built into the liberal theory in the nineteenth century in order to make it democratic, and as a way of linking them with the pre-liberal (or pre-market) Western tradition. Whether that Western tradition is traced back to Plato or Aristotle or to Christian natural law, it is based on the proposition that the end or purpose of man is to use and develop his uniquely human attributes or capacities. His potential use and development of these may be called his human powers. A good life is one which maximizes these powers. A good society is one which maximizes (or permits and facilitates the maximization of) these powers, and thus enables men to make the best of themselves.

It is important to notice that this concept of powers is an ethical one, not a descriptive one. A man's powers, in this view, are his potential for realizing the essential human attributes said to have been implanted in him by Nature or God, not (as with Hobbes) his present means, however acquired, to ensure future gratification of his appetites. The difference is important. It may be stated as a difference in what is included in each concept.

The ethical concept of a man's powers, being a concept of a potential for realizing some human end, necessarily includes in a man's powers not only his natural capacities (his energy and skill) but also his *ability* to exert them. It therefore includes *access* to whatever things outside himself are requisite to that exertion. It must therefore treat as a diminution of a man's powers whatever stands in the way of his realizing his human end, including any limitation of that access.

The descriptive concept of a man's powers, on the other hand, includes his natural capacities *plus* whatever additional power (means to ensure future gratifications) he has acquired by getting command over the energies and skill of other men, or *minus* whatever part of his energies and skill he has lost to some other men. This concept of powers does not stipulate that a man shall have the ability to use his human capacities fully. It does not require that a man shall have free access to that which he needs in order to use his capacities. It therefore does not treat as a diminution of a man's powers anything that stands in the way of his using his human capacities fully, or any limitation of his access to what he needs for that purpose. A man's powers on this view are the powers he has, not the powers he needs to have in order to be fully human. One man's powers, defined as his present means to get what he wants in the future, will include the command he has acquired over other men's energies and skills; another's will include merely what is left of his energy and skill after some of it has been transferred to others. On this concept of powers there is no diminution of a man's powers in denying him access to that which he needs in order to use his capacities, for his powers are measured after any such diminution has taken place.

One of the ways of transferring another man's powers to oneself is by denying him free access to what he needs in order to use his capacities, and making him pay for access with part of his powers. In any society where limitation of access has taken place on a large scale the resulting situation will appear differently depending on which concept of a man's powers is being used. On the ethical concept, there will be a continuous net transfer of part of the powers of some men to others, and a diminution of the human essence of those from whom power is being transferred. On the descriptive concept, there will be no net transfer of powers (since powers are defined as the means each man has acquired or has been left with), and no diminution of human essence (since the only idea of human essence that is at all implied in the concept of powers is that of man as consumer of satisfactions).

It was, I suggest, the ethical concept of a man's powers that was reintroduced into the Western tradition in the nineteenth century, and its reintroduction was what converted the liberal into the liberal-democratic theory. It is clearly apparent in T.H. Green, slightly less clearly in John Stuart Mill (who had, after all, to fight his way out of the Benthamite, i.e. Hobbesian, position). When this ethical concept was reintroduced in the nineteenth century it contained a more specific egalitarian assumption than it had contained in its ancient and medieval forms. It assumed not only that each individual was equally entitled to the opportunity to realize his human essence, but also (as against the Greeks) that men's capacities were substantially equal, and (as against the medieval tradition) that they were entitled to equal opportunity in this world.

Thus, when this ethical concept was reintroduced in the nineteenth century, by those who were seeking to humanize the market society and the pre-democratic liberal theory, it became a claim that the liberal-democratic society maximizes each individual's powers in the sense of maximizing each man's ability to use and develop his essentially human attributes or capacities.

This concept of maximizing men's human powers does not encounter the logical difficulty that besets the notion of maximizing utilities. Here there is no problem of measuring and comparing the utilities or satisfactions derived by different individuals from the receipt and consumption of the same things. True, the enjoyment one man gets from the use and development of his energies is incommensurable with the enjoyment every other man gets from his. But what is being claimed here is simply that the liberal-democratic society does provide the maximum freedom to each to use and develop what natural capacities he has. There is no need to compare incommensurable quantities of utility.

The difficulty in this claim lies deeper. It lies in the facts that the liberal-democratic society is a capitalist market society,[3] and that the latter by its very nature compels a continual net transfer of part of the power of some men to others, thus diminishing rather than maximizing the equal individual freedom to use and develop one's natural capacities which is claimed.

It is easy to see how this comes about. The capitalist market society operates necessarily by a continual and ubiquitous exchange of individual powers. Most men sell the use of their energy and skill on the market, in exchange for the product or the use of others' energy and skill. They must do so, for they do not own or control enough capital or other resources to work on, it being the nature of a capitalist society that the capital and other resources are owned by relatively few, who are not responsible (to the whole society or any section of it) for anything except the endeavour to increase their capitals. The more they increase their capitals, the more control they have over the terms on which those without capital may have access to it. Capital and other material resources are the indispensable means of labour: without access to them one cannot use one's skill and energy in the first business of life, which is to get a living, nor therefore, in the real business of life, which (on the second view of the essence of man) is to enjoy and develop one's powers. One must have something to work on. Those without something of their own to work on, without their own means of labour, must pay for access to others.' A society in which a man cannot use his skill and energy without paying others, for the benefit of those others, for access to something to use them on, cannot be said to maximize each man's powers (on the ethical concept of a man's powers).

The reason why this has not generally been seen should be clear from our analysis of the two concepts of a man's powers. It has not been seen because the two concepts have been confused. Twentieth-century economists (and most political writers) see no net transfer of powers in a perfectly competitive capitalist market society. They do not see it because, as heirs of the Hobbes-to-Bentham concept of man, they define a man's powers, in the way we have seen, to be whatever means a man has to procure satisfactions, that is, as much power as a man has already acquired, by his acquisition of land or capital, or as little as he is left with (his own capacity to labour) when others have acquired the land and capital. When powers are so defined there is no net transfer of powers in the labour-capital relation.

But this definition of powers is, as we have seen, quite inconsistent with the ethical definition of a man's powers, and it is the latter on which the claim of liberal democracy to maximize individual powers must logically be based.[4]

If then a man's powers must, in the context of the liberal-democratic maximizing claim, be taken to include his ability to use his natural capacities, it follows that the capitalist market society, which operates by a continual net transfer of part of the powers of some men to others, for the benefit and enjoyment of the others, cannot properly claim to maximize each individual's powers.

It may be objected that while the capitalist market model does necessarily contain a continuous net transfer of powers, our present Western liberal democracies do not do so because they have moved some distance away from the capitalist model. One result, it is commonly held, of the operation of the democratic franchise has been the emergence of the welfare state, whose characteristic feature is the massive continuous transfer payments from owners to non-owners, by way of state provision of free or subsidized services. It may thus be argued that the modern welfare state has, or can, offset the transfer of powers from non-owners that must exist in the capitalist model of society.

This argument cannot be sustained. We need not enter into the question whether the transfer payments of the welfare state have in fact altered the previously prevailing distribution of the whole social product between classes. We need only notice that the modern welfare state does still rely on capitalist incentives to get the main productive work of the society done, and that so long as this is so, any welfare state transfers from owners to non-owners cannot offset the original and continuing transfer in the other direction. This is fully appreciated by the strongest defenders of capitalism, who point out, quite rightly, that if welfare transfers were so large as to eat up profits there would be no incentive to capitalist enterprise, and so no capitalist enterprise.[5] We may conclude, therefore, that the existence of the welfare state does not cancel and cannot substantially alter the net transfer of powers from non-owners to owners which we have seen to be inherent in the capitalist model. The claim that the liberal-democratic welfare-state society maximizes human powers is therefore still unsustained.

23 JOHN DEWEY

Any American who has used a public library has been touched by the ideas and work of John Dewey (1859-1952). In his decades of teaching at the University of Michigan, the University of Chicago, and Columbia University, Dewey helped lay the foundations of progressive education and contemporary social science. Dewey was also quite active politically. As a leader of American Progressivism, he fought the belief that public institutions could not be used to solve social problems.

Morally and politically, Dewey was a pragmatist. He believed that the worth of a philosophy or an institution could be determined by watching that philosophy or institution in practice. Successful philosophies and institutions would solve moral and social dilemmas. Those which could not solve such dilemmas could be ignored. Dewey was not ruthless. He did not claim that *any* philosophy, because it offered apparent "solutions" to moral and political problems, was therefore "right." He did argue that the purpose of scientific and philosophical inquiry was to solve problems; consequently, those "ideal" systems of thought which could not be tested in real life situations were not worthy of attention.

Dewey's philosophy of education rested on this pragmatic foundation. The goal of public education was, in his view, that of creating citizens who could solve practical, technical, and social problems. The purpose of education was to replace habitual and superstitious thinking with a willingness to experiment and the knowledge necessary to interpret correctly the outcome of experimentation.

This confidence in experimentation, coupled with a refreshing open-mindedness, characterizes the following selection, taken from a series of lectures presented by Dewey at the University of Virginia in 1934.

LIBERALISM AND SOCIAL ACTION*

The Crisis in Liberalism

The net effect of the struggle of early liberals to emancipate individuals from restrictions imposed upon them by the inherited type of social organization was to pose a problem, that of a new social organization. The ideas of liberals set forth in the first third of the nineteenth century were potent in criticism and in analysis. They released forces that had been held in check. But analysis is not construction, and release of force does not of itself give direction to the force that is set free. Victorian optimism concealed for a time the crisis at which liberalism had arrived. But when that optimism vanished amid the conflict of nations, classes, and races characteristic of the latter part of the nineteenth century—a conflict that has grown more intense with the passing years—the crisis could no longer be covered up. The beliefs and methods of earlier liberalism were ineffective when faced with the problems of social organization and integration. . . .

The problem of achieving freedom was immeasurably widened and deepened. It did not now present itself as a conflict between government and the liberty of individuals in matters of conscience and economic action, but as a problem of establishing an entire social order, possessed of a spiritual authority that would nurture and direct the inner as well as the outer life of individuals. The problem of science was no longer merely technological applications for increase of material productivity, but imbuing the minds of individuals with the spirit of reasonableness, fostered by social organization and contributing to its development. The problem of democracy was seen to be not solved, hardly more than externally touched, by the establishment of universal suffrage and representative government. As Havelock Ellis has said, "We see now that the vote and the ballot-box do not make the voter free from even external pressure; and, which is of much more consequence, they do not necessarily free him from his own slavish instincts." The problem of democracy becomes the problem of that form of social organization, extending to all the areas and ways of living, in which the powers of individuals shall not be merely released from mechanical external constraint but

*Liberalism and Social Action (New York: Capricorn Books, 1963), pp. 28–55. Reprinted by permission of G. P. Putnam's Sons. Copyright 1935 by John Dewey; renewed 1962 by Roberta L. Dewey.

shall be fed, sustained and directed. Such an organization demands much more of education than general schooling, which without a renewal of the springs of purpose and desire becomes a new mode of mechanization and formalization, as hostile to liberty as ever was governmental constraint. It demands of science much more than external technical application—which again leads to mechanization of life and results in a new kind of enslavement. It demands that the method of inquiry, of discrimination, of test by verifiable consequences, be naturalized in all the matters, of large and of detailed scope, that arise for judgment.

The demand for a form of social organization that should include economic activities but yet should convert them into servants of the development of the higher capacities of individuals, is one that earlier liberalism did not meet. If we strip its creed from adventitious elements, there are, however, enduring values for which earlier liberalism stood. These values are liberty, the development of the inherent capacities of individuals made possible through liberty, and the central role of free intelligence in inquiry, discussion and expression. But elements that were adventitious to these values colored every one of these ideals in ways that rendered them either impotent or perverse when the new problem of social organization arose.

Before considering the three values, it is advisable to note one adventitious idea that played a large role in the later incapacitation of liberalism. The earlier liberals lacked historic sense and interest. For a while this lack had an immediate pragmatic value. It gave liberals a powerful weapon in their fight with reactionaries. For it enabled them to undercut the appeal to origin, precedent and past history by which the opponents of social change gave sacrosanct quality to existing inequities and abuses. But disregard of history took its revenge. It blinded the eyes of liberals to the fact that their own special interpretations of liberty, individuality and intelligence were themselves historically conditioned, and were relevant only to their own time. They put forward their ideas as immutable truths good at all times and places; they had no idea of historic relativity, either in general or in its application to themselves.

When their ideas and plans were projected they were an attack upon the interests that were vested in established institutions and that had the sanction of custom. The new forces for which liberals sought an entrance were incipient; the *status quo* was arrayed against their release. By the middle of the nineteenth century the contemporary scene had radically altered. The economic and political changes for which they strove were so largely accomplished that they had become in turn the vested interest, and their doctrines, especially in the form of *laissez faire* liberalism, now provided the intellectual justification of the *status quo*. This creed is still powerful in this country. The earlier doctrine of "natural rights," superior to legislative action, has been given a definitely economic meaning by the courts, and used by judges to destroy social legislation passed in the interest of a real, instead of purely formal, liberty of contract. Under the caption of "rugged individualism" it inveighs against all new social policies. Beneficiaries of the established economic regime band themselves together in what they call Liberty Leagues to perpetuate the harsh regimentation of millions of their fellows. I do not imply that resistance to change would not have appeared if it had not been for the doctrines of earlier liberals. But had the early liberals appreciated the historic relativity of their own interpretation of the meaning of liberty, the later resistance would certainly have been deprived of its chief intellectual and moral support. The tragedy is that although these liberals were the sworn foes of political absolutism, they were themselves absolutists in the social creed they formulated.

This statement does not mean, of course, that they were opposed to social change; the opposite is evidently the case. But it does mean they held that beneficial social change can come about in but one way, the way of private economic enterprise, socially undirected, based upon and resulting in the sanctity of private property—that is to say, freedom from social control. So today those who profess the earlier type of liberalism ascribe to this one factor all social betterment that has occurred; such as the increase in productivity and improved standards of living. The liberals did not try to prevent change, but they did try to limit its course to a single channel and to immobilize the channel.

If the early liberals had put forth their special interpretation of liberty as something subject to historic relativity they would not have frozen it into a doctrine to be applied at all times under all social circumstances. Specifically, they would have recognized that effective liberty is a function of the social conditions existing at any time. If they had done this, they would have known that as economic relations became dominantly controlling forces in setting the pattern of human relations, the necessity of liberty for individuals which they have proclaimed will require social control of economic forces in the interest of the great mass of individuals. Because the liberals failed to make a distinction between purely formal or legal liberty and effective liberty of thought and action, the history of the last one hundred years is the history of non-fulfillment of their predictions. . . .

The basic doctrine of early economic liberals was that the regime of economic liberty as they conceived it, would almost automatically direct production through competition into channels that would provide, as effectively as possible, socially needed commodities and services. Desire for personal gain early learned that it could better further the satisfaction of that desire by stifling competition and substituting great combinations of non-competing capital. The liberals supposed the motive of individual self-interest would so release productive energies as to produce ever-increasing abundance. They overlooked the fact that in many cases personal profit can be better served by maintaining artificial scarcity and by what Veblen called systematic sabotage of production. Above all, in identifying the extension of liberty in all of its modes with extension of their particular brand of economic liberty, they completely failed to anticipate the bearing of private control of the means of production and distribution upon the effective liberty of the masses in industry as well as in cultural goods. An era of power possessed by the few took the place of the era of liberty for all envisaged by the liberals of the early nineteenth century.

These statements do not imply that these liberals should or could have foreseen the changes that would occur, due to the impact of new forces of production. The point is that their failure to grasp the historic position of the interpretation of liberty they put forth served later to solidify a social regime that was a chief obstacle to attainment of the ends they professed. . . .

When it became evident that disparity, not equality, was the actual consequence of *laissez faire* liberalism, defenders of the latter developed a double system of justifying apologetics. Upon one front, they fell back upon the natural inequalities of individuals in psychological and moral make-up, asserting that inequality of fortune and economic status is the ''natural'' and justifiable consequence of the free play of these inherent differences. . . . I fancy that today there are but few who are hardy enough, even admitting the principle of natural inequalities, to assert that the disparities of property and income bear any commensurate ratio to inequalities in the native constitution of individuals. If we suppose that there is in fact such a ratio, the consequences are so intolerable that the practical inference to be drawn is that organized social effort should intervene to prevent the alleged natural law from taking full effect.

The other line of defense is unceasing glorification of the virtues of initiative, independence, choice and responsibility, virtues that center in and proceed from individuals as such. I am one who believes that we need more, not fewer, ''rugged individuals'' and it is in the name of rugged individualism that I challenge the argument. Instead of independence, there exists parasitical dependence on a wide scale—witness the present need for the exercise of charity, private and public, on a vast scale. The current argument against the public dole on the ground that it pauperizes and demoralizes those who receive it has an ironical sound when it comes from those who would leave intact the conditions that cause the necessity for recourse to the method of support of millions at public expense. Servility and regimentation are the result of control by the few of access to means of productive labor on the part of the many. An even more serious objection to the argument is that it conceives of initiative, vigor, independence exclusively in terms of their least significant manifestation. They are limited to exercise in the economic area. The meaning of their exercise in connection with the cultural resources of civilization, in such matters as companionship, science and art, is all but ignored. It is at this last point in particular that the crisis of liberalism and the need for a reconsideration of it in terms of the genuine liberation of individuals are most evident.

The enormous exaggeration of material and materialistic economics that now prevails at the expense of cultural values, is not itself the result of earlier liberalism. . . .

The underlying philosophy and psychology of earlier liberalism led to a conception of individuality as something ready-made, already possessed, and needing only the removal of certain legal restrictions to come into full play. It was not conceived as a moving thing, something that is attained only by continuous growth. Because of this failure, the dependence in fact of individuals upon social conditions was made little of. It is true that some of the early liberals, like John Stuart Mill, made much of the effect of "circumstances" in producing differences among individuals. But the use of the word and idea of "circumstances" is significant. It suggests—and the context bears out the suggestion—that social arrangements and institutions were thought of as things that operate from without, not entering in any significant way into the internal make-up and growth of individuals. Social arrangements were treated not as positive forces but as external limitations. . . .

[But] liberalism that takes its profession of the importance of individuality with sincerity must be deeply concerned about the structure of human association. For the latter operates to affect negatively and positively, the development of individuals. Because a wholly unjustified idea of opposition between individuals and society has become current, and because its currency has been furthered by the underlying philosophy of individualistic liberalism, there are many who in fact are working for social changes such that rugged individuals may exist in reality, that have become contemptuous of the very idea of individuality, while others support in the name of individualism institutions that militate powerfully against the emergence and growth of beings possessed of genuine individuality.

It remains to say something of the third enduring value in the liberal creed:—intelligence. Grateful recognition is due early liberals for their valiant battle in behalf of freedom of thought, conscience, expression and communication. The civil liberties we possess, however precariously today, are in large measure the fruit of their efforts and those of the French liberals who engaged in the same battle. But their basic theory as to the nature of intelligence is such as to offer no sure foundation for the permanent victory of the cause they espoused. They resolved mind into a complex of external associations among atomic elements, just as they resolved society itself into a similar compound of external associations among individuals. . . .

The crisis in liberalism is connected with failure to develop and lay hold of an adequate conception of intelligence integrated with social movements and a factor in giving them direction. We cannot mete out harsh blame to the early liberals for failure to attain such a conception. . . . [T]he controlled study of man in his relationships, is the product of the later nineteenth century. Moreover, these disciplines not only came into being too late to influence the formulation of liberal social theory, but they themselves were so much under the influence of the more advanced physical sciences that it was supposed that their findings were of merely theoretic import. By this statement, I mean that although the conclusions of the social disciplines were about man, they were treated as if they were of the same nature as the conclusions of physical science about remote galaxies of stars. Social and historical inquiry is in fact a part of the social process itself, not something outside of it. The consequence of not perceiving this fact was that the conclusions of the social sciences were not made (and still are not made in any large measure) integral members of a program of social action. When the conclusions of inquiries that deal with man are left outside the program of social action, social policies are necessarily left without the guidance that knowledge of man can provide, and that it must provide if social action is not to be directed either by mere precedent and custom or else by the happy intuitions of individual minds. The social conception of the nature and work of intelligence is still immature; in consequence, its use as a director of social action is inchoate and sporadic. It is the tragedy of earlier liberalism that just at the time when the problem of social organization was most urgent, liberals could bring to its solution nothing but the conception that intelligence is an individual possession. . . .

Humanly speaking, the crisis in liberalism was a product of particular historical events. Soon after liberal tenets were formulated as eternal truths, it became an instrument of vested interests in opposition to further social change, a ritual of lip-service, or else was shattered by new forces that came in. Nevertheless, the ideas of liberty, of individuality and of freed intelligence have an enduring value, a value never more needed than now. It is the business of liberalism to state these values in ways, intellectual and practical, that are relevant to present needs and forces. If we employ the conception of historic relativity, nothing is clearer than that the conception of liberty is always relative to forces that at a given time and place are increasingly felt to be oppressive. Liberty in the concrete signifies release from the impact of *particular* oppressive forces; emancipation from something once taken as a normal part of human life but now experienced as bondage. At one time, liberty signified liberation from chattel slavery; at another time, release of a class from serfdom. During the late seventeenth and early eighteenth centuries it meant liberation from despotic dynastic rule. A century later it meant release of industrialists from inherited legal customs that hampered the rise of new forces of production. Today, it signifies liberation from material insecurity and from the coercions and repressions that prevent multitudes from participation in the vast cultural resources that are at hand. The direct impact of liberty always has to do with some class or group that is suffering in a special way from some form of constraint exercised by the distribution of powers that exists in contemporary society. Should a classless society ever come into being the formal *concept* of liberty would lose its significance, because the *fact* for which it stands would have become an integral part of the established relations of human beings to one another.

Until such a time arrives liberalism will continue to have a necessary social office to perform. Its task is the mediation of social transitions. This phrase may seem to some to be a virtual admission that liberalism is a colorless "middle of the road" doctrine. Not so, even though liberalism has sometimes taken that form in practice. We are always dependent upon the experience that has accumulated in the past and yet there are always new forces coming in, new needs arising, that demand, if the new forces are to operate and the new needs to be satisfied, a reconstruction of the patterns of old experience. . . .

What I have called the mediating function of liberalism is all one with the work of intelligence. This fact is the root, whether it be consciously realized or not, of the emphasis placed by liberalism upon the role of freed intelligence as the method of directing social action.

Objections that are brought against liberalism ignore the fact that the only alternatives to dependence upon intelligence are either drift and casual improvisation, or the use of coercive force stimulated by unintelligent emotion and fanatical dogmatism—the latter being intolerant by its very constitution. The objection that the method of intelligence has been tried and failed is wholly aside from the point, since the crux of the present situation is that it has not been tried under such conditions as now exist. It has not been tried at any time with use of all the resources that scientific material and the experimental method now put at our disposal. It is also said that intelligence is cold and that persons are moved to new ways of acting only by emotion, just as habit makes them adhere to old ways. Of course, intelligence does not generate action except as it is enkindled by feeling. But the notion that there is some inherent opposition between emotion and intelligence is a relic of the notion of mind that grew up before the experimental method of science had emerged. For the latter method signifies the union of ideas with action . . . and action generates and supports emotion. Ideas that are framed to be put into operation for the sake of guiding action are imbued with all the emotional force that attaches to the ends proposed for action, and are accompanied with all the excitement and inspiration that attends the struggle to realize the ends. Since the ends of liberalism are liberty and the opportunity of individuals to secure full realization of their potentialities, all of the emotional intensity that belongs to these ends gathers about the ideas and acts that are necessary to make them real.

Again, it is said that the average citizen is not endowed with the degree of intelligence that the use of it as a method demands. This objection, supported by alleged scientific findings about heredity and by impressive statistics concerning the intelligence quotients of the average citizen, rests wholly upon the old notion that intelligence is a ready-made possession of individuals. The last stand of oligarchical and anti-social seclusion is perpetuation of this purely individualistic notion of intelligence. The reliance of liberalism is not upon the mere abstraction of a native endowment unaffected by social relationships, but upon the fact that native capacity is sufficient to enable the average individual to respond to and to use the knowledge and the skill that are embodied in the social conditions in which he lives, moves and has his being. There are few individuals who have the native capacity that was required to invent the stationary steam-engine, locomotive, dynamo or telephone. But there are none so mean that they cannot intelligently utilize these embodiments of intelligence once they are a part of the organized means of associated living.

The indictments that are drawn against the intelligence of individuals are in truth indictments of a social order that does not permit the average individual to have access to the rich store of the accumulated wealth of mankind in knowledge, ideas and purposes. There does not now exist the kind of social organization that even permits the average human being to share the potentially available social intelligence. Still less is there a social order that has for one of its chief purposes the establishment of conditions that will move the mass of individuals to appropriate and use what is at hand. Back of the appropriation by the few of the material resources of society lies the appropriation by the few in behalf of their own ends of the cultural, the spiritual, resources that are the product not of the individuals who have taken possession but of the cooperative work of humanity. It is useless to talk about the failure of democracy until the source of its failure has been grasped and steps are taken to bring about that type of social organization that will encourage the socialized extension of intelligence. . . .

Liberalism has to gather itself together to formulate the ends to which it is devoted in terms of means that are relevant to the contemporary situation. The only form of enduring social organization that is now possible is one in which the new forces of productivity are cooperatively controlled and used in the interest of the effective liberty and the cultural development of the individuals that constitute society. Such a social order cannot be established by an unplanned and external convergence of the actions of separate individuals, each of whom is bent on personal private advantage. This idea is the Achilles heel of early liberalism. The idea that liberalism cannot maintain its ends and at the same time reverse its conception of the means by which they are to be attained is folly. The ends can now be achieved *only* by reversal of the means to which early liberalism was committed. Organized social planning, put into effect for the creation of an order in which industry and finance are socially directed in behalf of institutions that provide the material basis for the cultural liberation and growth of individuals, is now the sole method of social action by which liberalism can realize its professed aims. Such planning demands in turn a new conception and logic of freed intelligence as a social force. . . .

24 THEODORE LOWI

This selection by Theodore Lowi builds on his earlier work, *The End of Liberalism*. Lowi's concern is less with political ideas than with political behavior. His position is that liberal ideas mean little if in fact they fail to motivate people in political life. His argument that liberalism has come to an end in America is really an argument that liberal institutions have become illiberal while liberal politicians have continued to publicly profess liberal concerns. For Lowi, American liberalism has become a sort of mythology, a collection of beliefs which justifies existing institutions even while the leaders of those institutions act in ways opposed to liberal values.

Lowi does not view American "liberal democracy" as based upon traditional liberal ideas. He argues instead that interest group pluralism is fundamentally different than the competitive factionalism of James Madison because the nature of the possible consequences of government action has changed. That is, the goal of political competition is not the same at the end of the twentieth century as it was at the beginning, and so, while American politics may still look basically the same (with political parties, lobbyists, and so forth), it is nevertheless very different. This selection illustrates Lowi's understanding of the nature of this change and of its consequences for American liberalism.

THE POLITICS OF THE SECOND REPUBLIC OF THE UNITED STATES*

Commonplace Characteristics of the First Republic—And Their Decline

The Traditional American republic—the "First" Republic—can be defined briefly by a few commonplace characteristics. But bear in mind that these commonplace items that are taken for granted every day actually point to the basis of authority in the traditional American republic. For example, it was a Federal Republic, with a weak national government and strong peripheral governments which the Constitution called *states*, drawing on a European theoretical concept precisely to indicate where most power and authority were expected to reside.

---

* "The Politics of the Second Republic of the United States," Edmund Janes James Lecture, Oct. 9, 1976, Department of Political Science, University of Illinois, Urbana, Ill. Reprinted by permission of the department and the author.

This is the way it proved to be in practice, because the second feature, commonplace though less well understood, is that the states actually did most of the governing in the First Republic. A glance at the annual session laws of Congress during the 19th Century will reveal that what little governing was done through the national government was about 99 per cent subsidy or "patronage." These policies of the national government to facilitate commerce were cumulatively important, but few involved fundamental social choices directing the coercive powers of government toward some selected goal. In the meantime, those fundamental social choices were being made by the state governments: all the property laws, the credit and exchange laws, the banking and insurance laws, the occupational laws, the family and estate laws, the health and safety laws, and virtually all other laws providing the governmental legal basis of modern life—from capitalism to the family. So fundamental were these state activities that they were called "police powers."

Another commonplace characteristic of the traditional system was that the national government was a Congress-centered government. Woodrow Wilson's basic text on American national politics, published in 1888, was quite properly entitled *Congressional Government*.

The beginning of the end of the traditional or first republic was the New Deal and its wake during the late 1940s and 1950s. The best known but least significant characteristic of the New Deal period was the increasing size of the national government, measured in budgetary terms. Although there was indeed an increase in size, it was not so large in relation to GNP, especially if one separates out defense expenditures during the 1940s and 1950s.

The most significant change during the New Deal was the change in the *functions* of the federal government. Subsidy policies were of course continued; in fact, growth in subsidies accounts for a large part of the general budgetary growth. However, in the process the Federal government was adopting two kinds of functions, new at least for the Federal government. First, a large number of important regulatory policies were adopted—i.e., the Federal government began to use the "police power." Second, the Federal government adopted an even more significant number of fiscal and monetary policies—grouped together as "redistributive" policies in this treatment.

There were precedents of course for both of these new types of functions, reaching back to the Interstate Commerce Act of 1887 and the Sherman Anti-Trust Act of 1892. However, the New Deal is distinguishable because of the number of such policies adopted and the establishment of the constitutional right of the Federal government to take on these new functions.

The important change implied by the taking on of these two new functions is that they involve direct and coercive use of Federal government powers on citizens—something that was extremely rare at the federal level during the entire 19th and part of the early Twentieth Century.

Another, and highly related, characteristic of this period is the rise of *delegated* power. The Federal government in effect grew by delegation. Although Congress did continue to possess the law making *authority*, it delegated that authority, increasingly in statute after statute, directly to an agency in the Executive Branch or to the President, who had the power to sub-delegate to an agency. At first this delegation of power was rationalized as "filling in the details" of congressional statutes. But ultimately, it was recognized for what it really was: "administrative legislation."

These very significant developments of the New Deal and the post-New Deal period should, however, be treated as transitional rather than final. There were many characteristics of that period other than the ones identified here. The Second Republic emerges after 1961, out of the pronouncement and validation of those few most salient characteristics.

The return of the Democrats to power in 1961 was accompanied by an entirely new attitude, and that new attitude is actually what validates certain New Deal characteristics, turning them into a new regime. This attitude was one of eagerness to establish and maintain a national government presence in all aspects of economic life. What had been done in the 1930s in the name of emergency and as necessary evils became, with the Kennedy Administration, positive virtues. If the 1930s had established a strong national state as politically feasible and constitutionally acceptable, the 1960s made the strong national state a positive virtue, desirable for its own sake.

Regulatory and redistributive policies were embraced as good things. The practice of delegation of power from legislature to executive was embraced as a good thing also. Legislative leaders were joined by career administrators and by professors of law and political science in singing hosannas to the superiority of technicians and to the inferiority of amateurs and legislatures trying to make laws. The new theory of the strong American national state relegated the legislator to the role of giving consent rather than making law. This amounted to budgeting authority, in a manner very similar to the way Congress was already budgeting money. The basis of the regime was indeed changing.

It is actually possible to pick two events in 1962 as the turning point in the practice and the theory of the Second Republic. The first of these was the economic report of the President in January of 1962, where President Kennedy requested from Congress a delegation of discretionary power over all public works and over the entire income tax structure of the Federal government. In effect, President Kennedy was asking (1) for personal discretion to make the laws controlling budget deficits and surpluses, (2) for personal discretion over the laws determining the level of public capital investment, and (3) to have personal discretion to manipulate the levels and rates that determine individual and corporate tax liability. President Kennedy did not get his requests. In fact his entire program had become immobilized months before his assassination in November of 1963.

But President Kennedy did establish beyond any doubt the basis for such requests for unlimited delegation of discretion to the President. And eventually, Congress would cooperate.

The second event of 1962 was the Yale Commencement Address delivered by President Kennedy in June. In this address President Kennedy argued as follows: "The central domestic problems of our time are more subtle and less simple. They relate not to basic clashes of philosophy or ideology, but to ways and means of reaching common goals—to research for sophisticated solutions to complex and obstinate issues." Thus, on the very eve of one of the most ideological periods in American history, President Kennedy had accepted the "end of ideology" thesis.

All of this was part of a reordering of American public philosophy. Not only did it include a general belief that a strong national government was basically in harmony with all of the interests in society. It went a good deal further than that. The new public philosophy also embraced the shift from a Congress-centered to an Executive-centered government and went still further to embrace a change from Executive-centered to White House-centered government.

Still another change in the emerging public philosophy was a redefinition of majority rule to make it appear as though the President, not Congress, was the true manifestation of the Real Majority. Congress was redefined as a useful collection of minorities. And once the presidency was redefined as the true representative of the Real Majority, the overwhelming inclination was to embrace the principle of embodying maximum *legislative* powers in the presidency.

It is possible to approve or to disapprove, but it is not possible to deny that these changes reflect fundamental shifts in the basis of authority. The everyday significance of these changes can be portrayed by a single case study—the Economic Stabilization Act of 1970, which instituted Federal controls over wages, prices, rents, and interest. This is one of the most far-reaching Federal enactments in American history. Its main provisions are as follows: "The President is authorized to issue such orders and regulations as he may deem appropriate to stabilize prices, rents, wages and salaries. . . . Such orders and regulations may provide for the making of such adjustments as may be necessary to prevent gross inequities. (Section 202) The President may delegate the performance of any function under this title to such officers, departments, and agencies of the United States as he may deem appropriate. (Section 203)"

The language of laws under the Second Republic is virtually the language of the Bible, expressing broad and noble sentiments, giving almost no direction or instruction at all. The Environmental Protection legislation of the same period might as well have been written as follows: "Whereas all Americans have a right to a healthy environment; and whereas the environment is growing more and more corrupt; now therefore let there come to pass rules and regulations from the President, who shall in his wisdom . . . etc."

In the *regulatory* field, new and highly discretionary policies will be found in wage and price controls, environmental protection, race relations, education, energy, narcotics, organized crime, domestic aspects of national security, commercial relations, communications, food and drug quality, credit and lending, labor relations, and industrial safety. In the *redistributive* field, new and enormously discretionary policies include the whole complex bundle of social programs first embodied in the Organization for Economic Opportunity; another is the system of tax credits to encourage investment; another is money and credit policy, a vast area the President shares with the Federal Reserve. Another, perhaps the most important, is the discretionary power of the Federal government to insure or underwrite private investment. With a mere signature on a paper guaranteeing repayment, the government can influence the decisions of private banks regarding long term loans at lower rates of interest or loans not otherwise available at any interest rate. The so-called Lockheed loan was no loan at all; it was a loan guarantee, part of a plan to shoreup the ailing defense sector. Some of these loan guarantees and investment insurance programs are across-the-board, extended without discretion to all members of a given sector. An example would be the Federal Deposit Insurance Corporation. But increasingly, these loan guarantees and insurance investment programs are discretionary, allowing the President or an agent to make each decision "on the merits."

So big is this discretionary insurance power that it gives the Second Republic its name: The State of Permanent Receivership. There is no time here to go into all of its ramifications and implications. Let a couple of items suffice: By our account, seventeen major Federal agencies have authority to grant loan guarantees and investment insurance. Also by our count, though not complete, there are at least 33 Federal loan guarantee and investment insurance programs. Soon there will almost certainly be another—loan guarantees and bond insurance for cities. Examples of discretionary investment insurance includes the five billion dollars of authority of the Maritime Administration. A more important example is of the field of mortgage guarantees; under FHA, VA, and other such agencies, over 40 billion dollars of home investment had been insured by the Federal government. Trillions of dollars in private investment decisions have been influenced by these guarantees, and the capacity of the Federal government to shape the economy through this technique is worthy of consideration as an emerging system of planning that would warrant description as "a state of permanent receivership."

Because so many of the new functions are put within presidential discretion or are based upon presidential authority, there is a tremendous clamor throughout the economy and society for decisions that can only be made at the presidential level. Our system is therefore highly centralized, but not because there is so much real power or knowledge at the center. It is rather because interests at the periphery and near the center come to feel that their own corporation or sector or agency can no longer operate without getting the privilege or support available only at the center. Thus, any impression of centralization in the Second Republic is not really a matter of central coordination of the economy but a continuous effort in the economy to *coordinate itself* in terms of perceived resources, privileges, and inclinations at the center.

It would be misleading to compare the Second Republic directly to European countries if only because of the fact that the positive national government in the United States has emerged *without a unitary bureaucracy*. Instead, we have a strong national government with a highly fragmented bureaucracy, fragmented not only in terms of legal insulation from central controls but also in terms of the freedom of each agency to form its own political alliances.

A related but still more important difference between the United States and the European governmental systems is that at the center of the American system there is no collective responsibility—not even a concept of collective responsibility. The President is virtually alone in his discretion, to such an extent that he is often held responsible for problems in the economy over which no person or institution should ever have been held responsible. For example, the American Cabinet is internationally famous as an institution of individuals, each with his or her own ambitions and sources of support. The American party system is equally well known as separate from the President. Moreover, there is no premier or other official intervening between the President and the legislature or between the President and the public. Therefore, no parliamentary bloc, whether a partisan one or simply a coalition, ever shares responsibility for the programs the President is responsible for implementing.

These factors do more than differentiate the contemporary United States from other industrial countries. They also bring into focus the particular problems of our new regime in action. Two dimensions of the regime in action must be analyzed: the administrative politics of the regime, and the electoral politics of the regime. In the end, some effort will be made to show how each of these relates to the other, conveying an impression of a bad republic.

Administrative Politics in the Second Republic

During the past century, virtually every important expansion in the Federal government has been accompanied or followed by a concerted effort at administrative reform. Beginning at the very time of the establishment of the first regulatory commission, two important commissions in administrative reform were established. These, and an important successor in 1910, concentrated primarily on questions of administrative efficiency and economy. This was obviously parallel to efforts in the private corporate world. In many respects, these efforts to achieve administrative efficiency culminated with the establishment of the Budget Bureau in 1921.

The enormous expansions of government during the early 1930s gave rise to one of the most important movements for administrative reform in American history, the President's Committee on Administrative Management. Although this Committee report opened with one of the most famous American appeals for administrative reform, "The President needs help . . .," actually the primary focus of the Brownlow Report of 1939 was on general administrative accountability. People in all parties and groups seemed to agree that the vast "alphabetocracy" had to be brought under control.

Quite consistent with the 1939 President's Committee were the Hoover Commissions of the 1950s, the dominant concern of which was for administrative accountability and departmental rationalization. Many proposals were made for regroupment of agencies within existing departments, and eventually President Eisenhower was responsible for the establishment of the first new domestic department, the Department of Health, Education and Welfare. This is altogether a case of administrative rationalization.

These efforts continued on into the 1960s—but with a great difference. The focus of administrative reform shifted from administration in general to the very top of the administrative hierarchy in particular. These efforts are best examplified in the Landis Report at the very time of Kennedy's inauguration, and the book by the scholar and former member of the Budget Bureau and the Truman White House, Richard Neustadt's *Presidential Power*. The overwhelming preoccupation of both documents is Presidential control—how the President deserves it, how he can achieve it, and how he can maintain it. This was absolutely necessary not only as the means of gaining administrative rationality and efficiency but also as a means of accomplishing the social programs to which the Federal government had been committed since the 1930s. These new proposals had external as well as internal goals, but either way their focus was upon the Presidency and the White House.

Recommendations flowing out of these considerations were adopted and pursued with vigor by President Kennedy and by President Johnson. Neither President got from Congress their desired reforms of the independent commissions, but Congress was more cooperative in other respects. Two new departments were created, Housing and Urban Development, and Transportation. But perhaps the most significant and meaningful administrative reform during the period was the creation of the Organization for Economic Opportunity, which was set up to coordinate, *from the White House,* the innumerable agencies and programs pertinent to welfare and social services, *regardless of the pre-existing departments within which those agencies were housed.*

These efforts of the 1960s culminated with the administrative reforms of Richard Nixon. In every respect, Richard Nixon's efforts to cope with the problems of the national bureaucracy were consistent with the efforts of Kennedy and Johnson. These began with the appointment of the Ash Council in 1969, culminating with the very dramatic recommendations in 1971 for *superdepartmentalization*— that is, the creation of four major cabinet departments and the regroupment of all constituent agencies according to the newly defined subject matter of each department. Congress did not give Mr. Nixon what he wanted in this regard, but Nixon proceeded to gain some of these requirements through his own administrative powers. By the end of his first Administration, Nixon had centralized administrative control in the White House beyond anything President Eisenhower had tried to do according to his military staff concepts, and beyond anything that Kennedy and Johnson had succeeded in doing through their years of preoccupation with "Presidential power." Given the innumerable revelations of the various Watergate investigating committees and commissions, it is unnecessary to document the extent of Presidential centralization or the extent of preoccupation with Presidential power during the last of the Nixon Administration. However, it would be wrong to draw from all of these facts an impression that President Nixon was disproportionately preoccupied with Presidential power. Everything about the history of the Presidency since 1961 indicates that this was the normal rather than the abnormal preoccupation. Even the last effort of President Nixon to reorganize his staff and Cabinet was consistent with the previous efforts by Kennedy and Johnson. If the Watergate scandal had not intervened, it is almost certain that the second Nixon Administration would have been [reorganized]. Four Cabinet officers were to be designated to serve jointly as Secretaries and as Presidential assistants. The Secretary of the Treasury would have served also as Presidential assistant for Economics; the Secretary of Health, Education and Welfare would have served jointly as Presidential assistant for Human Resources, and so on. Each of these four "super-Cabinet members" was to be given jurisdiction over the departments in which they served as Secretaries and over all other domestic departments and agencies with related areas of concern. Thus, the Cabinet in general was to be subordinated to the four super-Cabinet members. And the four super-Cabinet Secretaries would also serve as a new type of Cabinet, called the Domestic Council. Many of the previous members of the very large White House Staff were to remain in the White House while many others were to be reassigned to sensitive positions in all of the departments, presumably and probably maintaining their loyalties to the White House.

Thus, in order to gain and maintain Presidential control, President Nixon was proposing in effect a combination of Eisenhower concepts of military staff, Brownlow and Hoover concepts of administrative rationalization, and Landis-Neustadt concepts of Presidential power, all thrown together in an almost Prussian concept of an inspectorate made up of court eunuchs spread out among the various representatives of the crown. Many anti-Nixon partisans attacked his proposals as an effort by Nixon to insulate himself from Congress and the public, because of the fact that giving four Cabinet Secretaries appointments as personal advisors in the White House would have increased their rights to claim executive privilege against testifying before Congressional committees. This was probably one of President Nixon's motivations, but even this is consistent with the attitudes of all recent Presidents, that they are given mandates for four years and that it is basically not in the national interest for the public to know too much about their failures until they no longer have any time to redeem themselves.

Since Nixon's plan did not go into full effect, thanks to Watergate, we cannot evaluate these arrangements. Yet, since the responsibilities delegated to the President have not changed, it is almost certain that the next fully elected President of the United States will proceed in a manner consistent with his three elected predecessors. . . .

The Second Republic: A Plebiscitary Republic

Let me try to sum up these changes. Indeed, although Europe has never seen anything quite like our Second Republic, we can still best characterize it in European terms: We have developed a Bonapartist head of state; we have developed a plebiscitary presidency. We have a French Fifth Republic without de Gaulle and without a premier, a cabinet, or a party or parliamentary structure. The Second Republic is a plebiscitary republic in which the focus of national authority, national function, national power and national politics is upon a single, elected office.

"Plebiscitary" is intended to indicate centrally delegated power with an electoral base of authority, and in the Second Republic this relationship between President and public is close, sensitive, and daily rather than quadrennial. One cannot study the polls without being struck by the close relationship between President and public. But the actual pattern over the past twenty years or so is indicative also of the problem as well as the pattern of responses to the standard polling question, "Do you approve of the way the President is doing his job?" There is insufficient space and time to review the pattern in detail, but the tendencies are as follows:

1. The general tendency is for the rating of each president to decline, beginning well above the 50 per cent mark and, except for Eisenhower, dropping to well below the 50 per cent mark—to around 30 per cent for Truman and Nixon and to around 35 per cent for Johnson.
2. The general approval rating tends to jump up at the time of the general election, suggesting that each President begins with a fund of consent which he dissipates as he uses it. This is the popular basis of the "honeymoon."
3. The general approval rating tends to drop faster than the overall trend line whenever there is a major domestic event involving the Presidency, such as President Kennedy's sending troops to Mississippi during a civil rights demonstration, or President Ford's vetoing of an important labor regulation bill.
4. Except at the time of a general election, there is only one other occasion when the rating of a President jumps upward, and this is in the aftermath of a major international event. This event can be a fiasco, such as the U2 incident or the

Bay of Pigs; or it can be an event considered a triumph, such as the visit of a major international figure or the announcement of President Nixon that we were withdrawing from Vietnam. Whatever the international event is, the tendency of the public is to rally round the President. But the support does not last for long. Either the international event is forgotten, or further involvement in that situation begins to have domestic consequences and contributes toward the overall reduction of the President's approval rating.[1]

All of the data suggest that the President's relationship to the public is direct, sensitive, and generally downward. Aside from a deliberate involvement in an international incident, there is little a President can do deliberately and self-consciously to improve his position with the public. Perhaps this is why we have had a series of one-term Presidents since Eisenhower. President Kennedy's Administration was terminated by a single assassin's bullet, but it was clear to Kennedy and to others that his popularity was suffering greatly before his death. President Johnson was so unpopular at the end of his term of office that he considered himself unwelcome at the National Convention of his own party. President Nixon was reelected in an overwhelming victory in 1972 but was unable to complete his term of office—an event unprecedented in American history. Here lies the real measure of political change between the traditional and the Second Republic: In the Second Republic the sanction against presidential shortcomings is personal disgrace, not merely failure of reelection.

The Second Republic: A Bad Regime

If these various tendencies do constitute the "politics of the Second Republic," then they will very quickly be discovered by each President and, if rational, he will adjust his behavior accordingly. Even though we are early in the history of the Second Republic, it would be very useful to try to develop a model of Presidential behavior drawn from the knowledge of actual behavior that we already have—thanks especially to the various investigations of Presidents and the Presidency during the past four years.

This model of behavior can be based upon three well-established axioms:

(1) The ethical axiom: *with discretion comes responsibility*. Corollaries:
    (a) If the discretion is collective, the responsibility is collective;
    (b) If the discretion is individual, the responsibility is personal.

(2) The political axiom: *There is a very high probability of failure*. Corollary: The more a regime relies upon popular consent, the higher the probability of failure. (This is not only due to the false promises made by political candidates. It is also due to the need to simplify and to project by symbols and imageries. The general tendency in all mass political communication seems to be to raise the level of expectations, so that the probability of

failure is based upon the expectations of the public but also the actual expectations or criteria of people in public office.)

(3) A constitutional principle, new with the Second Republic, but nevertheless well established: Election to the Presidency of the United States is a mandate to govern for four years virtually without hindrance.

These three axioms are a formula for political disgrace when they become the context of presidential power. Nevertheless, this is the context, and within it we can deduce the basic strategies of each President, assuming rationality. Presidential behavior can be projected as a set of rational contingency plans.

First, the Rational President will try to succeed—sincerely and honestly. The reward for honest success in politics is very great, all the greater because of the heroic definition of the Presidency.

However, the Rational President will have to develop a contingency plan against any news leakages regarding failures and potential failures. It will be logical, rational, and imperative to suppress news of failures "as long as I have any time remaining in my four-year mandate." Therefore, it would be irrational not to have some important and skillful members of the White House staff to plug up the leaks of news about failure. It would be in bad taste and politically inept to give these especially sensitive people a separate title, such as "plumbers." However, that would indeed be their function. Perhaps we should call them "court eunuchs," because the Rational President would certainly wish to have in such positions individuals of such intense personal loyalty that they would be willing literally "to walk over my Grandmother's grave" for the President.

There must be a second contingency plan, since in any open society news leakages are possible. The Rational President will need to staff the White House with people who have the skill and knowledge to *redefine the news* so that it appears to be different, and better, than it actually is. The Rational President would therefore wish to have on his staff persons drawn from the advertising profession, because the advertising profession is based upon skill in the manipulation and redefinition of symbols.

However, effective as advertising techniques may be, there will still be news that escapes the White House and also manages to escape redefinition. Thus a third contingency plan is called for, and to meet it the Rational President will have to have on his White House staff persons who are skilled in redefining reality itself, to make failure appear to be less serious, or in fact often to convert failure into success. This is the quintessential professional skill of the lawyer—the ability to produce a particular reality through the prejudicial amassing of data. In Anglo-Saxon law this is called the adversary process, and it is based on the assumption that "When two men argue, as unfairly as possible, on opposite sides, it is certain that no important considerations will altogether escape notice." But that only proves the existence of the skill in question. It can be misused as well as used; what the Rational President needs is lawyers so skilled in the adversary process and so loyal personally to the President that they are able and willing to misuse the skill.

There is at least one other contingency plan, which each President must develop, but hopes never to use. *Suppression of dissent.* In the event that the news does leak and in the event that the realities of failure back of the news cannot be redefined by the ad men and the lawyers, the Rational President must be prepared to suppress those who might take dissenting actions on the basis of the news. Each Rational President, perceiving that he still has years, months, or weeks remaining in his mandate to make a success out of an apparent failure, will have to view as unfair and premature all dissenting actions aimed at him or his Administration. And, because active dissent will make his job harder to perform, the Rational President must ultimately view dissenting actions as contrary to national security. Once an action is defined as contrary to national security, directly suppressive actions by national police forces such as the FBI, CIA, and the Armed Forces, are justified. This also means that literally hundreds of actions that are otherwise illegal or impeachable, or both, suddenly become justifiable, acceptable, and in the national interest.

This five-step model may seem only to be an ironic way to describe the actual behavior of President Richard Nixon. But Nixon is the prototype President in the Second Republic, not the aberrant case. His style may have given every action an individual appearance, but the character of each was endemic, not idiosyncratic. President Johnson had already placed at least 100,000 civilians under surveillance by the Army—an illegal and impeachable act. President Johnson had also sought to suppress political dissidents by strategic use of conspiracy trials. Virtually all of the conspiracy actions taken by the Justice Department during the Vietnam period were taken under Johnson and his very liberal Attorney General Ramsey Clark. Both Kennedy and Johnson impounded funds. The bill of particulars could go longer, but there is, for the sake of brevity, one very good summary of the outlook and the behavior of Presidents in the Second Republic by one of the most important Presidential advisors ever to serve in the White House: ''[The President] vetoed minor bills that he did not like, impounded appropriated funds that he did not need, ignored restrictive amendments that he found unconstitutional and improvised Executive action for bills that would not pass.

''He did not feel obligated to risk unnecessary delay and possible defeat by sending every important international agreement to the Senate for approval as a formal, long-term treaty. Nor did he follow Eisenhower's precedent of seeking Congressional resolutions of approval for major foreign policy initiatives. He dispatched personal and official advisors on important missions abroad. . . . He invoked the claim of Executive privilege to prevent Congressional investigators from harassing State and Defense Department civil servants.''

It turns out that the Presidential councilor who made that statement was not John Ehrlichman or H.R. Haldeman defending President Nixon but was in fact Theodore Sorenson speaking for President Kennedy.[2]

These precedents from Johnson and Kennedy are in no way meant to soften the judgment history will make of President Nixon. They are meant rather to make the judgment of Kennedy and Johnson far more harsh. Yet, our concern should be for the regime, not for the men. If rationality in the Second Republic requires committing impeachable acts and to have contingency plans for still other impeachable acts, this is the measure of a bad republic. And if such a bill of particulars can be drawn on the Chief Executive of all modern republics, then all modern republics are bad republics.

The basis of republican government in the United States is the constitutionalist argument that a good republic is a republic whose constitution (small c) brings out the best of ordinary people. A constitutionalist does not seek a government by "good men" in the Greek sense but rather assumes that all people in politics are capable of good or bad, depending largely on a "good constitution." It follows that a bad regime is a regime whose constitution takes ordinary people and brings out their worst.

Many observers have come to agree that the problem of government in the United States is too much power in too few hands. But how shall we decentralize? To whom? For what?

For example, is there any real advantage to be gained from a movement to decentralize toward local governments? The urban crisis of 1975 should have broken the myth that local populations, especially urban populations, are capable of governing themselves. The rise of the Federal government in the first place was in large part a response to local incapacities and local incompetencies.

Shall we instead *deconcentrate,* turning back important powers to private hands in a new system of "neo-laissez-faire?" I personally can see considerable advantages in letting market mechanisms make some of the decisions that we are now trying vainly to make by governments. But deconcentration back toward private hands cannot be done without laying down some drastic conditions, conditions in the law that may be beyond the capacity of the modern United States Congress. Some substantial proportion of the modern paradox of inflation plus unemployment has to be attributable to a conspiracy between big labor and big capital. If modern government is to be deconcentrated, we will have to deconcentrate big labor and big capital as well, or we will be merely trading a leviathan for a behemoth.

Rather than trying to decentralize or to deconcentrate, perhaps we would find our solution by a *transference* of power—that is, by delegation of power not to the White House but to scientists and technologists whose skills and whose analytic capacities might produce better decisions more honestly, or without misleading the public. It seems to me that the answer is the other way around, that scientists and technologists, by virtue of their specialization, need the guiding hand of some central government. Our so-called crises of ecology, energy, transportation, and atomic proliferation provide evidence that a science community is much like a local community—well run but ungoverned—quite rational in terms of its own narrow interests but incapable, by virtue of its small size or its specialization, of seeing the whole society.

If there are solutions to the problems of the Second Republic, they will have to be found in a head-on confrontation with the constitutional and legal decisions that gave rise to the Second Republic. We might consider, for example, building some collective responsibility into the Presidency so that the heavy pressure of personal disgrace will be taken off the President. This might be done by a requirement that the entire Cabinet be submitted for "advice and consent" rather than individual nominees. Part of the same thing might be accomplished by establishing a Congressional practice of subjecting the entire Cabinet or any one or more members of the Cabinet to regular votes of confidence. As far as I can determine, this could be done without resort to a constitutional amendment. We might consider, by constitutional amendment, instituting the office of Premier, based on the theory and practice of the Fifth Republic of France.

Beyond any considerations of collective responsibility, we would also have to confront the problem of delegation by establishing strict limitations on how much and what type of delegation should be within Congress's power to make. In 1935 the Supreme Court did assert the power to declare statutes unconstitutional if they were so broad in their delegations that they provided no standards or guidelines for administrative implementation. This Court doctrine has never been reversed, even though it has not been employed on an act of Congress since the 1930s. If the Supreme Court did revive the doctrine we would then have a perfect method for deconcentrating power by preventing Congress from taking any action until it was fairly clear on what action it wanted to take.

However, the President could accomplish much the same thing by vetoing legislation that delegated too much discretion (personal responsibility) to him. His argument would be not only that such undefined delegation is unconstitutional. It is also unfair for the majority favoring the law or program not to share responsibility for its outcome. This sharing of responsibility between the President and a parliamentary bloc would take an enormous burden off the presidency.

But ultimately the only effective solution to the problem of a bad republic is widespread awareness of the problem itself. When one is living in an era of creeping illegitimacy, one is living in a time when theory is probably more powerful than practice. As long as our politicians live by and for popular consent, the one accusation they are least able to bear is the accusation of tyranny, of illegitimacy, of participation in arbitrary uses of power. Many specific reforms can and should be proposed. However, no proposal will mean very much until its precise purpose, and the context within which it is proposed, is clearly understood. If a

substantial step has been taken toward a definition of the character and consequences of the contemporary American regime, as the Second Republic, that is an
adequate accomplishment for the time being.

25 RICHARD WOLLHEIM

Many critics of liberalism and liberal democracy claim that liberalism is inher-
ently weak and unable to resist extremist movements because liberals lack absolute moral and ethical standards. They claim that it is necessary to ground or
justify political values and recommendations in metaphysical, transcendent, or
transhuman standards which will "prove" the "correctness" of liberal values.
Without such moral criteria politics will have no foundation and liberals will be
defenseless, subject to attack by those who are absolutely convinced of the moral
correctness of their actions. Others have argued that liberalism implies value neu-
trality, that liberals cannot have any real value preferences.

Richard Wollheim (b. 1923) disagrees with these positions. In this essay he
argues that neither doubt nor infinite metaphysical regress are necessary as a
foundation for liberty. Both positions are evasions of our basic problems. Rather,
he argues that we must make liberty itself our basic criteria or standard for measuring political values and actions.

Professor Wollheim teaches philosophy at the University of London.

WITHOUT DOUBT OR DOGMA:
THE LOGIC OF LIBERALISM*

There are two current theories about the foundations of liberalism. The first theory is that liberalism is based upon, is untenable without, a belief in some more
general system or order, in the law of nature or the scheme of things. The other
theory is that liberalism is the expression of, is acceptable only on the basis of,
total skepticism about ultimate values. One hears a great deal of both theories,
from defenders and opponents of liberalism alike, sometimes indeed from one

---

*"Without Doubt or Dogma: The Logic of Liberalism," *The Nation*, 183 (1956), pp. 74–76.
Reprinted by permission of *The Nation*.

and the same person: though I should have thought it quite apparent that they were in flagrant contradiction. . . .

Both theories are, I am convinced, fundamentally false. I do not wish to deny that someone might cleave to the principle of liberalism on account of some more general belief in the order of nature: or that he might come to it through skepticism. What I wish to deny is that either skepticism or the "public philosophy" is necessary as a justification of liberalism: or, what is the same thing in other words, that liberalism presupposes either.

I shall first consider the skeptical thesis. The argument runs something like this: According to liberalism anyone should be free to do what he wants to do or to say what he wants to say. But what a man wants to do might be wrong, and what he wants to say might be false. And so if the state allows him complete liberty, it might be permitting evil and error: indeed, since a man's actions and words can easily influence others, it might even be encouraging evil and error. Now clearly no one thinks it right that evil and error should be knowingly encouraged. Accordingly the only good reason the state could have for allowing the subject complete liberty is that it can never know, it can never be absolutely certain, that what it permits is evil or error. In other words, the sole justification for liberalism is skepticism on the great issues of truth and goodness.

Personally I find this argument rather more persuasive when directed against liberty of speech than when directed against liberty of action: so I shall consider it in this form. For here any attempt to brush the argument aside can be met by a charge of disingenuousness: "Consider," it will be said, "consider some simple case of error: a historical thesis, a mathematical conjecture that is definitely, beyond a shadow of doubt, known and proved to be false. Would you encourage its propagation? Surely not. If, then, you are prepared to allow complete liberty of speech in matters of morals or religion or social theory, this must be because you do not really believe that one can ever attain to certainty in these matters."

What can we say, what is a liberal to say to this challenge? In part, I think, its force depends upon a confusion, perhaps a deliberate confusion. For it runs together the beliefs that one thinks should be taught and the beliefs one thinks should be permitted. And it may well be that the first class of beliefs is somewhat narrower than the second. I do not know. But anyhow it is with the second class that I am here concerned. Still, even after this distinction has been made, enough of the challenge remains. What are we to say to it? One might capitulate to it, but I think that one need not. John Stuart Mill in his great essay *On Liberty* said that when a new opinion arises in opposition to accepted ways of thought, there are three possibilities. The new opinion may be true, it may be partly true, it may be false. But in all three contingencies alike, there is, Mill claims, a good, indeed an overwhelming, reason for tolerating the opinion. If it is true or partly true, the case for doing so is obvious. But if it is false, the case is no less strong. For unless the new opinion is tolerated, the received opinion will thereby suffer. It will be held by the majority of those who receive it "in the manner of a prejudice, with little comprehension or feeling of its rational grounds:" and, ultimately, it will come to be "a mere formal profession," a string of words, deprived or enfeebled of all meaning.

I should hesitate to describe this argument as conclusive: though personally I accept it. For my present purposes, however, the question of its acceptability is not the issue. All that matters is whether it is a reasonable argument. For if it is reasonable, then we here have definite proof that someone can without absurdity subscribe to liberalism and not subscribe to skepticism: which is what I set out to prove. And surely the argument *is* a reasonable argument. Liberalism, then, does not presuppose skepticism about ultimate issues. Indeed in a sense—I hope that it does not seem too trivial a sense—it may be said that they are incompatible. For there is at least one ultimate issue the liberal not merely need not, but must not, be skeptical about: and that issue is the value of individual liberty.

I want to turn now to the other current theory about the justification of liberalism: namely, that it depends on, that it is unplausible without, some more general belief about the universe and man's place in it, what Lippmann has called the "public philosophy." [1] I cannot see the force of this argument. Of course the liberal must believe in the principle of liberalism, and he must doubtless have reasons for believing in it; but why should it be thought necessary for him also to believe in some more general principle from which this principle can be inferred? Behind the idea that it is, there lurks, surely, the suggestion, the feeling, that the strength of a principle somehow depends upon the generality of the principle from which we can infer it. Those principles which follow from principles far more general than themselves are the best. But this feeling must be wrong. For ultimate principles are, by definition, those which cannot be inferred from more general principles: and surely no principles can have so strong a claim upon our allegiance as ultimate principles. In other words, the demand for a justification of a principle—in the sense of another principle from which it follows—seems to betray a certain uneasiness about, a certain dissatisfaction with, the principle as it stands. . . .

The justification of liberalism has a history, and a revealing one. In the seventeenth century, the principle of liberty was defended by Puritans by an appeal to the commandments of God: in the eighteenth century it was defended by the Encyclopaedists by an appeal to the order of nature: in the nineteenth century it was defended by John Stuart Mill by an appeal to the needs of human personality. At each stage, the distance across which the appeal is made contracts. To some this may seem tantamount to saying that at each stage the case for liberalism is weakened, its prestige reduced. But to me the opposite seems the case. For surely what has happened is that at each stage that which justifies human liberty, and all else, is seen as closer to human liberty, and human liberty as closer to it, and in consequence the value of human liberty is enhanced. And if the final stage in this history is, as I believe it is, to find the justification for the principle of liberty in liberty itself, then by this means the value of liberty is raised to the utmost: it becomes an ultimate value.

I should like to consider for a moment a particular version of the theory that liberalism rests upon, or presupposes, certain general assumptions about the nature of man and the universe: and that is the view that the principle of liberalism implies an "optimistic" conception of human nature. The fundamental error of the "children of light," as Dr. Reinhold Niebuhr calls traditional liberals, in opposition to the "children of darkness," the moral cynics, is a stupid, fatuous optimism. There is no doubt that many of the great classical thinkers of liberalism did hold very naive views about human psychology. But I do not think that such views are necessary to their liberalism: above all, I do not think that they are necessary to their belief in liberty of thought and speech. And yet the contrary view has often been urged. For, it is said, it would be against human reason to support complete toleration unless one believed that ultimately truth was likely to triumph over error. And so this must be what liberals believe. And if they believe this, they can believe anything.

But is this view that is attributed to them really so silly? Is it really so "optimistic" to believe that if people are allowed complete access to all opinions and all the evidence for them, they are more likely to accept those which are true than those which are false? If the current set of opinions is incomplete or the available stock of evidence inadequate, then mistakes are understandable. But otherwise they are surely the exception rather than the rule. To suppose differently is to take a very whimsical view indeed of the connection between evidence and true conclusion: as though it were a passage one was only likely to effect in consequence of some mysterious skill or luck: whereas in fact it is just the hall mark of a human being that, other things being equal, this is something he brings off quite naturally. I do not think it is true that, as some philosophers have urged, the truth on a particular matter of fact just is that conclusion which people move to when they have considered all the evidence. But I think that there is a sufficiently intimate connection between evidence and conclusion to make this a pardonable exaggeration.

I do not want to deny that there are dark instinctive forces that pull men into beliefs that they would not otherwise accept, or blind them to opinions they would otherwise accept. But surely the power that these forces exercise can be weakened by, perhaps only by, the continuous, uninterrupted, uncensored flow of evidence. It is often argued that the findings of modern psychology have obliterated the picture of man as a thinking, calculating being that is essential to the "optimistic" social thought of Condorcet or Mill. I do not think that this is really true. Indeed in some respects, paradoxical though it may be, modern psychology can

be said to have gone over the picture and freshened it. The phenomenon of repression, for instance, in a curious, oblique way testifies to the strength of the rational
process in man: for the fear in which the mind stands of uncomfortable evidence
is the tribute it pays to the power that this evidence if uncensored would exert over
it. And if psycho-analytical theory has at the same time laid bare the extent to
which the mind also consists of non-rational elements, the practice of analysis
shows the extent to which these elements can be subdued by reason. Modern
psychology, it seems to me, by making clear the true character of the powers of
unreason, so far from producing a case against liberty of discussion, demonstrates
in an empirical fashion that its existence is not a luxury but a necessity of civilized
life.

And now a final point. Confusion is often made between the presuppositions of
liberal theory and the prerequisites of liberal society. The presuppositions of liberal theory are the theories about man or nature or society or knowledge that are
entailed by liberal theory: that must be true if it is true. The prerequisites of liberal
society are the social conditions that are necessary for liberal society: that must
exist if it is to exist. The two things, though quite different, are often confused:
one reason being doubtless the widespread view that the prerequisite of liberal
society is a belief on the part of its members in the presuppositions of liberal
theory.

I have argued that there are no presuppositions of liberal theory. And I have
argued on grounds of logic. And appropriately. For the question is one of logic.
On the other hand, whether there are any prerequisites of liberal society is an
empirical question: not to be answered in that brisk *a priori* fashion in which it
ordinarily is. To some people, for instance, it seems obvious that liberal society,
if it is to work, must be composed of liberal citizens. But I doubt if that is so.
Montalembert once summed up the policy of his church *vis-à-vis* the world as
"When I am the weaker, I ask you for liberty, because it is your principle; but
when I am the stronger, I take it away from you, because it is not my principle."
Since Montalembert's day, churches other than his, religious and secular, have
embraced the same policy, but it is absurd to suppose that their members cannot
settle down in a liberal society in which they are fortunately outnumbered. They
are a permanent risk in any liberal society: but not its undoing.

The question, then, whether there are any prerequisites of liberal society can be
answered only by a careful investigation of the liberal experiment. It is often said
that nineteenth-century liberals in their folly thought that the precincts of Westminster could be reproduced in every dark corner of the world, and there would
be light: whereas now, in the modern age, we know better. It deserves to be
remembered, however, that John Stuart Mill, one of the least blinkered or cynical
of men, once thought that a good way of ridiculing certain thinkers was to suggest
that they advocated the extension of liberal institutions to Bedouins. It is

agreeable to realize that in politics also the cautious have no monopoly of the truth.

---

26 JERVIS ANDERSON

JEANNE KIRKPATRICK

DENNIS H. WRONG

There has always been a large amount of popular discussion of the meaning of liberalism. James and John Stuart Mill, John Maynard Keynes, and John Dewey wrote extensively for leading journals and newspapers. The following selections are taken from "A Symposium, What Is a Liberal—Who Is a Conservative?" published in *Commentary*, September 1976. They illustrate the role played by the press in explaining and analyzing liberalism.

Jervis Anderson works for the *New Yorker,* Jeane Kirkpatrick teaches political science at Georgetown University, and Dennis H. Wrong teaches sociology at New York University.

A SYMPOSIUM: WHAT IS A LIBERAL—WHO IS A CONSERVATIVE?*

Jervis Anderson

It is true . . . that the terms liberal and conservative are used rather loosely today. It is also true that certain positions once associated mainly with conservatives have lately found favor among liberals, and vice versa. In the circumstances, it is not surprising that a measure of confusion now exists in many minds over who can rightly be called liberal and who, conservative. I hope I do not

*"A Symposium: What Is A Liberal—Who Is a Conservative?" *Commentary,* 62 (Sept. 1976), pp. 35–36, 72–74, 111–13. Copyright 1976 by the American Jewish Committee. Reprinted by permission of *Commentary* and the authors.

surprise you too much by saying that I myself have managed to avoid being confused. This is because my own standards of definition are broad and resilient
enough to sustain occasional deviations; because I realize that the apparent ideological confusions we are now witnessing have occurred a number of times in the
past; and because, especially where liberals are concerned, I do not find these
developments at all astonishing. . . .

1. A lot may depend upon what motivates liberals and conservatives to adopt
positions that are not in harmony with the history or the background of their social
beliefs. In many cases, it may simply be that they have seen in these positions a
new opportunity to pursue old interests. For example, the advocacy by liberals of
decentralization and quotas is, indeed, problematic. It creates almost as many
problems for liberals as it solves. Not the least of the problems it creates is this:
suddenly called into question are both the consistency of the liberal belief in centralized administration and the integrity of what liberals have always said about
the more desirable ways of achieving equality. The latter end of this wicket is
probably the more sticky, because the espousal of anything resembling preferen-
tial treatment undermines the general principle of equality. However, when liberals are found taking such positions, it is often because they are stirred by plight,
and are acting out of a need to remedy or correct problems which do not respond
to conventional methods of solution. Conversely, when the conservatives advocate decentralization or oppose quotas, it is frequently because they are insensi-
tive to plight, hostile to the social objectives of centralized administrations, and
indifferent to the need for redress. In other words, the hand may at times be
Esau's, while the voice is still Jacob's.

2. The liberal persuasion has always seemed to accommodate fairly wide shad-
ings of social outlook; has always seemed unable to resist the challenge of
untested possibilities; and, as a result, has always lent itself to a good deal of risk
and experimentation. When one looks at some of the more admirable traditions
and achievements in American history, politics, and literature, one can only be
thankful that the liberal idea has always yielded to risk and moral adventure. On
the other hand, the ruins of many of its good intentions are by no means hard to
find. And yet, the mistakes and failures of liberalism—as it has sought to translate
itself into public policy—are almost worth celebrating, for they were consequences of some of its most appealing traits: its openness to a diversity of progressive dispositions; its willingness to undertake uncertain searches for uncertain
answers; and its awareness, as Lionel Trilling once said, of "complexity and
difficulty."

. . . Am I satisfied with the way the terms liberal and conservative are used
today—in light of the ideologically contradictory positions being adopted within
both camps? Because of my own standards of definition, I must reply that I am
neither satisfied nor dissatisfied. What are these standards? When I try to perceive
today who is liberal and who is conservative, it is not the occasional points at

which ideological positions merge or blur that I take chiefly into account. It is whether, despite certain apparent contradictions, those who call themselves liberal and those who call themselves conservative may still be seen to be upholding the central moral values and tendencies of their faiths.

Because I believe that it is the ultimate moral differences between liberal and conservative commitment that really count—and because I am inclined to wait and see who, in the end, remains available for a defense of what is decisive to liberal and conservative conviction—I believe it matters how the terms liberal and conservative are used, or how I use these terms. What are some of these ultimate differences? . . .

I would say that conservatives are not persuaded, on the whole, that humane ideals should influence the conduct of those who manage public affairs. Left to themselves, they would probably repeal the Bill of Rights and the philosophical premises of the American Revolution. They do not believe it is the duty of government to create what have been called "civilizing opportunities" for the general population. And their conduct, in government or in private, is more often shaped by their social irritabilities than by their social concern. Liberals look forward to making life somewhat more tolerable, somewhat more civilized, somewhat more just, and somewhat more decent for the general society. Their undertakings in the area of public policy are often animated by compassion and the instinct for redress. It is their conviction that social goals should be pursued democratically. They believe that government is the most effective instrument for providing the conditions under which social problems can be solved; and that civil liberties, freedom of speech, and freedom of the press are indispensable to the survival of a civilized community. . . .

Jeanne Kirkpatrick

The terms liberal and conservative are devoid of specific meaning, laden with affect, entangled in fashion, and involved in an ongoing power struggle of momentous importance.

These terms are not only affected by their social, historical, and political context; their *whole* meaning varies with the time, place, and speaker. This is the reason that Adam Smith, David Ricardo, and John Stuart Mill can be called liberals because they affirmed the importance of individual economic freedom, and Friedrich von Hayek can be called a conservative because he takes precisely the same position. . . .

It has been argued that liberalism has a core concern with individual freedom while conservative and radical philosophies emphasize collectivities (guilds, nations, races, classes, and so forth), and though a sizable literature in political philosophy reflects such a conception, contemporary usage, which often links liberalism with coercive social programs and détente with coercive nations, does not. It is also sometimes argued that liberal and conservative express orientations to change, so that a liberal is one who favors change *per se* and a conservative one who resists or opposes it. But a definition that positions people in relation to change regardless of the status quo in which they are situated, or of the direction in which they move, cannot be very useful in distinguishing among political types. Because the terms have no fixed referents, the liberalism or conservatism of specific policies—say, the Humphrey-Hawkins bill or the Jackson amendment—can only be settled arbitrarily, and not by rational inquiry or debate.

The terms Left and Right are, if anything, worse. In addition to their ambiguity, these terms also tacitly commit those who use them to an extraordinary philosophy of history according to which events and people can be arrayed on a simple universal political spectrum stretching through time and space—enabling us to locate any person or position on a single spectrum. Thus, of French politics it is said that Krivine is Left of Marchais who is Left of Mitterrand who is Left of Giscard who is Right of Chaban-Delmas who was Left of Pompidou. And of the Communist world it is said that Mao is Left of Fidel who is Left of Brezhnev who is Left of Berlinguer (or is he?). Descriptions such as these make dyslexics of us all.

An adequate effort to place political figures in relation to one another (more or less Left, more or less liberal) would begin from the fact that contemporary politics is multidimensional and that these dimensions do not necessarily hang together. At least four mutually independent dimensions are involved: first, a political dimension which includes attitudes toward competitive elections, tolerance of dissent, rule of law; second, an economic dimension which includes attitudes toward private property, distribution of wealth, public ownership, governmental regulation; third, a cultural dimension which includes attitudes toward authority and toward order in public and private spheres; fourth, a foreign-policy dimension which includes attitudes toward defense, supranational bodies, the Third World, détente, and related matters. And the problem of labeling these dimensions remains. Contemporary usage is consistent in terming as Left or liberal those economic positions which favor public control or ownership of resources and an egalitarian distribution of wealth. But what of the political spectrum—shall we call those positions Left which favor majority rule, minority rights, and rule of law, in which case the Communist governments are Right and we are Left, or should we reverse the labels? And what of the cultural dimension—shall we call Right those positions and organizations that favor hierarchy and order and Left those favoring more egalitarian distribution of status and loose, decentralized organization, in which case the Gaullist UDR is Left of the French Communist party? Finally, how do we label foreign policy: are those who support political freedom and free emigration and oppose political imprisonment Left, in which case Daniel P. Moynihan is a leading exponent of the Left, or do the PLO and IRA, George Habash and Idi Amin, represent the Left? The questions are not frivolous and their answers are by no means self-evident.

Does it really matter? Thoughts are no clearer than the words in which they are expressed and, as always, murky thinking obfuscates reality, causing that which is good to appear less good and that which is evil less evil. Political positions which would be perceived as morally untenable if clearly stated can be made to seem acceptable when they are clothed in the appropriately fashionable euphemisms. Godly people who would never dream of personally harming anyone support murder and kidnapping by terrorists conceived as Third World liberation movements, justify slave labor and starvation when it is called reeducation. The possibility of thinking clearly about development and international affairs dwindles when we lump together politically, economically, technically, culturally diverse peoples into the single category, Third World; the possibility of thinking clearly about southern Africa or anywhere else on that troubled continent declines when we describe dictatorships as majority rule; the possibility of thinking clearly about the Middle East decreases when we term Zionism racism; and the possibility of thinking clearly about the whole political world is diminished by our hapless efforts to fit complex realities into the meaningless yet misleading categories of Right and Left.

. . . Because they encourage us to focus on meaningless abstract attributes ("Leftness," "Rightness") instead of actual characteristics of persons and politics, the terms liberal and conservative, Left and Right, contribute to our disorientation in the political world and complicate the defense of human freedom.

Dennis H. Wrong

Terms like liberal and conservative, and Left and Right, have acquired such diverse historical associations that it would be remarkable if they were always used in a consistent manner. All of them are heavily freighted with positive or negative sentiments, inducing partisans to use them prescriptively in an effort to distinguish "true" liberalism or conservatism, or the "real" Left or Right, from what they see as usurpations of the label. Moreover, it is always in the interests of democratic politicians to gravitate to the Center by blurring the neat distinctions made by ideologists and intellectuals, just as it is often the aim of the latter to expose the politicians' rhetorical ploys and reinstate the distinctions. . . .

Despite the inevitable misuses of the terms, it remains the case that much of modern democratic politics can be seen as a struggle between liberals and conservatives, or Left and Right. Politicians, especially American politicians with their preference for maneuvering in the capacious and ambiguous Center, are given to making apparently oxymoronic claims that they are "progressive conservatives," "liberal traditionalists," or "Tory socialists." Yet some conception of a Left-Right spectrum or a liberal-conservative polarity is indispensable and creeps back even when the familiar tainted terminology is renounced, if only because the dictum that "if men define situations as real, they are real in their consequences" is especially applicable to political debate and the alignments it produces. Thus, to answer *Commentary*'s last question first, it matters how terms like liberal and conservative—and radical—are used. They are constitutive of political reality itself and, both as political actors and as analysts, we are compelled to define ourselves in relation to them.

Liberal-conservative and Left-Right have never been interchangeable distinctions in American political discourse, as *Commentary*'s questions seem to imply. The first derives from 19th-century British politics; the second, originally suggested by the seating arrangement of the first National Assembly at the time of the French Revolution, came to be favored in the following century by the rising socialist movement. In America, liberals and conservatives are seen as contestants in the main arena of party and electoral politics, whereas Left and Right are confined to smaller publics on the fringes—Marxist sectarians and Birchers, readers of *Dissent* and of *National Review,* the followers of Henry Wallace in 1948 and of George Wallace in 1968 and 1972. Of the four terms, liberal alone possesses some definite content, since the other three, except for indicating broadly different attitudes toward change, are definable only in relation to their opposites at any given time. Liberalism, of course, derives from "liberty" and affirms the widest possible extension of individual freedom from institutional authorities. In the nineteenth century, liberalism included advocacy of the economic freedoms of trade and enterprise and the term still retains Manchesterian overtones in much European political parlance.

In America, liberalism has since the New Deal acquired a social-democratic, collectivist tinge and one no longer hears opponents of the welfare state describe themselves as "Jeffersonian liberals." But even before the '30s, American liberals were for a more equal distribution of power, income, and status. There have been changes in the groups regarded as the most unjustly deprived and victimized by inequalities and the lack of full civil liberties, but liberals have continued to see unregulated capitalism, big business, or the corporations as their main political enemies and the federal government as the chief agency capable of reforming the society.

I apologize for mentioning these banal truths and do so only to cast doubt on *Commentary*'s suggestion that there are peculiar discontinuities in the way conventional political labels are used today. As for the assertion that "many positions which used to be called liberal are now called conservative," each of the positions adduced to support this conclusion requires separate discussion.

Quota systems: Liberals are by no means united on the issue of affirmative-action quotas in education and employment. In the past liberals unanimously opposed quotas that discriminated in favor of those already privileged. Affirmative-action quotas, however, discriminate in favor of groups that were formerly excluded, which is why some liberals have supported them as a temporary means of overcoming the disabilities these groups still suffer as a result of past discrimination. Obviously, this difference between past and present quota system explains why some liberals appear to have changed their positions. Liberal critics of affirmative action fear that the new quotas will create vested group interests that will make them hard to eliminate even if they succeed in fully achieving their equalizing purpose, which is also widely doubted. Whether or not these fears are well-founded, only the advocacy of *permanent* quotas favoring particular groups regardless of whether they still suffer disabilities resulting from past exclusion would amount to a reversal of traditional liberal principles. In any case, disagreements on the complex issue of affirmative-action quotas have not become a crucial dividing line between liberals and non-liberals.

Economic growth: When was support for economic growth ever a specifically liberal position? Though the term is of recent vintage, eulogists of American capitalism have always extolled its productivity, from those whom Veblen called at the turn of the century "votaries of the full dinner pail" to the oil companies in their institutional advertising today. Presumably, *Commentary* is referring to the vociferous support for environmental protection and zero population growth by segments of the counterculture and the New Left, and some prominent liberal intellectuals and academics, that emerged rather suddenly a few years ago. It was indeed something of a novelty to find these causes, especially neo-Malthusianism, embraced so ardently by liberals and leftists. Conservation and conservatism, after all, literally mean the same thing, and the founders of the conservationist movement early in this century were patrician Republicans like Theodore Roosevelt and Gifford Pinchot, although they belonged to the anti-business wing of the party. Environmentalism, however, is congruent with liberal-Left ideology in that pollution can be seen as another evil to be blamed on the corporations.

High rates of economic growth, as has often been noted, dampen down the class struggle by reducing dissatisfaction over inequalities in distribution. This applies internationally to conflict between rich and poor countries as well as domestically. . . .

. . . Although it undoubtedly appeals to a vastly larger constituency than a decade ago, environmentalism is reverting to the status it occupied before the recent flurry of interest in it, of being a special issue marginal to the major liberal-conservative differences and drawing supporters from both camps in addition to the concerned specialists, bucolics, cranks, and monomaniacs it has always attracted.

One need be neither a liberal nor a conservative, however, and certainly not a believer in the dubious computer models of the Club of Rome, to be persuaded that there *are* real limits to growth. The great boom from the end of World War II to 1970, which was so effective a solvent to domestic class conflicts, is over. In the Third World, the road to economic development now appears far rockier than it looked even a decade ago. At the very least, growth approaching the scale of the recent past can only recur if it is guided by environmental concerns and corrections for what economists call external diseconomies that are technically feasible but economically costly. Constant pressure on the private sector is necessary to insure that these concerns and corrections are taken into account even though the sheer physical limits to growth have been grossly exaggerated by the doomsday prophets.

Big government: Of the presidential candidates who most loudly denounced big government in their campaigns this year, I have never heard anyone call Ford, Reagan, or Wallace a liberal. Carter and Brown, the two most successful candidates in the Democratic primaries, also stressed this theme, but the media almost universally described them as centrists rather than as liberals. Writers for the *Village Voice,* surely a trendy beacon on the Left, repeatedly attacked both men as conservatives masquerading as moderates. Come to think of it, the *Voice* also attacked *Commentary* as the organ of a new "Right-Center" establishment. Is this perhaps the confusion of political categories that worries *Commentary*?

Support for decentralization and opposition to big government has a respectable liberal-Left heritage if one goes back before the New Deal. . . . The revival on the Left of suspicion of large centralized bureaucracies and of support for small-scale democratic participation was a healthy development. But there was always the danger that such an outlook might be professed by wind-sniffing politicians to give a new face to conventional opposition to federal social policies. This has happened to some extent in the '70s. Yet one permanent achievement of the '60s may have been the weaning of liberals away from an almost automatic reliance on federal policies and huge bureaucracies as the agencies most likely to implement their values.

One cannot classify every position on every political issue along a single dimension. Particular views may acquire a liberal or conservative coloration because they are espoused for a time by groups which are predominantly liberal or conservative on other issues, but their marginality to, or even contradiction with, positions on these other issues eventually becomes apparent. . . .

27 DONALD HANSON

Donald Hanson is professor of political philosophy at the University of Utah and a thorough student of liberal ideas. In the essay that follows, he attempts to separate the essential concepts and values of liberalism from ideas which are part of the tradition of liberalism but not suited to contemporary problems. In undertaking this task, Hanson demonstrates the vitality and flexibility of liberal thought and suggests the continuing importance of liberal concerns.

WHAT IS LIVING AND WHAT IS DEAD IN LIBERALISM?*

The aim of this essay . . . is to explore some of the chief defects and merits of the political philosophy of liberalism. More particularly, it undertakes the defense of what might be called a chastened liberalism, chastened by winnowing out some of the inessential accretions of a long and embattled doctrinal history. This amounts to a libertarian perspective that depends on only two essential ideas, complex though they are: that the cardinal principal of political value is individual freedom, and that this is most likely to be obtained through the tolerance of moral diversity.[1] This is obviously nothing new. Nor is there anything novel about the observation that ever since the nineteenth-century reaction to the French Revolution, criticism of liberalism has been frequent, voluminous, and sometimes cogent. Indeed, the critical assault of the nineteenth century was so vigorous that there is a tendency to overlook the fact that such criticism has obtained from the very beginning of the classical tradition of Anglo-American liberalism in seventeenth-century England.[2] In short, liberalism has never enjoyed undisputed supremacy. It is true that liberalism achieved its alliance with the idea of representative government and with the democratic impulse in the nineteenth century, and that it was then, too, that the only creative alternative—socialism—was produced. It is this coincidence in time that has led some observers to the perception of a paradox: that liberalism was just achieving its greatest triumph at the same time that it was being most resolutely rejected (Sartori, 1965: 357–58). The paradox, however, is only apparent, for the liberal philosophy of politics had long since acquired its standing as one of the permanent achievements of our intellectual history. The real paradox of nineteenth-century liberalism is quite different. Rather than characterizing that century in terms of the triumph of liberalism, it would be more accurate to say that it represented nothing so much as the beginning of a retreat from the values of classical liberalism, a retreat that has continued to our own time. In short, one of the most conspicuous features of political thought since the middle of the seventeenth century has been the multiplication of widely differing criticisms of liberalism. Moreover, so far has the attack pro-

*"What Is Living and What Is Dead in Liberalism," *American Politics Quarterly*, 2, no. 1 (Jan. 1974), pp. 3–37. Reprinted by permission of Sage Publications, Inc.

ceeded, as Cranston (1953) pointed out some years ago, that in America the very term "liberalism" has begun to acquire a pejorative connotation. Undoubtedly that movement in political rhetoric has accelerated (Wolff, 1969; Lowi, 1969).

But what is fashionable is not for that reason either accurate or reasonable, nor is the volume of criticism any measure of validity. Before there is undue celebration in anticipation of a new post-liberal orthodoxy, before we consign the literature of liberalism "to the flames," in Hume's phrase, it may be advisable to consider the problem on a wider plane than is normally the case of late. More particularly, it would be well to remember that classical liberalism began as a profoundly radical political theory. This simple reminder involves two important sets of considerations that ought to be taken into account in contemporary debate. First, the development of classical liberalism had a specific historical setting and, quite naturally, equally specific purposes and problems. Second, neither the early history of liberalism nor the history of subsequent modification can, by themselves, settle any important theoretical issues at stake today. The question of the merits and defects of liberalism is one, not merely of history nor, indeed, of evidence, but also one of examining and weighing the strengths and weaknesses of argument. In this essay, I propose to begin by examining the principal political purposes of the original liberals' demand for individual freedom in the English civil wars. I want to suggest that, by doing so, it will be possible to identify some historically conditional elements in the liberal tradition that, precisely because they are conditional, need not be considered indispensable components of a modern philosophy of individual liberty. I turn next to consider some aspects of the general problem of liberty. . . .

Seventeenth-Century Origins

The collection of general ideas that make up the substance of Anglo-American liberalism was fashioned in seventeenth-century England, largely during the course of the civil wars of the 1640s. Probably it would be generally agreed that the liberal philosophy of politics rests on the notion that government must be clearly distinguished from society. Certainly that distinction is fundamental, for a great deal else that is regarded as essential in liberalism is made to depend on that assumption. Indeed, so much a part of our outlook has this distinction become that it seems only natural to make it. No matter how natural it may seem, however, it does not refer to anything that belongs in the observable "furniture of the universe." The distinction is, of course, a claim, composed of both factual and normative elements. To see that it is not an ordinary factual proposition, it is enough to remember that no such distinction occurs in the political thought of classical antiquity. The important point, however, is to recognize that the distinction between society and government is an ideologically conditioned perception of political reality. I mean by this only that it expresses identifiable hopes and purposes.

The primary thrust of the idea seems clear enough: it is designed to assert that society is a meaningful and independent reality quite apart from government. But there is considerably more to it than this. In fact, the doctrine implies two other important assumptions, both of which are highly debatable, to say the least. In order to make the distinction plausible, it becomes necessary to assume that the social order somehow contains natural cohesive forces. Thus, in one stroke liberalism assumes away what Dahrendorf (1959: 157) has rightly said is "the most puzzling problem of social philosophy: how is it that human societies cohere?" The second assumption follows easily, and here the normative content is uppermost, and it is clear. This is the contention that government is an artificial contrivance and so, quite plainly, merely derivative. It is, of course, simply the instrument of the people who make up society. So much is generally shared. But it is worth noting that from this common point of departure, liberal opinion about government has taken a variety of forms, ranging from the expectation that eventually there would be no need for coercive institutions at all, to the view that government is necessary, if only in the negative sense that it can enhance social life. But the significant point concerns what is rejected—often, simply ignored— in all these formulations, as Wolin (1960: 286–94, 305–14) has rightly observed. And that, of course, is the point that Hobbes, in Chapter 13 of *Leviathan*, insisted on: that the absence of government is unthinkable; it would necessarily involve the terrors of the war of each against all.

Classical liberalism, then, assumed that men possess a native social virtue which would give rise to ordered existence naturally and spontaneously.[3] Given that assumption, the value of government could easily be depreciated. Obviously, however, this assessment produces a difficult problem of explanation in its turn. If men are thus virtuous and competent—quite capable, as Locke would have us believe, of identifying and pursuing their own best interests—how does it come to pass that the historical record is so bleak? Why is it that most men have lived out their lives in degradation, misery, and tyranny? Classical liberalism was not without an answer. Historically, men had been the victims of systematic miseducation. More specifically, priests and kings were responsible for what amounted to a monumental social swindle, for they were the interested sources of falsehood and ignorance (on this point, see Hazard, 1954: part 1, 1968: part 2; Gay, 1968). Hence, all that was required was elimination of the source.

One major form of political theory to emerge from the English civil wars rested on these assumptions. They inform the ideology of a revolutionary opposition. But for the purposes in hand here, the important point is that they represent a coherent set of responses to a particular traditional system. Precisely why should the revolutionary opposition insist upon just these assumptions, as against any other possibilities? It seems clear that the answer is to be found in the specific character of royalist ideas.

The basic claim of seventeenth-century English royalists was that a people without a single head simply could not be considered a people at all. The most any royalist would concede was that a society without a monarch was bound to be an inferior one. . . .

Moreover, this was not the only royalist doctrine that early liberalism was obliged to deal with. Royalist writers insisted, long before Hobbes, that law is and can only be the expression of the sovereign's will. Obviously, this idea is a natural enough corollary of the doctrine that social order is impossible without a sovereign. But in royalist hands, the imperative theory of law was developed in such a way as to goad the opposition into an elaborate counter-ideology. The really provocative notion was the royalists' insistence that, in the last resort, the will of the sovereign was arbitrary. . . .

It seems clear that these royalist doctrines provided the intellectual stimulus for liberal insistence upon institutionalized limitations of government, for the campaign, in short, to achieve constitutionalized government. Indeed, it might be said that the whole point of the constitutionalist tradition has been to deny the doctrine of sovereignty and its corollary, an arbitrary power of decision. The reply of the revolutionary opposition was both theoretical and institutional. The theoretical response turns on the idea that law is both anterior and superior to government. Hence an arbitrary, willful decision was held to be no law at all. In order to be genuine, a law must exhibit two essential characteristics: it must be both general and prospective. This view clearly entails two of the central ideas of the Anglo-American constitutional tradition, for it precludes bills of attainder and ex post facto legislation. In short, the opposition had replied to the imperative theory of law with the idea of a fundamental or constitutional law, which excluded the element of arbitrariness. However, this was not the end of the matter. The uncomfortable fact was that royalists could point to tolerably solid historical evidence that monarchy had been anterior to law. Indeed, it was the power of the royalist case from history that eventually drove the opposition from that level of discourse to the level of political philosophy. It is this weakness that accounts for the radically ahistorical reliance on contract theory and the idea of natural rights.

But serious institutional problems remained. Governmental decisions are often necessarily singular, rather than general. Moreover, in the ordinary course of affairs, an individual citizen is most likely to collide with his government in a court of law. And judges were appointed and removable by the king. Neither James I nor Charles I had hesitated to use their power of removal when it seemed essential to obtain a compliant bench. How were the gentlemen of the opposition to deal with these crucial problems of "executive" discretion? The answer is to be found in the remarkable reception of the antique doctrine of mixed monarchy, the division of executive, legislative, and judicial functions, and the general idea of checks and balances which it supports (concerning the points in this paragraph, see Hanson, 1970: ch. 10; Vile, 1967; Weston, 1960, 1956; Pargellis, 1938).

The primary normative concern that supplies the motive for all these theoretical and institutional ideas is, of course, the conviction that individual liberty could not be obtained otherwise (perhaps the best single expression of these views is to be found in the justly famous "Putney Debates," in Woodhouse, 1951: 1–24). But this is very far from self-evident. Just as in the case of the idea of the artificial and derivative character of government, libertarianism depended on very debatable assumptions. To begin with, the idea of individual liberty presumes that there ought to be a sphere of life that is distinctly private, not simply distinguishable from legitimate public concerns, but once and for all constitutionally insulated from governmental intrusion. But why was it supposed that liberty could be assured only in case governmental institutions were arranged in accordance with the idea of mixed monarchy and checks and balances? The answer is that classical liberalism assumed that the source of *all* coercion was government. Once this assumption is made, it then makes sense to think in terms of inducing governmental paralysis. For this purpose, the opposition could hardly have done better than to fasten on the idea of mixed monarchy. It was the perfect instrument for neutralizing the effects of a necessary evil. But why did the original liberals think that all coercion was governmental? Surely because their general theory involved the assumption that men are naturally virtuous and sociable creatures. Hence, the course of political evil had to be sought elsewhere, and in the seventeenth century it seemed reasonable to locate it in government, as, of course, it seems to some to the present day. Nevertheless, it is just this view which, after all, lies very near the ideological heart of liberalism that has rightly been identified as "the least defensible notion of classical liberalism: the identification of privacy, freedom, and choice with the non-governmental, while sanctions and force are entirely identified with governmental action" (Shklar, 1965: 56). For today only a little reflection is required in order to recognize the cogency of two contrary, but equally relevant points. On one side, it is perfectly clear that the effectuation of some libertarian goals requires governmental action, despite the risks involved. On the other hand, it is evident that the social order bristles with important coercive relationships of a non-governmental kind. The result appears to be a profound dilemma: the cause of liberty must simultaneously rely upon and mistrust the coercive powers of government.

The Problem of Liberty

Thus far, the argument has been designed to suggest that the general form of classical liberalism derives from ideologically conditioned perceptions, and that much of its content is a direct response to a historically specific set of ideas and institutions. But if one is prepared to recognize that historical specificity, it is then possible to dispense with those assumptions. Moreover, it is clear that there are good reasons for questioning the classical assumptions ancillary to the doctrine of liberty, quite apart from their historical contingency. If they are abandoned, then what remains is what Milton (1958: 223) called the religion of the revolutionary opposition—liberty, and the tolerance of moral diversity on which it depends. At any rate, that is what remains on the positive side. Negatively there is still the crucial dilemma of reliance upon and yet suspicion of government. But the existence of the dilemma does not detract from the desirability of liberty. In terms of that ideal, the principal problems seem to revolve around two questions: what are we to mean by "liberty," and according to what criteria are libertarian claims to be weighed against other sorts of claims?

It would seem that the leading tendency among those who have concerned themselves with the issue is to suppose that the primary intellectual problem is to frame a satisfactory definition. It is possible, however, that the importance of this task has been overestimated. A point often made, of course, is that such argumentation has been radically inconclusive. And while this is perfectly true, the value of the observation may well be doubted, for it suggests an erroneous conclusion: that since a satisfactory definition eludes us, the concept might best be abandoned. This conclusion seems doubly wrong. For it may be that the real problem is not one of definition in the first place. Secondly, inconclusive argumentation is not necessarily a sign of futility. On the contrary, it is much more likely to be an indication of the permanent importance of the issues at stake.

Much of the argument has been concerned with the question of whether the true meaning of liberty or freedom is to be sought in the negative or positive conceptions (see, e.g., the fascinating collection of conflicting definitions assembled in Cranston, 1953: 33–45). The negative conception involves the contention that liberty is rightly understood in terms of the absence of external constraints. The positive conception has not been similarly univocal, though it always involves something more than simple absence, such as positive action by the state, usually aimed at promoting the individual's fulfillment, his true interests, or genuine or potential self (for a careful discussion of a number of such theories, see Plamenatz, 1968: 22–61). There are important issues at stake here. But to what extent are they really definitional? To what extent does definitional controversy succeed even in illuminating, much less resolving, those issues? For, as Cranston (1953: 65) has so persuasively argued, any definition is bound to be historically contingent. . . . At a minimum, one must also know the answer to the question, "freedom from what? The answer to that question must hold the key to the intelligibility of any sort of liberalism" (Cranston, 1953: 67). The problem, then, is never simply one of discovering an eternally valid definition. On the contrary, the preoccupation with definition often amounts to an evasion of the substantive issues. This is not to say that definitional concern is never germane. Sir Isaiah Berlin (1958: 39–47 and throughout) has shown that there is still an important general point in insisting on the negative concept of liberty: it is an excellent way to deal with the problem of distinguishing between liberty and a variety of different and competing values. Liberty is not equality, participation, self-fulfillment, an integrated personality, and so on.

Furthermore, neither is it a formula. No more than with any other general principle, can a definition of liberty supply us with an easy and automatic answer to concrete problems. To suppose that it can or should is a mistake, and an important one, for it encourages the search for the automaticity of a formula. Indeed, much of the intellectual difficulty that has collected around the idea of liberty results from a mistaken search for a final formula, or for a settled definition. But it is important to recognize that these are not the only alternatives. What I wish to suggest is that liberty may be understood, instead, as a general principle of evaluation. Thus, when it is held to be the primary political value, its function as a principle is to express the adoption of a fundamental ethical postulate, and to lodge the normative claim that the minimization of external constraints ought generally to be preferred over other important claims—community, justice, equality, perhaps even order itself. The point here is to observe that the registration of such a claim is not at all the same thing as to assert that this will automatically settle an argument involving competing claims or countervailing circumstances; nor is it at all the same thing as to suppose that one's primary value leads easily and irresistibly to specific conclusions in complex situations of choice. On the contrary, it may be that in some circumstances one might be persuaded that his chief measure of political value ought to be modified, perhaps even subordinated or abandoned. For the function of a principle is to raise a presumption and to serve as a guide, rather than to masquerade as an infallible key. In short, the expression of one's primary postulate is the frame and the beginning of political argument, rather than the conclusion. As always, it is a matter of examining the case that can be made in a particular set of circumstances. . . .

However, even if one is prepared to acknowledge the difference between a principle and a formula, important conceptual difficulties remain. One of the most troublesome of these is raised by the libertarians' claim that freedom ought to be regarded as the primary political value. After all, first one must live in order to live well. How, then, can liberty be the highest political value? This is surely a pertinent objection. But it can be met by distinguishing between liberty conceived of as a goal, and liberty as a method. In the tradition of anarchism, liberty has been thought of as a goal, a condition to be achieved in a nonpolitical utopia. But liberalism can be interpreted to mean that freedom is primarily a method when considering this side of the problem. To be sure, as an evaluational principle, it is intended to serve as a measure of the worth of social institutions, to raise the question of how effectively those institutions promote and ensure individual liberty. But it need not be denied that the context is a political one, that the whole point of libertarian claims takes political order as granted. Its thrust, then, is not apolitical, not abolition of order, but continuous criticism and testing of the political order. It is, of course, free speech that at least allows for the possibility of correcting political error or blindness.

Nevertheless, there was and there remains a solid and important point in the anarchist contention. For it is anarchists who have best recognized the sharpest limitation of the liberal interpretation: that free speech may not be enough. Certainly it is not unreasonable to fear that government will refuse to practice tolerance, refuse to afford genuine protection for speech. Again, it is not absurd to claim that an anti-libertarian government cannot be overthrown by discussion. These are legitimate points. And upon them the issue is joined as between liberalism and anarchism. This is exactly the point at which liberals must recognize the difference between goal and method, the political context and limitations of their claims, and the generally ameliorative and moderate character of their doctrine. All this involves considerable amendment of the assumptions examined in the first section of this essay. For classical liberalism, both in the seventeenth and eighteenth centuries, was a genuinely radical political theory. Moreover, part of the reason for this was that it shared some of the expectations that later came to inform anarchism. More specifically, revolutionary liberalism embraced the view that liberty was a goal, a condition to be achieved. Just as in the case of anarchism later, that idea rested on the assumption that natural man was both virtuous and competent, that is, capable of deliberately and intelligently shaping his own social destiny. But monumentally disappointing political experience—particularly the French Revolution—was enough to destroy that faith in liberal quarters. Indeed, it is precisely a seriously amended conception of human nature that liberals are most apt to employ in rejecting anarchism. But liberals ought candidly to recognize that they are thus rejecting their historical selves. For a fundamental objection to anarchism (as well as to the anarchist element in classical liberalism) is that there is no reason to expect that the elimination of government would mean that natural man would, forthwith, enjoy liberty, harmony, and peace.

However justifiable this amendment of expectations may seem, it does deprive liberalism of its original radicalism. And that is why modern libertarian doctrine has no really satisfying answer to the charge that free speech may not be enough. The libertarian doctrine of John Stuart Mill is justly celebrated, but it does not address the problem of what the liberal critic is to do when the ideal of free discussion is insufficient. In short, modern liberalism has not framed a successful approach to the problem of justifiable resistance to government. It would be unfair to underestimate the difficulty of doing so. Certainly this essay makes no contribution to the problem. It is, nevertheless, an important problem, and a serious deficiency. At the same time, it seems fair to observe that there are no other modern political theories equipped with a satisfactory theory of resistance either. . . .

Thus, while it is clear that modern liberalism has in fact abandoned the classical faith in a virtuous human nature, and that it is this, above all, that accounts for its political moderation, it does not follow that liberals cannot continue to embrace the ideal of liberty. On this point, it is enough to recall that even Hobbes (*Leviathan,* ch. 21), who certainly cannot be accused of holding an exalted view of human nature, could nevertheless adopt a clear version of the negative doctrine of liberty. The crucial difficulty, therefore, does not occur at this abstract level. But serious problems of two kinds do arise as a result of the now modified conception of human nature in liberalism. The most important secondary contention in the general libertarian claim has been that it is the individual who knows his own interests best, that one man cannot choose another's good. But, in the first place, can this view be maintained without the assumption that natural man is virtuous? Secondly and more generally, can this view be maintained coherently in any case? This second point has two aspects. Is it not the case that one chooses for others when he chooses that they shall be free? After all, it is entirely possible that they may not wish to be free (this point is often insisted upon, e.g., by Fromm, 1965; see also remarks in Wolff et al., 1965: 30-35). Furthermore, even if everyone did choose to be free, it would surely be the case that libertarians would sometimes insist that others not be free—not free, for example, to take powerful drugs. The painful fact is, of course, that choosing, often for others, is simply unavoidable. And recognizing this involves a second aspect of the problem: such choosing structures human education, taking that word in its broadest sense. Hence, Marx (1959: 244) was clearly right to claim that "the educator himself needs educating." It is pointless to hide behind the notion that one can avoid choosing for others altogether, or the notion that educational processes (including, of course, law) are somehow neutral, mysteriously "unaffected by desire," in Aristotle's (1962: 1217a, 32) phrase, somehow beyond the reach of politics and morals (for a penetrating discussion of the political content of moral and legal theories, see Shklar, 1964).

All these difficulties are plainly acute, and modern liberalism ought to try to deal with them. As with the problem of justifiable resistance, however, this paper cannot pretend to have done so. Still, the first step is to acknowledge the problems. A small second step is suggested by combining the force of the two basic kinds of problems this essay has been concerned to explore. Abandonment of the historically specific assumptions of classical liberalism, and recognition of the problems discussed in this section, both suggest that modern liberalism will have to develop an unwonted political self-consciousness. The libertarian tradition has been implicitly or explicitly anarchic and, therefore, fundamentally apolitical, at least in the sense that the ideal condition hoped for has amounted to the eventual abolition of politics. But liberalism need not be apolitical. It may be necessary that it be anti-political, in the sense that insistence on the primacy of individual liberty implies a permanent mistrust of political power. As against the apolitical impulse, there is the alternative of accepting both the benefits and the liabilities of organized political life, and continuously engaging in the business of judging its adequacy in terms of the principle of liberty.

It is important to observe that mistrust of political power does not mean fastening on the conservative doctrine of laissez-faire (perhaps the most powerful advocate of this "conservative" liberalism, though he would deny the label conservative, is Hayek, 1960). To the extent that the libertarian tradition has come to be associated with the ideal of unfettered economic competition, it is to that extent involved in a departure from the original insistence on the priority of political freedom (for a general discussion, see Friedrich, 1955; Shklar, 1957: 235-56). . . . When the doctrine of laissez-faire has not been merely self-serving, it has rested on the claim that economic freedom is the indispensable precondition of political freedom (see Hayek, 1944). But this claim is both historically inaccurate and philosophically unconvincing. . . . Hostility to economic planning is a comprehensible thesis, but it simply does not demonstrate incompatibility between such planning and attachment to political freedom. On the contrary, in an age of massive concentrations of economic resources, it seems perfectly reasonable to observe that the promotion of political freedom will require far more control of irresponsible economic power than is currently provided for.[4] But this is not to say that libertarian suspicion of governmental power should be abandoned (for an argument in which liberal distrust is plainly abandoned, see Lowi, 1969). Rather than being a liability, the traditional liberal distrust of political power is an advantage, as against apolitical radicalism, for it acknowledges what seems clearly to be the case: that men will persist in abusing power. Certainly governmental power has undergone immense growth in the twentieth century, and that is enough to make "the liberal analysis more timely and correct than it was when it flourished as an ideology in the years before 1914" (Cranston, 1953: 81). The admittedly overdue recognition that coercion takes many nongovernmental forms is thus not a reason for arguing that the coercive power of the state is not there. Moreover, recent history does not offer any good grounds for supposing that that power is now benign.

As the arguments about the necessity of choosing and the political content of educational processes imply, the substance of debate should center on the question of which activities ought to be considered as of public concern, and which ones ought properly to be reserved to private life, these latter to be protected from political interference. This is, of course, a traditional concern, normally discussed in terms of John Stuart Mill's (1961: ch. 1) distinction between purely self-regarding and other-regarding actions. I suggest that this conception of an appropriate criterion may be usefully modified. Instead, the focus, as just suggested, ought to be the problem of a constantly shifting line between the public and private aspects of life. Obviously, this conception is no less abstract than

Mill's. It is intended to suggest a shift of emphasis. Mill's distinction has the effect of focusing attention too decisively in the direction of individual rights, whether these be considered natural or otherwise. In turn, this inclination produces a rather static conception of the task: the tendency to search for an essential human nature and its enduring rights. It seems clear that these emphases abet the generally apolitical drift of liberalism.

In view of Mill's (1961: 261-62; 1924: 201-2) preoccupation with the problem of protecting the creative role of the intellectual against socially imposed uniformity, this outcome is not surprising. But it is not the only possible angle of vision, even if one restricts himself to classical liberalism. One need not accept the frailties of a specific version of the liberal philosophy. More particularly, it is not the case that liberalism *must* be accompanied by a lack of regard for the public order. Consider the case of Bentham, who, after all, is often regarded as one of the most uncompromising exponents of the liberal idea of freedom. Thus, "no law can be made," according to Bentham (Bowring, 1843: 2, 493), "that does not take away something from liberty."[5] One could not very well ask for a clearer expression of the negative doctrine. But it is less often remembered that Bentham was also perfectly clear on the point that the general security had first to be established. This did not alter his contention that any law is a restriction of liberty. But his argument is that "the liberty which the law *ought* to allow of . . . is the liberty which concerns those acts only, by which, if exercised, no damage would be done to the community as a whole; that is, either no damage at all, or none but what promises to be compensated by at least equal benefit." What is to be maintained, he insists, is consistency "with the greatest good of the community" (Bowring, 1843: 2, 505-6). Thus the paladin of negative liberty.

In short, liberalism need not involve neglect, much less hostility to the general interest (for some recent efforts to supply content for the idea of the public interest, see Flathman, 1966; Barry, 1967, 1965: 173-285). On the other hand, Mill's famous principle suggests only left-handed recognition of the public order at best. Drawing the distinction in terms of the contrast between public and private allows much more easily for centering debate where it belongs—at the level of self-conscious political choice. To be sure, it does not make the problems any easier; indeed, it may make them more difficult. It does set them in their proper context. . . .

References

ARENDT, H. (1963) Between Past and Future, Cleveland: World.
——— (1959) The Human Condition. Garden City, N.Y.: Doubleday Anchor.
ARISTOTLE (1962) Politics (E. Barker, trans.). Oxford, Eng.: Oxford Univ. Press.
ARON, R. (1968) The Industrial Society, New York: Simon & Schuster.
——— (1962) The Opium of the Intellectuals. New York: W. W. Norton.
BARRY, B. (1967) "The public interest," pp. 112-126 in A. Quinton (ed.) Political Philosophy. Oxford, Eng.: Oxford Univ. Press.

—————— (1965) Political Argument. London: Routledge & Kegan Paul.

BERLIN, I. (1969) Four Essays on Liberty. Oxford, Eng.: Oxford Univ. Press.

BENTHAM, J. (1950) The Theory of Legislation (R. Hildreth, trans.). London: Routledge & Kegan Paul.

—————— (1945) The Limits of Jurisprudence Defined. New York: Columbia Univ. Press.

BLOCH, M. (1961) Feudal Society, Chicago: Univ. of Chicago Press.

BOWRING, J. [ed.] (1843) The works of Jeremy Bentham. Edinburgh: William Tait.

COBBAN, A. (1960) In Search of Humanity. New York: George Braziller.

COX, H. (1966) The Secular City. New York: Macmillan.

CRANSTON, M. (1953) Freedom: A New Analysis. London: Longmans, Green.

CRICK, B. (1967) "Freedom as politics," pp. 194-214 in P. Laslett and W. G. Runciman (eds.) Philosophy, Politics and Society. Oxford, Eng.: Basil Blackwell.

CROCE, B. (1915) What Is Living and What Is Dead in the Philosophy of Hegel. (Ainslie, trans.). London: Macmillan.

DAHRENDORF, R. (1959) Class and Class Conflict in Industrial Society, Stanford: Stanford Univ. Press.

FILMER, R. (1949) "The anarchy of a limited or mixed monarchy." p. 277 in P. Laslett (ed.) Patriarcha and Other Political Writings of Sir Robert Filmer. Oxford, Eng.: Basil Blackwell.

FLATHMAN, R. E. (1966) The Public Interest. New York: John Wiley.

FORSETT, E. (1606) A Comparative Discourse on the Bodies Natural and Politique. London.

FRIEDRICH, C. J. (1955) "The political thought of neo-liberalism." Amer. Pol. Sci. Rev. 49: 509-525.

FROMM, E. (1965) Escape from Freedom. New York: Avon.

GAY, P. (1968) The Enlightenment. New York: Vintage.

—————— (1964) The Party of Humanity. New York: Alfred A. Knopf.

GOUGH, J. W. (1956) John Locke's Political Philosophy. Oxford, Eng.: Oxford Univ. Press.

HANSON, D. W. (1970) From Kingdom to Commonwealth: The Development of Civic Consciousness in English Political Thought. Cambridge, Mass.: Harvard Univ. Press.

HAYEK, F. (1960) The Constitution of Liberty. Chicago: Univ. of Chicago Press.

—————— (1944) The Road to Serfdom. Chicago: Univ. of Chicago Press.

HAZARD, P. (1968) The European Mind. Cleveland: World.

—————— (1954) European Thought in the Eighteenth Century. London: Hollis & Carter.

HEER, F. (1963) The Medieval World (J. Sondheimer, trans.). New York: NAL.

HOBBES, T. (1962) Leviathan. New York: Collier.

KOLKO, G. (1962) Wealth and Power in America. New York: Frederick A. Praeger.

KRAMNICK, I. (1967) "An Augustan reply to Locke: Bolingbroke on natural law and the origin of government." Pol. Sci. Q. 82 (December): 571-594.

LASLETT, P. [ed.] John Locke: Two Treatises of Government. Cambridge, Eng.: Cambridge Univ. Press.

—————— [ed.] (1949) Patriarcha and Other Political Writings of Sir Robert Filmer. Oxford, Eng.: Basil Blackwell.

LIPPMANN, W. (1937) The Good Society. Boston: Little, Brown.

LOWI, T. J. (1969) The End of Liberalism. New York: W. W. Norton.

LOWITH, K. (1967) From Hegel to Nietzsche (D. E. Green, trans.). Garden City, N.Y.: Doubleday Anchor.

McILWAIN, C. H. [ed.] (1918) "Trew law of free Monarchies," p. 68 in The Political Works of James I. Cambridge, Mass.: Harvard Univ. Press.

MACPHERSON, C. B. (1962) The Political Theory of Possessive Individualism. Oxford, Eng.: Oxford Univ. Press.

MARCUSE, H. (1964) One-Dimensional Man. Boston: Beacon

MARX, K. (1959) "Theses on Feuerbach," in L. S. Feuer (ed.) Karl Marx and Friedrich Engels: Basic Writings on Politics and Philosophy. Garden City, N.Y.: Doubleday Anchor.

MILL, J. S. (1961) "On liberty," Chapter 1 in M. Cohen (ed.) The Philosophy of John Stuart Mill. New York: Modern Library.

——— (1924) Autobiography. New York: Columbia Univ. Press.

MILTON, J. (1958) "The ready and easy way to establish a free Commonwealth," in K. M. Burton (ed.) Milton's Prose Writings. London: J. M. Dent.

NISBET, R. A. (1962) Community and Power. Oxford, Eng.: Oxford Univ. Press.

PAPANDREOU, A. (1972) Paternalistic Capitalism. Minneapolis: Univ. of Minnesota Press.

PARGELLIS, S. (1938) "The theory of balanced government," in C. Read (ed.) The Constitution Reconsidered. New York: Columbia Univ. Press.

PLAMENATZ, J. P. (1968) Consent, Freedom and Political Obligation. London: Oxford Univ. Press.

RIEFF, P. (1961) Freud: The Mind of the Moralist. Garden City, N.Y.: Doubleday Anchor.

SARTORI, G. (1965) Democratic Theory. New York: Frederick A. Praeger.

SHKLAR, J. N. (1968) "Facing up to intellectual pluralism," pp. 275-295 in D. Spitz (ed.) Political Theory and Social Change. New York: Atherton.

——— (1965) "The political theory of utopia." Daedalus 94 (Spring): 367-381.

——— (1964) Legalism. Cambridge, Mass.: Harvard Univ. Press.

——— (1957) After Utopia. Princeton, N.J.: Princeton Univ. Press.

SKINNER, B. F. (1972) Beyond Freedom and Dignity. New York: Vintage.

SPITZ, D. (1966) "The pleasures of misunderstanding freedom." Dissent 13.

——— (1964) Essays in the Liberal Idea of Freedom. Tucson: Univ. of Arizona Press.

TANZER, M. (1971) The Sick Society: An Economic Examination. New York: Holt, Rinehart & Winston.

THOMAS, K. (1965) "The social origins of Hobbes's political thought," in K. C. Brown (ed.) Hobbes Studies. Cambridge, Mass.: Harvard Univ. Press.

VILE, M. J. C. (1967) Constitutionalism and the Separation of Powers. Oxford, Eng.: Oxford Univ. Press.

WALZER, M. (1966) "On the nature of freedom." Dissent 13.

——— (1965) The Revolution of the Saints. Cambridge, Mass.: Harvard Univ. Press

WESTON, C. C. (1960) "The theory of mixed monarchy under Charles I and after." English Historical Rev. 75: 426-443.

——— (1956) "Beginnings of the classical theory of the English Constitution." Proceedings of the Amer. Philosophical Society 100: 133-144.

WOLFF, R. P. (1969) The Poverty of Liberalism. Boston: Beacon.

——— B. MOORE, Jr., and H. MARCUSE (1965) A Critique of Pure Tolerance. Boston: Beacon.

WOLIN, S. S. (1960) Politics and Vision. Boston: Little, Brown.

WOODHOUSE, A. S. P. [ed.] (1951) Puritanism and Liberty. Chicago: Univ. of Chicago Press.

WORMUTH, F. D. (1949) The Origins of Modern Constitutionalism. New York: Harper.

——— (1939) The Royal Prerogative 1603-1649. Ithaca, N.Y.: Cornell Univ. Press.

Suggested Readings

Those interested in reading further should begin by tackling in their entirety the essays or books from which we have taken our individual selections. Beyond those, however, are the following sources.

Primary readings

Addams, Jane. *The Social Thought of Jane Addams*, ed. by Christopher Lasch. Indianapolis: Bobbs-Merrill, 1965.

Beveridge, William H. *Social Insurance and Allied Services*. New York: Macmillan, 1942.

Beveridge, William H. *Full Employment in a Free Society*. London: George Allen and Unwin, 1944.

Douglas, William O. *A Living Bill of Rights*, New York: Doubleday, 1961.

Douglas, William O. *The Anatomy of Liberty: The Rights of Man Without Force*. New York: Trident Press, 1963.

Galbraith, John Kenneth. *American Capitalism*. Boston: Houghton Mifflin, 1956.

Galbraith, John Kenneth. *The New Industrial State*. Boston: Houghton Mifflin, 1967.

Haller, William, ed., *Tracts on Liberty in the Puritan Revolution*. New York: Columbia University Press, 1934.

Hobhouse, L. T. *Liberalism*. London: n.p., 1911.

Hobson, J. A. *The Crisis of Liberalism: New Issues of Democracy*. London: n.p., 1909.

Milton, John. *Areopagitica, A Speech for the Liberty of Unlicenced Printing*, 1644.

Milton, John. *The Tenure of Kings and Magistrates*, 1649.

Milton, John. *The Ready and Easy Way to Establish a Free Commonwealth*, 1660.

de Montesquieu, Charles Louis. *The Spirit of the Laws*, 1748.

Ricardo, David. *Principles of Political Economy and Taxation*, 3d edition, 1821.

Sumner, William Graham. *What the Social Classes Owe to Each Other*, 1883.

de Tocqueville, Alexis. *Democracy in America*, Vol. 1, 1835, Vol. 2, 1840.

Woodhouse, A. S. P., ed. *Puritanism and Liberty*. Chicago: University of Chicago Press, 1951.

Wolfe, Don M. *Leveller Manifestoes of the Puritan Revolution*. New York: Humanities Press, 1967.

Secondary Sources and Collections

Berlin, Isaiah. *Four Essays on Liberty.* London: Oxford University Press, 1969. See especially the "Introduction" and "Two Concepts of Liberty".

Bullock, Allan and Maurice Shock, eds. *The Liberal Tradition: From Fox to Keynes.* London: Adam and Charles Black, 1956.

Freeden, Michael. *The New Liberalism: An Ideology of Social Reform.* Oxford: Clarendon Press, 1978.

Grampp, William D. *Economic Liberalism.* New York: Random House, 1965.

Hartz, Louis. *The Liberal Tradition in America, An Interpretation of American Political Thought Since the Revolution.* New York: Harcourt, Brace and World, 1955.

Laski, H. J. *The Decline of Liberalism.* London: Oxford University Press, 1940.

The Relevance of Liberalism. Ed. by the staff of the Research Institute on International Change, Zbigniew Brezinski, director. Boulder, Colo.: Westview Press, 1978.

de Ruggiero, Guido. *The History of European Liberalism,* trans. by R. G. Collingwood. London: Oxford University Press, 1927.

Salvadori, Massimo, ed. *European Liberalism.* New York: John Wiley and Sons, 1972.

Salvadori, Massimo, ed. *The Liberal Heresy: Origins and Historical Development.* London: Macmillan, 1977.

Schapiro, J. Salwyn, *Liberalism: Its Meaning and History.* Princeton: D. Van Nostrand, 1958.

Spitz, David. *The Liberal Idea of Freedom.* Tucson: University of Arizona Press, 1964.

Volkomer, Walter E., ed. *The Liberal Tradition in American Thought.* New York: Capricorn Books, 1969.

Notes

Introduction

1. For a view that liberalism essentially embodies the Western tradition, see Frederick Watkins, *The Political Tradition of the West* (Cambridge, Mass.: Harvard University Press, 1948).

2. As a political label the word *liberal* apprently comes from the name of a late eighteenth-century Spanish political party, "Liberales." See David G. Smith "Liberalism" *International Encyclopedia of the Social Sciences* (New York: Macmillan, 1968), vol. 9, p. 276. As a political term, however, liberal is much older. See Adam Smith, *The Wealth of Nations* (New York: Modern Library, 1937) p. 628. Thomas Jefferson often used this word also. For a complete discussion see *The Oxford English Dictionary* (Oxford: Clarendon Press, 1933), vol. 6, pp. 237-38, and *A Supplement to the Oxford English Dictionary* (Oxford: Clarendon Press, 1976), vol. 2, pp. 657-58.

3. For Milton Friedman see especially *Capitalism and Freedom* (Chicago: University of Chicago Press, 1962) and *An Economist's Protest* (Glen Ridge, N. J.: Thomas Horton, 1972). For Ayn Rand see especially *Capitalism, The Unknown Ideal* (New York: New American Library, 1966) and *The Fountainhead* (Indianapolis: Bobbs-Merrill, 1968).

4. George H. Sabine, *A History of Political Theory* (New York: Holt, Rinehart and Winston, 1961) p. 704.

5. Modification of Sabine, p. 704.

6. We have borrowed the term "reform liberal" from Kenneth M. Dolbeare and Patricia Dolbeare, *American Ideologies* (Chicago: Markham, 1973) p. 86ff. The actual usage, however, is ours and bears little resemblance to theirs.

7. On the continent, positive freedom was sometimes defined as achieving your real self or real interest through recognizing and doing your duty or merging into a higher form of organization or collective consciousness. Real reason and liberty existed only in the collectivity, whether that was society, state or nation. It is in this sense that the Rousseau of the *Social Contract* is sometimes called a liberal, even though he attempted to transcend individualism through the General Will. Negative and positive liberty, however, blur at the edges, especially in the Anglo-American tradition, and we should not make too rigid of a distinction between them.

8. Donald Hanson, "What Is Living and What Is Dead in Liberalism?" *American Politics Quarterly,* 2 (January 1974), p. 10.

9. Harold J. Laski, *The Decline of Liberalism* (London: Oxford University Press, 1940), p. 15.

10. See Francis W. Coker, "Some Present-Day Critics of Liberalism," *American Political Science Review,* 47 (1953), p. 4ff. Cf. critiques by Walter Lippmann, *Essays in The Public Philosophy* (New York: New American Library, 1956) and José Ortega y Gasset, *The Revolt of the Masses* (New York: W. W. Norton, 1932). The French liberal Alexis de Tocqueville argued that there was a conflict between democracy and liberalism in America. See his *Democracy in America,* the first volume of which was published in 1835. See especially vol. 1, chapter 21, vol. 2, book 4. There are many modern editions of this work.

11. Majority rule lies at the heart of John C. Calhoun's (1782-1850) defense of states' rights and slavery in the Southern states. Calhoun rejected all notions of natural rights in favor of those rights which a community gives to its members.

12. Cf. Richard John Newhaus, *Commentary,* 62, no. 3 (September 1976), p. 84.

1. The Putney Debates

All footnotes for this selection are from *The Clarke Papers* unless noted by "editor's footnote."

1. Reprinted in A. S. P. Woodhouse, *Puritanism and Liberty* (Chicago: University of Chicago Press, 1951) pp. 422-26. (Editor's footnote)

2. Donald Hanson, *From Kingdom to Commonwealth* (Cambridge: Harvard University Press, 1970) p. 310, states that this was the first time since classical antiquity that such issues were debated. (Editor's footnote)

3. Rainborow's argument seems to be: God gave man reason that he might use it, and though the poorest man may have no property yet he has reason and he was meant to use it. It may be a small right but it is something, and you are not justified in taking from him any right God has given him. See the same argument stated by the agitators in *The Case of the Army Stated,* October 15, 1647.

4. This part of Rainborow's speech is too fragmentary to follow his arguments, but see his comments immediately after Pettus and Ireton.

5. Limited to possessors of freeholds worth 40 shillings a year. Cowling is giving his theory of the object of the statute of Henry VI limiting the franchise to persons having free land or tenement to the value of 40 shillings a year.

6. Should be, "to constitute, i.e. to legislate, according to the just ends of government, not simply to maintain what is already established."

7. Rainborow.

8. Wildman's speech came near the end of the debate on October 29. In it he reported on his meeting with some of the other regimental agents and reflects the kinds of ideas which many of the rank and file soldiers held about rights, participation and government. (Editor's footnote)

9. The three passages given in brackets are supplied from *The Case of the Army Stated.*

3. James Harrington

1. Adult males were organized into a militia to better protect their liberties and the commonwealth.

2. England, Ireland, and Scotland.

4. John Locke

1. Paragraph 142 requires that there be "one rule for rich and poor, for the favourite at court and the countryman at plough."

7. Thomas Jefferson

1. In this and the following two letters Jefferson refers to Shays' Rebellion which broke out in Massachusetts in 1786-1787, during a depression. This movement occurred among small landowners to prevent seizure of their lands for unpaid debts and taxes. Jefferson was living in Paris, as Ambassador to France when he wrote these letters.

2. In this letter Jefferson discusses the proposed revision of the Virginia Constitution.

9. Jeremy Bentham

1. Note by the author, July 1822. To this denomination has of late been added, or substituted, the *greatest happiness* or *greatest felicity* principle: this for shortness instead of saying at length *that principle* which states the greatest happiness of all those whose interest is in question, as being the right and proper, and only right and proper and universally desirable, end of human action: of human action in every situation, and in particular in that of a functionary or set of functionaries exercising the powers of government. . . .

2. These circumstances have since been denominated *elements* or *dimensions* of value in a pleasure or a pain.

14. John Rawls

1. As the text suggests, I shall regard Locke's *Second Treatise of Government,* Rousseau's *The Social Contract,* and Kant's ethical works beginning with *The Foundations of the Metaphysics of Morals* as definitive of the contract tradition. For all of its greatness, Hobbes's *Leviathan* raises special problems.

19. John Stuart Mill

1. Mill is referring essentially to voting rights and representation.

22. C. B. Macpherson

1. On the distinction between liberal democracy and other types, see my *The Real World of Democracy* (Toronto, 1965; Oxford, 1966).

2. This is of course a very different view of man's powers from that contained in the liberal-democratic (and pre-seventeenth-century) notion of maximization of human powers. For the importance of the distinction, see below, section 3.

3. I argue at the end of this section that the rise of the welfare state has not altered this equation.

4. It would take too long here to demonstrate, what I hope to demonstrate in a subsequent study of nineteenth-century theory, that the same confusion between the two concepts of powers is the root of the inadequacy of Mill's and Green's theories.

5. A not unreasonable speculation by some economists that capitalist entrepreneurs might continue to operate even in those circumstances is acknowledged (and shown to be irrelevant) in Essay 4, section 2, p. 84.

24. Theodore Lowi

1. For more of the actual figures, see Lowi, *American Government: Incomplete Conquest* (Hinsdale: Dryden Press, 1976), pp. 438-44.

2. Theodore C. Sorenson, *Kennedy* (New York: Harper and Row, 1965), p. 347.

25. Richard Wollheim

1. Walter Lippmann, *The Public Philosophy: Essays in the Public Philosophy* (Boston: Little, Brown, 1955).

27. Donald Hanson

1. This limited form of liberalism informs the argument in Shklar (1964), to which I would like to acknowledge a general and deep indebtedness. A similar kind of emphasis is to be found in Spitz (1964).

2. That is the force, for example, of the writings of Sir Robert Filmer, which originated not in connection with the liberalism of John Locke, but during the course of debate in the civil wars. Filmer's writings were resuscitated by the Tory faction during the crisis over the Exclusion Bill, which was, presumably, the occasion of Locke's treatises as well (see Laslett, 1960: 45-66, 1949; Gough, 1956: 120-35). Moreover, as Walzer (1965) has rightly insisted, the English Puritans were not concerned with the idea of liberty. For a most interesting account of philosophical criticism and rejection of liberalism in eighteenth-century England, see Kranmick (1967). On the primacy of the value of liberty in England in and after the civil wars, see Wormuth (1949: 163–68 and throughout).

3. This point is well made in Walzer (1965: 302-3). For a general critique, see Wolin (1960: 239-351).

4. The literature drawing attention to the facts of economic concentration is, of course, growing rapidly. Much interesting information is ably deployed in Kolko (1962). For two recent and profoundly critical accounts, see Tanzer (1971) and Papandreou (1972).

5. Nor is there any doubt at all that Bentham insisted on this point again and again (see, e.g., Bentham, 1950: 94-95; 1945: 139; 1843, II: 503, 505-6).